NOW NEEDLEPOINT

A Joyous New Approach to Creative Designing

Jan Orr

 VAN NOSTRAND REINHOLD COMPANY
New York   Cincinnati   London   Toronto   Melbourne

To my husband Garry,
who lived through all the stages of this book
with love, faith and patience.

Van Nostrand Reinhold Company Regional Offices:
New York Cincinnati Chicago Millbrae Dallas

Van Nostrand Reinhold Company International Offices:
London Toronto Melbourne

Designed by Jean Callan King/Visuality
Published by Van Nostrand Reinhold Company
A Division of Litton Educational Publishing, Inc.
450 West 33rd Street, New York, N.Y. 10001

16 15 14 13 12 11 10 9 8 7 6 5 4 3

Library of Congress Cataloging in Publication Data

Orr, Jan, 1920–
   Now needlepoint.

   Includes index
   1. Canvas embroidery. I. Title: Now needlepoint.
TT778.C3077   746.4'4   74-7779
ISBN 0-442-26301-5

All color photography (with the exception of Figs. C-27 and C-59)
and black and white photography of patterns and finished items are by
Garrett P. Orr, Sr.
   All other black and white photographs, diagrams and drawings are
the work of the author. The jacket was designed and worked by the
author. It is a variation of the Orr Weave Carnival. (Figs. 7-32 and
C-119.)

Acknowledgments

My heartfelt thanks:

To my husband, Garry—professionally, for taking the numerous photographs of my stitches and for many helpful suggestions along the way; personally, for living with quiet patience in a home where stitch projects appear everywhere, and for just plain listening by the hour while my ideas unfolded and gradually developed into the material for this book.

To my loving and loyal friend, Jacqueline Enthoven, whose enthusiasm for my designs has never ceased to amaze me. Her gentle but determined urging that I share my ideas was one of the persuasive factors which resulted in my decision to write this book.

To my editor, Estelle Silbermann, for her many helpful technical suggestions and for accepting my joyous, but lengthy and detailed, approach to writing directions. And to Jean Callan King, for her excellent design.

To the editors of *House Beautiful* for granting permission to include some of my designs featured in the article "Instant Needlepoint" and for allowing me to reproduce the interiors photographed by Ernest Silva which appeared in the publication.

To Connie Lischy, who typed the manuscript with love and enthusiasm as well as patience and care.

To Bessie Sanchez, Mary Malvezzi, Mary Claire Malarky and her assistants, and to the many, many gracious individuals whose warm reactions to my designs spur me on continuously to do more.

And lastly to the late Karnig Paternayan, whose death occurred during the period when this book was being prepared for publication. Karnig, a color technician, was one of the founders of Paternayan Bros. Inc., manufacturers of the Pat Rug Yarn which I used for the majority of patterns and finished items featured throughout this book. Many years ago when I first became involved in the needlework business, I visited the Paternayan Bros. headquarters, in a loft building uptown in New York City, and was completely overwhelmed by the delightful sight which greeted my eyes, a blazing rainbow of colored yarns which stretched from the floor up to the high ceiling, and seemed to extend for miles before disappearing off on the horizon. Up to that time I had only been aware of the subtle grayed colors of the traditional crewel yarns. It was a cherished moment for I knew that I had to accept the creative challenge which the magnificent colors afforded. From that day on my needle has consistently been threaded with bright color, as is evident in my designs. Karnig Paternayan was responsible for developing the range of colors which first inspired me to create with the needle and seriously start my needlework designing career. I shall be eternally grateful to him.

Contents

Introduction

My husband, Garry, and I live in an old home built in 1790. A brook runs close by and there is a waterfall. Actually, they are on our neighbor's property, but we can enjoy the sight of them along with the musical sound of rushing water. We live in a country atmosphere, surrounded by good neighbors and woods filled with little animals, birds and all the wonders of nature. Garry—an art director, portrait painter, watercolorist—works in the studio over mine. The two studios are in a wing separate from the main part of the house and both are in a constant "state," for they are functional most of all. We love the beamed ceilings, fireplaces and many windows that bring the outdoors indoors. There is much to inspire creativity and I often feel as if my cup runs over. I have a strong need to share my blessings and the joyous rewards I find in my needlework. This book is an invitation to visit with me. In these pages you will learn of a unique new method for creating your own designs that I call Now Needlepoint and which I sincerely believe can prove to be joyous and rewarding for you too!

My basic purpose in writing this book, which I hope is expressed in the title, is to present a lighthearted creative approach to needlepoint for today, tomorrow, the immediate future, *for now!* An approach which is elastic and can be manipulated to encompass all types of décor and personal tastes. Specific patterns and finished articles will be presented, but only as sample suggestions. All can easily be adapted to colors of your own choice in order to reflect your individual preferences.

The information represents a compilation of the many discoveries I made while experimenting constantly with stitches, yarn, canvas, design and color. There are not iron-clad rules to follow. You can bend any of the directions or suggestions to suit your personal needs if you can find an easier method. I am not declaring, "This is the only way!" Use my explanations and instructions to start you down the avenue of becoming a creative designer. They are merely tools, at your disposal, but *you* must pick them up and make them work for you. And please, do not let that word "creative" make you cringe. For some reason, it seems to send panic through many people. They immediately think, "I could never be creative." *You can!* Hopefully, this book will show you how easy it is to accomplish this goal. Start this minute, start *now*, believing this. Read on with a joyous, positive attitude. Become aware. When you do this, it is like a light switching on in a dark room. You begin to see all the various items within the room. So press your "aware button" and before you know it you will be thinking creatively!

Now Needlepoint is very different in appearance from the usual needlepoint. It can be designed for contemporary use in bold brilliant colors and patterns, or, if you wish, toned down for traditional use. The choice is yours. It is much like weaving without a loom. Textures and eye interest are created immediately by the very personality of the individual stitches and the choice of colors. The slight imperfections or variations which are formed because of the twisting, turning and placement of the heavy yarn have a charm of their own, like the ridges on handwoven materials or the bumps on pure silk. The overall concept is basically geometric, but some of the stitches can be made to walk in a variety of directions which do create softer patterns with daintier effects. From the minute you pick a stitch to master and decide on the colors you wish to use, you are creating. You experience a good feeling as you see the texture emerge so quickly before your eyes. The canvas is large, the yarn heavy, so the work progresses rapidly. *House Beautiful* magazine called it "Instant Needlepoint," which gives you an indication of how quickly the work goes.

It can be a joy for women—and men too! The large-size stitches with their rather rugged look have a definite masculine appeal. Even boys can be enticed to try it when you explain that it is more like weaving than sewing. Each member of a family can get involved and create an item. Specific suggestions for décor are given later but the point I wish to make here is that a family can work together on a project to enhance the home. Instead of a loom, it is the heavy canvas that controls the size of the stitches which create the patterns. Easily seen by people with sight problems, the large canvas is also wonderful for those who are on in years but young at heart. The therapeutic value for confined persons is incalculable; faces light up at the very sight of the bright wool and canvas. Even under difficult conditions, long dreary hours and days, like magic, can become filled with creative and productive experiences.

This book is not a dictionary of many stitches. In fact, you will no doubt be startled when you discover how few stitches are involved. The few stitches, however, are presented with detailed, complete instructions plus drawings and step photographs, which even the novice can follow. But there are also many, many patterns and suggestions for finished items which can all be produced when the basic mechanics are mastered. The unique construction directions make it possible to produce finished items completely in Now Needlepoint stitches if you so desire—without the use of your own sewing machine or a professional seamstress. Once you have mastered the details necessary for construction, you can design your own item in the stitch, color and size you wish. Throughout, the basic patterns and designs are purposely keyed to "stretch" to cover any size area. You are in complete control as the designer. Do you grasp the potentials? No more endless searching for that hard-to-find packet or kit design to fill your specific needs. Simply pick out the stitch and the colors, and cover the canvas to the size desired in the pattern you like. Isn't it an exciting prospect? How this is accomplished is explained in detail later, but I feel it is one of the most important aspects of the creative approach which should be pointed out immediately. Because the large stitches cover the canvas quickly, items like headboards, valances, bench tops—which would take a lifetime in the finer canvas and yarn—become feasible. The design potentials are limitless. One of my greatest problems in assembling the information for this book was not thinking up new designs but eliminating and selecting the ones to use.

I have very strong convictions concerning adequate and clear directions. From careful study of students in my classes, I realized that some had learning problems in one area while others sailed over that same area with ease and had difficulty at another point. In a class you can give individual students attention as the problems arise. In a book you must attempt to anticipate all the problems and include sufficient explanations so that the majority of students can sail over the learning hurdles with ease. So often in books the little helpful suggestions which a "live" teacher would inject along with the mechanical directions are dispensed with in an effort to make the instructions *appear* to be simple and easy. But omission of vital information can cause much frustration. It is my firm belief that a how-to book should live up to its claims, and so I have made every possible effort to present instructions which are understandable and complete.

Learning from the printed page has many strong points in its favor. For instance, you can learn at your own pace. Sometimes the competition of quick learners in a class can be extremely disturbing to those who learn at a slower pace. I personally learn mechanical steps slowly and with difficulty. Until the steps of any process become completely automatic to me, I truly struggle. Then there is that wonderful moment of understanding. The pains of mastering the fundamentals are over and the enjoyment starts. The length of time it takes an individual to arrive at this point is not an important factor. Also, the printed page is constantly available, at your side or perched on your bookshelf. You need only to reach for your teacher at the time most convenient for you to proceed with your studies.

The detailed instructions are not cut-and-dried, for I have added my supplementary thoughts whenever I thought they would give a clearer understanding of how to proceed. Also, sometimes a lighthearted touch makes the necessarily dull "down-in-1-and-up-in-2" routine instructions easier to read. To ease the learning kinks, I explain what you are doing, that is, "working around a hole" or "over a crossed bar of canvas." Students become so involved in the "up-in-something and down-in-something" that they completely lose sight of the particular stitch's basic principle which so simplifies the learning process. I carefully outline what each stitch does best: some "walk" naturally in a diagonal direction while others are naturally vertical or horizontal walkers. I explain what each stitch is best suited for and why. In many instances, step photographs taken during the production of patterns or finished items are included so you can actually see the work in progress and compare the photograph with your own project.

The first chapter, Creative Awareness: Design and Color, is the most important one of all! Opening your eyes and truly *seeing* the wonders surrounding you can produce a joyful approach to life in general, not only in the needlework world. Creative rewards are close at hand—you need only reach out. Hold on to this thought while you diligently strive to master the stitch mechanics.

Chapter 2, General Information, should be read carefully, for its subject matter relates to all of the Now Needlepoint stitches. If there is something unusual regarding a particular stitch, it will be explained in the individual stitch chapters; otherwise this chapter will cover all. It also has the instructions for a few extra-fancy stitches, which will be useful for you to know, and a short list of page numbers so that you can quickly find some cross-references that frequently come up in the later chapters.

The individual-stitch chapters follow and include information about each stitch's personality, the directions in which the stitch can be worked, design and color potentials, suggested uses, plus step-by-step instructions for producing the stitch. The written instructions, accompanied by drawings and photographs outlining the mechanical steps, are presented in a manner that a beginner can follow. Directions for both patterns and sample finished items are also included. The instructions can be easily followed if you advance one step at a time. Wait until you actually have the necessary canvas, needle and yarn ready before you get involved in the step-by-step directions. It is like learning a new language or getting to know a new friend, so it is wise to take each step as it comes.

Construction and Finishing, the last chapter, encompasses a number of the Now Needlepoint stitches and some of the patterns presented throughout the book. There is one sample with detailed instructions shown for each specific *type* of article, and all of the steps necessary to produce the finished item are included. You can substitute any stitch pattern or design of your choice suitable for the article. For instance, there are directions for constructing a bellpull worked in the French Stitch. The same procedure can be followed using a different stitch and pattern for any-size wall hanging. This chapter will make it possible for you to complete Now Needlepoint items with boutique professional touches. Instructions are included for such items as tassels, cording and fringe.

The many ideas and thoughts which flow continuously through my mind concerning Now Needlepoint have been pulled into focus and presented in this book. Please keep in mind that what you read is not intended to appear as profound, irrefutable statements or strict procedures but rather bits of information and discoveries which I am sharing with you. Hopefully, you will open your mind, press your aware button and your creative potential which has been waiting to blossom will begin to do so through the Now Needlepoint approach to designing!

I should point out that the Now Needlepoint creative approach is a golden opportunity for needlework teachers. Many learners find it helpful to actually see the stitch in progress as a clarification of the written instructions. Also, there are many who need the discipline of attending classes at a designated time. If you are a teacher, you can make a number of working samples while *you* are mastering the stitches and patterns and these can be used later for display during class sessions. Local shop owners usually welcome an arrangement with a teacher who has something new and creative to interest their customers—and the shop can be a convenient source of materials for you and your students. Determine what heavy yarn is sold in the shop and use it for any samples to be displayed. This will also serve as a test to make certain it covers the canvas properly if it is not the same yarn shown in the samples of this book.

The Now Needlepoint approach to needlepoint can also be a boon to shop owners, allowing them to promote and move the heavy rug yarn which so often sits on a shelf because customers are not certain how it should be put to use. Some bright, finished samples and a display of a number of stitch patterns can quickly catch the eye of customers and if there is an instructor available, as just mentioned, considerable creative excitement can be produced in a shop. Shopowners can start with a fairly limited inventory of yarn colors and increase their palette as interest develops. Since items are completed quickly, customers are back within a week or so to purchase more materials for the next project.

As for interior decorators, the potentials for custom designing with Now Needlepoint are staggering because of the very exciting unusual décor that can be created. The chapter on design and color points out many of the possibilities. Interior decorators can readily key designs to their own specifications and color combinations, although finding someone to carry out the designs in stitches sometimes presents a problem. The answer might be the local needlework shop, where able needlewomen who would welcome the opportunity to produce the finished item at a fair price could be found. Also, there are many handicapped or confined people who could be trained to execute the designs.

The color, texture and patterns of this needlepoint method can be used for a fine art approach and could therefore appeal to artists. You can literally paint with the texture and stitches and produce magnificent wall hangings. The overall effect of the needlepoint stitches lend themselves beautifully to abstract designs, but realism can also be introduced, as you will see when you read about the Wiggly Chain design motifs. The Wiggly Chain can be made to work overtime for you. The motifs shown had to remain simple and uniform in order to present drawings that the reader could reproduce. But an artist can improvise and wiggle them in an irregular manner with delightful results. With surface stitches, you add additional texture and eye interest. Experiment a bit and you will quickly become aware of the endless possibilities.

1.

Creative Awareness: Design & Color

I had been a professional designer in the needlework field for a very short time when I noticed a visitor to my studio looking around, carefully examining my original needlework designs on display. When I inquired if I could help her, she startled me with the request: "Yes, Jan, please make me creative!" My first thought was "Only the Lord can do that!" but her plea kept swimming around in my head. And then one day the idea for a new approach, one which could greatly increase an individual's creative ability, started to unfold. I realized I couldn't *make* anyone creative but perhaps I could guide a bit, suggest a bit, help by pointing out certain basic facts. Perhaps I could provide motifs or patterns which the individual could manipulate and combine to create original designs. It is my firm belief that we are *all* creative to some degree. True, certain of us are more so than others, but this is due to the fact that our minds are open and we have learned to be constantly aware of the wonders surrounding us. So many times I have received the reply, "I never thought of it that way" after calling attention to something fairly obvious.

I personally feel as if a guardian angel on my shoulder keeps opening idea doors along the way. The door opens but I must take the initiative by wondering: "What would happen if I tried???" That particular question has preceded any new discovery I have made. "I wonder what would happen if . . ." Then I start to experiment. With needlepoint, the question led to blowing the work up slightly in size, then more and more, trying different stitches, different yarns, giving new twists to old stitches, designing with color, figuring out how I could explain the process to other people so that they could experience enjoyment too. Anything new involves a certain amount of risk, and along with the successes there are the attempts which must be discarded for numerous reasons. I have a drawer full of rejects—experiments which did not come up to my standards. I had about given up on the

Chain Stitch and was ready to settle for very limited design potentials, when a new door flew open and "I wonder what would happen if I tried . . ." was answered with endless possibilities and the Wonderful Wiggly Chain and the Design Motifs were born. A book could be written on that stitch alone. This is the miracle of discovery! The possibilities are always right there waiting for us to discover them. We simply walk through the idea door and wonder. Creative discovery does not necessarily take great intellect or special genius or tons of talent; sometimes it is evoked by sincere curiosity and quiet faith which spurs the individual to take a slight risk and experiment.

My husband claims I have serendipity. Maybe you do too! I admit to discovering some things by happenstance. One day I gathered together some scrap yarn in an attempt to tidy up my working table—always such a chore since I am so anxious to start on the next project after completing the last one. I threw the scraps together in a pile and there they stayed for an hour or so. Walking through my studio later, I happened to glance down at the scrap pile and, behold, there was a delightful combination of colors, the answer to a design interpretation that I had been searching for for some time. It appears in the book but I won't mention which one it is; I will indulge myself in letting you think it was carefully and methodically worked out. Actually it is one of those things which, for no explainable reason, simply pleases the eye. If serendipity touches you, be aware of it; hold on to it by making quick notes on paper. Don't let it slip away—swoosh—out of your mind.

Learn to be inspired by the world you live in daily; develop the habit of *seeing*. We can all be guilty of looking but not truly seeing. Nature abounds with amazing examples of design, harmony, graceful rhythms, and yet, our sophisticated eye looks past these miracles.

One morning my husband and I were having our coffee

break out on the patio. We could hear the brook rushing by and the whole moment was very good! He brought to my attention the *feel* of many arches formed by the graceful growth of the trees, a whole series of semicircles swooping around, letting you peek through to a section of the woods where, lo and behold, would be another arch farther off, so far off it left you wondering what was beyond that distant one. I became intrigued with this rhythm so much like music. I had looked at that scene hundreds of times, but this was the first time I became aware of the rhythm of the arches. It made me know the importance of taking a quiet moment in this world of rush to *see* and *study*.

How does this relate to needlepoint? It points out how we can easily discover myriads of ideas for design inspiration if we will learn to become aware. One summer afternoon I looked carefully around my small garden and wondered what could be interpreted in Now Needlepoint. The Wiggly Chain Design Motifs in Chapter 6 show you what evolved. The motifs can be combined on canvas in such a way that an overall rhythm is formed to create a finished item such as the bee pillow (Fig. 6-49).

Train yourself to look at the world with new eyes, as if you were seeing it for the first time. Start to be conscious of color and design patterns. We are born with an innate curiosity which needs only a drop of nourishment to make it grow by leaps and bounds. Once you have carried out the initial task of planting some thoughts in your mind, your creative awareness will blossom forth with amazing speed. A certain amount of discipline is necessary in the beginning as you open your mind and learn to observe in a creative manner, but you will be astonished how quickly the new thought approach jells and becomes habit. Soon your mind will develop an insatiable appetite for information, and you will probably find it necessary to joyously feed it for the rest of your days. And not only at the appropriate, called-for times, for creative thinking goes on constantly once it has taken root. It becomes an integral part of your everyday existence and enters all facets of your life.

There are numerous places where you will find sources for design and color inspiration to spark your creative awareness. You should visit bookstores and build up your personal library. Purchase as many books on design and color as you can afford. The books are like rows of friendly instructors, always ready with a helpful answer and bulging with inspiration. You needn't feel extravagant when you purchase books—even the very expensive ones—since the process of learning is immeasurably encouraged by having material for quick reference on your own bookshelf.

Public libraries are another wonderful source of information. I couldn't exist without the cooperation of the helpful group that runs our local library. For years I did not make use of our small local library; I had the notion that the rather unusual books which I needed from time to time would not be available there. How mistaken I was. Here in New Jersey requests for books are sent to a magical place referred to as "The County" where they are answered within a short time. There is actually a reciprocal arrangement between all the libraries in the county to exchange books on request, thus increasing the scope of the small local library tremendously and making it possible to obtain books otherwise unavailable. It would be worthwhile for you to check in your locality to determine the extent of your facilities. In addition, the large urban libraries usually contain row after row of excellent books on design and color waiting to be read. This source is also very easy on your pocketbook. And, while you are in the library, take a glance at the art magazines. Most libraries subscribe to a number of art publications which you can peruse to familiarize yourself with the current happenings in the art and design world. You might want to subscribe to some periodicals if you find them particularly interesting.

You could also spend months uncovering exciting themes in museums, which are overflowing with suggestions for design. There is usually some significant style or look about each culture, and with a little imagination you can capture the feel of it and express it with needle and yarn. Think of Greek borders or the distinctive Indian designs sprinkled with chevrons and zigzags. Many could be expressed so beautifully in Now Needlepoint stitches. Visits to museums will provide you with food for creative thoughts and keep the thoughts constantly growing and expanding.

But the primary source of all inspiration is nature. Open the doors and windows in your mind and heart and begin to appreciate the wonders of nature. Try looking around you with a fresh eye: magnificent design formations start to appear. The color is breathtaking—brilliant combinations or subtle blends. You can find whatever pleases your taste or the current vogue demands. If you live in the country, you need only walk outdoors. If you are a city dweller, take a walk in the park, or visit a botanical garden, or peer in the window of a florist shop, or, even better, buy an inexpensive bouquet of flowers. Study and think about the rhythm of growth, the placement and shape of petals, leaves, branches and stems. The miracles are all there, gracious suggestions to inspire creative thoughts.

Design and color are the two components you should study, but they become so fused in the mind that it is difficult to separate them for the purpose of explanation. As in a happy marriage, two supposedly separate entities have thoroughly blended. The end product is seen as a whole and it is almost impossible to detect where one ends and the other begins. The *design* pattern is formed through the proper use of *color*. Each is extremely dependent on the other and they must be compatible if the overall finished design is to be a success.

This is especially true in the Now Needlepoint approach. The majority of the patterns and designs in this book are produced entirely by color changes within the stitches themselves. In contrast to the traditional needlepoint where the designs are painted on canvas in advance, Now Needlepoint patterns unfold as the work progresses. The only markings needed for all of the samples shown were small yarn ties used in the corners to indicate the area to be covered or at starting spots for repeat designs and individual motifs. The texture formed by the various stitches must also be taken into consideration since it becomes an integral part of the overall design and produces additional eye interest.

It takes a lifetime of study to arrive at a deep understanding of design and color. Creative artists and designers are constantly experimenting, trying unique approaches, testing new materials. It is like a never-ending voyage, with new discoveries always before you.

With the information that follows and the help of the patterns, you can begin to create with confidence and to key your own designs in Now Needlepoint. The facts which will best equip you to start designing immediately have been pinpointed, but they should be supplemented constantly with additional information if you wish to continue to develop your understanding.

CREATIVE DESIGNING

A former student stopped in my studio one day and, overflowing with pride, showed me a pillow she had completed in Now Needlepoint. She fairly shouted, "The best part of all is there isn't another pillow exactly like this one anywhere in the world." She was right. She had designed it herself in the colors of her choice, and this was something very special to her, as it is to us all. We live in homes with walls, ceilings, chairs, tables all basically alike and we spend our lives attempting to make them distinctive—make them proclaim our difference, that our family lives here, that we are special. We constantly search for ways to express our own individuality or that of our family as a group.

Personal taste is an important factor in creative designing. Each of us develops unique, definite likes and dislikes in clothes, home décor and all things that become part of our existence. We like any color if it is turquoise. We like big, bold designs and find small grayed designs dull and uninteresting; yet others are happiest with muted restful colors. We should not lose touch with these individual tastes, since we are much better creative designers if we are working with patterns and colors that please us and

happier people when living with them. In certain instances it is wise to defer to the collective taste of the family; also, keep in mind the taste of the receiver if the finished product is to be a gift to an individual. If the recipient is a hot-pink–orange person, then design the item in those colors, even if you are a blue–green person yourself. The joy of giving comes from the sincere attempt to please the other person. Once you have decided on the size and type of article you wish to make, Now Needlepoint will let you key the design and perfectly express your individual taste and make easy choices concerning stitch, pattern and color.

In the majority of the samples shown throughout the following pages, the patterns are formed by the manner and direction in which the stitches are worked and by the changes of color. Of the number of factors to consider while keying your design, the first should be to determine in your mind the overall impact you wish to create. Through your choice of stitch, pattern and color, you can achieve a restful, subtle blend of stitches and color—or a dazzling eye-stopper with bold, brilliant color. Study the information on color magic in this chapter and the sample patterns in the later chapters so you can produce the overall message you wish. The finished item should fit in the décor where you intend to place it.

Choose stitches and colors that suit the function of the finished item. Your design should also be keyed with thought to harmony and balance. The blank canvas is your challenge. Most of the patterns presented in the stitch chapters remain entertaining to the eye when repeated or stretched to cover large areas. Generally speaking, you should establish a symmetrical balance on the outer edges of repeat patterns: tops and bottoms should balance and the two sides should correspond. For instance, if you start with a green stripe on the left, end with a green stripe on the right. But this does not always hold—when you are keying asymmetric designs, for example, exact balance is not important.

When you key designs that involve the Wiggly Chain Design Motifs, place them in such a way as to break background area up into interesting shapes. By making the little working samples suggested in Chapter 6, you can better visualize the spacing and placement. Switch them around—experiment a bit—try various arrangements. Remember to allow for the rollback around knife-edge pillows (those without gussets). Glance at the finished samples and you will see how the area around the edge of a knife-edge pillow is lost to the eye. Sufficient background area must be worked completely around to properly frame the design area, like a mat on a watercolor painting. When the design area is completed, a good trick is to place the canvas over a pillow of the approximate size you wish to make, so you can determine how much solid background area is necessary.

You should learn several more designing tricks. As one of the meanings for the word "trick" the dictionary lists "a quick or artful way of getting results," and that is exactly what these little aids accomplish. They are so marvelously unscientific, work like charms and save mountains of time.

The Squint Test. To squint is to look or peer with eyes partly closed. It is difficult for me to understand how anyone designs or paints or makes color choices without the use of the Squint Test. Try it. Squint your eyes very tightly so only a thin slit is left to peer through. Glance around the room. A weird transition takes place. Specific objects literally disappear and only masses or areas of light and dark remain—areas rather than things. You can see clearly whether patterns and colors stand out against those in surrounding areas. Try it with this printed page. Squint and you see only blurred gray rows: the individual letters and words blend and one continuous pattern or line forms in your eye. Your Now Needlepoint stitches and patterns are like words. When you squint, your eye simplifies areas and makes it easier for you to determine correct value contrast in color and proper balance in placement of designs. This trick is especially valuable with the Wiggly Chain Design Motifs. After you've switched them around and found a satisfactory arrangement, squint. For some wonderful reason, you then quickly discover corrections you wish to make. You might want to move the motifs slightly to one side so they will balance. When the motifs are completed, hold the proposed background yarn close to them and squint. If everything blends together, the value contrast is probably not strong enough. Since the motifs must stand out against the background, the value should be darker or lighter, depending on the colors involved.

This is but one example when the squint test is helpful. I suggest you use it on many occasions throughout the book. As you advance and are faced with numerous creative decisions, you will find it a valuable judge.

You can also put it to good use when you discover an interesting pattern during a museum trip or in a book. While you are asking yourself, I wonder what would happen if I interpreted that design in stitches, give it the squint test. The physical matter in which the pattern is expressed seems to slip away and you can quickly evaluate how the design could be simplified and expressed in Now Needlepoint stitches.

The squint test can sometimes produce an amusing situation. Once, while waiting to cross the street in New York City, I glanced up and discovered a fascinating frieze with a delightful repeat design. I squinted and wondered and squinted for some time. When I returned to reality, I discovered I had a group of people around me—yes, all looking up and, strangely enough, squinting!

I gave them a weak smile and went on my way, leaving them to their unsatisfied curiosity.

Mirror, Mirror on the Wall. Long ago, artists discovered the detective qualities of a mirror on the wall. Along with telling who is the fairest of them all, a mirror uncovers imbalance in a design in a flash. Hold up a partially worked design in front of a wall mirror; the reflected image is reversed and this makes it possible for the eye to detect design flaws. This trick is invaluable when keying asymmetrical designs, and it also helps you to double-check balance of light and dark and color, especially if you combine it with the Squint Test. It is amazing how quickly, with the use of these tricks, it becomes evident that one little white flower is needed on the left or perhaps one additional row of background should be worked across the top.

Another good mirror trick is to hold up a sample pattern or motif so it touches the mirror at a right angle, folding back the excess or unworked canvas. This causes the sample to be repeated in the mirror as if it were one continuous image. With a few squints you can see the negative space which would be formed between the motifs. You can try them closer together or farther apart by folding back the canvas at various spots until you find the spacing most pleasing to the eye. If your project involves an overall repeat pattern, you can hold it to the mirror when you are halfway through, folding back the unfinished portion, and the finished half will be repeated in the mirror—letting you have a preview of how the item will appear when completed.

Grids for Keying Designs. We are all familiar with the grid system of dividing areas into small squares which is used for enlarging or reducing designs. By breaking up the overall area into smaller sections, it is easier to determine proper placement for design purposes.

The following system utilizes grids in a slightly different manner and can be extremely helpful in keying designs. A delightful timesaver, it eliminates the necessity of taking measurements and the complications of numerical dividing which can be troublesome when there are many fractions involved.

First, cut out a piece of paper—regular brown wrapping paper is good—to the exact size of the area to be covered. You can fold it into any number of equal sections. One horizontal fold plus one vertical fold gives you the exact center (where they cross) and divides the space into four equal quarter sections. By making additional folds, you can divide each of the four sections into as many equal spaces as you need for keying your design. Or, you can start with diagonal folds (from corner to corner) and you will end up with interesting triangular shapes. Experiment with a practice piece of paper, for there are many possibilities. If you want a solid area around a central design that is equidistant from the edges, you can indicate the area to keep free of design by making a few folds.

After you have made the desired number of divisions, place the paper *under* your canvas and you are ready to start keying your design. The folds are visible through the large canvas and it is a great comfort to be able to glance through and know immediately where the exact center is or what spot is one-quarter distance in from the side edge. (Again, this is especially valuable when keying designs which involve the Wiggly Chain Design Motifs.) If you have made up working samples, you can place them under the canvas on top of the paper grids, moving them for proper balance. Tie yarn markers (see p. 40) on the exact spots where you will start to work motifs. If you will be repeating a motif—or motifs—a number of times at equidistant intervals, it is wise as a double-check to count bars or canvas holes between after you have tied the markers.

A Quick Divider. Another trick to remember gives you the easiest and quickest way in the world to find the center between any two points. Make two marks on the edge of a piece of paper indicating the length of the distance to be divided in half. Fold the paper once so the two marks are matched. Clearly define the fold with your fingernail. Open the paper flat and the fold will be in the exact center. Anyone who is a precisionist may be appalled by this method, but it is amazingly accurate.

COLOR MAGIC

Color is by far the most exciting area. With color, artists and designers can wield an unbelievable degree of visual and emotional power. Like the effect of a beautiful chord on the ear, the eye finds beauty and entertainment in harmonious combinations of color. Signals are sent to the brain and emotions are stimulated.

We have strong associations with color, some of which are universal. Warm color variations of yellows, oranges and reds make us think of bright sunshine or brilliant flowers. Cool colors such as greens and blues remind us of water, sky and deep woods; white of clean and sparkling things; black of darkness and night. Personal associations each of us have had with color can also influence our emotional reaction. A color takes on importance for numerous reasons—sometimes simply because we feel good when looking at it, wearing it or living with it. If you had the best time of your life while wearing a blue dress, that could explain blue becoming your favorite color; you associate it with happy times. This is an important factor which should be carefully considered when you design: do your best to follow your personal color preferences.

Think of color as being alive with personality traits, just like people. Certain colors are far more friendly than others and can live in close harmony with a variety of relatives and neighbors. They adapt to varied personalities and varied environments, always creating a happy atmosphere. However, there are other colors with erratic qualities, and they must be dealt with in a special manner. They can behave beautifully in specific situations, but can cause havoc if they are not in the proper setting. Some colors can have an adverse effect on each other when placed side by side. Brilliant colors can fade or wash out more subtle colors while other combinations of brilliant and dull colors create delightful contrast and beauty. *Color is entirely at the mercy of its environment.* At times, like a chameleon, it can completely change in appearance because of the surroundings.

Back in the eighteen-thirties a problem arose with the production of the famous Gobelin tapestries. Even in those days it was possible to produce brilliant, vibrant colors with the available dyes. However, a strange thing happened when the bright yarns and threads were woven into tapestries. They became dull and drab looking. This was a serious problem for the industry, since the tapestries were known for their brilliant color. M. E. Chevreul, a noted scientist, was asked to investigate. In the process of tracking down the source of the trouble, he discovered many wondrous things about the harmony of color. Chevreul's findings revealed that the dull appearance of the colors in the Gobelin tapestries was due to the juxtaposition of colors and was not the fault of the dyes. When the combinations of colors were corrected, the brilliance returned.*

Color magic is everywhere, waiting to be noticed. There was a time when the use of blues and greens together in fashion items or décor was not considered to be in good taste. Then the late talented textile designer, Dorothy Liebes, must have looked out her window and become aware of the blue sky and green grass which so pleases the eye in nature. She introduced that combination in her designs and, as you probably know, it became a trademark which helped to make her famous. Today, the combination is accepted without question.

While visiting my studio one day, a very traditional stitcher voiced disapproval of the floral design I was keying which was all hot pinks, oranges and bright yellows. Her taste definitely ran toward the typical, subtle crewel colors and, being rather outspoken by nature, she said she did not care for the "garish modern colors" used

*Chevreul's magnificent *The Principles of Harmony and Contrast of Color*, long out of print, was reprinted in 1967 by Reinhold Publishing Co. It is a record of the science and harmony of color, and one needs only to glance through its pages to gain insight into the vast scope of the science of color.

today. After quietly explaining that the colors were not necessarily "modern," that there is a Designer who has made use of them for ages, I led her to my kitchen window beyond which we saw my small garden ablaze with brilliant, breathtaking zinnias. She agreed they were beautiful and that a bouquet of them would enhance any décor. A look of amazement appeared on her face when I pointed out that the colors were the same as those in my design.

Incidentally, if you have never examined the structure of zinnias with a magnifying glass, you are missing a treat. In addition to being dressed in eye-catching color, they are delightful miracles of formation. Some have a circle of tiny flowerets around the center, each one symmetrically perfect. One cannot help but wonder whether each of those tiny, bright flowerets in turn contains a circle of smaller flowerets and whether this form continues to infinity.

You can feel free to interpret the magnificent colors of nature and the amazing design formations in any way you wish for there are no copyrights or any restrictions whatsoever concerning use.

Many people have mistaken, dogmatic ideas about color—rules they feel should not be broken. For example, they believe that only subtle colors can be used for traditional décor and that bright, strong color must be reserved for contemporary settings. Ridiculous! The warm glow of antique furniture can be made to sing if combined with strong, rich color. If you are happier with muted colors, fine. But if you like strong color, you can drop it into all types of décor as long as you use good judgment.

Colors go a long way to create that initial, overall impact as you enter a room. In designing décor, consider the environment. Being on the south side of the house, my living room is extremely bright and sunny. All day long, especially in winter, the sun pours in through the large antique windows. I am a blue-green person—a lover of the sea—and so I chose turquoise, blues, greens and a touch of purple for my décor. In this extremely bright room, my cool colors are set off to advantage. Imagine what the impact of a hot, sunny afternoon in midsummer would have been if I had chosen brilliant oranges and yellows. This demonstrates the psychological and emotional effect which can be produced by choice of color. If a room is shady and cool, you can introduce a feeling of sunlight through the use of warm reds, pinks, oranges and yellows. Use bright, warm colors wisely, for otherwise they can be overpowering. A few Now Needlepoint pillows worked in bright colors can produce quite a glow!

The color combinations presented at the beginning of the color section (C-2 through C-10) have been keyed to assist you in Now Needlepoint designing. Many of them appear in the finished samples shown throughout this book. Actual yarn samples were used to make it easier for you to visualize the combinations in needlepoint stitches.

I attempted to place the color combinations in groupings which can be used in various décor schemes. In general they run from warm golds, yellows and oranges to pinks, reds, purples and then to yellow greens, greens and blues. The combinations loosely follow the sequence around the color wheel. A few interspersed examples show what happens when you drop black or white or both into a combination. Then there follows a potpourri of "color medleys" which have pleasing possibilities in Now Needlepoint. Any of these combinations can take the place of those used for actual patterns in the individual stitch chapters, but make certain there is the necessary value contrast to properly interpret the particular pattern.

Each designer has an individual style or look, like his handwriting, and naturally my designs and color combinations have my stamp on them. The combinations are presented to help you—especially the beginners—but do not feel bound by them. I hope to stimulate your creativity so you can eventuallly produce your own look. Try not to be a mimic. I always feel deeply disappointed when an exact duplication of the look or stamp of a teacher is evident in a student's work. An influence is perhaps natural, but, technically, the student's creativity begins to develop at the point where his own stamp takes over. The Thought Guide toward the end of this chapter will help you bring your designing thoughts into focus. Once you have thoroughly digested the general information in Chapter 2 and have mastered the stitch mechanics, you can follow the guide and start to create!

Test for Color Harmony. The success of a project greatly depends on whether or not a harmonious effect is produced, so it is wise to test the juxtaposition of colors before making your final decisions. There is an extremely helpful test you can use when keying the yarn colors. Place the hanks of selected yarn close together. Then place a single strand from each of the hanks side by side over your forefinger. Do this gently so that the hank is not disturbed. Hold them at arm's length and squint. You can determine whether you have the impact you want, the right harmony and whether the value contrast is correct. You have to put the color samples together, *away* from the other colors. It is difficult to key properly your own creation from a color chart, especially when the snips of yarn or color swatches are at opposite ends of the chart. And merely placing the large hanks together will give you an indication of whether the colors harmonize, but it is not enough of a test for my critical eye when keying a design.

Make your color choices when you find the combination which pleases you, but do keep loose and elastic in this area for you might wish to make slight changes as the work progresses. There are times when the final project ends up very different from the original concept. Leave room for the unexpected disclosure, the happenstance, the delightful serendipity which may surprise you.

There are certain basic things you should know about color, even before you start to design. Think of each color as having three personality traits:

Hue. This is the color itself, such as blue, red, green, etc.

Value. This refers to the amount of dark or light in a color. An example of a deep value is black; of a middle value, gray; and of a light value, white. There must be value contrast for your eye to distinguish and isolate shapes; the more contrast in value, the quicker your eye picks out an area. The extreme example would be white flowers on a black background. For instance, you can see a value change if you start with a pot of deep blue paint and add some white paint, then take a sample; add more white paint and take a sample. As you continue doing this, the blue swatches will get lighter and lighter in value.

Intensity. This refers to the brightness or dullness of a color. Think of a brilliant yellow and a very dull gold. The brilliant yellow is high while the dull gold is low in intensity.

As already pointed out, the appearance of individual colors depends entirely on the neighboring color or colors. You must place colors together in such a way as to create a happy atmosphere. There are occasions when you purposely wish to produce an exciting look or cause some static, but in most instances the designer is intent on creating a harmonious result which pleases the eye. You can accomplish this by learning some of the basic reasons that cause certain color combinations to be more harmonious than others. Once you understand why and when they are happy, you can make colors perform as you like in your designs.

White is by far the friendliest of all colors and becomes a delightful addition to most color schemes. You will notice it has been included in so many of the sample color combinations. It enhances all the neighboring hues and creates an overall clean sparkle.

But black is inclined to be a bit fickle, so use it with caution. In many instances it is an excellent accent, especially when both black and white are dropped into a color scheme, but it can also destroy a desired impact if it is not properly controlled. Because black is so deep in value—deeper than any color— the texture formed by Now Needlepoint stitches is almost lost to the eye in the areas where black is used. This is true of all very deep-value colors. The highlights and shadows are not distinguishable; your eye sees only the silhouette of the area or a stripe.

Black should be used as a background only when the motifs or designs are so interesting and entertaining that they can get by on their own merit. A fascinating thing happens with a black background: it becomes air or space in which the design motifs are suspended. Instead of becoming part of the color scheme, as with all other background colors, the black background literally slips away from eye consciousness and becomes space. Glance at any picture with a black background and you will see. This phenomenon has exciting possibilities, so muster up your courage and try it sometime, but keep in mind that the texture of the individual stitches disappears.

You are on safe ground in designing when you use a **single-color scheme.** This entails using one color with variations in value only—from deep to pale. Technically, this is termed "monochromatic color." With this color scheme, you can key a design in several values of one color and be assured that the end result will be pleasing to the eye. You can't miss if you have the necessary value contrast to properly interpret the stitch and pattern.

Some manufacturers dye their wool in "families" consisting of four or five values of one color. The finer yarn used for delicate crewel shading is usually merchandised in this manner, but this is not always true of the heavier rug yarns. The Pat Rug Yarn, which is used for the majority of the samples in this book, is available in families in a great variety of colors. But if the particular yarn you have in mind is not available in families, many times a slight variation in the color can produce the effect of a single-color scheme. You can pick out a deep-value green, a middle green and a very pale green as close to the same hue as possible and end up with a pleasing result. Since this is not as safe as when you stick to the same color family, do be certain to give your combination the Squint Test so that your eye can judge the success of the harmony.

Any color on the color wheel can be used for single-color schemes. If you use close values, they will blend in your eye; the greater the value contrast the more your eye will hold the edge. You can blend close values to create a feeling of dimension or you can cause stripes and designs to pop out by strong value contrast. For a quick, complete change of appearance, introduce white or black, or maybe both, depending on the single color involved. Try out your combination by squinting at it!

You should also experiment with **related-color combinations.** Artists and color specialists refer to these as analogous colors. The term "related" is self-explanatory; related colors appear close together on the color wheel and, like relatives in a family, they have some similar characteristics. Each color shown on the wheel contains a portion of its neighbor on each side, and your

Text continues on page 34.

C-1. COLOR WHEEL.

C-2

| 413 | 441 | 421 | 958 | 259 | 239 | 233 | 672 | 632 | 356 | 731 | 738 | 718 | 559 | 545 | 550 |

C-3

| 413 421 968 550 | 441 434 433 | 413 421 172 050 | 421 545 | 988 978 968 958 | 421 968 259 |

C-4

| 632 237 259 968 | 239 237 958 259 | 219 239 259 279 | 237 259 | 632 279 | 237 731 | 672 632 |

C-5

| 550 731 | 728 550 | 718 731 545 413 | 748 738 728 718 | 550 738 632 718 | 550 738 559 731 |

C-6

| 239 434 413 | 545 259 413 728 | 738 259 413 632 | 738 550 259 632 | 413 550 958 632 |

C-7

| 632 421 413 | 510 239 279 | 550 259 | 413 738 | 738 050 | 550 279 632 | 279 545 |

C-8

| 6 | 7 | 8 | 11 | 17 | 24 | 32 | 30 | 37 | 38 | 43 | 46 | 47 | 55 | 61 | 64 | 78 | 84 |

C-9

| 7 11 | 24 11 7 | 17 38 11 | 47 38 17 | 32 38 | 46 47 | 84 64 61 | 78 84 |

C-10

| 7 38 64 84 | 61 32 | 47 32 84 | 11 38 47 | 38 61 | 64 61 78 | 64 84 38 47 | 84 38 |

THE COLOR BANDS IN FIGURES C-2 TO C-7 USE PAT RUG YARN, WHILE THE COLOR BANDS IN FIGURES C-8 TO C-10 USE NANTUCKET 6-PLY CABLE YARN. IN BANDS C-2 TO C-7 THE WHITE IS NUMBER 005, AND IN BANDS C-8 TO C-10 THE WHITE IS NUMBER 1.

C-11. FIG. 3-14.

C-15. FIG. 3-18.

C-19. FIG. 3-22.

C-12. FIG. 3-15.

C-16. FIG. 3-19.

C-20. FIG. 3-23.

C-17. FIG. 3-20.

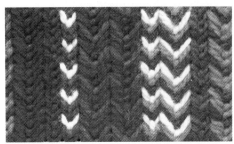

C-21. FIG. 3-24.

C-13. FIG. 3-16.

C-14. FIG. 3-17.

C-18. FIG. 3-21.

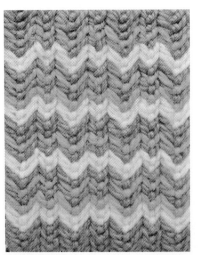

C-22. FIG. 3-25.

C-23. FIG. 3-26.

C-24. FIG. 3-27.

C-25. FIG. 3-28.

C-26. FIG. 3-29.

C-27. PHOTOGRAPH COURTESY OF *HOUSE BEAUTIFUL.* COPYRIGHT 1967, THE HEARST CORPORATION. PHOTOGRAPHER, ERNEST SILVA.

C-28. FIG. 3-38. DESIGN COURTESY OF *HOUSE BEAUTIFUL.* COPYRIGHT 1967, THE HEARST CORPORATION.

C-29. FIG. 3-33. DESIGN COURTESY OF *HOUSE BEAUTIFUL.* COPYRIGHT 1967, THE HEARST CORPORATION.

19

C-30. FIG. 3-34.

C-31. FIG. 3-36.

C-32. FIG. 3-35.

C-33. FIG. 3-39.

C-34. FIG. 4-19.

C-37. FIG. 4-22.

C-35. FIG. 4-20.

C-38. FIG. 4-23.

C-36. FIG. 4-21.

C-39. FIG. 4-24.

C-40. FIG. 4-25.

C-44. FIG. 4-29.

C-41. FIG. 4-26.

C-45. FIG. 4-30.

C-42. FIG. 4-27.

C-46. FIG. 4-32.

C-43. FIG. 4-28.

C-47. FIG. 4-33.

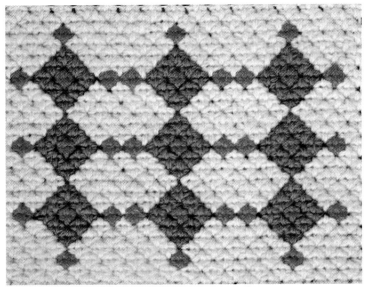

C-48. FIG. 4-35.

C-51. FIG. 4-38.

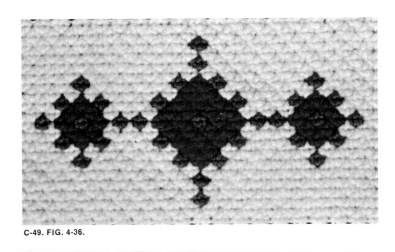

C-49. FIG. 4-36.

C-50. FIG. 4-37.

C-52. FIG. 4-39.

C-53. FIG. 4-40.

C-54. FIG. 4-41.

C-55. FIG. 4-42.

C-56. FIG. 4-44.

C-57. FIG. 4-45.

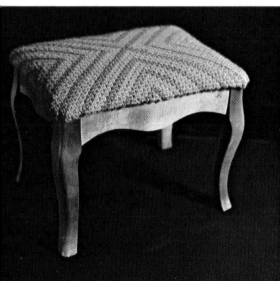

C-58. FIG. 4-46.

C-59. PHOTOGRAPH COURTESY *HOUSE BEAUTIFUL*. COPYRIGHT 1967, THE HEARST
CORPORATION. PHOTOGRAPHER, ERNEST SILVA.

C-60. FIG. 4-47. DESIGN COURTESY OF *HOUSE BEAUTIFUL*.
COPYRIGHT 1967, THE HEARST CORPORATION.

C-61. FIG. 4-48. DESIGN COURTESY OF *HOUSE BEAUTIFUL*.
COPYRIGHT 1967, THE HEARST CORPORATION.

C-64. FIG. 5-9.

C-63. FIG. 5-7, RIGHT.

C-65. FIG. 5-10, TOP.

C-66. FIG. 5-10, BOTTOM.

C-67. FIG. 5-11.

C-68. FIG. 5-12.

C-69. FIG. 5-13.

C-70. FIG. 5-14.

C-71. FIG. 5-15.

C-72. FIG. 5-19.

C-75. FIG. 5-29.

C-76. FIG. 5-30.

C-77. FIG. 5-35.

C-73. FIG. 5-21.

C-74. FIG. 5-23.

C-78. FIG. 5-31.

C-79. FIG. 5-33.

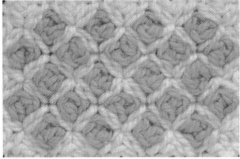

C-80. FIG. 6-2.

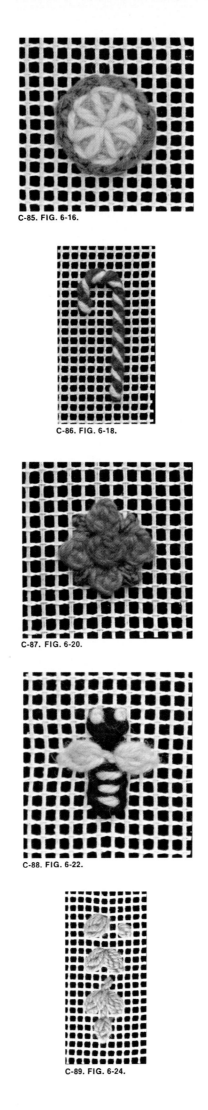

C-85. FIG. 6-16.

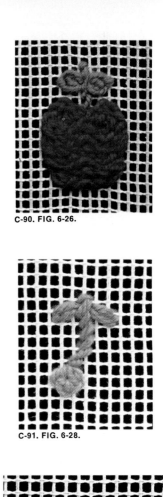

C-90. FIG. 6-26.

C-81. FIG. 6-3.

C-86. FIG. 6-18.

C-91. FIG. 6-28.

C-82. FIG. 6-4.

C-87. FIG. 6-20.

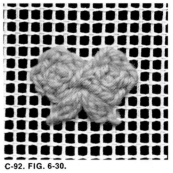

C-92. FIG. 6-30.

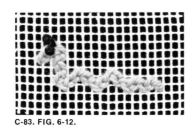

C-83. FIG. 6-12.

C-88. FIG. 6-22.

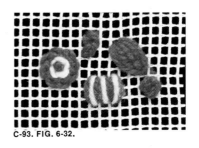

C-93. FIG. 6-32.

C-84. FIG. 6-14.

C-89. FIG. 6-24.

C-94. FIG. 6-34.

C-95. FIG. 6-37.

C-98. FIG. 6-45.

C-102. FIG. 6-53.

C-99. FIG. 6-47.

C-103. FIG. 6-55.

C-96. FIG. 6-41.

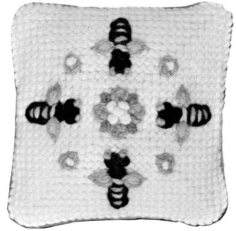
C-100. FIG. 6-49.

C-104. FIG. 6-57.

C-97. FIG. 6-43.

C-101. FIG. 6-51.

C-105. FIG. 6-59.

29

C-106. FIG. 7-15.

C-111. FIG. 7-24.

C-107. FIG. 7-16.

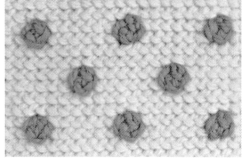

C-114. FIG. 7-27.

C-108. FIG. 7-17.

C-112. FIG. 7-25.

C-115. FIG. 7-28.

C-113. FIG. 7-26.

C-109. FIG. 7-18.

C-116. FIG. 7-29.

C-110. FIG. 7-20.

C-117. FIG. 7-30.

C-118. FIG. 7-31.

C-119. FIG. 7-32. (SEE ALSO JACKET.)

C-120. FIG. 7-33.

C-121. FIG. 7-35.

C-122. FIG. 7-37.

C-123. FIG. 7-39.

C-124. FIG. 8-22.

C-125. FIG. 8-29.

C-126. FIG. 8-30.

C-127. FIG. 8-37.

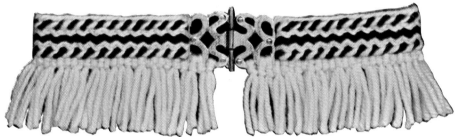

C-128. FIG. 8-43.

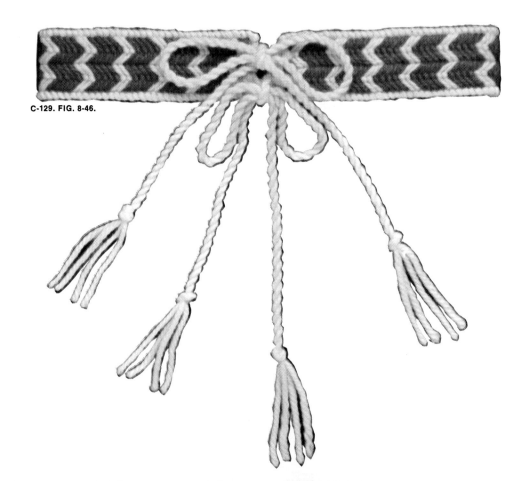

C-129. FIG. 8-46.

eye finds pleasure in the harmony produced when they are placed together. A related color scheme is also a safe one, for the colors consistently live happily side by side. It is not necessary to stick to brother colors—those side by side on the wheel—but you can use cousin colors, skipping colors between, and still have related harmony. If you place the colors in your design in the order they appear on the wheel, you will find the results extra-pleasing. The values can be adjusted to suit your needs for a specific design.

You are taking a more adventurous path when you use **opposite-color combinations.** Technically called "complementary colors," these appear opposite each other on the color wheel. While the related colors blend harmoniously when placed together, opposite colors have powerful effects which are magnificent when used in correct proportions but tricky when not controlled. With opposite-color combinations you are constantly discovering color magic.

You can add an extra zing to a design when you use an opposite color. (See color wheel, Fig. C-1.) By introducing a touch of the opposite color on the wheel to the predominant color used in the design, you can create excitement. But it must only be an accent: proportion is the key to success. The predominant color usually likes only a dash of its opposite color. If you use equal proportions, each fights so for dominance that neither wins and instead of a sparkle, you get a dull effect.

Vibrations in the eye can be created by juxtaposing opposite colors of the exact same value. Years ago I was introduced to this phenomenon while working on a creative stitchery with a red velvet background. It was a bull's eye design made up of a series of circles. The outer circle of stitches needed a bit of softening. So I held up a turquoise yarn, gave it the Squint Test and decided that would do the trick in a splattering of tiny seed stitches (straight stitches which resemble dots) around the outside edge. The turquoise was the exact same value as the background and the opposite color on the wheel. While working the seed stitches, I realized my eyes were acting strangely. I thought I needed new glasses because I could not get the work in focus. But that was not the trouble. My eyes were simply reacting to the combination of opposite colors: there was actually an eerie pulsing sensation taking place. I still have the stitchery and it still vibrates around the edge if you stare at it for a moment. Those innocent-looking little turquoise dots on the red background are like touches of magic causing tremendous excitement. Once a designer or artist understands how to control this magic, he truly gains considerable power.

There are numerous other color schemes that involve a mixture or hodgepodge of colors which do not fall under basic classifications, and these will be referred to as **color medleys**. As the words indicate, they represent a mixture of color and pattern themes used in the same design. The term "medley" is often used in music when several little tunes are played one right after the other.

It is difficult to give rules or guides for medleys. However, there is one very important thing to remember which helps you to produce a successful design. Because of the variety of colors and patterns, there must be some single force which pulls the design together; otherwise you end up with a design made up of scattered unrelated areas. This force can be a solid background color which surrounds motifs or weaves through patterns, or, in a geometric design, it can be a balanced repetition of one predominant color. This color does not necessarily have to be repeated in a symmetrical manner as long as it balances, to please the eye.

To illustrate this point, imagine a patchwork design made up of squares of different colors and patterns. The squares can be of different sizes if you wish, as in a Mondrian painting. But there should be one rather strong color repeated in all or at least most of the individual areas—sometimes just a touch or accent of the color will suffice. Another suggestion would be to completely outline all of the squares or areas in one color. The lattice effect thus produced automatically causes the individual areas to become an integral part of the whole.

While the individual colors in a medley should be placed so they balance throughout, in most instances it is best to keep the proportion of each color uneven. One color should predominate, with various smaller portions of the other colors, and perhaps a few tiny accents of one color for sparkle. However, don't consider this a rigid rule since much depends on the type of design.

And don't forget that friendly white. There are times when it should be used sparingly, but it can make a design sing if it is sprinkled throughout. Use the squint test as your pattern unfolds. Keying a color medley may take a little more effort and is perhaps not as safe as some other color combinations, but, like anything involving a bit of risk, the rewards can be great—and fun for the designer too!

Another color effect is that of **color fusion**. It may sound technical, but in reality it is very easy to create. When fusion is introduced, a color becomes charged with vibrations which add extra zest to a design. It is a delicious design secret, for most viewers are not conscious of how the effect is created—they only see the result. The effect is achieved by using two or more closely related colors of exactly the same value, which, when placed side by side, your eye fuses or blends into one vibrant color. If one color is darker or lighter than the others in value, fusion will not take place.

In the Fly Stitch pattern for the bench top (Fig. 3-38), color fusion takes place. Along with the related color scheme, color fusion is used by placing red and deep shocking pink of the same value side by side in a number of places. It is difficult to show on the printed page how successful the fusion is, for part of the impact is lost in reproduction. Like your eye, the camera blends, but in its own way. It is much more vibrant and exciting when the eye of the viewer does the fusing.

You can create this phenomenon with a variety of related color combinations—the closer the colors, the better for this purpose. Blues and greens, yellows and pinks, purples and blues, oranges and yellows, yellows and yellow-greens . . . you could go on and on. But remember: in a regular, related-color scheme, the colors can be of any value; if you wish to produce fusion in a particular area, then the related colors must be of the *same* value.

Many artists have used color fusion in painting. George Seurat painted with tiny dots and let the eye of the viewer do the blending. Pierre Bonnard, my very special favorite, sprinkled areas of his paintings with myriad brush strokes of colors of the same value which miraculously fused, simulating a blanket of sunshine. Study the work of these artists in your library or, better still, in a museum. This color technique must be greatly simplified when you use it in Now Needlepoint, but just a touch of this magic will add sparkle.

This chapter presents only a few tidbits of information pertaining to design and color. Only facts necessary for keying designs in Now Needlepoint have been included. These merely touch the surface and should definitely be supplemented by further study. Read at least one book on design and composition and one on color. Your power as a designer will increase as your understanding of the basic principles develops.

Before you can reap the rewards of designing, you will have to become thoroughly familiar with the methods involved in Now Needlepoint and exercise discipline to learn the stitches. But think on the happy side; think of how few stitches there are to master in order to produce the many patterns and samples presented throughout this book.

I will constantly be urging you to consider the patterns and finished items merely as suggestions. Because I want to emphasize the creative approach, I will repeatedly point out design potentials after instructions so that you can elaborate on and utilize the basic patterns to key your own designs.

Following is a summary which you can use as a kind of guide when you are about to key a design. Use it to bring your thoughts into focus.

THOUGHT GUIDE SUMMARY FOR KEYING CREATIVE DESIGNS

1. Type of Item. Decide on whether it will be pillow, bellpull, bench top or some other item.

2. Overall Impact. What is the overall impact you wish to create? Where will the item be used? What will be the environment? Should it be subdued or attention-getting?

3. Size. Establish the size desired. Anticipate and allow for any necessary construction. If the item is to be a pillow or pin cushion, will there be a fancy Now Needlepoint backing in the same novel needlepoint technique as you used on the front?

4. Stitch or Stitches. Choose the suitable stitch or stitches. Be careful to consider how the item will be used.

5. Design Motif and Color. Select the design motif or pattern and choose the colors. But keep an open mind, since slight changes may be necessary as the work progresses and the design unfolds.

Note: Your creative ideas can form at any time during the day or night, so keep a pad and pencil handy at all times to make thumbnail sketches when an idea pops in your mind. Make lots of sketches and don't throw away the unused ones after your final decision. File them in a safe place, for they can be of great help in future designing. Start a small treasure file of design ideas.

Once you have made the vital decisions, you are ready to purchase the necessary materials and follow the specific instructions for completing the project. This book is full of information to assist you. The labor pains will quickly go away as you become familiar with the various steps. Proceed with joy as you keep in mind the wonderful thought: I am creating!

A FESTIVAL OF COLOR

The following color combinations will give you a condensed concept of the eye excitement which can be achieved through the use of color. If you allow your eye the luxury of slowly traveling over the rows of brilliant yarn swatches, you can literally become intoxicated by the miracle of color magic.

Because color is so affected by neighboring colors, each suggested combination should be viewed separately. Make yourself an expandable viewer, with the following directions. When you place the viewer on the color

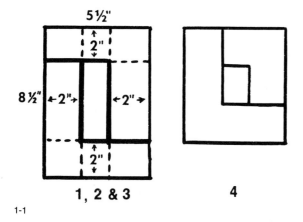

1-1

1, 2 & 3   **4**

page, the center opening can be expanded or reduced to accommodate the size of each individual color combination.

How to Make an Expandable Color Viewer.

1. Cut out a piece of black mat-finish paper, 8½ in. × 5½ in. If black paper is not available, a fairly heavy-weight piece of opaque white paper can be substituted (one-half sheet of 8½ in. × 11 in.).

2. Measure and draw lines 2 inches in from each of the four sides—crossing them at the corners as indicated in Figure 1-1.

3. Cut *only* along the indicated solid lines in the drawing so that there are two "L"-shaped sections 2 inches wide. Discard the middle section.

4. Move the bottom "L" up, overlapping the upper left corner and the bottom right corner of the top "L".

The overlapped "L"-shaped sections form a mask with an expandable opening in the center. This enables you to view each color scheme separately as you block out the immediate surroundings. The series of colors interspersed with white can be viewed individually with white, or, by expanding the opening, with any number of the neighboring colors on either side. The colors are placed on the band in the same sequence as they would appear on the color wheel, so a related color scheme results when neighboring colors are included.

These combinations represent only a partial selection from the wide color ranges available in each of the two types of yarns that were used—Pat Rug Yarn and Nantucket 6-Ply. They are suggestions from which you can move onward and upward as your knowledge and understanding develop. These are the colors which I find exciting and pleasing and they are presented to stimulate your sense of color—to start you thinking of color as a powerful designing force. Use the combinations freely until you acquire color confidence, and then do your own thing.

There are many delightful combinations waiting for you to discover them!

The Color Wheel. Pat Rug Yarn was used for the color wheel. (Fig. C-1.) Only the primary and secondary colors are shown to explain the basic theory behind the circle of different colors. The yarn colors on the wheel are as close to the basic colors as the color range permits. Most of you will be familiar with the theory, but let's review it for creative Now Needlepoint purposes.

Primary Colors. The triangle of colors comprising red, yellow and blue represents the three basic primary colors from which all other colors are derived.

Secondary Colors. The triangle of colors orange, green and violet represent the secondary colors. Each of the secondary colors is a mixture of its two neighboring primary colors. Orange is a mixture of yellow and red. Green is a mixture of blue and yellow. Violet is a mixture of blue and red.

Each of the endless possible nuances of color occupies a spot on the color wheel. Yellow-orange would fall between yellow and orange—and so forth around the wheel.

Opposite Colors. The colors which are directly opposite each other on the wheel are the opposite (complementary) colors referred to on page 34 which can cause color magic when properly used. The French Knots demonstrate how just a touch of the opposite color can cause a brilliant sparkle. Use the expandable viewer to cover up the surrounding colors and view each color section separately to prove this point.

Most art books on color include a color wheel that shows a large number of hues. Color wheels are also available in art stores at a small cost. If you wish to use the opposite-color magic in your Now Needlepoint designing, obtain a color wheel that will enable you to match as closely as possible the yarn color you have chosen to the swatch on the color wheel and then determine the color which is its opposite.

In the Color Bands A through I (Fig. C-2 through Fig. C-10) in the color pages, numbers for each color are given over the yarn, so that you can duplicate the exact color if you wish. The bands in Figure C-2 to Figure C-7 use Pat Rug Yarn.

Color Band A. (Fig. C-2.) This band of color loosely follows the sequence around the color wheel. Starting clockwise with yellow at the top, if they were in a circle, the colors would end with yellow-green on the left of the yellow. Each color is related to the colors on both sides. When you use the expandable viewer on the band, reduce the space so you can see the effect of an individual color with friendly white—or expand it to include any number of colors. By moving the viewer along the band you can key an endless number of safe, related color combinations.

Color Bands B, C and D. (Figs. C-3, C-4, C-5.) These bands of color also very loosely follow the color sequence around the color wheel. They have color groupings which are suitable for specific décor schemes. Suggestions for gold and orange décor are shown in Figure C-3; pink, red and purple in Figure C-4; blues and greens in Figure C-5. View separately each suggested group with the expandable viewer. There are related-color schemes and single-color schemes—some with white, some with black and white. In most instances a color can be eliminated, if you wish, without destroying the effect.

Color Bands E and F. (Figs. C-6 and C-7.) These happy color medleys will brighten any décor. No rhyme or reason—they simply delight the eye.

Color Bands G, H and I. (Figs. C-8, C-9 and C-10.) Nantucket 6-Ply Cable Yarn was used for these bands. The band of color in Figure C-8, which loosely follows the color wheel, is similar to the band in Figure C-2. If you glance at Color Band H (Fig. C-9), you will see that this band of

suggested combinations also very loosely follows the sequence of the color wheel. Color Band I (Fig. C-10) shows bright color medleys in the Nantucket Yarn. Take particular notice of the last two groupings on the right, which show how easy it is to delete several colors in a color combination and create an entirely new impact. Turquoise and purple were deleted in the last group.

Because color plays such an important part in the formation of Now Needlepoint designs, all of the patterns and finished items are shown in the color section so that you can see the full impact of Now Needlepoint. I designed the patterns using color to its full advantage and purposely dismissed restrictive thoughts concerning reproduction in black and white. All patterns and finished items are duplicated in the black and white photographs which are placed close to the directions for easy reference. But the black and white camera eye is fickle. Unless there is strong contrast in value, in many instances the defining line between colors is lost. Also, two entirely different colors can photograph alike in black and white. Filters were used whenever necessary to force value contrast, making it possible for you to see the pattern outline when you are following the directions. Therefore, you will find the value contrasts in some of the patterns are different from the color versions.

2.

General Information

Now Needlepoint is extremely different from traditional finer needlepoint. You do not follow an outline marked on the canvas in advance. You work the designs on the bare canvas in such a way that the stitches and variations of color form the texture and patterns. The patterns literally grow in rows—out from the center, from side to side, from top to bottom, depending on the design involved. In many instances you need only count zigs or zags in the first row. Then you automatically follow the same contour across the canvas, making proper color changes to create the pattern. As soon as the basic pattern is completed in repeat designs, you can close the book and merrily travel on, for the worked area becomes your guide. You simply repeat it over and over for desired coverage. This process eliminates the necessity of fussy counting. What could be easier! There are, of course, more complicated patterns included which do require a certain amount of counting, but you will find even those steps become automatic after working a small area.

You start by familiarizing yourself with the array of facts in this chapter which are presented to help you make friends with this different approach to needlepoint.

ALL ABOUT THE YARN

There are many excellent, heavy wool rug yarns available on the market today. The color ranges and the quality are improving constantly. Synthetic yarns with amazing, unique, durable qualities are also being developed by manufacturers. To be suitable for use in Now Needlepoint a yarn should be:

1. Heavy enough to properly cover the canvas.

2. Durable enough to withstand wear and tear—not soft like the yarns used for knitting.

3. Colorfast with a good range of colors. The color range is extremely important; it is impossible to create pleasing designs with dull, drab colors.

The two types of yarn used in the samples shown throughout the book, Pat Rug Yarn and Nantucket 6-Ply Cable Yarn, are different in weight—one much heavier than the other—and are also completely different in personality. Both yarns are colorfast, extremely durable and come in breathtaking color ranges. Although I heartily recommend them, I don't in any way wish to exclude other excellent yarns which might qualify. If you substitute another yarn, purchase a small amount and experiment to determine if it properly covers the canvas before you invest in large quantities for extensive projects. There must be a happy marriage between the canvas and the yarn if your designs are to be successful. Figure 2-1,

2-1

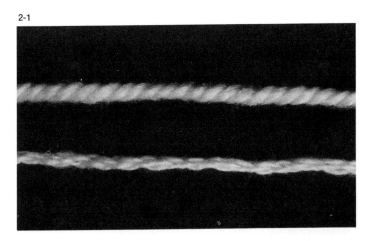

which shows the actual size of the yarns, gives you a criterion for judging the yarn weight. The heavier weight on top is the Pat Rug Yarn and the lighter weight on the bottom is the Nantucket 6-Ply Cable Yarn.

Information pertaining to the yarn is presented throughout to assist you in keying designs in the proper colors and in determining how much yarn to purchase. The actual color numbers and the approximate number of strands used for all the finished items are included and are designated in the directions by "str." It is always good insurance to purchase sufficient yarn from the same dye lot to completely cover a solid background—even a little extra—since any slight difference in a plain area is quickly detected by the eye. The manufacturers miraculously match their colors, so you do not have to be too concerned in most designs where over-all patterns are concerned—only in the solid areas.

Pat Rug Yarn is a heavyweight 3-ply yarn with remarkable resilience and durability. You need only rub it between two fingers to *feel* the wearing quality. It is available in a magnificent range of over two hundred colors which run the gamut from the subtle grayed to the brilliant colors. Almost all of the colors come in families of four and sometimes five different values. A designer's dream come true!

Nantucket 6-Ply Cable Yarn is lighter in weight than the Pat Rug Yarn and, as the name implies, resembles a cable in texture. The yarn is available in over fifty colors but not in families. However, the colors are among the most unique and brilliant ones on the market today. There are unusual, superb grayed colors too. This yarn's palette is also a designer's delight and the overall texture produced by the cable twist is smashing! It covers the canvas beautifully when worked in the Fly, French and Chain stitches, but due to the lightweight quality of the yarn, a special version of the Orr Weave stitch called the "Double Orr Weave" must be used. The additional step quickly becomes automatic and the result is well worth the extra effort. Shops and companies which sell Pat Rug Yarn and the Nantucket Cable are listed at the back of the book.

Both yarns are available in ¼-lb. hanks. The following information shows the approximate number of strands—not yards—in a ¼-lb. hank of each of the two types of yarns. This will help you to determine how many ¼-lb. hanks of yarn will be necessary to complete any of the finished samples, since the number of strands used are listed throughout. Even if the count goes slightly over the indicated number, you should purchase an additional ¼-lb. hank. The excess yarn can always be put to good use in future projects.

Pat Rug Yarn has approximately 35 1¾-yd. strands in each ¼-lb. hank.

Nantucket 6-Ply Cable Yarn has approximately 43 1¾-yd. strands in each ¼-lb. hank.

Rough Rule of Thumb for Coverage. A very rough rule of thumb is that ½ lb. of yarn covers approximately one square foot of canvas. This varies to some degree with each stitch, and, of course, you must purchase yarn in the number of colors necessary to interpret the pattern, but do tuck this information away in the back of your mind for it can allow you to estimate quickly the amount of yarn necessary for coverage.

How to Convert 1¾-Yd. Strands into a Yard Count. For example:

Question: How many yards are there in 15 strands?

Answer: Since there are 1¾ yds. (or 1.75 yds.) in each strand, therefore 15 × 1.75 yds. = 26.25 yds.—or in round numbers, approximately 27 yds.

With this simple formula, you can easily convert strands to yards when you wish to substitute other yarns.

Cutting Strands of Yarn. Both the Pat Rug Yarn and the Nantucket 6-Ply Cable Yarn are merchandised in ¼-lb. hanks of approximately the same size. My system for cutting yarn in working strands is to cut off the knot connecting the two ends and cut once through the entire hank. Then cut the finer piece of yarn which you will find encircling the hank, so the strands can be separated easily.

Note: If you are planning tassels or fringe, keep in mind that you must reserve uncut yarn for trimmings which require one continuous length or specified shorter lengths.

It is important that you understand that 1¾ yds. is a long strand. When the strand is new and long, double it over three quarters of the length while you work the stitches. You may prefer working with shorter strands. I suggest you cut a few 1¾ yd. lengths and try them before slicing the whole hank. Shorter lengths should be used when learning the stitches, and the long strand can be cut in half for this purpose.

I always use the long strand for a number of reasons. The most important one is that it reduces the number of stops and starts, thus eliminating excess bulk and bunching which might occur on the wrong side. Another good reason: it is so easy to give one slice through the hank rather than continually having to measure individual lengths. Also, it is rather a nuisance to have to end a strand and start a new one too frequently. There are experts who will no doubt be horrified at my suggesting this length, but with very few exceptions all of my students have used the long length with favorable results.

One point: If the design pattern you are using involves continual similar runs across or down the canvas, you *can* establish the necessary length (measure the strand before you work it and deduct any excess) and cut your strands accordingly. By using this method you eliminate stops and starts except at the beginning and end of each row. A bit of waste might be involved, since you must be certain the length will be sufficient to work the stitches through to the end of the row or you have defeated the purpose.

Threading the Needle with Ease. The age-old system of moistening the thread in your mouth doesn't work with the heavy yarn—it just leaves you with the feeling that you have been chewing on sweaters—but you can easily slip the heavy rug yarn through the eye of the needle as follows:

1. Hold the needle and yarn as shown in Figure 2-2 with approximately ½ in. of yarn extending to the left beyond the eye of the needle.

2. Tightly clamp the end of the yarn around the needle with the fingers of your right hand as shown in Figure 2-3. Keeping the fingers clamped together, slip the loop up off the top of the needle.

3. Still holding the loop tightly clamped, push it through the eye of the needle. Release your fingers as in Figure 2-4. Pull the loop through the eye of the needle with the left hand.

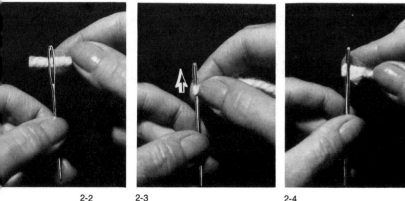

2-2   2-3   2-4

Keep the Yarn Untwisted at All Times: This is the golden rule for all needlework. Nothing destroys working pleasure or the appearance of the work more than twisted, kinked-up wool. Some of us are twisters and some are untwisters. This rule also holds true for the stitches: the yarn should always be worked in its natural, relaxed state for a pleasing end result. To twist or untwist—whichever is necessary—simply hold the canvas up, right side down, and let the needle and yarn dangle free for a moment. Sometimes a little help is needed, but usually the yarn will twist or untwist to its natural state.

Tension of Yarn. Each yarn has a distinct personality of its own which should be evident in the finished work. If

you have never worked with large canvas and heavy yarn, you will notice a completely different feel and sometimes a slight tug on the yarn. The yarn should be pulled through the canvas with a slow, steady movement. Do not pull the yarn through in fits and starts or you will tear the yarn.

Let the personality of the yarn live, so it retains its texture and remains fluffy. This you accomplish by correct tension. Work the yarn so it is loose enough to show the texture, but not so loose that the formation of the stitch is lost. Experiment a bit. Practice is the secret, and in a short while you will develop a steady, even rhythm much like that of a weaver.

Starting and Ending Strands of Yarn. No knots—absolutely no knots!—if you want to prevent excess bunching of yarn on the wrong side. Because of the heavy quality of the rug yarn, knots tend to create cumbersome wads and so they are never used in Now Needlepoint. Avoid a concentration of yarn when you run it under on the wrong side by not using the exact same spot for both start and stops. Do not run the yarn under along the edge. When beginning and ending a row of stitches, it is best to run the yarn under a row of stitches on the wrong side toward the outside edge for starts, and away from the outside edge when the row is completed. This prevents having excess wool in areas along the edges where construction will take place.

To Start Strands. When you wish to start the first stitch on the canvas or when there is no worked area close at hand, leave a tail of yarn on the wrong side at least 6 in. long to be woven in later and proceed with the stitches. For a regular start, run the needle threaded with yarn under a row of stitches on the wrong side for at least 1 in. Pull the yarn through, leaving a ½ in. tail. Bring the needle up to the surface on the right side in the correct spot to start a stitch. Proceed with the stitches.

To End Strands. When a strand is almost used up, complete the last step of the stitch by bringing the needle through the canvas to the wrong side. Run the yarn under the worked area for at least 1 in. Remove the needle and snip off the yarn end, leaving a ½ in. tail.

Note: In certain instances it is advisable to end a strand on a particular step of the stitch, rather than waiting to complete it, in order to retain the formation. Whenever this is necessary, it will be called to your attention.

Yarn Tie Markers. The only markers that were used for all the samples shown were ties made of 3-in. lengths of scrap yarn. These are done by simply tying one simple half knot (Fig. 2-5) or, if you wish, making a loose square knot. It should be loose, for the yarn tie is removed

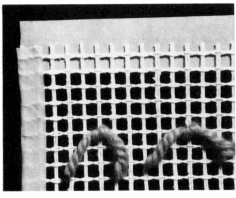

2-5

immediately before the particular spot is covered with a stitch. And don't remove it too far in advance or you will lose the spot. Tie these markers over crossbars or on straight bars—whichever pinpoints the spot most clearly.

Remember always to place a yarn tie marker at the top of the canvas before you start to work the stitches. As soon as you have placed the masking tape around the raw edges, tie the marker close to the edge of the side which will be the top. This instruction is not repeated throughout the book, but please make it a habit. It is very easy to pick up the canvas and start stitching in the wrong direction without the top marker.

The markers can be used to indicate spots where you wish to start Wiggly Chain Design Motifs, and at corners to indicate the exact area you wish to cover, as the following directions explain.

To place yarn tie markers at corners when you are using overall repeat patterns, measure the area you wish to cover on the canvas and tie a yarn marker diagonally over each of the four crossbars which will be your guides for the corners. The corner stitches of the area to be covered will be worked *over* these crossbars of canvas or as close to them as the particular stitch permits. As already explained, you should remove the markers immediately before working the corner stitches. Using the four corners as guides, you can cover the area with a particular design of your choice. Keep in mind that overall repeat patterns require a specific number of bars of canvas to correctly center and balance the design. To insure balance at the top and bottom, and the side edges, it often takes a bit of planning and counting of bars at this point to key designs involving patterns of zigzags or stripes. You should make certain in advance that the pattern you have chosen can be maneuvered to fit properly in the specific area, especially if you must adhere to exact measurements.

In order to place yarn tie markers for background areas after the central design has been completed, you should:

1. Count up (or down) from the central design the number of horizontal canvas bars you wish to cover with background. Place a finger on this horizontal bar.

2. Count out to the side from the central design the number of vertical bars you wish to cover with background. Place a finger from your other hand on this vertical bar.

3. Run both fingers toward the corner and place a yarn tie marker diagonally over the crossbar where they meet.

Repeat this procedure for the four corners. The top and bottom markers should be on the same vertical bar on each side—the two top markers on the same horizontal bar and the two bottom markers on the same horizontal bar. The corner stitches will be worked over these crossbars or as close to them as the particular stitch permits.

Note: If you feel you need to completely outline the outside edges, purchase a tube of the acrylic paint used by artists in a deep yellow which will show on the canvas. Dilute it with water and mark your area. *Let it dry thoroughly* before stitching over it. But before you attempt to use any of the felt tip markers, investigate and determine if they are colorfast—even test them yourself. Remember that dry cleaning is recommended for Now Needlepoint items. "Colorfast" can be a very elastic term. Such factors as how the canvas is sized and what type of cleaning fluid will be used seem to have an important bearing on whether or not markers will "bleed" under certain conditions. You might find one which will serve your purpose beautifully, but do put it through a rigid test before you use it. Hours of effort can be ruined too quickly.

Single Strand Doubled. Thread a needle with a strand of yarn. Pull the ends even and work the double strand as one. (Fig. 2-6.) A single strand of yarn is used doubled when single strands would not properly cover the canvas or when a heavy textural effect is desired. *Do not use two strands.* Four strands plus the needle would have to be pulled through the canvas and this is not feasible with the heavy yarn.

When you use a single strand doubled, place the pointer finger of your left hand under the spot where the yarn comes *out* of the canvas before tightening the loop to

2-6

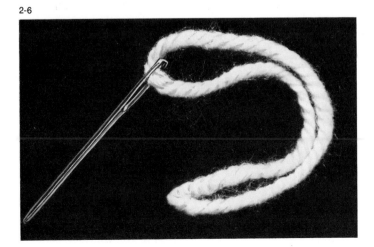

complete a stitch step. For some reason, the two strands tend to fall neatly in place side by side if you follow this procedure. After a few stitches this step will become automatic. As mentioned before, it is especially important to keep the wool untwisted at all times.

Correction with the Needle. Slight irregularities which might occur in the stitches can be corrected with a little help from the needle. By pulling a bit more wool to the surface you can usually correct an uneven look. You can well afford a bit of time to pamper the stitches when necessary since they progress so very rapidly.

ALL ABOUT THE CANVAS

Two sizes of canvas are used for the samples shown throughout the book. Figure 2-7 shows the 3 to the inch (sometimes referred to as 3½ to the inch) on the top and the 5 to the inch canvas on the bottom. The double sets of bars in the 5 to the inch canvas are treated as single bars. Always place the needle in the large holes unless you are otherwise instructed. Both sizes can be worked lengthwise or crosswise and are stiff enough to control the shape of the large stitches. The canvas takes the place of a cumber-

2-7. *Top:* 3 to the inch canvas.
Bottom: 5 to the inch canvas.

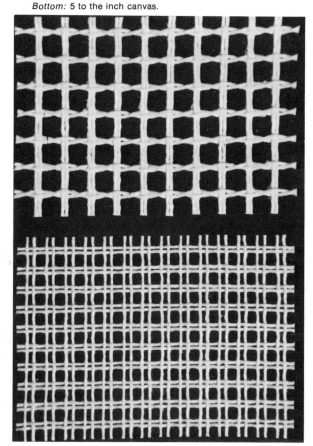

some loom and becomes your guide for uniformly working the stitches. Both sizes of canvas are sold by the yard in 40 in. widths, but they can usually be purchased in smaller amounts in most shops.

Think Plan for Purchasing Canvas and Cutting it to Size. Make a quick think-plan drawing to establish the overall measurements, so you can determine how much canvas to purchase. Approximately 2 in.—at the very least 1½ in.—of canvas should be added on all sides for construction. A small portion of this excess will be cut off after you machine zig zag to prevent unraveling. It is always wise to allow an extra canvas bar or two in case you decide to work a braid stitch completely around after you have completed the area.

We will use a 12 in. pillow top as an example. The first drawing (Fig. 2-8) is for the top only—the second is for when a backing is included. The drawing shows the area to be covered with Now Needlepoint in the middle plus the necessary surrounding excess canvas. By making this drawing you can quickly see you would need a piece of canvas with the following dimensions: 16 in. (2 in. + 12 in. + 2 in.) × 16 in. (2 in. + 12 in. + 2 in.). You would need to purchase ½ yd. of canvas to cut out the 16 in. square.

If a backing is to be included, you would need a piece of

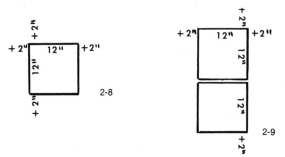

2-8

2-9

canvas with the following dimensions (Fig. 2-9): 16 in. (2 in. + 12 in. + 2 in.) × 28 in. (2 in. + 12 in. + 12 in. + 2 in.). Both types of canvas are sold 40 in. wide so you would need to purchase ½ yd. to cut out the 16 in. × 28 in. piece.

Cut the canvas to size with sharp scissors. Carefully cut between the bars following the row exactly for the desired length. The selvage is removed after the work is completed.

This think-plan can be used for all Now Needlepoint items. *Note:* Leftover pieces can be used in future items. Save any small scraps for practice stitches or samples for designing.

Preparing the Canvas for Work. Cover all raw edges with masking tape before commencing work. (See Fig. 2-5.) Cut a strip of 1 in.-wide masking tape the length of one side of canvas. Place it sticky side up on a flat surface. Then place the canvas down on half of the width as shown—and fold the remaining half down over the edge of the canvas and press firmly in place. Snip off the tape ends so they are even. Continue around this way until all raw edges are covered. The selvage can remain as is. If the selvage is included, it can be used to indicate the top. Otherwise place a yarn tie marker near the edge in the center of a side which will be the top.

Treat the canvas gently. As your experience increases, try to develop a method of working where you do not constantly clutch and crumple the canvas. The stitch instructions explain how to work the stitches from the surface, and with help from your free hand you can easily proceed without mangling the canvas. It isn't necessary to do so and if you do, it destroys the stiffness of the canvas which controls the shape of the stitches.

Machine Zig Zag Before Construction. Because of the nature of the very open weave of the large canvas, it is essential that you work a double row of machine zig zagging on the *third bar of canvas outside the Now Needlepoint area* before construction. This system allows extra canvas for construction and prevents unraveling. Specific instructions are given throughout the book for this step, but the basic general procedure is:

1. Remove the masking tape if it is close to the worked area. In many instances it will be far enough away so that it will not interfere with machine stitching and therefore can be left in place.

2. Use heavy-duty sewing thread. Machine zig zag completely around on the third bar of canvas outside the worked area (the third set of double bars on the 5 to the inch canvas). Make a second machine zig zag on the same bar (or bars) of canvas.

3. Carefully cut off the excess canvas *outside* of the machine zigzagging.

Needles. Use large-eyed tapestry needles for all of the Now Needlepoint stitches. The needle should have a round point and the eye must be large enough to accommodate the heavy yarn.

Masking Tape. The 1 in. masking tape used for covering raw edges of canvas while the work is in progress can be obtained in stores where artists' supplies are sold.

No Blocking. All Now Needlepoint stitches have cross tension play which results in an even pull in opposite directions. This makes blocking unnecessary. None of the samples shown in the following chapters have been blocked in any way other than their being carefully pulled into shape *immediately* before construction takes place. If a stitch tortured the shape of the canvas, I discarded it for use in the heavy wool and it does not qualify to be included in Now Needlepoint. It never ceases to amaze me when my eyes fall on canvas painstakingly worked in a delightful design but so pulled out of shape by the stitch that it has the look of a tortured lopsided diamond even after blocking and construction have taken place. To me this result would be a disaster in the heavy yarn and large canvas.

Some of the stitches do produce a slight pull in one direction, but only slightly so if the tension is correct. The secret is to pull the area carefully into shape with several tugs while holding the item in your hands at diagonally opposite corners. Pull in one diagonal direction—then pull in the opposite diagonal direction. By using this method you can easily square off the sides. It is sometimes necessary to give several extra tugs in one direction.

This lining-up process must take place *immediately* before construction. For instance, a pillow top would be pulled into shape directly before it is placed face down to be attached to the pillow backing. As soon as the construction takes place, the pillow is held in shape. It will also hold any distorted shape if it has not been corrected before being attached to the backing.

An imbalance can be caused while you work the stitches if the tension in one direction is stressed to a greater extent than that in the opposite direction. If you discover your canvas is being pulled out of shape to a great degree, quickly correct the tension and the problem will be resolved.

If you wish to get rid of a rumpled look—some of us are rambunctious workers—or correct a distortion due to incorrect tension, you can cover a flat clean surface with brown paper. Pull the article in shape and place it right side down on the brown paper. Use a warm steam iron —not hot, since we are dealing with wool—and steam the wrong side, touching the wool as little as possible. Steam the work enough to slightly dampen the canvas and wool. Then turn the item over and place it right side up on the surface. Again, pull it in shape, very carefully this time. (Pushpins can be used to hold the work in shape if necessary, but be certain to place them outside of the worked area for they cause rust spots. The flat surface material would then have to be something which would take the pins.) Having the item face up gives the heavy wool a chance to fluff and breathe while it dries. Let the item dry *thoroughly* before you move it. This takes considerable time with the heavy wool. The canvas stiffens again as it dries so it is important to have the item remain in the desired shape as this process takes place.

Caution: Do not substitute aluminum foil for brown paper, since it sometimes has a strange chemical effect on the yarn dyes and can cause a slight "bleeding" of colors.

Dry Cleaning. As mentioned before, dry cleaning is recommended for all Now Needlepoint items. Remove the stuffing from the pillows when possible. If pillows or pincushions have Now Needlepoint backings, they can be successfully dry cleaned if they have been stuffed with Poly-Fil. The manufacturer assured me that this product is dry cleanable as long as you point out that the item is stuffed with polyester. Check with your local cleaner if your items have been stuffed with other material.

Many times you can freshen up an item with a soft cloth and some cleaning fluid. There are a number of cleaning products on the market which should work well. But keep in mind that you are dealing with wool and experiment on some of your sample stitches before tackling a finished item.

Throughout these pages you will be encountering some terms which I use frequently and with which you may not be familiar:

Keying a Design. Dictionaries list several meanings of the word "key": to attune; to regulate the musical pitch of; to bring into harmony. Perhaps it is stretching a point and coining a slightly new meaning, but you are "keying" a design during the period when you are considering what stitch to use, how large the item should be, deciding on the proper colors or, in general, making all the decisions needed to produce harmony in the end result. Consider the design "keyed" when you are ready to start the actual stitching.

Zig. Diagonal downward direction from left to right: ↘

Zag. Diagonal downward direction from right to left: ↗ Perhaps you can best remember the directions if you associate the "i" in "zig" with the "i" in the word right.

Four Stitch Zig Zag. Four stitches in each diagonal direction. Count stitches at points each time. (Fig. 2-10.)

2-10

Four Stitch Square. Four stitches on each side. Count stitches at corners each time. (Fig. 2-11.)

2-11

Thumbnail Sketch. A rough little sketch made quickly to record a design or an idea on paper for future references. A thumbnail can be made anytime on any handy piece of paper whenever an idea flashes through your mind.

Think Plan. A quick little plan jotted down on paper to formulate plans for construction or to determine the exact mathematical dimensions for cutting canvas to proper size, as described on page 42.

Touch Stitch. Many of the stitches described in this book are worked over more than one bar or crossbars of canvas. It is necessary to work them out from a point so that each succeeding stitch or row of stitches touches the preceding stitch or row of stitches. The French Stitch is a good example of a Touch Stitch. You cannot work one row of zig zag stitches down the left side and then jump to the right side and work a row. It is practically impossible to determine the exact spot where the row on the right should be started, so that there will be the proper number of bars and holes between to fill in the rows with French Stitches. If you wish to create symmetrical balance, you should start with a row in the exact center and work out to each side so that every row is worked directly next to and touching the preceding one.

The Orr Weave is an example of a stitch that is *not* a Touch Stitch. Because only one crossbar of canvas is used to complete each individual stitch, you can jump to another area to start a parallel row of stitches and subsequently fill in the area between.

There are several decorative stitches to learn which you use to embellish many of the patterns and finished items. They are delightful little additions which produce sparkle and textural interest in the Now Needlepoint designs. The stitches are worked after the area stitches are completed and you can learn them quickly with a bit of practice.

Back Stitch for Decorative Purposes. The Back Stitch is worked *between* already-worked rows of stitches and produces a decorative outline. As an example, see the rockets on the turquoise pillow in Figure 3-36.

The Back Stitch is worked on both 3 and 5 to the inch canvas. Follow Figure 2-12. The Stitch is worked from right to left. (Turn the canvas to the correct position so that the stitches can be worked in this direction.)

2-12

1. Bring the needle up to the surface in hole 1.

2. Place the needle down in 2—going under 2 bars of canvas—and up in 3 in one motion.

3. Place the needle down in 4 and up in 5 in one motion. Continue working the stitch for desired length.

Lazy Daisy Stitch for Surface Stitching. A series of simple chain stitches worked *out* from a center point like magic produce a daisy. The petals can be made any length you wish. They can be uniform or irregular and at times can be worked in a semicircle, simulating the side view of a daisy. Take a close look at some daisy pictures or, better still, examine live ones. There are many charming irregularities which appear in nature and which make it unnecessary to produce painstaking uniform stitches when you are attempting to capture a feeling. Daisies appear to dance in the fields, so let your stitches do the same. This version of the chain stitch is open and lacy and so is excellent for surface stitching since it allows the underneath texture to peek through. The stitches are worked on the surface of overall textural background stitches such as the Chain Stitch or the Orr Weave, but are not suitable for use with stitches which have very definite patterns, such as French or Fly stitches.

To work a Lazy Daisy Stitch, follow Figure 2-13.

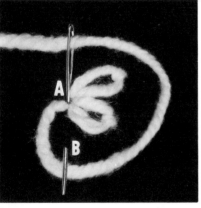

2-13

1. Bring the needle up to the surface in A.

2. Place the needle down in A—or close to A—and bring the needle up in B in one motion as shown in the photograph. (This step is where you control the size of the finished daisy. The greater the distance between points A and B, the larger the daisy.) Pull the needle and yarn so that the loop of yarn is caught underneath.

3. Work a small tie-down stitch over the end of loop and bring the needle up close to A in the correct spot to start the next petal. The stitches can be worked around in either direction. Your spacing and the length of the loops create the look and size of the finished daisy. A French Knot of a contrasting yarn worked in the center (or a

group of knots if you allow space) is the finishing touch which spells "daisy" to your eye.

Fabulous French Knots—So Obliging! They become tiny buds, centers of flowers, polka dots, berries, and even eyes on bugs. They produce that extra touch so often needed to make a design sing. They can be worked in a variety of sizes: Small (single strand—around the needle once); medium (single strand—around the needle twice); large (single strand doubled—around the needle once); extra large (single strand doubled—around the needle twice).

The procedure for working the French Knot with the single strand is:

1. Bring the needle and yarn up to the surface in the spot where the French Knot is to be placed. Hold the needle in your right hand. To work the knot around the needle once, wind the yarn over the needle once with the left hand as in Figure 2-14. To work the knot around the needle twice, wind the yarn over the needle twice with the left hand as in Figure 2-15.

2. Place the point of the needle down in the spot close to where the yarn comes through to the surface. (It is necessary to work over either a bar of canvas or some yarn at this point to prevent the knot from slipping through to the back when the knot is closed. This step will become automatic in no time, especially after a few knots have slipped through to the back.) See Figure 2-16. Pull the yarn gently and slowly with your left hand, so that it

2-14

2-15

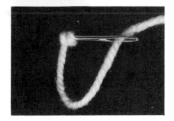

2-16

45

closes around the needle. Don't pull too tightly since the needle and the yarn have to be pulled through the center.

3. Pull the needle slowly through the twisted yarn to the wrong side until the surface knot is formed. Shape it with your fingers if necessary. Bring the needle up to the surface in the place where the next knot is to be placed. I catch once on the wrong side if there is an extra-long run between the knots. If they are very far apart, end the yarn and start in a new spot. Let discretion be your guide.

The heavier knot—the French Knot with the single strand doubled—is worked exactly like the single-strand knot. Keep the yarn untwisted at all times and work slowly, especially during step 3, when the knot is actually being formed. Irregularities in the final knot can be eliminated by gently pulling a loose single strand from underneath. The single-strand-doubled knot takes a bit of practice but the chunky, heavy, textural effect it produces is worth the extra effort.

Note: Once in a while a knot will not behave. Don't let it frustrate you; it happens to all of us. Pull the needle and the yarn up to the surface, carefully untie the knot and make a fresh start.

Finally, we have come to the nitty-gritty— the learning of the stitch mechanics. If you happen to be familiar with some of the stitches, you can decide on your project, stitch, colors and get off to a flying start. Those who are complete novices and those who wish to learn how to make the stitches perform should proceed by first obtaining the following:

Canvas. Invest in at least ¼ yd. of each of the two sizes of canvas. Each piece can be cut in half to make two 9 in. × 20 in. pieces—and halved again if you prefer for four 9 in. × 10 in. smaller practice pieces. Place masking tape around the outside edges of the canvas.

Yarn. Purchase Rug Yarn—¼ lb. each of white, a middle-value color and of a deep-value color. Pick colors which please you.

I prefer students to use good-quality rug yarn even while they are learning the stitches. You constantly use the samples for reference once you start planning your own projects. However, if you are frugal by nature, inexpensive rug yarn available in most chain stores can be substituted during the learning process. But be certain it is rug yarn. The soft knitting yarns, which are not manufactured to withstand the pull on the heavy canvas, are not suitable and only cause confusion. Cut the yarn according to previous instructions. Cut a few long strands in half for learning purposes.

Needles. Purchase at least three large tapestry needles —one for each color yarn.

Pick the stitch you wish to master first and *begin!*

Remember, those labor pains will vanish in no time.

The stitches are most easily worked from the top surface, and the photographs of the actual stitch in progress show how to do this. There are times when the needle is pulled through to the back—for instance, when working through several thicknesses of canvas for the edges or construction, or at the end of a row—but usually the needle goes down and up in one motion. Some of the stitches require numerous turns of the canvas, but these turns quickly become automatic as you progress and become interested in the textures you are forming with the stitch.

Help all you can with your free hand. You will notice hands are not shown in any of the photographs of the stitch steps. The reason is that each of us has our own way of holding needles and assisting with our free hand. It would be confusing to the student for me to dictate, "Hold the needle thus and so." Only the steps need be outlined, so that you can form your own natural way of producing the stitches.

Practice the stitch diligently until you have mastered the mechanics—until you can work it without referring to the drawings. Do not be too concerned with tension in the early learning stages. Get the stitch steps under control—then work on the tension. If, as with the French Stitch, a stitch walks in many directions, master the one or two natural directions before getting involved in the other, more difficult, directions. Keep practicing. A point will soon come when you will sail along without thinking of all the steps involved. This is when the enjoyment starts.

Once you have mastered the mechanical steps and the correct tension I suggest you pick a simple pattern using the stitch and plan your first project. It is best to keep this project on the small side so you can quickly experience the satisfaction of completing it. After the project is completed, you will be on intimate terms with the stitch. Then, be daring and experiment on a practice piece of canvas. Make that stitch dutifully walk in all possible directions. This practice will give you an idea of the stitch's potentials for creative designing. Work a number of sample patterns similar to the ones shown in the book, so that you understand how the patterns are formed. Spark your awareness by giving thought to additional design and color combinations which could be interpreted in the stitch. Make rough thumbnail sketches with color notes.

Move on to the next stitch chapter. Repeat the foregoing procedure until you have mastered the mechanics and are on friendly terms with each of the stitches. You will end up with a vocabulary of stitches, working sample swatches, thumbnail sketches and a head full of ideas —all of which will be invaluable when you key future designs.

Helpful Aid to Keep Track of a Long Series of Directional Changes. Cut a section out of a 3 in. × 5 in. piece of paper to form an "L" shape. Place the "L" down on the page of directions, using the inside of the "L" as a guide. As you complete each color change or step, move the paper to the proper position for the next change or step.

Length of Strand. Throughout the stitch chapters, the approximate amount of yarn is given for all finished items. The abbreviation "str." designates strands. The length of a strand is 1¾ yds. long. The figure indicates the approximate number of 1¾-yd. strands used for each color. (See p. 39 if you wish to convert strands into a yard count.)

A Final Note: In the section on the finished items in the individual stitch chapters, there are frequent references to instructions in other chapters, especially the last chapter on construction and finishing. Although you can find the cross-references easily enough by flipping through the cited chapter or find the exact pages by looking up the subject in the index, here is a short list of the most often-mentioned subjects, with the pages on which they are discussed:

3.

The Facile Fly Stitch:
A Spirited Chevron

3-1. The Fly Stitch.

Personality. The Fly Stitch has a distinct look, a personality all its own. Like distant birds in flight, it forms a chevron—a stylized version of the letter Y—two arms that reach upward at angles with one small tie-down stitch at the bottom to hold them in place. It is easy to master the mechanics, for once you have established the width and angle of the first stitch you can walk the stitches in step, one right under the other, down to the bottom of the row. Unlike the crewel Fly Stitch worked on material where you must constantly gauge size with your eye, the bars of canvas act as guides to a uniform look. If you control your tension correctly, the stitches fall evenly in place and produce a very professional appearance.

Two versions or sizes of the Fly Stitch are presented, so that you will be able to vary the angle and width of the chevrons, thus adding greatly to the designing potentials of this stitch:

The *4-Bar Fly Stitch* is a large chevron with a deep angle worked over 4 bars of canvas.

The *2-Bar Fly Stitch* is a small chevron with a shallow angle worked over 2 bars of canvas.

Will Travel. The stitches are *always* worked in a downward direction, from the top of the canvas to the bottom, and the normal procedure is to work rows from left to right. However, the rows can also be worked from right to left. This is helpful if you wish to center a row of stitches for designing purposes and then work the subsequent rows out from the center to each side.

Note: The Fly Stitch is a Touch Stitch; several bars of canvas are used for each stitch.

Design and Color Potentials. Push your aware button and think of the myriad possibilities for the chevron motif. Turn the stitches one way and they become little rockets shooting upward into the atmosphere. Turn them in the opposite direction—add suggestions for stem and leaves plus a few French knots for stamens—and presto, they become stylized flowers. Think also of the look of Indian designs where the chevron motif appears constantly. Glance at the patterns in this chapter. Notice what happens when you introduce delightful French knots between the rows of Fly Stitches. Rosebuds magically appear, producing a very feminine and pretty effect. Surface whipping through the tie-down stitches creates wiggly curved patterns—a pleasant contrast to the stitch's straight, regimented appearance.

3-2

You can form waves that run across a design by repeating a color at the exact same spot in each row—so easy to follow once you have keyed the first row. By varying the width of the rows and introducing pleasing color, you can easily produce endless design patterns. You can go wild, as in Pattern #11 used for the bench top, and end up with a very modern, striking effect. (See Fig. 3-24.) Every row appears to be different and, with the use of color fusion, your eye literally dances across the Now Needlepoint. The orange stitches were worked in the same spot in each row throughout and were connected in one continuous wave across the area. While you may not be conscious of this magic, the busy pattern is solidified by the net of orange waves. This is a designing device well worth remembering.

Color Changes. With the Fly Stitch they are easy and fun—yes *fun!* Glance quickly at some of the patterns in the chapter. Most of them are created with very few colors and are simple to produce. Look at the bench top again. All those colors! Even with so many colors involved the technique for changing the colors is not complicated once you understand it. You don't have to end and start yarn strands constantly. You simply work as many stitches in a color as required for the pattern, skip under on the wrong side and bring your needle up to the surface in the hole where the color will be reintroduced. Then place the needle and yarn over to the left out of the way. Work the necessary number of stitches in the next color and repeat the same process by anticipating where the second color will be reintroduced. This is the way it goes; it only requires that you end and start colors once in a row (except when the yarn is used up). The technique is like using bobbins in knitting—remember the argyle-sock days?—but it is far less complicated for the yarn and needles can be placed over to the side, out of the way, and do not dangle and become twisted.

Suggested Uses. Fly Stitches lie flat and are held securely by the little tie-down stitches, but the arms of the 4-Bar Fly do reach for a considerable distance, creating a rather long run of yarn. Therefore, the Fly Stitch is recommended for the full gamut of items, with one exception—rugs. Heels might get caught in the long runs of the Fly Stitch arms, so it is best to use one of the stitches that are closely woven and hug the canvas for rugs.

MECHANICS FOR
4-BAR FLY AND 2-BAR FLY STITCHES

Both sizes of the Fly Stitch are worked on 5 to the inch canvas, and both versions are always worked in rows from the top of the canvas to the bottom. The normal procedure is to start at the upper left corner and work the rows from left to right. Rows can also be worked from right to left if it is necessary for designing purposes.

Fill-in Stitches. Because of the formation of the Fly Stitch, you will have to work fill-in stitches at the top and bottom of each row to cover the exposed canvas and produce an even edge. The top Fill-in Stitches are worked immediately after the first stitch is worked and the bottom ones after the last stitch is completed.

To Work the 4-Bar Fly Stich, Follow Figure 3-2.

1. Start at the upper left. Bring the needle up to the surface in hole 1, leaving a 6 in. tail on the wrong side to be woven in later.

2. Count 4 bars to the right. Place the needle down in 2 and up in center hole 3 in one motion, catching the yarn under the needle as shown in Figure 3-3, p.50. Pull the yarn through to the surface so a flat V is formed.

3. The needle is up in 3. Go over the yarn and bar of canvas and place the needle down in 4 and up in 5 in one motion. Pull the yarn through to the surface to form the first chevron.

Note: At this point we have jumped up to 5 to fill in the exposed canvas.

4. Place the needle down in 6 and up in 7 in one motion.

5. Go over the yarn and bar of canvas. Place the needle down in 8 and up in 9 in one motion.

6. Go over the bar of canvas only. Place the needle down in 10 and up in 11 (over to the left) in one motion.

Note: The Fill-in Stitches are completed. From now on work the stitches one directly under the other. There are only two steps involved in the formation of the Fly Stitch once the Fill-in Stitches are worked:

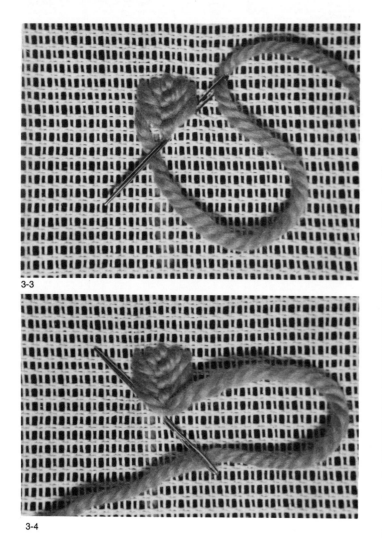

3-3

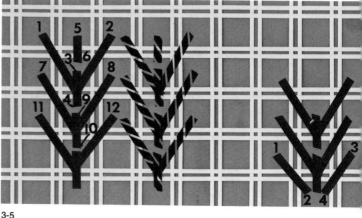

3-5

Second Row. Start the second row at the top, to the right of the first row. The second row is indicated by striped stitches in the stitch diagrams. Bring the needle up in the same hole 2 that was used for the right side of the first row. Repeat the first row.

To Work the 2-Bar Fly Stitch, Follow Figure 3-5.

1. Start at the upper left. Bring the needle up to the surface in hole 1, leaving a 6 in. tail on the wrong side to be woven in later.

2. Count 2 bars to the right. Place the needle down in 2 and up in center hole 3 in one motion, catching the yarn under the needle, as shown in Figure 3-6. Pull the yarn through to the surface so a flat V is formed.

3. The needle is up in 3. Go over the yarn and bar of canvas. Place the needle down in 4 and up in 5 in one motion.

Note: At this point the exposed canvas at the top is filled in.

4. Go over the bar of canvas only. Place the needle down in 6 and up in 7 in one motion.

Note: This completes the Fill-in Stitch. Only two steps are involved in the formation of the 2-Bar Fly, as follows:

3-4

7. You are up in 11. Go down in 12 and up in center hole 13 in one motion, catching the yarn under the needle as shown in Figure 3-3.

8. Go over the yarn and bar of canvas. Place the needle down in the center hole 14 and up in 15 in one motion as in Figure 3-4. Keep repeating Steps 7 and 8 until the row is completed. The stitches walk in steps down to the bottom, one directly under the other. Make certain you do not skip holes along the sides. Sometimes it is necessary to peek under the yarn to find the next free hole.

To End the Row. Use Fill-in Stitches to form an even edge at the bottom of the row, as shown at the right of Figure 3-2. Complete the last stitch in the row, but do not end the yarn.

1. Bring the needle up in 1. Place the needle down in 2 and up in 3.

2. Place the needle down in 4—skip under on the wrong side—and bring the needle up in 5 over to the right.

3. Place the needle down in 6 and up in 7.

4. Place the needle down in 8. Pull the yarn through to the wrong side. End the yarn.

To End Strands. Pull the yarn through to the wrong side upon completion of a stitch. Run under at least 1 in. of worked area. Snip off the yarn, leaving a ½ in. tail.

To Start Strands. Run under at least 1 in. of worked area on the wrong side. Bring the needle up in the correct hole to the left, directly under the last stitch.

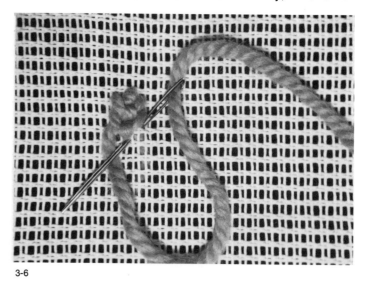

3-6

50

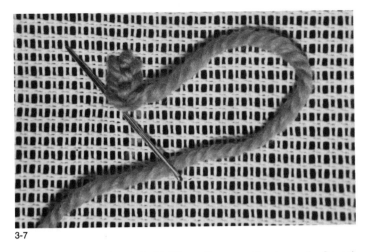

3-7

5. The needle is up in 7. Place the needle down in 8 and up in 9 in one motion, as in Figure 3-6.

6. Go over the yarn and bar of canvas. Place the needle down in center hole 10 and up in 11 in one motion. (Fig. 3-7.) Keep repeating 5 and 6 until the row is completed.

To End Row. The Fill-in Stitches form an even edge at the bottom of the row as shown at the right of Figure 3-5. Complete the last stitch in the row. Do not end the yarn.

1. Bring the needle up in 1. Place the needle down in 2 and up in 3.

2. Place the needle down in 4. Pull the yarn through to the wrong side. End the yarn.

Note: To end and start strands, use the same procedure that was described for the 4-Bar Fly.

Second Row. Start the second row at the top to the right of the first row. The second row is indicated by striped stitches. Bring the needle up in the same hole 2 as was used for the right side of the first row. Repeat the first row.

Single Surface Whipping.

A yarn of contrasting color is used to work surface whipping on 4-Bar Fly Stitches.

1. Bring the needle up to the surface at the top center of the row of 4-Bar Fly Stitches. Place the needle through the first center single Fill-in Stitch from right to left, as shown in Figure 3-8.

2. Place the needle through the next center tie-down stitch from left to right as shown in Figure 3-9, leaving a small decorative loop.

Continue to the bottom of the row, alternating the direction of the surface whipping to form the pattern shown in the photographs.

Double Surface Whipping.

1. Work single whipping from top to bottom of the row.

2. Start at the top and work down the row, using the same tie-down stitches but reversing the direction of the single whipping. (Figs. 3-10 and 3-11.) Small loops are formed on the side opposite those in the row of single whipping.

Continue to the bottom of the row, alternating the direction to form the pattern shown in the photographs.

Note: Different effects can be obtained by changing the size of the loops. The loops should be uniform once you decide on the length you wish.

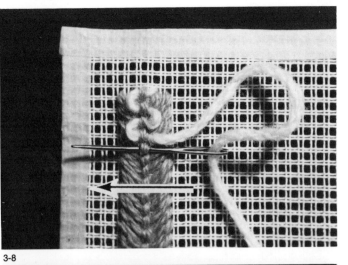

3-8

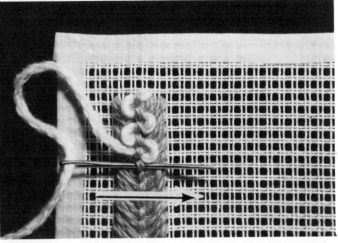

3-9

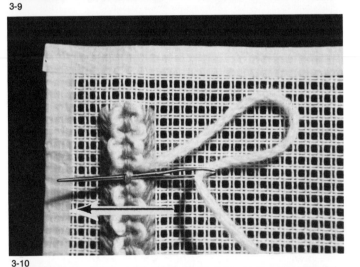

3-10

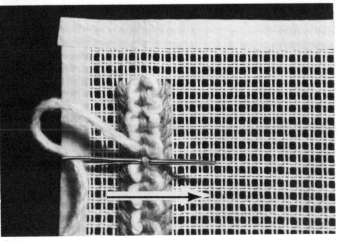

3-11

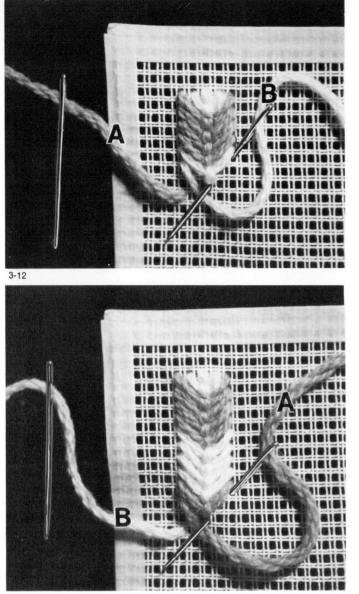

3-12

3-13

Color Changes with the Fly Stitches. Figures 3-12 and 3-13 show how to make color changes when working the 4-Bar Fly Stitch. (The same method is used for the 2-Bar Fly Stitch). The photographs show how the changes of color are accomplished for the pink and white chevron in Pattern 1. (See Fig. 3-14.) Follow the same process for all Fly Stitch patterns involving color changes.

1. Start at the top. Work the desired number of stitches in Color A. When the stitches are completed, do not bring the needle up to the surface directly underneath the last stitch worked. Instead, *anticipate* where the color will be introduced again by counting down holes along the left (the number will depend on the pattern) and bring the needle up in the proper hole. The correct number of holes must be left free so the second color can be worked in between.

Place needle A over to the left, out of the way of the working area as shown in Figure 3-12.

2. Bring the needle threaded with Color B up to the surface on the left under Color A stitches. Work the desired number of stitches of Color B directly under Color A stitches. *Anticipate* where Color B will be introduced again by counting down holes along the left. Bring Needle B up in the proper hole.

Place Needle B over to the left out of the way of the working area as shown in Figure 3-13.

3. Pick up Needle A and work the desired number of stitches under Color B. Continue to the bottom of the row, making necessary color changes to produce the pattern.

Note: The color of the Fill-in Stitches at the top and bottom of the rows will vary according to the design. Work the Fill-in Stitches in the proper color to preserve the pattern.

There you have the key to Fly Stitch color changes —simple and quick! The needles threaded with different color yarns are *always* brought to the surface in the exact spot where the next stitch in that particular color will be worked. If you leave them hanging loose on the wrong side, you will end up with a tangled mess. They wait on the left side, so quietly you can introduce any number of colors with ease, with the result that the pattern possibilities are limitless. But it is not advisable to have too great a distance between where a color ends and where it is introduced again because of the run the yarn must take on the wrong side.

A happy note. If you key a design such as the large wavy pillow in Pattern 12 (Fig. 3-25), life becomes free and easy after the first row. In that particular pattern, the waves or changes in color continue across from side to side. You can follow the color changes in the first vertical row when working the second and all subsequent rows. It is wonderful to work while watching television or chatting with a friend!

PATTERNS FOR 4-BAR FLY AND 2-BAR FLY STITCHES

All color changes for the patterns are worked in the same manner as will be described for Pattern 1. The necessary color changes can easily be made, once you are familiar with the technique. The system is new, so sufficient details have been included to help you interpret the early patterns. However, in the later patterns, only the color changes will be indicated.

Pattern 1. Alternating chevrons of 4 pink and 4 white stitches are worked in 4-Bar Fly. (Fig. 3-14.)
Nantucket 6-Ply Cable Yarn: shocking pink #38; white #1.

Follow the detailed directions for color changes as given earlier; see Figures 3-12 and 3-13. Shocking pink is the Color A and white is the Color B.

1st Row.

1. Start at the upper left. Work four 4-Bar Fly Stitches in shocking pink (Color A). (Do not work Fill-in Stitches at the top.) When you complete the last stitch, count down on the left side and bring the needle up to the surface in the fifth hole down. Place the needle over to the left out of the way.

3-14. Pattern 1.

3-15. Pattern 2.

2. Use white yarn (Color B). Work the fill-in area at the top. Bring the needle up in the first free hole to the left under the 4 pink stitches.

3. Work 4 white stitches. Count down and bring the needle up to the surface in the proper hole to leave space for 4 pink stitches. (Count the hole where the pink yarn has been brought through to the surface as No. 1.)

Continue this way to the bottom of area. Work Fly Fill-in Stitches at the bottom in the proper contrasting color to preserve the chevron design. The pink and white chevrons are repeated twice in the pattern shown.

2nd Row. Alternate the color of the chevrons. Start with the white yarn next to the top pink chevron in the first row. Continue to the bottom of the row, with the result that opposite-color chevrons will be next to each other.

Continue in rows from left to right across the canvas for desired coverage, alternating the chevron colors in each row.

Pattern 2. Saucy white 4-Bar Fly chevrons stand out against a bright orange background. Rows of white 5 stitch chevrons are worked with solid orange rows between. (Fig. 3-15.)
Pat Rug Yarn: orange #958; white #005.

1st Row.

1. Start at the upper left. Use orange yarn. Work one solid row of 4-Bar Fly orange stitches, working Fly Fill-in Stitches at the top and the bottom—16 stitches in the sample. (The bottom Fill-in Stitches have not been worked in the sample.)

2nd Row.

1. Use white yarn. Work 5 stitches. Upon completion of the last stitch, bring the needle up to the surface, leaving space for 3 orange stitches. (Do not work the Fill-in Stitches in white.)

2. Use orange yarn. Work the Fill-in Stitches at the top. Bring the needle up to the surface to the left, directly under the 5 white stitches.

3. Work 3 orange stitches. Bring the needle up to the surface, leaving space for 5 white stitches.

Repeat the pattern to the bottom of the row—5 white stitches with 3 orange stitches between. The bottom edge should balance the top. If your design starts close to the top edge, plan the bottom so the point of the chevron also runs to the edge. If you wish to have a solid area of orange surrounding the design, work a number of orange stitches before starting the white chevrons. This would be repeated at the bottom. (Additional solid rows of orange can be added on the sides for balance if necessary.)

Continue the rows from left to right across the canvas, alternating one solid row of orange with one row of chevron patterns.

Design Note: This basic idea of alternating solid rows with patterned chevron rows has endless possibilities. The chevrons can run down an item, or across an item or sail up like little rockets. (See the finished pillow, Fig. 3-33.) Begin to be aware of chevrons in designs and experiment with interpreting them in Fly Stitches.

You will notice that the last solid row of orange to the right of the sample was worked in reverse to create a different, interesting effect. This is achieved by turning the canvas upside down while you work the solid rows of

3-16. Pattern 3.

orange. To keep the background from becoming too busy, only one direction should be used for this pattern—either one or the other. The two methods are shown together in Figure 3-15 for instruction purposes only.

Pattern 3. Alternating blue and white 4-Bar Fly Stitches form a herringbone pattern. (Fig. 3-16.)
Pat Rug Yarn: blue #731; white #005.

1st Row.
1. Start at the upper left. Work 1 blue stitch. Drop down and bring the needle up to the surface to the left, so there is space left for 1 white stitch. (Do not work the top Fill-in Stitches at this point.)
2. Work 1 white stitch. Work a Fill-in Stitch directly above the first blue stitch. (A small single stitch in the top center will be worked in blue later to preserve the pattern.) Drop down and bring the needle up to the surface to the left in the hole so that there is space left for 1 blue stitch.
3. Work 1 blue stitch. Jump up to the top on the wrong side and work a single, small, center Fill-in Stitch. Drop down and bring the needle up to the surface to the left so there is space left for one white stitch.
Repeat the alternating blue and white stitches to the bottom of the row; 17 stitches are shown in the sample. Work Fill-in Stitches at the bottom in the correct colors to preserve the pattern.

2nd Row. Start with 1 white stitch to the right of the top blue stitch in the first row. Work stitches down to the bottom so opposite colors are next to each other. The top and bottom Fill-in Stitches must preserve the color pattern.
Continue working rows from left to right for the desired coverage, reversing the color sequence in each row.
Note: When you are thoroughly familiar with the pattern, you can complete the stitches in one color down to the bottom of a row—leaving spaces between for the second

3-17. Pattern 4.

color—and then work the entire row of contrasting color stitches between. This eliminates the need for constantly changing needles and yarn. But please work a row or two alternating the colors as outlined before you try this method. You can then decide which method you prefer.

Pattern 4. White waves form horizontal stripes across a bright green background. (Fig. 3-17.) The 4-Bar Fly and 2-Bar Fly Stitches meet to create an interesting irregular effect.
Pat Rug Yarn: green #569; white #005.

1st Row.
1. Start at the upper left. Work four green 4-Bar Fly Stitches, including the Fill-in Stitches at top. Drop down on the left and bring the needle up to the surface in the third hole under the last green stitch, leaving space for 2 white stitches.
2. Work two white 4-Bar Fly Stitches. Drop down on the left and bring the needle up to the surface in the fifth hole under the last white stitch, leaving space for 4 green stitches. (Count the hole where the green yarn comes through to the surface as No. 1.)

3. Work four green 4-Bar Fly Stitches. Drop down on the left and bring the needle up to the surface, leaving space for 2 white stitches.

Continue to the bottom of the row, alternating 2 white stitches and 4 green stitches. End the row with 4 green stitches to balance the top; there are 22 stitches in the sample shown. Work the bottom Fill-in Stitches in green.

2nd Row. The second row is an exact duplicate of the first row. It is smooth sailing from now on. No counting of stitches is necessary: the pattern is keyed and the preceding row becomes an easy guide for the color changes.

3rd Row. Follow the same color changes as in the first two rows. Work the row from top to bottom in 2-Bar Fly Stitches. This creates the interesting change in the dip of the stripes across the pattern.

Note: You must work 5 green stitches plus Fill-in Stitches at the bottom of the 2-Bar rows (but only 4 in the 4-Bar rows) to form an even edge.

To summarize the pattern, the stitches are 4 green, 2 white; the rows are 2 of 4-Bar Fly, 1 of 2-Bar Fly. Continue working the rows from left to right for desired coverage. A good design should end with two rows of 4-Bar Fly if the design is symmetric and starts that way. If the design is asymmetric, this balance is unnecessary.

Design Note: The concept represented by this pattern can be varied if you increase or decrease the number of stitches worked in each color. It is best to create interest by having more stitches of one color which become background and less of the second color which forms stripes, as shown in the sample. If you reverse the colors you will have a white pillow with green stripes waving across, which would be quite delightful too! You can also change your work's appearance by varying the combination of 4-Bar and 2-Bar rows.

Pattern 5. Uniform black and white horizontal stripes run across a blue background with white French Knots for texture. (Fig. 3-18.)
Pat Rug Yarn: blue #760; black #050, white #005.
The 4-Bar Fly Stitches are used throughout.

1st Row.
1. Start at the upper left. Work 3 blue stitches including Fill-in Stitches at the top.
2. Work 1 black stitch.
3. Work 1 white stitch.
4. Work 1 black stitch.
5. Work 5 blue stitches.
Repeat steps 2–5 to the bottom of the row, ending with 3 blue stitches (instead of 5) to balance the top, as shown in the sample. Work the Fill-in Stitches in blue. Increase the number of stitches at the top and bottom if you want larger areas of solid color.

3-18. Pattern 5.

For the second and subsequent rows, repeat the first row as many times as necessary for desired coverage.

French Knots. Use white yarn. Work one French Knot single strand (around the needle twice) at the center point of each white chevron.

Pattern 6. Alternating vertical stripes of green and white 4-Bar Fly Stitches with whipped centers produce a stunning effect. (Fig. 3-19.)
Nantucket 6-Ply Cable Yarn: green #84; white #1.

3-19. Pattern 6.

1st Row. Start at the upper left. Use green yarn. Work one complete row of 4-Bar Fly Stitches with Fill-in Stitches at the top and bottom. (The sample has 17 stitches.)

2nd Row. Use white yarn. Work one complete row of 4-Bar Fly Stitches with Fill-in Stitches at the top and bottom.

Continue the rows from left to right across the canvas for desired coverage, alternating one row of green and one row of white. End with the same color as in the first row.

Surface whip the center tie-down stitches from the top to the bottom of each row, using contrasting color. (See the instructions for single whipping.)

A delightful pattern of curves forms down the center of each vertical stripe in pleasing contrast to the straight arms of the stitches.

Design Note: This basic concept can be varied in a number of ways. For example, two vertical rows of solid color, plus one contrasting whipped row, can be repeated across the canvas. To solidify the design it is best to use the color of the contrasting stripes (or a very closely related color) for the whipping. Otherwise, the areas will become isolated segments and the overall effect will not be as pleasing to the eye. Choose a fairly strong value contrast or the pattern formed by the whipping will be lost. This design is easy to work and can be used in any décor—contemporary or traditional—where a striped pattern is suitable.

Pattern 7. White 4-Bar Fly Stitches combined with stripes of French Knot rosebuds create a pretty and feminine effect. (Fig. 3-20.) The sample shows three color variations plus a multicolor version.
Nantucket 6-Ply Cable Yarn: white #1; green #84; shocking pink #38; turquoise #64; yellow #6.

1st Row. Work one complete row of white 4-Bar Fly Stitches with Fill-in Stitches at the top and bottom. (The sample has 17 stitches.)

2nd Row. Leave one exposed double bar of canvas to the right of the completed row for the rosebud stripe. Repeat the first row.

Continue working white rows from left to right across the canvas for desired coverage, leaving one double bar of canvas exposed between rows for the rosebud stripes.

Follow the detailed directions in Chapter 8 for rosebud stripes on 5 to the inch canvas.

1. Work diagonal stitches of green from top to bottom on rows of exposed canvas.

2. Work French Knots of desired color (single strand —around the needle twice).

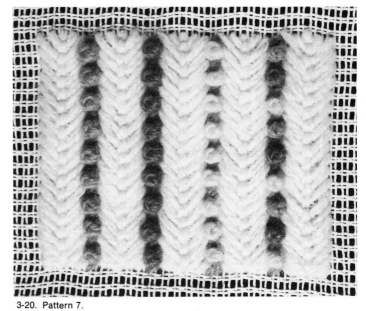

3-20. Pattern 7.

Design Note: The stripes of rosebuds make for a feminine, dainty effect, especially if you use a white background as in the sample, or an extremely light value of color. Such items are perfect for bedroom décor touches. A maxi pincushion for the dresser with a matching pillow for a boudoir chair or bed will delight ladies of all ages.

Several rows of solid white can be worked on the left and right sides if you wish the stripes to be centered. These rows would be worked side by side with no exposed canvas left between them.

Each of the next three patterns (8, 9 and 10) has an overall impact all of its own. Each is worked in the 4-Bar Fly Stitch but with a completely different pattern which is formed by the color changes and value contrast. Each one is extremely effective and so easily worked! Once the first row is completed you repeat it across the canvas as many times as you wish for desired coverage.

Pattern 8. Three related colors very close in value are teamed up with deep orange. (Fig. 3-21.) All rows are worked in the 4-Bar Fly Stitch.
Pat Rug Yarn: yellow #413; light orange #421; deep orange #968; yellow green #550.

1st Row. Work the top and bottom Fill-in Stitches in the correct color or colors to preserve the pattern if you want an overall pattern effect.

1. Start at the upper left. Work 1 yellow stitch.

2. Work 2 light orange stitches.

3. Work 1 deep orange stitch.

4. Work 1 yellow-green stitch.

Repeat steps 1–4 as many times as necessary to the bottom of the row. (They are repeated four times in the sample.)

3-21. Pattern 8.

2nd Row. The second row is an exact duplicate of the first row. Color changes are easy to follow with the first row as your guide.

Continue the rows from left to right for desired coverage.

Pattern 9. Two related colors plus beige and black are worked in the 4-Bar Fly Stitch. (Fig. 3-22.)
Pat Rug Yarn: beige #496; gold #440; taffy #433; black #050.

3-22. Pattern 9.

1st Row. Work the top and bottom Fill-in Stitches in the correct color or colors to preserve the pattern if you want an overall pattern effect.

1. Start at the upper left. Work 2 beige stitches.
2. Work 2 gold stitches.
3. Work two taffy stitches.
4. Work 1 black stitch.

Repeat steps 1–4 as many times as necessary to the bottom of the row. (They are repeated three times in the sample).

2nd Row. The second row is the exact duplicate of the first row. Color changes are easy to follow with the first row as your guide.

Continue the rows from left to right for the desired coverage.

Pattern 10. A new multicolored mod look is created with the 4-Bar Fly Stitch. (Fig. 3-23.) The Nantucket yarn colors chosen for the sample are extremely brilliant and cause vibrant excitement when placed together.
Nantucket 6-Ply Cable Yarn: shocking pink #38; green #84; turquoise #64.

3-23. Pattern 10.

1st Row. Work the top and bottom Fill-in Stitches in the correct color or colors to preserve the pattern if you want an overall pattern effect. Start at the upper left. Work stitches down to the bottom of the row in the following color sequence:

2 shocking pink stitches, 1 green stitch, 2 turquoise, 3 green, 1 shocking pink, 1 turquoise, 1 green, 3 shocking pink, 1 turquoise, 1 green, 1 shocking pink, 3 turquoise, 2 green, 2 shocking pink, 1 turquoise, 1 green.

Design Note: All (or a portion) of this color pattern for the first row can be repeated for desired coverage. Better still—you can key your own combination of colors. One color can be made to predominate by introducing it more often than the other colors. Follow the basic suggestions outlined in Chapter 1, so that you make the appropriate choice of colors for the impact you want to create. Use the Squint Test from time to time as the work progresses to make certain there is a pleasant balance of color. A staggering assortment of patterns can be produced by using different color combinations and controlling the width of the horizontal waves with the number of stitches worked in each color. Any equal number of stitches of one solid color (including the Fill-in Stitches) can be worked at both the top and bottom to create a background area. As if you had waved a magic wand, the color used at the top and bottom becomes background and the other colors appear to be stripes.

2nd Row. The second row is the exact duplicate of the first row. Color changes are easy to follow with the first row as your guide.

Continue the rows from left to right for desired coverage.

━━━━━━

Pattern 11. Wild! The 4-Bar Fly and 2-Bar Fly Stitches unfold in a blaze of color with surprise accents of friendly white. (Fig. 3-24.) The sample shown measures 6¼ in. from side to side. (The bench top with this design motif appears among the finished items; see Fig. 3-38.)

3-24. Pattern 11.

Note: Figure 3-24 shows an actual sample I presented to the *House Beautiful* editors and decorators to give them an idea of what I had in mind for a brilliant bench top to be featured in an article. It is more vivid viewed in person for some of the brilliance is lost in reproduction. The first ten rows to the left of the bench top are worked exactly as shown in the sample and can be repeated as many times as necessary for desired coverage. However, this is not the method I used. It was truly a joyous project for me. There are no actual repeat motifs in the bench design; I worked each row as the ideas for color and size came to me. You can travel the same road. Use the pattern that follows as a starter and then continue and create your own pattern to cover the desired area.

The color combinations cause much eye excitement. Deep pink and red placed together produce color fusion. Many different color combinations can be substituted to harmonize with your décor. A special feature used for this pattern which can be helpful to you when keying your own design are the orange stitches which wave consistently across from side to side and integrate and solidify the design formed by the color changes. Throughout you work one orange stitch, then two stitches in another color or colors, one orange stitch—continuing on to bottom of the row. The uniform placement of these orange stitches, which are worked in identical spots in each row, forms a net of color which keeps your eye from jumping in all directions.

Pat Rug Yarn: orange #958; light pink #259; deep pink #239; cherry red #237; white #005.

The color pattern for the ten rows shown in the sample are given below. Each row starts with the top orange stitch and the color key for the next two stitches which form the pattern is given. The pattern for each row is repeated as many times as necessary for desired coverage. (The sample has 17 stitches.) The type of stitch—4-Bar Fly or 2-Bar Fly—is also indicated. Orange stitches are always worked next to orange stitches in the preceding row. Fill-in Stitches at the top and bottom of the rows are worked in the proper colors to preserve the overall pattern.

1st Row. (2-Bar Fly), 1 orange, 2 light pink.

2nd Row. (4-Bar Fly), 1 orange, 2 red.

3rd Row. (2-Bar Fly), 1 orange, 2 red.

4th Row. (2-Bar Fly), 1 orange, 1 white, 1 deep pink.

5th Row. (4-Bar Fly), 1 orange, 1 red, 1 deep pink.

6th Row. (4-Bar Fly), 1 orange, 1 red, 1 deep pink.

7th Row. (2-Bar Fly), 1 orange, 1 white, 1 pale pink.

8th Row. (4-Bar Fly), 1 orange, 1 white, 1 pale pink.

9th Row. (2-Bar Fly), 1 orange, 2 deep pink.

10th Row. (4-Bar Fly), 1 orange, 2 pale pink.

Pattern 12. Rippling waves of turquoise, yellow-green and white are formed by combining 4-Bar and 2-Bar Fly Stitches. (Fig. 3-25.) Key the first row and you can sail across the canvas, since the color pattern is the same throughout.

Pat Rug Yarn: yellow-green #550; turquoise #738; white #005.

3-25. Pattern 12.

1st Row. Use the 4-Bar Fly. Start at the upper left.

1. Work 2 yellow-green stitches (work the top Fill-in Stitches in yellow-green), 1 turquoise, 1 yellow-green.
2. Work 2 white stitches.
3. Work 1 yellow-green, 1 turquoise, 1 yellow-green, 1 turquoise.
4. Work 2 white stitches.

Repeat steps 1–4 for desired coverage. The pattern consists of Steps 1 through 4—two different patterns of yellow-green and turquoise stitches between each pair of white stitches. In order to balance the top, the pattern can be ended after any two white stitches by adding two yellow-green stitches and working the bottom Fill-in Stitches in yellow-green.

2nd Row. Use the 2-Bar Fly. Repeat the color pattern of the first row.

Continue working the rows from left to right, alternating the 4-Bar Fly and the 2-Bar Fly rows across the canvas for desired coverage. Once the color pattern of the first row is completed you need no longer refer to the written instructions since the first row becomes the guide for subsequent rows.

Design Note: Many different color schemes can be substituted, but there must be sufficient value contrast if the waves are to be defined as in the sample.

Pattern 13. An inverted pattern of 4-Bar Fly Stitches creates deep waves of turquoise and yellow. (Fig. 3-26.)

Pat Rug Yarn: turquoise #738; yellow #413.

The 4-Bar Fly Stitch is used throughout.

1st Row. Start at the upper left.

1. Work 1 turquoise stitch (do not work Fill-in Stitches).
2. Work Fill-in Stitches at the top in yellow. Work 3 yellow stitches.
3. Work 1 turquoise stitch.
4. Work 3 yellow stitches.

Repeat from steps 3 and 4. (The pattern just consists of these two steps.) Continue to the bottom for desired

3-26. Pattern 13.

coverage ending with 1 turquoise stitch and working the Fill-in Stitches in yellow.

2nd Row. Turn the canvas upside down so that the top becomes the bottom. The second row is worked to the left of the first row. Be certain to find the correct hole on the left where you start the first stitch.

1. Work 3 yellow stitches (do not work the Fill-in Stitches).

2. Work 1 turquoise stitch. At this point work 1 turquoise Fill-in Stitch above the 3 yellow stitches. Work the single, center Fill-in Stitch in yellow to preserve the pattern.

Note: In this particular pattern it is best to work the overall pattern directly to the top and bottom edges. Otherwise it is very difficult to create a balanced effect. Check your pattern match. The turquoise stitch must be worked with the needle going down on the right side in the same hole where the turquoise stitch was worked in the first row.

3. Work 3 yellow stitches. These, too, must correspond to the yellow stitches in the first row; the difference is that the chevrons now run in the opposite direction because of the turn of the canvas.

Continue to the bottom of the row. In the sample, one yellow stitch (including the yellow Fill-in Stitches) was worked after the last turquoise stitch.

3rd Row. Turn the canvas back to its original position. Work to the right of the second row, repeating the first row.

4th Row. Turn the canvas to its upside down position. Work to the left of the third row and repeat the second row.

Continue for desired coverage. Remember to turn the canvas before you start each new row.

Note: This procedure sounds more complicated than it is when you are actually working the pattern. When you are on familiar terms with the stitch mechanics—I would not suggest this for a first project using the stitch—you can easily master the technique, which will become automatic after the first few turns of the canvas.

Pattern 14. Decorative orange arrows on a yellow background connected by shocking pink French Knots create colorful textural stripes. (Fig. 3-27.)
Pat Rug Yarn: orange #968; yellow #413; deep pink #241.
The 4-Bar Fly and 2-Bar Fly Stitches are used.

1st Row. Start at the upper left, using the 4-Bar Fly.

1. Work 2 orange stitches (do not work the top Fill-in Stitches).

3-27. Pattern 14.

2. Work 2 yellow stitches. Work Fill-in Stitches above the orange stitches in yellow.

3. Work 2 orange stitches.

4. Work 2 yellow stitches.

Repeat Steps 3 and 4 to the bottom for desired coverage and end with 2 orange stitches. Work the bottom Fill-in Stitches in yellow.

2nd Row. Use the 2-Bar Fly. Work the entire row in yellow, including the top and bottom Fill-in Stitches.

3rd Row. Repeat the first row.

4th Row. Repeat the second row.

Continue from left to right across the canvas for desired coverage, alternating the patterned row of 4-Bar Fly with the solid yellow row of 2-Bar Fly.

French Knots. Use deep pink yarn. Work two French Knots over the centers of yellow stitches between the orange chevrons (single strand—around the needle once). Do not place the knots too close to the top and bottom edges if the material backing is to be used, since they would interfere with construction. Work only one knot at the top of the row.

Design Note: The orange and shocking pink in the pattern are close in value, and so they form a continuous stripe of arrows and texture. A completely different effect can be achieved when there is strong value contrast between the chevrons and the knots. If the finished item is a pillow, start and end with solid yellow 4-Bar Fly rows of stitches. This allows for a construction area on both sides which will not interfere with the pattern. Otherwise, you would have to crop into the patterned row, which would destroy the item's uniform effect.

3-28. Pattern 15.

Pattern 15. Brilliant red and purple multi-flowers grow on a sparkling white background. (Fig. 3-28.)
Nantucket 6-Ply Cable Yarn: white #1; red #32; purple #47; green #84.

The 4-Bar Fly Stitch is used throughout. (The sample has 24 stitches in each row.)

1st Row. Use white yarn. Work one complete row, including the top and bottom Fill-in Stitches.

2nd Row. Work 4 white stitches (including the top Fill-in Stitches), 2 red, 2 white, 2 red, 2 white, 2 red (total: 3 red chevrons), 4 white, 1 green, 1 white, 1 green (total: 2 green chevrons), 3 white (including the bottom Fill-in Stitches to duplicate the pattern).

Note: If you wish two rows of flowers across the item, as in the tulip motif in Figure 3-29, work 6 white stitches under the last green stitch and repeat the multi-flower and green leaves. If you make the larger, double-row version, work at least 8 white stitches at the top and bottom (as in the tulip-motif pillow, Figure 3-35), and work 2 rows of solid white stitches down each side to allow for the rollback of the knife edge pillow.

3rd Row. Use white yarn. Work one complete row, including the top and bottom Fill-in Stitches.

4th Row. Repeat the second row but substitute purple yarn for the red.

Continue working the rows from left to right across the canvas, alternating the chevron colors and working one solid row of white between the motifs. It is best to end with a row of red chevrons on the right as on the left, but this is not absolutely necessary if it is not possible in the overall area you wish to cover. You must, however, end with the solid row (or rows) of white. The solid background area can be greatly increased on all sides if you wish the row (or rows) of motifs centered by adding extra stitches at the top and bottom of the rows, and extra rows along each side.

Green Stems. See Figure 3-30 which relates to the gold tulip motif of Pattern 16. Use green yarn. Surface whip the center tie-down stitches on the white 4-Bar Fly stitches *between* the red and purple chevrons. Start under top chevron and whip down, skipping under the chevrons on the wrong side. Continue whipping down to the bottom green-leaf chevron.

French Knots. Alternate the colors, working two French Knots (single strand—around the needle once) directly in the center at the top of each motif and one French Knot on each side of the stems between the colored chevrons. Check the photograph of the pattern for the exact placement. Purple knots go on the red chevron motifs—red knots on the purple chevrons.

Pattern 16. It's tulip time! Stylized gold and yellow tulips look Scandinavian on the white background. (Fig. 3-29. See the finished pillow, Fig. 3-35.)
Pat Rug Yarn: white #005; gold #440; green #545; yellow #413.

The 4-Bar Fly Stitch is used throughout. (The sample has 36 stitches in each row.)

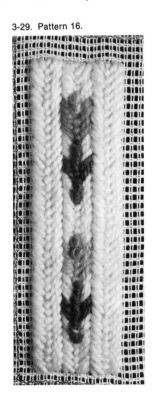

3-29. Pattern 16.

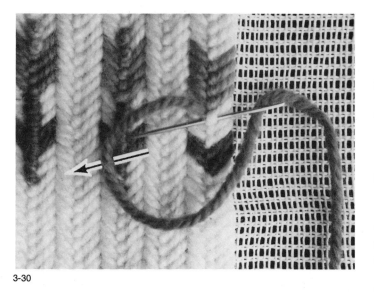

3-30

3-31

3-32

1st Row. Start at the upper left. Use white yarn. Work one complete row, including the top and bottom Fill-in Stitches.

2nd Row. Work 4 white stitches (including the top Fill-in Stitches), 4 gold, 3 white, 2 green (end of the top motif), 8 white, 4 yellow (start of the bottom motif), 3 white, 2 green (end of the bottom motif), 6 white (including the bottom Fill-in Stitches).

3rd Row. Use white yarn. Work one complete row, including the top and bottom Fill-in Stitches.

4th Row. This is not shown in the sample. Repeat the second row, but work the top flower motif in yellow and the bottom motif in gold.

Continue across the canvas from left to right, alternating the flower motif colors in each patterned row and working one solid row of white between. The end row should be white.

Stems. See Figure 3-30. Use green yarn. Bring the needle up to the surface directly under each flower motif, as shown in the photograph. Working in a downward direction, surface whip each center tie-down stitch, including the two white stitches under the green chevron (3 white, two green, two white). The arrow indicates the needle must go *under* the loop of yarn, not through it. Slowly pull the yarn so that it closes around the tie-down stitches to simulate a stem.

French Knots. See Figures 3-31 and 3-32. Work French Knots (single strand—around the needle once) in the correct colors—yellow knots on the gold motif and gold knots on the yellow motif—over the two white center tie-down stitches directly above each flower motif. Now your eye tells you the motifs are tulips—created with several colored chevrons and a few knots! The fly stitches can be completed and the entire area covered before you work the surface whipping and knots. However, I usually work several rows and then work the surface stitches. I find it more satisfying to be able to glance at the finished motifs while I work the remaining stitches.

Design Note: This pattern will harmonize beautifully with many different types of décor. The flower motif can be worked in any bright color on the white background—or reverse the value contrast and have white tulips on a colored background. You might have to change the value of the green depending on the background color you use. You can easily manipulate the size of an item. You could design a delightful pincushion or mini pillow with one row of three motifs running across and a solid row between the motifs. One point to remember when keying your own design is that two of the white stitches at the bottom of each motif are used for the stem. You must add these to the number of background stitches between the motifs and also at the bottom. Allow sufficient background area for the roll of knife-edge pillows. Think of the design possibilities and have some fun! Through your use of color and decorative touches, you can easily manipulate the 4-Bar Fly Stitches to create the illusion of stylized realism.

FLY STITCH FINISHED ITEMS

White Chevrons sail upward on a deep orange background. (Fig. 3-33.) Size: 17 in. × 10 in. Pillow design courtesy of *House Beautiful.*
Pat Rug Yarn: orange #958 (38 str.); white #005 (17 str.).

The 4-Bar Fly is used throughout. Start at the upper left. The rows are worked from left to right.

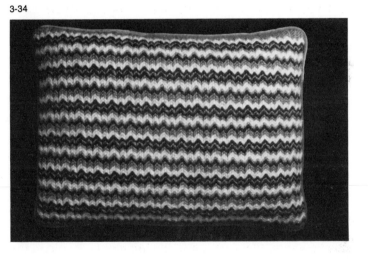

3-33. Design courtesy of *House Beautiful.*
Copyright 1967, The Hearst Corporation.

1st Row. Use orange yarn. Work a solid row of 47 stitches, including the top and bottom Fill-in Stitches.

2nd Row. Work one orange stitch plus the top Fill-in Stitches. See Pattern 2 (Fig. 3-15) for detailed directions to work white chevrons on the orange background. Using white and orange yarn, work the same pattern down until there are 6 white chevrons. Work 1 orange stitch at the bottom, including the Fill-in Stitches.

3rd Row. Use orange yarn. Work one solid row, including the top and bottom Fill-in Stitches.

Repeat the rows from left to right across the canvas until there are 10 rows of white chevrons with single solid rows of orange between them. End with a solid row of orange for a total of 21 rows (11 solid orange—10 with white

chevrons). Turn the item upside down and the chevrons will point skyward.

See Chapter 8 for the directions for attaching material backing.

Decorative turquoise, yellow-green and white waves splash across an oversized pillow. (Fig. 3-34.) Size: 16 in. × 22 in. The backing on the sample is yellow-green velvet with matching material cording.
Pat Rug Yarn: yellow-green #550 (49 str.); turquoise #738 (27 str.); white #005 (36 str.).

Alternating rows of 4-Bar Fly and 2-Bar Fly were used. Start at the upper left. The rows are worked from left to right.

3-34

1st Row. Use the 4-Bar Fly Stitch. See Pattern 12 (Fig. 3-25) for detailed instructions. Continue working the pattern down the canvas until there are 12 sets of 2 white stitches. Then work 3 yellow-green stitches including the bottom Fill-in Stitches.

2nd Row. Use the 2-Bar Fly Stitch. Repeat the same color pattern used in the first row.

Continue the rows across the canvas from left to right, alternating the 4-Bar Fly and the 2-Bar Fly rows until there are eighteen 4-Bar Fly rows with seventeen 2-Bar Fly rows between—for a total of 35 rows. The same color pattern is used for all the rows.

See Chapter 8 for the directions for attaching material backing.

A Saucy gold and yellow tulip pillow has a Scandinavian air. (Fig. 3-35.) Size: 17½ in. × 9½ in. The backing on the sample is gold velvet with matching material cording.
Pat Rug Yarn: white #005 (43 str.); gold #440 (5 str.); yellow #413 (5 str.); green #545 (6 str.).

The 4-Bar Fly is used throughout. Start at the upper left.

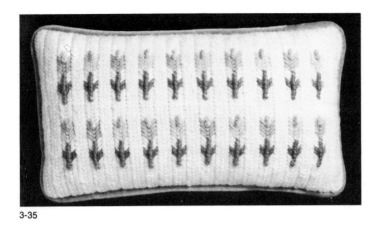

3-35

3-36

1st and 2nd Rows. Use white yarn. Work 2 solid rows of 46 stitches, including the top and bottom Fill-in Stitches.

3rd Row. See Pattern 16 (Fig. 3-29) for the detailed directions. Work one row of the tulip pattern, increasing the background stitches at the top and bottom as follows: Work 8 white stitches including the top Fill-in Stitches, 4 gold, 3 white, 2 green (end of the top motif), 8 white, 4 yellow (start of the bottom motif), 3 white, 2 green, 10 white, including the bottom Fill-in Stitches.

4th Row. Use white yarn. Work one solid row, including the top and bottom Fill-in Stitches.

5th Row. Repeat the second row but reverse the colors in the flower motifs: 4 yellow in the top motif—4 gold in the bottom motif.

Continue working the rows across the canvas from left to right, alternating the flower motif colors in each patterned row and working one solid row of white in between until there are 10 vertical rows of tulips. When the 10th patterned row is completed, work 2 solid rows of white to balance the beginning for a total of 23 rows.

Stems and French Knots. Follow the detailed directions under Pattern 16 (Figs. 3-30, 3-31, and 3-32) for surface whipping stems and French Knots.

See Chapter 8 for the directions for attaching material backing.

━━━━━━

Up, Up and Away! A turquoise pillow has double rows of white and yellow rockets and oversized two-color macramé tassels. (Fig. 3-36.) Size 9½ in. × 17 in. The backing on the sample is made of good-quality turquoise felt.

Nantucket 6-Ply Cable Yarn: Pillow top, turquoise #64 (50 str.); white #1 (14 str.); yellow #7 (15 str.). Four tassels, optional, yellow #7 (Color A), 12 yds. uncut yarn; white #1 (Color B), 87–88 yds. uncut yarn.

The 4-Bar Fly is used throughout. Start at the upper left.

1st and 2nd Rows. Use turquoise yarn. Work 2 solid rows of 47 stitches, including the top and bottom Fill-in Stitches.

3rd Row. Work 1 turquoise stitch, including the top Fill-in Stitches. See the directions under Pattern 2 (Fig. 3-15) for the orange and white chevrons. Substitute turquoise yarn for the orange. Work the chevron pattern down until there are 6 white chevrons. Work 1 turquoise stitch, including the bottom Fill-in Stitches. The pattern consists of 5 white stitches with 3 turquoise between them, plus 1 turquoise stitch at the top and bottom of the row.

4th Row. Use turquoise yarn. Work 1 solid row, including the top and bottom Fill-in Stitches.

5th Row. Repeat the third row with the chevron pattern.

6th and 7th Rows. Use turquoise yarn. Work 2 solid rows, including the top and bottom Fill-in Stitches.

Continue across the canvas from left to right until there are 4 groups of double rows of white chevrons. Then work 2 solid rows of turquoise to balance the beginning.

Your key for working the rows is: 2 solid turquoise, 1 chevron pattern, 1 solid turquoise, 1 chevron pattern. Repeat this 4 times for the pillow top. Then work 2 solid turquoise rows for a total of 22 rows.

Surface stitches for the rockets. (Fig. 3-37.)

1. Use yellow yarn. Backstitch on either side of the white rockets, including 1 turquoise stitch at the bottom points. (See detailed directions for the Back Stitch under Fig. 2-12.) The extra Back Stitches at the bottom points of the rockets add a slight suggestion of movement.

2. Use yellow yarn. Double surface whip the center tie-down stitches on the white chevrons. (See detailed directions with Figures 3-10 and 3-11.) Pull the yarn so that it loosely closes around the tie-down stitches.

3. Use yellow yarn. Whip 3 times over the turquoise center tie-down stitch directly above the top point of each white chevron.

Note: It is not necessary to end the yarn after each of these procedures. Pull the needle and yarn through to the

3-37

3-38. Design courtesy of *House Beautiful.*
Copyright 1967, the Hearst Corporation.

wrong side when a step is completed and bring it to the surface in the correct spot to start the next step.

See Chapter 8 for the directions for attaching material backing.

Optional. If you like, you can add 4 extra-large macramé two-color tassels. Use yellow (Color A) and white (Color B) yarn for the outer macramé casing, and white for the center. Make 4 two-color tassels according to the detailed directions in Chapter 8. Use a 6 in. card and go around the card 40 times for the tassel center. Use a 20 in. tie for the top.

Note: Solid-color tassels of any one of the three colors used in the pillow would also be appropriate. The touch of yellow with the white was used in this sample to repeat the rocket colors.

▼▼▼▼▼▼

This dazzling bench top could brighten any décor. (Fig. 3-38.) Courtesy of *House Beautiful.* This sample measures 16 in. × 22 in. and is combined with material for construction.
Pat Rug Yarn was used for the sample; colors used are given under the detailed directions for Pattern 11 (Fig. 3-24).
The item is worked in 4-Bar Fly and 2-Bar Fly Stitches.
The exact measurements for desired coverage must be taken, so the first step is to purchase the bench. I suggest you only work the flat top in Now Needlepoint. Suitable material in a matching color was used for the side construction and cording. When taking the measurements for the Now Needlepoint area, allow at least ¼ in. extra on all sides for construction cropping. Unless you are extremely proficient in construction, it is best to place the finishing problems in the hands of a good local upholsterer when the Now Needlepoint area is completed.

Pattern 11 is used for the first ten rows on the left side of the bench top. From that point on I improvised, striving constantly for an asymmetric arrangement of color throughout. A creative challenge like this one results in an individual design—so the rewards are great. If you are not so daring, you can repeat the basic pattern as many times as needed for the proper coverage. Use yarn tie markers at the corners to indicate the area you wish to cover.

You can change the color scheme to make it blend with your particular décor. It is impossible to estimate the yarn requirements; they depend entirely on the size of the area and the color key you use for the pattern. I recommend this helpful guide: In general, the very rough rule of thumb for yarn requirements for Now Needlepoint is that ½ lb. of yarn covers 1 square foot. Figure the overall approximate requirements and then break the total down into color requirements. If you want one color to predominate, such as the orange in the sample, you will need a larger amount of that color and less of the others. It is best to purchase sufficient yarn, even if there is some left over at the end, since it can always be used for small projects. Be brave and have fun! This project was one of my most enjoyable ones because of the engaging manner in which the pattern unfolded.

▼▼▼▼▼▼

A charming textural yellow-green pincushion or mini pillow has stripes of tiny white flowers. (Fig. 3-39.) Size: 4½ in. × 7 in. The cushion has a matching Now Needlepoint backing.
Pat Rug Yarn: yellow-green #550 (18 str.); white #005 (6 str.); deep green #559 (2 str.). Divide these numbers in half if you do the front side only.

The 4-Bar Fly is used throughout. Rows are worked from left to right. The backing is an exact duplicate of the top except for the substitution of diagonal white stitches

3-39

3-40

for the French Knot flowerets. This makes it possible to work both the top and backing at one time; all you have to do is skip under one double bar of canvas between the areas and then continue down to the bottom. This procedure eliminates excessive ending and starting of strands. However, if you prefer, the entire top can be completed before you start the backing. In either case the one double bar of canvas between the areas must be left exposed as shown in Figures 3-40 and 3-41.

1st and 2nd Rows. Start at the upper left. Use yellow-green yarn. Work 2 solid rows of 19 stitches each, including the top and bottom Fill-in Stitches.

Important Note: To eliminate confusion the directions are given for the top area only. When you have completed the bottom Fill-in Stitches of each row of the top area, do not end the yarn. Skip under on the wrong side and bring the needle up to the surface so that one double bar of canvas is left exposed; then repeat the top portion exactly. You will then have one long continuous row which runs down through the top and back areas, with a break in the middle as shown in Figure 3-41. Leave one vertical double bar of canvas exposed to the right of the completed second row.

3rd, 4th, 5th and 6th Rows. Use yellow-green yarn. Work 4 solid rows, including the top and bottom Fill-in Stitches. These 4 rows are worked side by side as were the first two rows. (Exposed canvas is only left between the second and third rows and between the sixth and seventh rows.) Leave one vertical double bar of canvas exposed to the right of the completed 6th row.

7th and 8th Rows. Use yellow-green yarn. Work 2 solid rows including the top and bottom Fill-in Stitches. (The

keying is: 2 solid rows, exposed canvas, 4 solid rows, exposed canvas and 2 solid rows for a total of 8 rows.)

The exposed canvas bars are filled in as follows. Follow the detailed directions in Chapter 8 for rosebud stripes on 5 to the inch canvas. Work deep-green stitches on the exposed double bars of canvas on the top and the back. (See Fig. 3-40.) For the top, use white yarn. Work French Knots (single strand—around the needle twice) between the deep green diagonal stitches on the top area only. For the back, use white yarn. Work diagonal stitches between the deep-green diagonal stitches.

Special Braid Construction. Use white yarn. Follow the procedure outlined in Chapter 8 for constructing the pink and white rosebud mini pillow, but substitute the Special Braid Stitch, which is worked on 5 to the inch canvas.

Design Note: Many different color combinations can be used successfully to produce a feminine-looking item. You can easily blow up the overall size by increasing the rows of background area and perhaps run two or three floweret stripes along each side. You can run a row of flowerets between each pair of 4-Bar Fly Stitches and create a delightful overall effect.

The Zig and Zag of Now Needlepoint: The Fabulous French Stitch

4-1. The French Stitch.

Personality. Individual stitches form small diamond-shaped motifs which blend to produce a knubby, textural effect. The French Stitch normally walks in a diagonally downward direction—to the right or left—making possible endless versions of eye-catching zig zags. When this stitch comes to mind, train yourself to think of diagonals—of zig zags—of diamonds. Most design motifs which consist of diagonal lines can be interpreted beautifully: small zig zags; large zig zags; irregular combinations of two sizes; zig zags that run vertically from top to bottom and which, by turning the canvas 90 degrees while working the stitches, can be made to run horizontally from side to side. The zig zags can also be easily worked to form diamond-shaped areas of all sizes.

The stitches are worked in rows touching each other. Once the initial shape of the zig zag is keyed, you merely follow the contour outline.

And that isn't all! By working two basic diagonal rows which cross in the middle (see Pattern 9, Fig. 4-27), you can key numerous effective designs. You work each of the four individual areas created by the cross separately in diagonal rows. The rows become smaller and smaller as the work progresses until the area is completely covered. There's no tiresome counting involved.

A beautiful knubby effect is produced when you work the stitch in one solid overall color. The stitches are worked in diagonal rows, but one color is used throughout. Individual stitches can also be worked in two colors to produce an unusual woven effect.

The French Stitch is a Touch Stitch worked around a hole of canvas.

Will Travel. The two downward diagonal directions in which the French Stitch walks are *zig*—downward right diagonal direction—and *zag*—downward left diagonal direction. Use these two directions whenever the design permits. The French Stitch can be made to walk in two upward diagonal directions: diagonally up to right and diagonally up to left. It also climbs in four straight directions. The word "climb" is used advisedly because the stitch is normally a diagonal walker and must be urged to walk the straight paths. With a bit of practice, you utilize the straight directions, working single stitches to add sparkle to a design, as in Pattern 15 (Fig. 4-35). Do not be concerned with the straight directions until you master the mechanics of the diagonal walks. But think of it —eight different directions!

Vertical rows are normally worked across the canvas from left to right, but rows can easily be worked in the opposite direction, from right to left. This makes it possible to work rows out from a center design motif toward each of the side edges—a process which is valuable when interpreting certain designs.

Horizontal rows are achieved by turning the canvas 90 degrees and working the stitches in vertical rows. The top of the canvas becomes the right side while the work is in progress. When the stitches are completed, turn the canvas back to the original position and the rows run horizontally across the canvas.

Design and Color Potentials. Fortune will smile favorably on you as a designer if you use this stitch properly. Once you have mastered the working mechanics you can have a ball. You need only study the patterns and samples in this chapter to realize the wide scope of interpretation this stitch affords. Press your aware button. If I am not mistaken, your world will be filled with exciting zigs, zags, diagonals and diamonds. You will wonder how you have lived so long and never noticed them before. Keep that aware button pressed down for there is inspiration on all sides. One day while attending a magnificent exhibition of Navaho blankets I was so inspired that I wanted to run home and start stitching. How beautifully those primitive Navaho blanket designs could be interpreted in this stitch. The patterns are made to order.

There is one facet to the personality of this stitch which is like an added dividend. By working only one half of the stitch—either the upper or lower half—you can form a straight horizontal edge which will make it possible for you to produce the half diamond or triangular shape so often used in Indian and Peruvian designs.

I chose the French Stitch to show how a delightful effect results when you use the same design theme for a variety of items. The large pillow, the mini pillow or pincushion and the bellpull (Figs. 4-44, 4-45 and 8-30) all use Pattern 7 (Fig. 4-25). The same basic pattern was adapted to fill different-shaped areas. Don't apply the same design to too many items or you will destroy the charm of having interesting design notes and create a jumble instead. If this kind of repetition is not overdone, it can do much to integrate the décor of a room and please the eye.

The results can be bold designs with dazzling color— eye-stoppers, perfect for contemporary use. Use softer colors—perhaps related colors combined with white— a smaller pattern and the overall effect of the item would make it suitable in most décors, traditional or modern. Glance at the large variety of patterns. They are all accomplished without huge graphs and constant counting of squares. The stitches grow out from each other—touching, so that each one becomes a guide for its neighbors. The patterns are created by the direction in which the stitches are worked and the changes in color. *You* create the effect with your decisions regarding design and color. The power is all yours and so are the rewards when your unique project is completed.

Suggested Uses. Textural and closely woven, with no loose runs of yarn, the French Stitch is suitable for the full range of items. I feel it is one of the most versatile of all the stitches. Marvelous for many types of upholstery, such as chair seats, valances and headboards, loose seat pads and window seats, it can also be used for rugs, pillows, pincushions, bellpulls and various hangings. I could go on and on!

MECHANICS FOR THE FRENCH STITCH

The French Stitch is worked on 3 to the inch canvas. *Very important.* Always place a yarn tie marker at the top of the canvas when you work the French Stitch.

As mentioned before, the stitches are normally worked in rows from the top to the bottom of the canvas in two downward diagonal directions:

Zig: Downward right diagonal direction. ↘

Zag: Downward left diagonal direction. ↙

The rows are normally worked from left to right, but can easily be worked from right to left when necessary.

The French Stitch literally consists of two little uneven crosses worked closely together to form a small diamond-shaped unit. Keep in mind that you are making the two little cross stitches *around a hole of canvas*—one on the top and one on the bottom. On the last step of each stitch, concentrate on bringing the needle up to the surface in the correct hole so that you can start the next stitch in the direction you want to proceed.

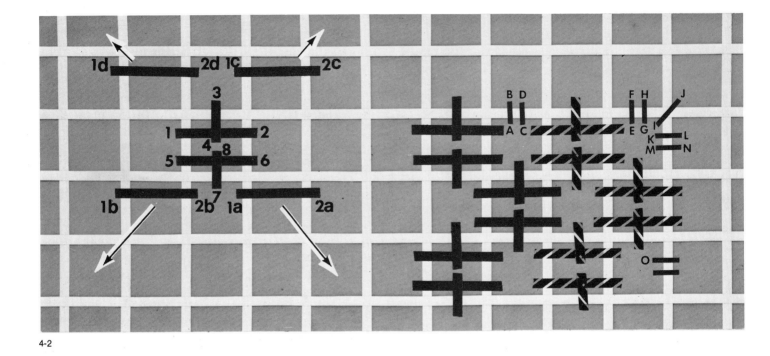

4-2

Follow the steps shown for the completed center stitch at the left of Figure 4-2. The 4 single bars with arrows represent the starts for the second stitch in each of the 4 diagonal directions. Figures 4-3 to 4-9 show you the actual steps in progress.

Zig. Work in the downward right diagonal direction.

1. Start at the upper left. Bring the needle up to the surface in hole 1, leaving a 6 in. tail on the wrong side to be woven in later. Go to the right over one hole of canvas; place the needle down in 2 and up in 3 in one motion. (See Fig. 4-3. The white dot indicates the hole around which the stitch will be worked.)

2. Go over a bar of canvas and yarn; place the needle down in 4 and up in 5 in one motion. This completes the top half of the stitch.

3. Go to right over a hole of canvas; place the needle down in 6 and up in 7 in one motion.

Note: These basic 3 steps are always the same. The fourth and last step differs according to the direction in which you wish to travel. The fourth step completes the stitch and brings the needle up in the correct hole for starting the next stitch.

4. Follow the arrow for the downward right diagonal direction. Place the needle down in 8, going over the bottom canvas bar and the bottom run of yarn, and come

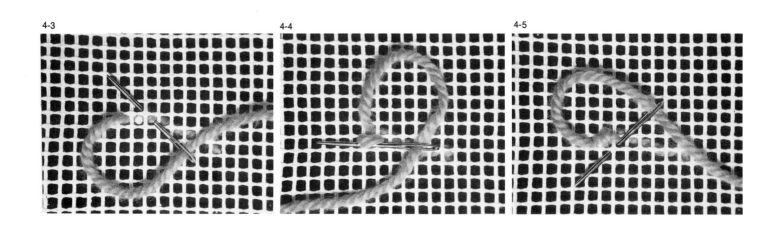

4-3   4-4   4-5

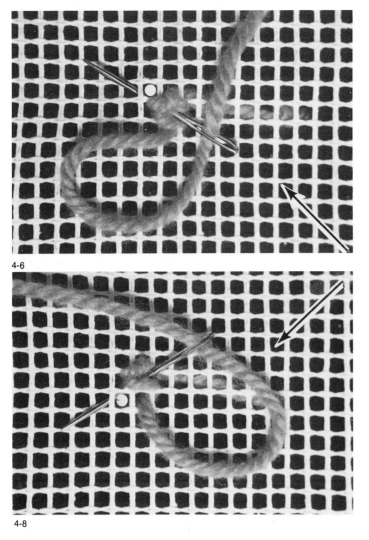

4-6

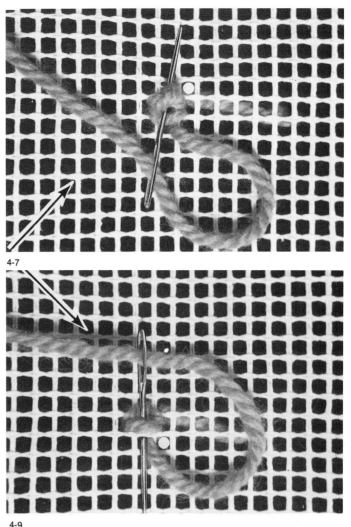

4-7

4-8

4-9

up in 1a—the same hole as 7 and directly underneath the completed stitch. (See Fig. 4-9. The white dot indicates the hole around which the next stitch will be worked.)

Continue repeating the stitches according to Figure 4-2. Bring the needle up to the surface in the hole directly under the completed stitch to start the next stitch. Please don't get discouraged; there are happy times ahead once you master the mechanics and the patterns and texture start to emerge.

Zag. Work in the downward left diagonal direction. Complete Steps 1, 2 and 3 as outlined for the right direction.

4. Follow the arrow for the downward left diagonal direction. Place the needle down in 8, going over the bottom canvas bar and the bottom run of yarn, and up in 1b to the left. (See Fig. 4-8. The white dot indicates the hole around which the next stitch will be worked.)

Continue repeating the stitches according to Figure 4-2. Bring the needle up to the surface in the correct hole to the left for starting the next stitch.

A suggestion for working Step 4 in all directions may be helpful to you. Especially in the beginning, when you are learning, place a finger on the hole around which the next stitch will be worked before you complete the fourth step. Somehow this seems to send a message which clears your mind and enables you to proceed with ease. It also quickens the mechanical learning process, since it is always the next diagonal hole which points to the direction you are traveling.

Second Row. The second row is indicated by the patterned lines at the right of Figure 4-2. It is worked directly to the right and shares the holes with the first row shown in solid black. Follow the contour of Row 1. First learn to work the rows from left to right. When you have mastered this technique, practice working the rows from right to left.

Upward Right Diagonal Direction. Complete Steps 1, 2 and 3 as outlined in the preceding instructions.

4. Follow the arrow for the upward right diagonal direction. Place the needle down in 8, going over the bottom bar of canvas and the bottom run of yarn, and come up in 1c, the hole directly above the completed stitch. (See Fig. 4-7. The white dot indicates the hole around which the next stitch will be worked.)

Continue repeating the stitches according to Figure 4-2. Bring the needle up to the surface in the hole directly above the completed stitch to start the next stitch.

Upward Left Diagonal Direction. Complete Steps 1, 2 and 3 as outlined in the preceding instructions.

4. Follow the arrow for the upward left diagonal direction. Place the needle down in 8, going over the bottom bar of canvas and over the bottom run of yarn, and up in 1d to the left. (See Fig. 4-6. The white dot indicates the hole around which the next stitch will be worked.)

Continue repeating the stitches according to Figure 4-2. Bring the needle up to the surface in the correct hole to the left to start the next stitch.

Special French Fill-in Stitch to Even Outside Edges. An irregular outside edge results because of the diamond shape formed by the individual stitches. You don't need to use the Special French Fill-in if the finished item will be combined with material when construction takes place. Cropping half of the edge stitches—approximately ¼ in.—during construction prevents exposed canvas from peeking through. You do need to even up the outside edges if you plan to use the unique Now Needlepoint construction method where the Regular Braid Stitch is worked around the completed area for trimming and construction purposes.

To learn the mechanics for the Special French Fill-in, look at the Fill-in Stitches indicated by letters at the right of Figure 4-2. Work Fill-in Stitches from left to right. The yarn is looped twice over the exposed canvas between the completed French Stitches. The instructions take you around a corner so you can continue along the next side.

1. Run yarn under the worked area on the wrong side and bring the needle up to the surface in hole A. (This can be any spot along the edge.) Place the needle down in B (looping the yarn over and under the exposed canvas bar) and up in C in one motion. (Fig. 4-10.)

4-10

2. Place the needle down in D (looping the yarn over the canvas bar and going under the stitch to the right) and up in E in one motion. (Fig. 4-11.)

Follow Figure 4-2 for the corner. Notice that there is an extra diagonal trip of yarn to cover the corner crossbar of canvas I to J. Five trips are worked out of the same hole.

4-11

Note: Because of the diagonal nature of the stitch, two types of corners occur. One type of corner is that which is formed by the two top patterned stitches to the right of Figure 4-2 and is filled in as instructed. The other corner involves a single stitch in the corner hole, such as the top and bottom stitches to the left of the grouping. When this occurs, work one diagonal only—for example, I to J—to cover the exposed bar of canvas and proceed according to instructions.

When you have worked the corner, turn the canvas 90 degrees and continue along the next edge from left to right. Continue until all the exposed canvas between the stitches is covered. These instructions cover items with solid color backgrounds which do not involve color changes in the edge stitches.

French Fill-in When One or More Color Changes Occur Along Top and Bottom Edges. You must use your own discretion about the proper placement of the different-color Fill-in Stitches. If the pattern is a zig zag, the Fill-in Stitches must be placed so they continue the pattern. Squint and your eye will quickly tell you whether or not you have chosen the correct placement for a Fill-in Stitch in a particular color. If it is wrong, pick it out and move it to the correct spot.

If the color repeats are close together, you can finish the item and then work the Fill-in Stitches. Each color is worked separately. Skip under on the wrong side and bring the needle up to the surface where the color is repeated. Catch the yarn once on the wrong side if necessary.

But there are alternatives to this method. For example, if there are many color changes and the repeats are far apart, when starting a row involving a change of color, work the first stitch and right then and there work the necessary Fill-in Stitch in the right spot. Drop under on the wrong side and bring the needle up to the surface in the proper hole to start the second stitch. When the row of color is completed, work the Fill-in Stitch in the correct spot at the bottom before ending the yarn. After completing the Now Needlepoint area, work the Fill-in Stitches down each side edge in the correct colors to preserve the design pattern.

See the instructions under Figure 4-18 regarding the use of half stitches for the straight top and bottom edges. The two sides are filled in as just described.

The French Stitch Climbs in Four Straight Directions. Complete Steps 1, 2 and 3 as outlined in preceding instructions and shown in Figure 4-2. Then:

4. Follow Figure 4-12. You are up in 7. Place the needle down in 8—completing the stitch—and up in the proper hole 1 for whichever direction you wish to take. Follow the chart carefully, since the needle has to travel under the canvas for a considerable distance to come up in the correct hole for some of the directions.

Note: I suggest you use the straight directions only when small touches or accents are needed to spark a design. As mentioned before, the normal way for this stitch to travel is in a diagonal direction.

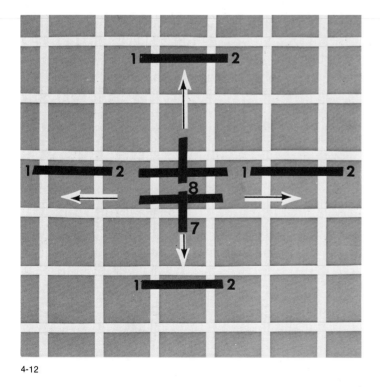

4-12

Three Methods of Working French Stitch "Around a Diamond." In all three methods the outside row is worked first, and the subsequent rows are worked in toward the center.

Method A. (Fig. 4-13.)

1. Start at the top. Work the desired number of stitches in a zig direction—downward right diagonal.

2. Work the desired number of stitches in a zag direction—downward left diagonal.

3. Work the desired number of stitches in an upward left diagonal direction.

4. Work the desired number of stitches in an upward right diagonal direction.

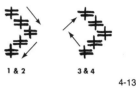

1 & 2   3 & 4

4-13

Method B. (Fig. 4-14.)

1. Start at the top. Work the desired number of stitches in a zig direction—downward right direction.

2. Work the desired number of stitches in a zag direction—downward left diagonal.

Turn the canvas upside down, so that the top becomes the bottom, and:

3. and 4. Repeat steps 1 and 2, closing the diamond shape.

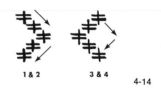

1 & 2   3 & 4

4-14

Method C. (Fig. 4-15.) Use this method when you work large diamond-shaped areas. The stitches are most uniform when all are worked in either a downward right or a downward left diagonal direction. Method C makes this possible. Do not use for small diamond-shaped areas, which would involve numerous stops and starts.

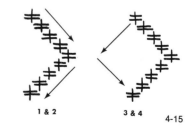

1 & 2   3 & 4

4-15

1. Start at the top. Work the desired number of stitches in a zig direction—downward right diagonal.

2. Work the desired number of stitches in a zag direction—downward left diagonal. End the yarn.

3. Again start at the top. Work the desired number of stitches in a zag direction—downward left diagonal.

4. Work the desired number of stitches in a zig direction—downward right diagonal closing the diamond shape.

Note: In the beginning I would advise you to use the method I recommend for working the French Stitch around a diamond which is given in the directions for patterns and finished items. As you advance and become thoroughly familiar with the travels of the French Stitch, you can substitute the method you prefer.

Individual Two-Tone French Stitches. In this version, the top half of each stitch is worked in Color A and the bottom half in Color B. A wonderful tweedy appearance results which softens the effect of the hard-edged zig zags (see Patterns 17 through 20, Figs. 4-37 to 4-40). Endless combinations of color are possible. It is easy to work the two colors once you are on friendly terms with the basic mechanics.

1. Follow the solid line at the left of Figure 4-16. Use Color A yarn. Start at the upper left. Work the top half only of the stitches down to bottom of the row.

2. Follow the patterned lines at the right of Figure 4-16. Use Color B yarn. Complete the bottom half of the stitches down to the bottom of the row as shown in Figure 4-17.

Note: The down-and-up in-one-motion steps should be similar to those used for the regular French Stitch. Figure 4-16 shows the steps for a Two-Stitch Zig Zag to make clear how the change of direction is worked. Figure 4-17 shows a Five-Stitch Zig Zag in progress.

Straight Horizontal Lines. You can produce straight horizontal lines within a design—or straight outside edges along the top and bottom of an overall area— by working a half French Stitch between completed stitches, as shown in Figure 4-18. The half stitches are indicated by the striped lines. The bottom halves are used along the *top* of an area to produce a straight edge and the top halves are used along the *bottom* of an area to produce a straight edge.

Sounds like double-talk but that's the truth! This technique is handy to know when you are interpreting the triangular-shaped motifs used in so many Indian designs, for it enables you to divide a diamond-shaped area in two with ease. The half stitches would also have to be used in the adjacent area of color—above or below—to hold the straight horizontal line.

Important Point: Half stitches can be used at the top and bottom of outside edges instead of Special French Fill-in Stitches. After you become thoroughly familiar with the mechanics of the French Stitch, you can easily start and end each row with the correct half stitch, automatically producing even edges along the top and bottom as you work each row. The two side edges are filled in with Special French Fill-in Stitches in the correct color (or colors, if there is a pattern involved) after the area is completed.

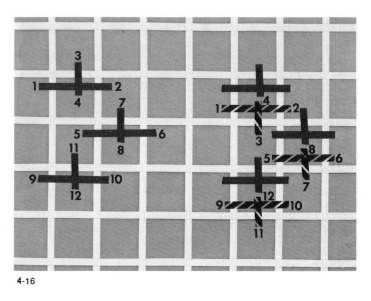

4-16

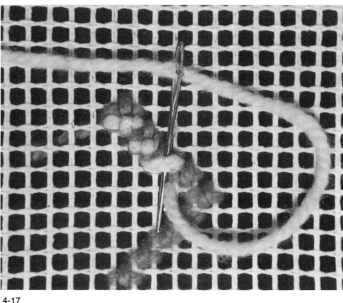

4-17

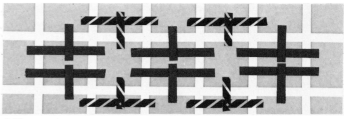

4-18

FRENCH STITCH PATTERNS

The following four patterns show how the overall design can be completely changed by increasing the number of stitches in the zig zags and through the use of color.

Pattern 1. A Two-Stitch French Zig Zag has a shocking pink, orange and gold rickrack pattern. (Fig. 4-19.) Pat Rug Yarn: shocking pink #259; orange #968; gold #421.

1st Row. Start at the upper left. Use pink yarn.
1. Work two French Stitches in a zig direction.
2. Work one French Stitch in a zag direction.
3. Work one French Stitch in a zig direction.

Note: You are forming a Two-Stitch French Zig Zag pattern, which is not as obvious as in the patterns that follow where more stitches are involved. This pattern merely wriggles down the canvas resembling rickrack.

Repeat the zig zag pattern to the bottom of the row. (The sample has 13 stitches.)

2nd Row. Use orange yarn. Repeat the Two-Stitch Zig Zag directly to the right of the first row.

3rd and 4th Rows. Use gold yarn. Work two rows. This completes the pattern.

4-19. Pattern 1.

To continue the pattern, repeat the first through fourth rows from left to right across the canvas for desired coverage. The pattern is repeated twice in this sample, plus one row of pink and one row of orange to balance the beginning.

⚫⚫⚫⚫⚫

Pattern 2. This Three-Stitch French Zig Zag pattern has related colors yellow and yellow-green with beige and soft brown. (Fig. 4-20.)
Pat Rug Yarn: beige #496; brown #433; yellow-green #550; yellow #413.

1st Row. Start at the upper left. Use beige yarn.
1. Work three French Stitches in a zig direction.
2. Work two French Stitches in a zag direction.
3. Work two French Stitches in a zig direction.

Note: You are forming a Three-Stitch French Zig Zag pattern. Remember to count the stitches at the points of the zig zags each time. There should always be three stitches in each direction. Repeat the zig zag pattern to the bottom of the row. (The sample has 13 stitches.)

2nd Row. Use brown yarn. Repeat the Three-Stitch Zig Zag directly to the right of the first row.

3rd Row. Use green yarn. Repeat the Three-Stitch Zig Zag directly to the right.

4th Row. Use yellow yarn. Repeat the Three-Stitch Zig Zag directly to the right. This completes the pattern.

To continue the pattern, repeat the first through fourth rows from left to right across the canvas for the desired coverage. The pattern is repeated twice in this sample plus the first 3 rows, ending with the yellow-green row. This balances the spacing of the brown rows which are accented by the value contrast. Work single yellow

4-20. Pattern 2.

stitches along both sides so that the pattern is continued to the edges.

Read about a helpful designing trick under the next pattern. One color can easily be made to appear as background.

⚫⚫⚫⚫⚫

Pattern 3. This Four-Stitch French Zig Zag has bright blue and white zig zag stripes on a yellow-green background. (Fig. 4-21.) With the easy trick that follows, behold, one color becomes the background!

4-21. Pattern 3.

4-22. Pattern 4.

Design Note: The zig zags will create an overall pattern in Pattern 2 and in the purple and white finished pillow (Fig. 8-29) if you wish. To accomplish this, you must continue the pattern to the very edge. Sometimes only single stitches in a particular color are necessary along the edges to preserve the pattern. If you wish predominant colors—usually bright colors with strong value contrast—to stand out as stripes, simply fill in the two side areas solidly in the color you wish to be the background. At this point, you must use good judgment and perhaps a Squint Test or two. Let me explain my thinking in keying this design. The sharpest value contrast is between the bright dark-blue and the white. Your eye is immediately attracted to the areas where these two colors are side by side. Look at the pattern and you will understand. The stripes of blue and white jump out. The contrasting edge between them is what your eye sees first and the message goes to your brain, telling you they are stripes. The green middle value is a natural for the background color. You can help this image along by starting and ending your design with green zig zags at either side, and filling in the side areas solidly with the same color as shown in the pattern. You can easily increase the feeling of background color by working several rows of background color side by side in your pattern and adding additional rows at either side. You can isolate patterns, as in some of the later patterns, by working areas of the background color at the top and bottom too. You can force any color to become the background color but try to choose the natural one; usually the middle value is best since its use produces the most effective impact.

Pat Rug Yarn: yellow-green #550; blue #731; white #005.

1st Row. Start at the upper left. Use green yarn.
1. Work four French Stitches in a zig direction.
2. Work three French Stitches in a zag direction.
3. Work three French Stitches in a zig direction.
Note: You are forming a Four-Stitch French Zig Zag pattern. Remember to count the stitches at the points of the zig zags each time. There should always be four stitches in each direction. Repeat the zig zag pattern to the bottom of the row. (This sample has 13 stitches.)

2nd Row. Use blue yarn. Repeat the Four-Stitch Zig Zag directly to the right of the first row.

3rd Row. Use white yarn. Repeat the Four-Stitch Zig Zag directly to the right. This completes the pattern.

To continue the pattern, repeat the first through the third rows from left to right across the canvas for desired coverage. The pattern is repeated three times in the sample; add one row of yellow-green to balance the beginning. Work green stitches along both sides so that green is continued to the edges.

Pattern 4. In this irregular French Stitch Zig Zag pattern, Six-Stitch Zigs are combined with Three-Stitch Zags in black, green and turquoise rows. (Fig. 4-22.)
Pat Rug Yarn: black #050; green #569; turquoise #738.

1st Row. Start at the upper left. Use black yarn.
1. Work six French Stitches in zig direction.
2. Work two French Stitches in a zag direction.
3. Work five French Stitches in a zig direction.
Note: You are forming an irregular zig zag pattern, so there are six stitches in the zig direction and three stitches in the zag direction. Remember to count the stitches at the point of the zig zags each time.

Repeat the zig zag pattern to bottom of row. (The sample has 20 stitches in each full row.)

2nd Row. Use green yarn. Repeat an irregular zig zag directly to the right of the first row.

3rd Row. Use turquoise yarn. Repeat an irregular zig zag directly to the right. This completes the pattern.

To continue the pattern, repeat the first through the third rows from left to right across the canvas for desired coverage. The pattern is repeated twice in the sample. Work portions of rows as necessary to continue the pattern to the right edge as shown in the sample.

4-23. Pattern 5.

To fill in the area on the left side of the first row, reverse the order of colors and work portions of rows as necessary to continue the pattern to the left edge as shown in the sample.

Pattern 5. This pattern is made up of peppermint stripe diagonals in red and shocking pink with sparkling white. (Fig. 4-23.)
Pat Rug Yarn: white #005; red #237; shocking pink #259.

Note: All rows are worked in a zag direction—the downward left diagonal. Mark the corners of the area to be covered with yarn tie markers so you will know when you reach the outside bars of canvas. (This sample uses 15 bars of canvas from top to bottom and 23 bars across.) The directions get you started in the top left corner and specify the number of stitches in the first few rows. From there on you let the number of stitches grow in each row for desired coverage. They increase by two stitches in each row until you reach the bottom bar of canvas. Then continue across from left to right working the same number of stitches in each row until you reach the top right-corner marker. The number of stitches will then decrease until you reach the bottom right-corner marker.

1st Row. Start at the upper left corner. Use white yarn.
1. Place your finger on the upper left corner hole of canvas. Move the finger over one hole to the right. Work one French Stitch around this hole.
2. Work the second stitch in a zag direction. The first row has only two stitches. The tails from the starting and ending of the yarn can be woven in later in the worked area.

2nd Row. Use red yarn. Starting directly to the right of the first row, work four red stitches in a zag direction.

3rd Row. Use pink yarn. Starting directly to the right, work six pink stitches in a zag direction. This completes the pattern: one row each of white, red and pink, in that order.
Continue working the rows in the correct color sequence, increasing the number of stitches in the rows for desired coverage. The sample shown is a helpful guide. When you work the French Stitch in straight diagonal rows, there is often a slight pull on the canvas. An extra tug or two with the fingers might be necessary to make

certain the edges are straight and the canvas squared off before construction takes place.

Note: Up to this point the French Stitch patterns have involved only the two downward diagonal directions—to the right or to the left. The designs which follow involve all four diagonal directions. Practice a bit and master the mechanics of walking the stitches in the two upward diagonal directions before you work the patterns.
There are a number of ways in which the stitches can be worked to interpret the patterns. I will outline the procedure I prefer so you can follow my suggestions in the beginning. As previously explained, I find the two downward diagonal directions the easiest to work, so I use them whenever possible. In most instances, I keep the top of the canvas on top while working the stitches. When you have completed a few projects, you may discover favorite ways of your own. You may wish to turn the canvas while the work is in progress or you might discover a more convenient place to start. Feel free to develop the working process which you find easiest, but do be certain that you are thoroughly familiar with the stitch mechanics before you solo.
It is important to keep in mind that this is a Touch Stitch. Most of the patterns are worked from the center out in all directions, and each stitch is worked so it touches a preceding stitch that is already completed. The designs literally grow out from the center. Do not attempt to work an isolated row far removed from the already worked area.

Pattern 6. The diamond-shaped bull's-eye has a deep purple and blue design. The pattern produces an 8 in. square. (Fig. 4-24.)
Pat Rug Yarn: purple #632; blue #760.
Find the exact center hole by folding the canvas in quarters. The first stitch is worked around the hole directly above the center hole.

1st Row. For the basic center diamond, use purple yarn. The first row in this pattern consists of the basic-center purple diamond shape made up of four French Stitches worked as follows:

Basic Center Diamond.
1. Work one stitch around the hole directly above the center hole as just explained.
2. Work one stitch in a zig direction.
3. Work one stitch in a zag direction.
4. Work one stitch in an upward left diagonal direction. This last stitch fills in the area to the left of the other three stitches, forming the basic diamond shape around which the rows will be worked.

4-24. Pattern 6.

Note: The actual stitch count for each side of the diamond is given for the first four rows. From then on only the number of the row and the proper color will be indicated. The first stitch of each row is started directly above the top stitch in the preceding row. Place a finger on the first completely free hole directly above: this is the hole around which to work the first stitch.

2nd Row. Use blue yarn. Start at top of the diamond after finding the correct hole. Work 4 French Stitches in a zig direction. Work 3 stitches in a zag direction. Work 3 stitches in an upward left diagonal direction. Work 3 stitches in an upward right diagonal direction. This completes the row around the diamond. There should be 4 stitches on each side.

3rd Row. Use purple yarn. Start at the top of the diamond and work one row around similar to the second row but with 6 stitches on each side of the diamond.

4th Row. Use purple yarn. Start at the top of the diamond and work one row around with 8 stitches on each side of the diamond.

5th Row. Use blue yarn. Start at the top and work one row around.

6th Row. Use purple yarn. Start at the top and work one row around.

7th Row. Use blue yarn. Start at the top and work one row around. This completes the last unbroken row around for the pattern. The outer four points of the blue diamond formed by the seventh row key the size of the sample pattern. You can easily determine the corners by running your fingers along these bars toward each corner and placing yarn tie markers on the crossbars where they meet.

Corners.

1. Use purple yarn. Keeping within the area keyed by the blue diamond points, work one row of purple consisting of 12 stitches. The diagonal direction will depend on the particular corner you are working.

2. Use blue yarn. Work 5 rows of blue stitches—the number of stitches will decrease by 2 in each row—until you reach the corner. When the rows become very short, run the yarn under on the wrong side to reach the correct spot for starting a new row.

Design Note: This pattern can be keyed in many different color combinations. The width of the rows can vary by working 1, 2 or 3 (or more) rows of one color next to each other. Also the overall square area can grow and grow to any size if you add as many complete rows around as is necessary for desired coverage before you work the corner areas. You can use the alternate Method C for working rows around a diamond, described on page 73, when the rows grow longer.

Pattern 7. The French Stitch special! A turquoise background is ablaze with multicolored zig zags—in green, shocking pink, bright yellow and crisp white. (Fig. 4-25.)

Because of the happy versatility of this special pattern, it was chosen as an example of a theme which could be used for a number of items of various sizes and shapes.

4-25. Pattern 7.

See the pincushion and large pillow (Figs. 4-44 and 4-45) among the finished items—pillows of all sizes can be keyed in a flash— and the bellpull in the last chapter (Fig. 8-30). The basic design is extremely adaptable and the possibilities of color combinations are endless. Size of pattern: 5½ in. × 10 in.
Pat Rug Yarn: turquoise #738; white #005; yellow #413; shocking pink #279; green #550.

The pattern is worked from the center out to each side.

To create the center diamonds around which the zig zag stripes are worked, find the center hole along the top of the canvas. Drop down to start the first stitch, so that a border of at least 5 bars of canvas is left free along the top.

Top Diamond. Use turquoise yarn.

1. Work one French Stitch around the correct hole of canvas described in the preceding paragraph. Work 4 additional stitches in a zag direction, a total of 5 stitches.

2. Work 4 stitches in a zag direction.

3. Work 4 stitches in an upward left diagonal direction.

4. Work 4 stitches in an upward right diagonal direction. This will close the outside row of the diamond with 5 stitches on each side.

5. Start at the top of the inside opening. Work the first stitch directly under the outside top stitch of the diamond. Work stitches completely around the diamond directly inside the outer first row—3 stitches on each side of the inside diamond.

6. Fill in the center opening with one stitch. This completes the top diamond.

Bottom Diamond. Work the first stitch directly under the stitch in the bottom point of the top diamond. Repeat steps 1 through 6. When you have completed the center diamond shapes, the contour is set for the zig zag stripes on either side. It is not necessary to count stitches. Follow the contour of the center diamond-shaped areas and work the rows of stripes in the colors indicated.

Zig Zag Stripes. For the color sequence to the right of the center diamond, start at top, to the right of the top turquoise stitch. Work the rows from the right of the diamonds to the right edge in white, yellow, shocking pink, green, white, turquoise.

Note: Use the right-side points of the completed turquoise zig zag to establish the side edge. Fill in the two corners and the middle side areas left open by the zig zag pattern as follows. Work stitches in diagonal rows at the corners (the rows decrease by 2 stitches in each row). Follow the contour of the zig zag in the center open area. Work the rows of stitches until the area is filled in and the right edge stitches line up one under the other.

For the color sequence to the left, work the rows from the left side of the diamonds to the left edge, repeating the sequence: white, yellow, shocking pink, green, white,

turquoise. Follow the same instructions for filling in the areas on the right-side edge to form a straight edge along the left side.

Note: If you wish to increase the background area on the sides, work additional turquoise zig zag rows before filling in the corners and middle areas.

Design Note: I feel as if I should take a deep breath before describing the potentials of this pattern! It can grow to any size or shrink obligingly as shown in the finished examples. It is all accomplished like magic with a series of simple tricks. The overall area can be long and skinny, square or rectangular-shaped—whichever you choose. The design can be manipulated to fill specific areas in a manner which gives the finished items that professional custom-designed look. You can add zig zag stripes; delete stripes; change the size of the center diamonds; work two or more rows of background color and repeat the sequence of color stripes a second or third time; close the zig zags so that they meet at the top and bottom of the center diamonds (as in the large pillow); drop a white stripe between the zig zag colors. You can use "ice cream" colors, related colors, bold brilliant colors with sharp value contrast. You could literally work this pattern in colors that would jump off the wall if this pleases you and would be at home in your décor. One factor to remember in keying your designs: a row (or rows) of background color interspersed between zig zag stripes immediately isolates the groupings of colors on each side, transforming them into separate bands. This pattern can be used very successfully for luxury items that have the "expensive look." Picture a long, solid-colored couch with three oversized pillows similar to the large pillow in Figure 4-45, perhaps with a deeper value contrast and extremely brilliant colors. On the opposite side of a coffee table, there's a long bench with one continuous version of the same design—or perhaps a valance for a picture window across the room. Very exciting thoughts! Not too many items or you will destroy the charm of design accent. Draw some thumbnail roughs of the possibilities and your excitement will mount as your creative ideas emerge.

Pattern 8. French Stitch chevrons of deep old bronze with black French Knots stand out against a bright daffodil-yellow background. (Fig. 4-26.) Size of pattern: 5 in. × 9 in.
Nantucket 6-Ply Cable Yarn: bronze #11; yellow #7; black #120.

Find the center hole by folding the canvas in quarters. The first stitch is worked around the hole directly above the center hole.

1st Row. Use bronze yarn. Follow the instructions under Pattern 6 (Fig. 4-24) for the basic Four-Stitch Center Diamond (steps 1 through 4).

4-26. Pattern 8.

Note: The first stitch of each of the next two rows is started directly above the top stitch in the preceding row. Place a finger on the first completely free hole directly above and this will be the hole around which to work the first stitch.

2nd Row. Use bronze yarn. Start at the top of the diamond as instructed.

    1. Work 4 French Stitches in a zig direction.

    2. Work 3 French Stitches in a zag direction.

    3. Work 3 French Stitches in an upward left diagonal direction.

    4. Work 3 French Stitches in an upward right diagonal direction. The diamond should have 4 stitches on each side.

3rd Row. Use bronze yarn. Start at the top of the diamond, as instructed, and work one row around similar to the second row, but with 6 stitches on each side.

This completes the center diamond. The easiest way to proceed is to complete the design area and then fill in the surrounding background.

Area to Right of Center Diamond. Start the first stitch to the right of the top stitch in the point of the center diamond. Work the rows toward the right-side edge.

1st Row. Use yellow yarn. Work one zig zag row following the contour of the right side of the center diamond, ending with a stitch to the right of the bottom point.

2nd Row. Use bronze yarn. Work one row to the right so that the top and bottom stitches are flush with top and bottom points of the center diamond (see Fig. 4-26).

3rd Row. Work one similar row of yellow.

4th Row. Work one similar row of bronze.

5th Row. Work one similar row of yellow. This brings you to the right edge of the pattern. If you want a longer design, simply continue the alternate rows for the desired coverage.

Area to the Left of the Center Diamond. Start at the spot to the left of the stitch in the top point of the center diamond. Repeat rows 1 through 5, as described, to the left edge, so that the color pattern is duplicated on the right side as shown in Figure 4-26.

Background Area. Use yellow yarn. The outer points of the two side yellow zig zags (fifth row) key the left and right edges. Work the yellow background around the center design motif by continuing the rows in diagonal directions—either upward or downward. Using yellow yarn, extend one of the bronze chevrons following the diagonal directions—3 stitches upward, 3 stitches downward—and you will key the top and bottom edges. Use the top and bottom stitches as guides, plus the two side points, and place yarn tie markers in each corner. (Run your fingers along the canvas bars toward each corner and place a marker on the crossbar where they meet.) You must be a little inventive to figure out the best way to fill in the small background areas around the central design. Whenever possible I run the yarn underneath on the wrong side to bring the needle up to the surface in the spot where additional stitches will be worked. This eliminates a number of stops and starts of yarn for the short runs. Continue filling in the yellow background, working the stitches in diagonal directions, until the top and bottom areas are covered and the corner areas are completed.

French Knots. Use black yarn. Place a French Knot (single strand—around the needle once) in the center of each stitch at the top, bottom and points of the chevrons, and in each corner stitch of the center diamond.

Design Note: This pattern can grow and change according to the size of the center diamond and the size and number of chevrons used. The pattern can be repeated across or up and down as many times as you wish. Any number of color combinations could be substituted. There should be sharp value contrast between the background and the design area. The pattern shown can be used for a mini pillow or a maxi pincushion.

Each of the next three patterns 9, 10 and 11 are started with one large basic cross or X. Once you have worked the two diagonal rows of stitches—crossing them *exactly* in the center—you can produce innumerable variations of the patterns. The four triangular shaped areas formed are individually worked in rows of color following the contour of the X. The patterns can grow to any size or proportion. Mark the four corners of the area you wish to cover with the yarn ties, find the exact center hole and you are in business. Simply work the four arms of the Basic X from the center out until the bars of canvas representing the edges are reached. In a perfect square the extending arms of the X will hit exactly in the corners, but not so with a rectangle. The side areas extend beyond the basic cross, as explained in the directions for Pattern 11.

Pattern 9. This pattern of uniform stripes in two values of yellow-green with white lives happily in many different types of décor, both traditional and contemporary. (Fig. 4-27.) White can be used with two values of just about any color you can name. Size of sample: 7 in. square.
Pat Rug Yarn: deep yellow-green #550; light yellow-green #580; white #005.

Find the exact center hole of the canvas by folding the canvas in quarters. The first stitch is worked around this center hole.

4-27. Pattern 9.

For the **Basic Big Center Cross,** use deep green yarn.
   1. Work one French Stitch around the center hole.
   2. Not counting the center stitch, work 11 stitches in a zig direction. End the yarn.
   3. Start back at the center stitch. Not counting the center stitch, work 11 stitches in a zag direction. End the yarn.
   4. Start back at the center stitch. Not counting the center stitch, work 11 stitches in an upward right diagonal direction. End the yarn.
   5. Start back at the center stitch. Not counting the center stitch, work 11 stitches in an upward left diagonal direction. This completes the basic center cross.

The four areas formed by the big cross are worked individually in rows which follow the contour of the basic cross and become smaller and smaller as the work progresses. This method requires that you keep the yarn tie marker indicating the top on top as you work all the stitches.

Two Side Areas. These are both worked in a zig zag fashion in downward diagonal directions. Stay inside the boundaries of the basic cross. In this pattern which forms a square, the ends of the arms are the corners.

Top and Bottom Areas. These are worked in both the downward and upward diagonal directions. For the top area you start at the left and work the rows downward to the center, then upward. For the bottom area, start at the left and work the rows upward to the center, then downward.

Color Pattern for All Four Individual Areas. 1st Row, light green; 2nd Row, white; 3rd Row, deep green; 4th Row, light green; 5th Row, white. This completes the rows for the pattern shown. Repeat rows 3, 4 and 5 as many times as necessary for larger areas. The number of stitches in the basic cross must be increased accordingly.

There is an alternative method for working large areas. As I have mentioned, I prefer the downward diagonal directions, so I use these directions whenever possible, especially if the area to be covered is large and the rows long ones. The downward diagonal directions can be used throughout as follows. For the top area, start at the top on the left and work the stitches diagonally down to the center. End the yarn. Start at the top on the right and work the stitches diagonally down to the center, completing the row. For the bottom area, start at the center. Work stitches in a zig direction. End the yarn. Start at the center and work stitches in a zag direction. End the yarn. Continue both areas following the color pattern. (The two side areas are always worked in the same manner—downward diagonal directions.) When the rows become very short, I resort to the combination of downward and upward directions to avoid too many starts and stops of yarn. Use your own judgment regarding the method which is best for you.

Pattern 10. Hurrah for the Red, White and Blue! Two different patterns of stripes are used to fill in the areas surrounding the big X. (Fig. 4-28.) Size of sample: 7 in. square.
Nantucket 6-Ply Cable Yarn: red #32; blue #61; white #1.

Find the exact center hole by folding the canvas in quarters. The first stitch is worked around this center hole.

4-29. Pattern 11.

4-28. Pattern 10.

Basic Big Center Cross. Use red yarn. Follow steps 1 through 5 for the basic big center cross in Pattern 9.

In this pattern, the top and bottom areas are worked in one pattern of stripes and the two side areas in a different pattern. Follow the instructions as outlined under Pattern 9 for working four areas formed by the big cross.

Color Pattern for Two Side Areas. 1st Row, white; 2nd Row, blue; 3rd Row, red; 4th Row, white; 5th Row, blue. Repeat the color pattern of rows of white, blue and red as many times as necessary for larger areas. The number of stitches in the basic cross must be increased accordingly.

Color Pattern for Top and Bottom Areas. 1st and 2nd Rows, white; 3rd Row, blue; 4th and 5th Rows, white.

Repeat the color pattern of 2 rows white and 1 row blue as many times as is necessary for the larger areas. The number of stitches in the basic cross must be increased accordingly.

Note: The 12 in. square pillow shown under the finished items (Fig. 4-41) is an example of how this pattern looks when it grows to a larger size.

●●●●●●

Pattern 11. A way-out effect is achieved with bold and brilliant color! (Fig. 4-29.) The big X is used to form a rectangular-shaped area. Size of sample: 5 in. × 7 in.

Nantucket 6-Ply Cable Yarn: shocking pink #38; green #84; yellow #7.

Find the center hole by folding the canvas in quarters. The first stitch is worked around this hole.

Basic Big Center Cross. Use pink yarn. Follow Steps 1 through 5 for the basic big center cross under Pattern 9 with one exception. Not counting the center stitch, work 8 stitches instead of 11 in all four diagonal directions.

In this pattern, the top and bottom areas are worked in solid pink. The two side areas are worked in a striped zig zag pattern. Follow instructions as outlined in Pattern 9 for working the four areas formed by the big cross, substituting the colors indicated.

Two Side Areas. To form the overall rectangular shape, the side areas are continued to each side *beyond* the basic cross. This is accomplished by starting the top first stitch of each zig zag row directly next to and flush with the top stitch of the basic cross and working down until the bottom stitch in each row is flush with the bottom stitch in the cross. You can continue doing this and the rectangle will increase along the sides to any width you choose. When it is the desired size, fill in the open side areas within the last zig zag and the edge will be formed. (In the pattern, only the green row is worked in this manner to show how the shape can be extended.)

Color Pattern for Two Side Areas. 1st Row is green. Extend this row to either side of the basic cross as explained in the preceding paragraph. 2nd Row, yellow. To duplicate the pattern, start to form the side edges with this row. Stitches in rows will decrease from this point on. 3rd Row, pink; 4th Row, green; 5th Row, yellow.

Repeat the color pattern of green, yellow and pink as many times as necessary for larger areas.

Color for Top and Bottom Areas. Fill in the top and bottom areas with solid pink, following the instructions for the top and bottom areas under Pattern 9.

Design Note for Three Big X Patterns 9, 10 and 11: I believe the three big X patterns speak for themselves regarding color potentials. Three entirely different effects are presented and these only touch the surface of the possibilities. One of the finished items, the footstool (Fig. 4-46) is another example. Give some thought to an over-sized contemporary square hassock with wide startling stripes of strong contrasting colors. What an impact that could produce! And wall hangings and long bench tops. You will imagine an endless stream of designs if you press that aware button. Keep one thought in mind. The larger the area, the greater the possibilities of variations. When space allows, you can work a number of rows of one color together and produce wider stripes. This gives you the opportunity to key a greater variety of widths in the stripes, so that the areas can be broken up into interesting design patterns.

The following two lattice patterns also start with one large basic cross. The first pattern is a white lattice holding small four-stitch diamonds of background between its lines (2 stitches on each side). The second is a more open white lattice which creates larger two-color diamonds (four stitches on each side).

Pattern 12. A white lattice with a bright green background is cool and fresh-looking. (Fig. 4-30.) Size of pattern: 6½ in. square.
Pat Rug Yarn: white #005; green #569.

Find the exact center hole by folding the canvas in quarters. Work the first stitch around this hole.

4-30. Pattern 12.

Basic Big Center Cross of the White Lattice Pattern. Follow Steps 1 through 5 for the basic big center cross in Pattern 9.

Note: The stitches are worked out in all directions from the basic cross to form the lattice pattern. Space is left between the parallel lines for a four-stitch diamond (two stitches on each side) which will be filled in later in green. The pattern is an exact square, so the ends of the four arms of the basic cross form the corners. Figure 4-31 shows a small section of the basic cross—where it crosses at the center—to help you start the lattice pattern. When you have formed several of the lattice crosses, the pattern will be evident and you can continue on your own. Count the stitches out from the center and check constantly to make certain the crosses are uniform and all the rows equidistant.

To form the lattice pattern. Use white yarn. Work on diagonal A–B. (Fig. 4-31.) Start at the center stitch. Not counting the center stitch, count down to the third stitch and work a diagonal row of stitches in a left downward direction to the bottom edge (No. 1). Using the same

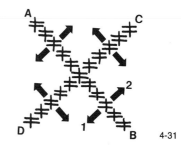

4-31

stitch as your guide, continue working the diagonal row in an upward right direction (No. 2) to the side edge. Continue working the rows parallel to 1–2, leaving 2 stitches in between until you reach the corner. Repeat the process from the center stitch up to the corner in the direction of A. This will complete the crossbars of white on line A–B of the big cross.

Important: Space for two stitches should be left free between the lattice crosses in all directions. Now work on line C–D. Repeat the same process you followed for line A–B, working the rows in the diagonal direction indicated by the arrows. When you reach a stitch which is already completed, skip under on the wrong side and bring the needle up to the surface in the proper spot beyond the stitch to continue the row in the same direction. Continue working the diagonal rows of white stitches until the lattice pattern is keyed over the entire area.

Background Diamonds. Use green yarn. Fill in the spaces between the lattice pattern with four-stitch diamonds—two stitches on each side. Work stitches in a clockwise direction. You can easily jump from one open diamond space to the next on the wrong side until you use up a strand of yarn. Fill in any portion of edge diamonds necessary to continue the pattern.

Pattern 13. The Lattice pattern grows! A background of two bright, related colors glow like warm sunlight. (Fig. 4-32.) Size of pattern: 6½ in. square.
Pat Rug Yarn: white #005; yellow #413; orange #421.

Find the exact center hole by folding the canvas in quarters. The first stitch is worked around this hole.

4-32. Pattern 13.

Basic Big Center Cross of the White Lattice Pattern. Use white yarn. Follow the instructions under Pattern 9 for the basic cross. Follow instructions in Pattern 12 for the lattice with the following exception. Start at the center stitch and, not counting the center stitch, count down to the fifth stitch; then work the diagonal in a left downward direction to the bottom edge. Continue following the directions but leave space for four stitches between the lattice pattern throughout. This leaves space for a background diamond shape with four stitches on each side.

Background Diamonds.

1. Use yellow yarn. Work one row of stitches in clockwise direction around each area formed by the lattice pattern. The diamond has four stitches on each side.

2. Use orange yarn. Work a four-stitch diamond in the center area (two stitches on each side).

Note: When filling in the diamond-shaped areas, you can skip under on the wrong side to come up to the surface in the hole where the same color will be introduced again. Catch the yarn once or twice on the wrong side if the run is extra long.

Design Note for Lattice Patterns. The openings in the lattice pattern can grow to any size. An entirely different effect would be produced if you worked the lattice in a dark value against a light background. The two related colors in this pattern are close in value so they tend to blend in your eye, but you can easily accent the small diamond in the center of each area by introducing a sharp value contrast. Both patterns 12 and 13 can be interpreted in color schemes too numerous to mention with as much value contrast as you wish.

Diamonds, diamonds, diamonds are a designer's good friend! Patterns 14, 15 and 16 show how the placement, size and color of diamond shapes can completely change the overall effect. Still the little ol' diamond, but how different it looks!

Pattern 14. In pleasing colors white and green and pink, diamonds nestle closely together and form a compact design motif which can grow to any size or proportion. (Fig. 4-33.) Size of pattern: 6 in. × 8 in.
Pat Rug Yarn: white #005; green #550, shocking pink #279.

4-33. Pattern 14.

Note: Each of the alternating green and pink diamonds have three stitches on each side and one white stitch in the middle. Work the center green diamond first. The others progress outward from the center diamond, which acts as the key for the placement of the stitches. Remember, this is a Touch Stitch. Start the first stitch of each new diamond directly next to an already-worked stitch.

Find the exact center hole by folding the canvas in quarters. The first stitch is worked around the second hole directly above the center hole.

Center Vertical Row of Green Diamonds. Use green yarn. Work the middle diamond, starting in the hole just indicated. Start in a zig direction and work stitches clockwise to form a diamond with 3 stitches on each side. (There will be a space in the center for a white stitch, which will be worked later.)

For the top diamond, work a green stitch directly above the top stitch of the center diamond. Starting in an upward left diagonal direction, work around clockwise to form the second green diamond directly above the center diamond.

For the bottom diamond, work a green stitch directly beneath the bottom stitch of the center diamond. Work the third green diamond directly below, following the same method you used for the center diamond. This completes the center row of three green diamonds. The pattern of pink and green diamonds grows out to each side from this center row. Follow the color pattern shown in Figure 4-34. When the pink and green pattern is completed, fill in the single white stitches in the center of each diamond. Also, work the six single green outside stitches as indicated in the drawing. This completes the design area.

4-34

Background. Use white yarn. The background in the sample pattern is worked so there is one white stitch beyond the outside points on all sides of the design. (This can easily be increased if you want a larger background area.) Work the background in diagonal rows from the design area out to the edges. Once the top, bottom and two side edges are established, work the background out to the corners where the edge bars of canvas cross. You can use yarn tie markers to indicate the corners.

Pattern 15. Brilliant turquoise and shocking pink diamonds on a white background delight the eye. (Fig. 4-35.) Size of pattern: 9½ in. × 7 in.
Nantucket 6-Ply Cable Yarn: turquoise #64; shocking pink #38; white #1.

4-35. Pattern 15.

Note: The center vertical row of three turquoise diamonds is worked first. Since the French Stitch is a Touch Stitch, the two single stitches of shocking pink between the rows must be worked to establish the proper locations for the vertical rows of turquoise diamonds on either side.

Find the exact center hole by folding the canvas in quarters. The first stitch is worked around the second hole directly above the center hole.

Center Row of Turquoise Diamonds. Follow the instructions for the center row of three green diamonds in Pattern 14, substituting turquoise yarn. Following Figure 4-35 for the placement, fill in single shocking pink stitches as follows: one stitch in the center of each turquoise diamond; two stitches side by side at the left and right points of each diamond; one stitch at the top of the row; one stitch at the bottom of the row.

Two Side Rows of Turquoise Diamonds. Use turquoise yarn. Use the outer pink stitches as guides. Start the first turquoise stitch next to the pink stitch. Work the stitches clockwise around each diamond. Form an identical row of turquoise diamonds on each side of the center row. Fill in the single shocking pink stitches in each side row as follows: one stitch in the center of each turquoise diamond; one stitch at the top and bottom of the row and at each of the outer side points of the diamonds. This completes the design area.

Background. Use white yarn. The background is worked so there is one white stitcl. beyond the outside points on all sides of the design. (This can easily be increased if you want a larger background area.) I started in the central background areas, working in my favorite downward diagonal directions whenever possible. Skip under the design areas on the back to continue the rows to the edges. Fill in the top areas later. The design areas are small in this pattern so this procedure is feasible and avoids numerous stops and starts of yarn. Once the top, bottom and two side edges are established, work the background out to the corners where the edge bars of canvas cross. Yarn tie markers can be used to indicate the corners.

Pattern 16. Purple and red are the epitome of pageantry. You can almost hear the trumpets! (Fig. 4-36.) Size of pattern: 6 in. × 11 in.
Pat Rug Yarn: red #237; purple #632; white #005.

4-36. Pattern 16.

Note: Work the large center red diamond first. Then work the center and surrounding single purple stitches. The two purple stitches placed side by side next to the right and left points of the large diamonds establish the correct locations for the two smaller red diamonds.

Find the exact center hole by folding the canvas in quarters. The first stitch is worked around the second hole directly above the center hole.

Large Red Center Diamond. Use red yarn.

1. Work the first stitch in the hole mentioned. Start in a zig direction and work around clockwise to form a diamond with three stitches on each side. (There will be an open space in the center where the purple stitch will be worked later.)

2. Work a stitch directly above the top stitch in the diamond. Start in a zig direction and work around clockwise to form a larger diamond with five stitches on each side.

Purple Accents of Single Stitches. Use purple yarn. This process is a bit tricky and sounds confusing, but it is really quite simple once you get started. Study Figure 4-36. Notice that there are two single purple stitches (one on top of the other) at the top and bottom points of the large red diamond and two purple stitches next to each of the right and left points, with alternating white and purple single stitches along the sides. Start at the top of the red diamond. Work one purple stitch directly above the top stitch in the diamond. Work a second purple stitch directly above the first stitch. Drop down and catch the yarn on the wrong side under the worked area. Proceed in a downward right diagonal direction. Leave space for one stitch; work one purple stitch; leave space for one stitch; work a second single purple stitch; leave space for one stitch; work a third single purple stitch. This purple stitch falls directly to right of the point of the red diamond. Work a second purple stitch directly to the right. Keep referring to Figure 4-36. Catch the yarn on the wrong side and continue around in a clockwise direction, working the two single stitches as directed at each point, and leaving space on the sides for the alternating white stitches. Work a single purple stitch in the center.

Two small Side Diamonds. Use red yarn. Use the outer side purple stitches as your guide for starting the first stitch of red diamonds on the same horizontal line. Work around clockwise to form the two smaller red diamonds with three stitches on each side. Work single purple stitches around the outside of the small diamonds, leaving space for white stitches between. Work a single purple stitch in the center of each.

Background. Use white yarn. The background is worked so there is one white stitch beyond the outside points on all sides of the design. (This can easily be increased if you want a larger background area.) Work the background in diagonal rows. Start in the central design area and work out toward the edges. Skip under the design area on the wrong side when possible to prevent numerous stops and starts of yarn. Once you have established the top, bottom and two side edges, work the background out to the corners where the edge bars of canvas cross. Yarn tie markers can be used to indicate the corners.

Design Note for Three Diamond Patterns: Patterns 14, 15 and 16 can be used as is for delightful mini pillows. But if you wish, you can extend the background area considerably and produce larger pillows. The designs will then become more isolated. Don't go too far or they will appear to be lost in the background space. The patterns can grow to any size in any direction. By turning them on their sides, any of the three designs could be extended and keyed for long skinny bellpull shapes. A startling number of patterns can be created by using the contrast of small diamond accents against the larger diamond-shaped areas. Make the color work for you. Small touches of contrasting color can add much zing to the overall effect. Think Diamonds. Keep your aware button pressed down and you will find diamond shapes sprinkled all over. Make little rough thumbnail sketches and experiment. You can isolate shapes or nestle them together. You can increase the size of the diamonds by working more rows around. You can use multiple colors, related colors or single-color schemes. Be certain there is sharp value contrast between the background and the design pattern. Your eye should quickly be able to define the edges for the best effect in this particular type of design.

When you use a Two-Tone French Stitch, a whole new world springs up. Softer edges produce a woven tweedy effect. Each of the following three patterns (17, 18 and 19) are worked in a Five-Stitch Zig Zag design. To form the zig zags, follow basic instructions under pattern 3 (Fig. 4-21) for the Four-Stitch Zig Zag but increase the count to five stitches in each direction and repeat for desired coverage. The Five-Stitch Zig Zag is repeated twice in each of the three patterns, making a total of 17 stitches from top to bottom in each row. (See Figs. 4-16 and 4-17 for detailed directions for working the Two-Tone French Stitch.) The rows are worked from left to right. To work the rows of two-tone stitches, complete the top half of the stitch from the top of the row to the bottom; then fill in the bottom half of the stitch. Although the yarn colors used in the patterns are listed, I give the color changes for the rows in terms of value so that you can easily substitute different colors. Pattern 20 also uses the two-tone stitches but is worked in diagonal rows.

Pattern 17. Burnt orange and white form a pattern of uniform zig zag stripes. Size of pattern: 5 in. × 6 in.

4-37. Pattern 17.

Pat Rug Yarn: orange #417 (deep value); white #005 (light value). Start at the upper left.

Color Pattern for the Five-Stitch Zig Zag. 1st Row—solid deep value; 2nd Row—solid light value; 3rd and 4th Rows—two-tone. In the two-tone stitch, the top is light value and the bottom is the deep value. 5th Row—solid light value.

Repeat Rows 1 through 5 for desired coverage. To duplicate the pattern, work Rows 1 through 5, then repeat Rows 1 through 4. Fill in the side areas, using the right color changes to continue the overall pattern.

Pattern 18. Two-tone stitches worked in various combinations of turquoise, yellow-green and white produce textural eye interest. (Fig. 4-38.) Size of pattern: 5 in. × 6 in. Pat Rug Yarn: turquoise #728 (deep value); yellow-green #550 (middle value); white #005 (light value).

Start at the upper left.

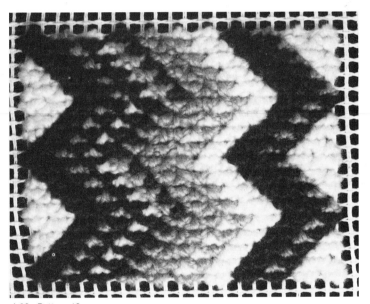

4-38. Pattern 18.

Color Pattern for the Five-Stitch Zig Zag. 1st Row—solid deep value; 2nd Row—two-tone (the top is the middle value and the bottom is the deep value); 3rd Row—two-tone (the top is the light value and the bottom the deep value); 4th Row—two-tone (the top is the deep value and the bottom the middle value); 5th Row—solid middle value; 6th Row—two-tone (the top is the light value and the bottom the middle value); 7th Row—solid light value.

Repeat Rows 1 through 7 for desired coverage. To duplicate the pattern, work Rows 1 through 7, then Rows 1 and 2. Fill in side areas in a light value as shown in the pattern. If you wish, the design can be continued to the edge in the correct color changes for producing the overall pattern.

4-39. Pattern 19.

Pattern 19. A combination of two values of shocking pink and a touch of white results in textural charm. (Fig. 4-39.) Two values of any color can be substituted. Size of pattern: 5 in. × 6 in.

Pat Rug Yarn: shocking pink #239 (deep value); shocking pink #279 (middle value); white #005 (light value).

Start at the upper left.

Color Pattern for the Five-Stitch Zig Zag. 1st Row—solid deep value; 2nd Row—two-tone (the top is the middle value and the bottom the deep value); 3rd Row—solid middle value; 4th Row—two-tone (the top is the light value and the bottom the middle value).

Repeat Rows 1 through 4 for desired coverage. To duplicate the pattern, work Rows 1 through 4 twice; then work Row 1. Fill in the side areas, using the correct color changes to continue the overall pattern.

Pattern 20. Texture on the diagonal is created with solid stripes of green combined with two-tone areas of gold and white. (Fig. 4-40.) Size of pattern: 3½ in. × 8 in.

This pattern is worked in the same manner as Pattern 5. (See Fig. 4-23.) Mark the corners with yarn ties for the desired coverage as suggested. Follow the general instructions under Pattern 5 but substitute the following colors:

Pat Rug Yarn: yellow-green #545 (deep value); gold #440 (middle value); white #005 (light value).

1st Row. Place two stitches in the upper left corner. The two-tone stitches are a light value at the top and a middle value at the bottom.

2nd Row. Use a solid deep value.

3rd, 4th and 5th Rows. Use two-tone stitches that are of a light value at the top and a middle value at the bottom.

Thus the color pattern is: one row deep solid value and three rows two-tone, with the top the light value and the bottom the middle value.

Repeat this color pattern for the desired coverage.

Design Note for all Two-Tone French Stitch Patterns. The number of possible combinations of design and color is endless. Keep in mind that you should insert some plain, solid rows to produce the hard edge that contrasts with the soft woven look. Break up the area to form different widths to create interest for the eye. You can produce marvelous effects of blending by using related colors which are close in value. Combine these with a sharp value contrast and your pattern will have zing! You need not stick to repeat patterns; you can improvise the rows of color patterns as you work along. Use the Squint Test constantly if you proceed in this fashion. Watch your color and value balance. While the areas can vary in size, shape and color, there should be a balance of lights and darks or your design will appear to be lopsided. It can be asymmetric, yes, but the overall effect should balance. Asymmetric designs take a bit of courage, but the rewards are great when the extra effort results in a delightful finished product that is distinctively yours!

FRENCH STITCH FINISHED ITEMS

Pattern 10 grows to a 12 in. square pillow. (See Fig. 4-28.) The pillow is backed in red velvet with matching material cording. (Fig. 4-41.).

4-40. Pattern 20.

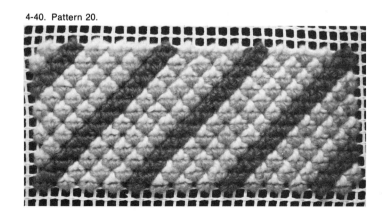

4-41

Pat Rug Yarn: blue #731 (16 str.); red #237 (13 str.); white #005 (27 str.).

Follow the basic instructions under Pattern 10. To increase the area size, make the following changes:

Basic Big Center Cross. Not counting the center stitch, work 20 stitches in four diagonal directions to form the basic cross.

Two Side Areas. Repeat the color patterns for the rows three times in white, blue and red. Fill in the single red stitch in the center of the last small red zig zag.

Top and Bottom Areas. Repeat the color pattern for the rows three times (2 white, one blue stripe). Fill in the single blue stitch in the center of the last small blue zig zag.

See Chapter 8 for directions for attaching material cording and backing. No Fill-in Stitches along the edge are necessary. Half of the edge stitches are cropped in construction to produce an even look.

The brightest pillow for miles around is worked in a Six-Stitch French Zig Zag in shocking pink with red and deep purple. (Fig. 4-42.) Size of sample: 9 in. × 17 in. The long rectangular-shaped pillow has saucy macramé tassels and a shocking pink felt backing.

4-42

Nantucket 6-Ply Cable Yarn: Pillow top—shocking pink #38 (33 str.); deep purple #47 (24 str.); red #32 (15 str.). Tassels (optional)—shocking pink #38, approximately 18–20 yds. of uncut yarn for each tassel or a total of approximately 80 yds. for four.

Start at the upper left. Work stitches from the top to the bottom in vertical rows from left to right. The entire pattern is worked in a Six-Stitch Zig Zag. Follow the detailed directions under Pattern 3 (Fig. 4-21) for the Four-Stitch Zig Zag but increase the count to 6 stitches in each zig and zag.

1st Row. Use red yarn. Work one row in the Six-Stitch Zig Zag until there are three zig zags from the top to the bottom. This first row sets the contour of the pattern.

2nd Row. Use purple yarn.

3rd and 4th Rows. Use pink yarn.

Repeat this color pattern for the rows—one red, one purple, two pink—six times across the canvas to the right. Then work one red, one purple and one pink. Fill in the side areas with the left side in solid pink, and the right side in pink and one single red stitch in each area to continue the overall pattern.

French Knots. Use purple yarn (around the needle once—single strand doubled). Work two French Knots to the right and left of each of the points formed by the purple zig zags. (Fig. 4-43.) The first knot is worked so it touches the point—the second is about ¼ in. distance from the first. Fill in the space between with a straight

4-43

stitch in purple to connect the knots. Along the side edges, work only one knot. Correct placement of the knots gives the zig zags extra movement as well as added textural interest.

Attach material cording and backing. No French Fill-in Stitches along the edge are necessary since half of the edge stitches are cropped during construction.

Macramé Tassels. The macramé tassels shown are fat and chunky. You can choose a different size or type if you wish. The following instructions are for those in the finished item. Use shocking pink yarn and follow the basic directions for macramé tassels in Chapter 8 but with these changes.

1. Cut 10 lengths of yarn 24 in. long, so that there will be 20 cords 12 in. long or *five* groupings of 4 cords each for the square knot pattern.

2. Follow Step 2 of the basic macramé-tassel directions but increase to 6 rows worked on the spool instead of 4.

3. Cut the cardboard 4 in. deep. Wind around it 40 times. Make four tassels and attach them to the corners as directed.

The French Stitch Special (Pattern 7—see Fig. 4-25) is adapted to a mini pillow or a large pincushion. (Fig. 4-44.) Size of sample: 7 in. square. The item has yarn cording of heavy white braid and a Now Needlepoint solid color turquoise backing.

Pat Rug Yarn: pillow top—turquoise #728 (12 str.); white #005 (5 str.); yellow #413 (3 str.); shocking pink #279 (3 str.). Braid: white #005 (9 str.). Backing: turquoise #728 (19 str.).

4-44

Topside. Work the small, turquoise Four-Stitch diamond in the center first. Using this center shape as a guide, work the rows of color, progressively larger and larger, around it. Find the center hole of the topside area. The first stitch is worked around the hole directly above the center hole.

Center Turquoise Diamond. Use turquoise yarn. The four stitches worked to form the center basic diamond are considered the first row. Follow the directions under Pattern 6 (Fig. 4-24) for the basic center diamond, Steps 1 through 4.

The second through sixth rows are worked from the center out in a sequence of white, yellow, shocking pink, white and turquoise, which is the background color.

Background. The outer points of the diamond formed by the last turquoise row in the color pattern are the guides

for the edges of background area. Use turquoise yarn. Working in diagonal rows, fill in each corner area out to the corner points where the canvas bars along the edges cross. Run your fingers along the bars and place yarn tie markers to indicate the corner crossbars if you wish. The diagonal rows can run in either a downward or upward direction. As I have explained, I use the downward diagonal runs whenever possible. Keep the top yarn marker on top or you will have a mix-up of stitches. If you plan to use a material backing, you can stop at this point. But if you plan to work a Now Needlepoint backing and braid stitch cording as in this item, work French Fill-in Stitches completely around the top area to produce even edges.

Now Needlepoint Backing. Use turquoise yarn and follow the directions in Chapter 8 for Now Needlepoint backings. Remember to leave one exposed bar of canvas between the two areas. Work the backing in diagonal rows and duplicate the size of the top area exactly. I started at the upper left corner of the back area, using the stitches in the upper left corner of the top area as guides. I worked the rows in a zag direction— two stitches in the corner row, four stitches in the next row to the right. Count the number of canvas bars down the side in the top area and place yarn tie markers on the crossbars where the bottom corners will fall, and you will know where to end the rows. Work French Fill-in Stitches completely around the backing area.

Heavy White Braid Construction. Follow the basic directions for braid construction and stuffing pillow given for the rosebud mini pillow in Chapter 8. Use white yarn (single strand doubled). Work the Regular Braid Stitch (Start A). The single strand doubled quickly eats up the yarn. Carefully weave in the ends as instructed, so that the ends and starts are not detectable.

The French Stitch Special (Pattern 7—Fig. 4-25) is adapted to a large pillow. (Fig. 4-45.) Size of sample: 13 in. × 19 in. The pillow has turquoise velvet cording and backing.

Pat Rug Yarn: turquoise #728 (60 str.); white #005 (15 str.); yellow #413 (6 str.); shocking pink #279 (6 str.); green #550 (7 str.).

Turn the canvas 90 degrees while the work is in progress so that the right side becomes the top and you can work the three turquoise center diamonds in a vertical row. With the canvas in this working position, place the yarn tie marker at the top. The three center turquoise diamonds are worked first, with the center one first, the bottom one second and the top one last. The multi-colored zig zag design rows are then worked around the three diamonds. The background is filled in after the design area is completed.

4-45

Find the center hole by folding the canvas in quarters. The first stitch is worked around the fourth hole directly above the center hole. Use turquoise yarn for the three diamonds.

Center Turquoise Diamond.

1. Work one French Stitch around the hole indicated. Work 4 additional stitches in a zig direction, making a total of 5 stitches.

Follow steps 2 through 6 under Pattern 7 (Fig. 4-25) to form the center diamond with 5 stitches on each side.

Bottom Turquoise Diamond. Work the first stitch directly under the stitch in the bottom point of the middle diamond. Repeat the instructions for the center diamond.

Top Turquoise Diamond. The start is different for the top diamond.

1. Start the first stitch directly *above* the top stitch in the center diamond. Work 4 additional stitches in an upward left diagonal direction.

2. Work 4 stitches in an upward right diagonal direction.

3. Work 4 stitches in a zig direction.

4. Work 4 stitches in a zag direction. This completes the outer row. Fill in the center rows in the same manner as with the center and bottom diamonds.

Multicolored Zig Zags. The rows of zig zags are worked around and follow the contour of the center diamond motifs. I prefer to start the rows at the top, directly over the top stitch in the previous row, and work in the downward zig zag directions on one side of the design. Then I

end the yarn and go back up to the top and work down the other side. The alternative is to work completely around in a clockwise direction, working in the two upward diagonal directions along one side. Using the method you prefer, work the zig zag Rows 1 through 6 in the color sequence of white, yellow, shocking pink, white, green and white. The design grows larger and the rows longer as the work progresses. This completes the multicolored zig zags.

Turquoise Background. Use turquoise yarn for the background. Work three rows completely around the central design motif in the same manner as you worked the stripes. The outer points on all sides of the last turquoise row establish the outside edges. Fill in the open areas on the sides of the turquoise zig zags to form straight edges. Run your fingers along the edge bars toward the corners and place yarn tie markers on the crossbars where they meet. Work stitches in diagonal rows until you have filled in the corner areas.

See Chapter 8 for directions for attaching material cording and backing. No French Fill-in Stitches are necessary, since half of the edge stitches will be cropped during construction.

This easy pattern for a footstool or bench top stretches or shrinks to any size and will live happily in many types of décor, both traditional and contemporary. (Fig. 4-46.) The sample is worked in purple and turquoise, but there are endless possibilities of two-color combinations.

4-46

Pat Rug Yarn: purple #632 (deep value); turquoise #724 (light value). The amount of yarn necessary depends on the size of the area to be covered.

Take careful measurements of the area. Cut out a paper pattern if necessary or, better still, cut out a pattern from an old sheet. Make certain the area to be worked is sufficient to roll around and under the top so that raw canvas will not show. If the top is flat and will be combined with material as in Figure 3-38, allow for ¼ in. extra worked area on all sides which will be cropped when construction takes place. Place the pattern down on canvas and tie yarn markers in the four corners as guides for area coverage.

Follow the procedure outlined under Pattern 9. (See Fig. 4-27.) Work the basic big center cross in a deep-value yarn, working out from the center until you reach the edge bars of the area to be covered. Follow the directions for filling in the four areas formed by the big cross in the color pattern: two rows in light value, one row in deep value. Unless you are an expert, it would be best to place the construction problems in the hands of a good upholsterer.

4-48. Design courtesy of *House Beautiful.*
Copyright 1967, The Hearst Corporation.

4-47. Design courtesy of *House Beautiful.*
Copyright 1967, The Hearst Corporation.

A bold and unique design made of zany asymmetrical zig zags was used for a valance and matching headboard. (Figs. 4-47 and 4-48.) Both designs are courtesy of *House Beautiful.* Size of samples: valance, 9 in. × 30 in.; headboard, 18 in. × 30 in.

These items call on the personal ingenuity and inventiveness of you, the designer, for each zig zag is different. Your primary purpose is to work uneven, broken zig zags. The colors used proved to be a very happy combination.

Pat Rug Yarn: white #005; orange #421; gold #441; yellow #413; taffy #433. The amount of yarn necessary depends on the size of the area to be covered.

Place the yarn tie markers in the corners to indicate area coverage. Make the necessary allowance for construction cropping. A pattern can be cut as suggested in the directions for the footstool.

Figures 4-47 and 4-48 can be helpful guides for keying your own patterns. The items were worked in the positions shown— from top to bottom. My system was to work one very irregular—and I mean irregular—white zig zag from the top to the bottom. This zigs and zags unevenly—it almost reaches the edge at times—and acts as the basis for the irregular short runs. If you study the photographs you can find the white irregular row in each design which runs the full length of the item. From this point you are on your own. You face a challenge which continually keeps you thinking, planning, testing and creating as the unique pattern unfolds like a joyous adventure! Use the Squint Test throughout. Keep loose and work a variety of shapes and lengths, but remember to balance your colors and deep values so that the end result will be pleasing to the eye.

There are directions for two additional finished items worked in the French Stitch in the last chapter. (See Figs. 8-29 and 8-30.)

5.

Chain Reaction: A New Charm for the Age-Old Chain Stitch

A brand-new personality springs from the simple, old Chain Stitch known to us all. Used for centuries in embroidery on cloth, the stitch takes on an interesting Now Needlepoint effect when you work a zig, a zag or a wiggle on the large canvas with the heavy yarn. The result is a marvelous, rough texture with a handwoven look which is extremely pleasing to the eye.

The mechanics of the basic Chain Stitch can be mastered in a few minutes. It is one of the easiest stitches to learn, and many of you might already be familiar with the steps involved. All based on the simple Chain Stitch, the instructions and designs will include:

The Single Zig Zag Chain. A One-Stitch Zig and a One-Stitch Zag—one stitch in each downward diagonal direction.

The Double Zig Zag Chain. A Two-Stitch Zig and a Two-Stitch Zag—two stitches in each downward diagonal direction.

Reversed Zig Zags with Center Interest.

Single Zig Zag Chain Square Motif.

Single Zig Zag and Double Zig Zag Chain Personality. Like waving a magic wand, designs with little waves of zig

5-1. The Chain Stitch.

zags, deeper waves, with closely related colors that blend in your eye, or colors with sharp contrast that cause excitement and zing, can all be keyed with ease. The zig zag chain patterns are excellent to use for beginners' projects—they are so simple to work and can be very effective if keyed in colors which live happily together.

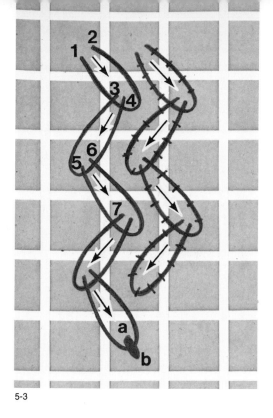

5-3

Will Travel. The stitches are worked in zigs and zags from the top of the canvas to the bottom. Rows are normally worked from left to right. However, they can also be worked from right to left when you wish to key a design by working from the center out to each side. If you want to have a design run horizontally across the finished item —from side to side—plan your working area on the canvas to best utilize the yardage. Happily, the 3 to the inch canvas accepts the stitches in either direction. Turn the canvas 90 degrees while the work is in progress so that you can work the stitches in a downward direction. (Fig. 5-2.)

5-2

Design and Color Potentials. In both versions of the Zig Zag Chain, the overall impact is completely controlled by the use of color. By studying the pattern photographs, you can discover how easily a design can be altered with the addition of a color or two. Add black and white and behold the change. (See Patterns 3 and 3A, Fig. 5-10.) Notice what happens in Patterns 1 and 1A when you surface-whip the stitches. (Fig. 5-7.) Instead of stripes, a lattice motif appears.

Suggested Uses. Because of the closely woven quality plus the thick padding on the wrong side, the Zig Zag Chains are suitable for a variety of items ranging from small pincushions to pillows, bench covers, wall hangings, valances, headboards and rugs. When worked in the proper tension, the equalized cross-pull produced by the alternate zigs and zags prevents any distortion of the canvas. A trim, professional appearance results.

MECHANICS FOR THE SINGLE ZIG ZAG AND DOUBLE ZIG ZAG CHAIN STITCH

All versions of the stitch are worked on 3 to the inch canvas.

Single Zig Zag Chain. Follow Figure 5-3. There is one stitch in each zig and each zag.

The stitches are worked from top to bottom in a zig and a zag.

The rows are normally worked from left to right. The rows can also be worked from right to left for designing purposes.

1st Row. The first stitch is worked in a zig direction.

1. Start at the upper left. Bring the needle up to the surface in 1, leaving a 6 in. tail to be woven in later.

2. Place the needle down in 2 (same hole as 1) and up in 3 in one motion. The needle goes under the crossbar of

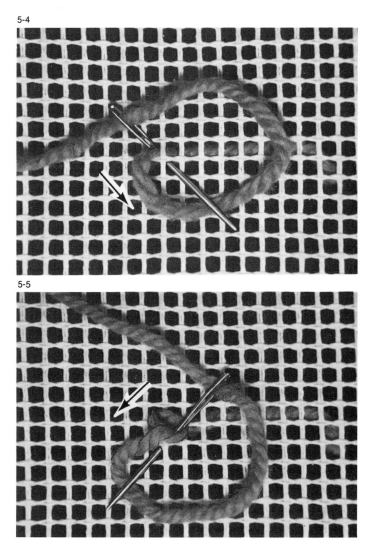

5-4

5-5

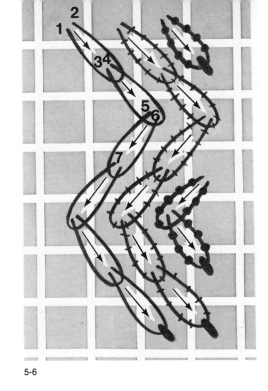

5-6

canvas in a downward right diagonal direction. It comes up in 3 and goes over the loop of yarn. (Fig. 5-4.) Pull the yarn slowly to close the loop of yarn. Form the habit of following the direction of the stitch when you pull the yarn through the loop.

The second stitch goes in a zag direction.

3. Place the needle down in 4 (in the loop of the first Chain Stitch where the yarn comes up to the surface) and up in 5 in one motion. The needle goes under the crossbar of canvas in a downward left diagonal direction. It comes up in 5 and goes over the loop of yarn. (Fig. 5-5.) Pull the yarn slowly in the direction of the stitch to close the loop.

The third stitch goes in a zig direction.

4. Place the needle down in 6 and up in 7 in one motion (same direction as the first stitch).

Continue alternating zigs and zags down to the bottom of the row for desired coverage.

To End the Row. Follow Figure 5-3 at the bottom of the first row. The yarn will be up to the surface in "a". Go over the loop of the last chain and down in "b". Pull the yarn through to the wrong side. Weave under for 1 in. Snip off the remaining yarn, leaving a ½ in. end. Do not pull too tightly or the last stitch will be drawn under to the wrong side. Pull the stitch to the surface with your needle if necessary after ending the yarn. Rows can be ended on either a zig or a zag.

2nd Row. Follow Figure 5-3, where the second row is indicated by cross lines on the stitches. Start at the top. Bring the needle up to the surface in the hole directly to the right of where the first row was started. Follow exactly the zigs and zags of the first row.

Continue the rows from left to right across the canvas for desired coverage.

To End Strands. End the yarn as you would at the bottom of a row.

To Start Strands. Weave under for at least 1 in. on the wrong side. Bring the needle up to the surface in "a"—up through the center of the last chain. Proceed with the next stitch in the correct direction.

Note: Ends and starts can be made on either a zig or a zag. No Fill-in Stitches are necessary for the Single Zig Zag Chain.

Double Zig Zag Chain. Follow Figure 5-6. There are two stitches in each zig and each zag.

The stitches are worked from top to bottom in a zig and a zag.

The rows are normally worked from left to right. Rows can also be worked from right to left for designing purposes.

1st Row. The first two stitches are worked in a zig direction.

1. Start the first stitch at the upper left. Bring the needle up to the surface in 1, leaving a 6 in. tail to be woven in later.

2. Place the needle down in 2 (same hole as 1) and up in 3 in one motion. The needle goes under the crossbar of canvas in a downward right diagonal direction. It comes up in 3 and goes over the loop of yarn. Pull the yarn slowly in the direction of the stitch to close the loop.

3. For the second stitch, place the needle down in 4 (in the loop of the first Chain Stitch where yarn comes up to the surface) and up in 5 in one motion. This stitch is worked in the same direction as the first stitch. Pull the yarn slowly in the direction of the stitch to close the loop.

The third and fourth stitches go in a zag direction. Continue down to the bottom of the row for desired coverage, working two stitches in each zig direction and two stitches in each zag direction.

Note: The rows are ended and the strands are ended and started in the same manner as with the Single Zig Zag Chain.

2nd Row. Follow the row with the small cross lines in Figure 5-6. Start directly to the right of the first row. Follow the countour of the zigs and zags in the first row.

Continue the rows from left to right across the canvas for desired coverage.

Special Fill-in Stitches for the Double Zig Zag Chain. Because of the deep waves formed by the Double Zig Zag Chain it is necessary to work Fill-in Stitches along the sides to form straight edges. Follow Figure 5-6. The Fill-in Stitches are indicated by the lines with dots at the right. Start at the top. Fill in the corner with one zig stitch. Go over the loop as at the bottom of a row, but do not end the yarn. Drop down past the right point of the Double Zig Zag Chain pattern and work two single stitches—a zag and a zig—in that order, as shown. Go over the loop but do not end the yarn. Continue down to the bottom of the row until all open spaces are filled and a straight edge has been formed. You can make one catch on the wrong side between jumps if you wish. Repeat the process on the left side, working 2 single stitches in each opening—a zig and a zag, in that order. The corners are filled in with single stitches.

Color Note: Fill-in Stitches are usually worked in the color yarn used in the outside rows on each side. However, there might be an occasion when you wish to continue an overall pattern out to the very edge. If this is the case, use the correct color to preserve the pattern.

Tension Note: Learn to control the tension so that each chain stitch remains neatly on the surface next to its neighbor. Pulling the yarn in the direction of the stitch when you close the loop helps to produce even stitches. If a stitch does happen to pull through to the back, pull it immediately to the surface with your needle before you start the next stitch.

ZIG ZAG CHAIN PATTERNS

The patterns in this section use consecutive rows of Single or Double Zig Zag Chains. With the exception of 1A, Patterns 1 through 8 can be worked in either the Single or Double Zig Zag Chain. The difference is in the depth of the waves. The stitches are worked from top to bottom in rows from left to right across the canvas. All the patterns are started at the upper left. The color changes are given according to rows.

Pattern 1. Single rows of turquoise and white stripes. (Fig. 5-7, left.)
Pat Rug Yarn: turquoise #738; white #005.

5-7. *Left:* Pattern 1.
  Right: Pattern 1A.

Color Pattern for Rows of Single Zig Zag Chain. 1st row, turquoise; 2nd row, white.

Repeat the rows for desired coverage (repeated 6 times in the sample) plus one row of turquoise at the end to balance the beginning.

Pattern 1A. Create a turquoise and white lattice design with the quick magic of surface whipping. (Fig. 5-7, right.)
Pat Rug Yarn: turquoise #728; white #005.

Color Pattern for Rows of Single Zig Zag Chain. It's the same as in the previous pattern. A deeper-value turquoise was used in the lattice-pattern sample to produce more value contrast.

Surface Whipping. Use white yarn. Weave under on the wrong side for 2 in. and bring the needle up to the surface at the top of the first turquoise row. Working in a right-to-left direction, slip the needle under the first Zig Chain Stitch. Go under the two sides of the chain which are on the surface. Do not catch the canvas. Continue down the row surface, whipping each stitch in a zig direction, as shown in Figure 5-8, skipping the zag stitches between. Repeat this on each turquoise row across the worked area.

5-8

Pattern 2. Shocking pink with white stripes. (Fig. 5-9.)
Pat Rug Yarn: shocking pink #259; white #005.

Color pattern for Rows of Single Zig Zag Chain. 1st, 2nd and 3rd Rows, shocking pink; 4th Row, white. Repeat the first 4 rows for desired coverage (repeated 3 times in the sample). End with three rows of pink to balance the beginning.

5-9. Pattern 2.

Pattern 3. Related colors form pleasing stripes. Two middle-value colors—burnt orange and green—and one light-value color—yellow—are used. (Fig. 5-10, top.)
Pat Rug Yarn: green #545; burnt orange #417; yellow #413.

5-10. *Top:* Pattern 3.
       Bottom: Pattern 3A.

Color Pattern for Rows of Single Zig Zag Chain. 1st Row, green; 2nd Row, burnt orange; 3rd Row, yellow.
Repeat the first 3 rows for desired coverage (repeated 4 times in the sample). End with a green row to balance the beginning.

Pattern 3A. A new personality is produced with the addition of black and white. (Fig. 5-10, bottom.)
Pat Rug Yarn: black #050; green #545; burnt orange #417; yellow #413; white #005.

Color Pattern for Rows of Single Zig Zag Chain. 1st Row, black; 2nd Row, green, 3rd Row, burnt orange; 4th Row, yellow; 5th Row, white.
Repeat the first 5 rows for desired coverage (repeated 3 times in the sample). End with a black row to balance the beginning.

Pattern 4. Offbeat colors close in value fuse pleasantly in the eye. (Fig. 5-11.)
Pat Rug Yarn: orange #421; green #565; shocking pink #279; lavender #672.

Color Pattern for Rows of Single Zig Zag Chain. 1st Row, orange; 2nd Row, green; 3rd Row, orange; 4th Row, pink; 5th and 6th Rows, lavender; 7th Row, pink.
Repeat the first 7 rows for desired coverage (repeated twice in the sample). End with 1 orange, 1 green and 1 pink row to balance the beginning.

5-11. Pattern 4.

Pattern 5. Turquoise, green, deep purple and white form an interesting variety of stripes. (Fig. 5-12.)
Pat Rug Yarn: turquoise #738; purple #632; white #005; green #569.

Color Pattern for Rows of Single Zig Zag Chain. 1st Row, turquoise; 2nd Row, purple; 3rd and 4th, turquoise; 5th, white; 6th, green; 7th, turquoise; 8th, green; 9th, purple; 10th, turquoise; 11th and 12th, white; 13th, turquoise; 14th, purple; 15th, white; 16th, purple; 17th, green; 18th, turquoise; 19th, white; 20th, turquoise.

Repeat the first 20 rows—or a portion thereof—for desired coverage. The pattern as shown measures 6 in. across.

5-13. Pattern 6.

5-12. Pattern 5.

Pattern 6. Hot Colors in a potpourri of stripes create exciting entertainment for the eye. (Fig. 5-13.)
Pat Rug Yarn: orange #958; gold #434; light shocking pink #259; deep shocking pink #239; deep cherry red #237.

Color Pattern for Rows of Single Zig Zag Chain. 1st Row, orange; 2nd and 3rd, gold; 4th, light pink; 5th and 6th, red; 7th, orange; 8th, gold; 9th and 10th, orange; 11th, light pink; 12th, deep pink; 13th, red; 14th, gold; 15th and 16th, light pink; 17th and 18th, gold; 19th, orange; 20th, red; 21st, light pink; 22nd, gold; 23rd and 24th, orange; 25th and 26th, deep pink; 27th, orange.

Repeat the first 27 rows—or a portion thereof—for desired coverage. The pattern measures 8 in. across and is shown with the Regular Braid Stitch (single strand doubled) along the left edge. This pattern would be especially exciting if worked in the Double Zig Zag Chain.

Pattern 7. Bright and gay! Double Zig Zag stripes of shocking pink and green wave through the sparkling white background. (Fig. 5-14.)
Nantucket 6-Ply Cable Yarn: shocking pink #38; green #84; white #1.

Color Pattern for Rows of Double Zig Zag Chain. First grouping—1st and 2nd Rows, white; 3rd, pink; 4th, green; 5th, pink; 6th, green; 7th, pink. Second grouping—1st and 2nd Rows, white; 3rd, green; 4th, pink; 5th, green; 6th, pink; 7th, green.

Alternate the groupings across the canvas for desired coverage. End with 2 rows of white to balance the beginning. It is best to end with the same grouping used for the start of the design. One grouping only can be repeated across if you wish. The pattern shown measures 7 in. across. Work white Fill-in Stitches (see Fig. 5-6) down each side to form straight edges, as shown on the right side of the pattern.

5-14. Pattern 7.

Pattern 8. A striking color combination of blues and green with white forms salty waves. The stripes can run vertically or horizontally across an item. (Fig. 5-15.)
Pat Rug Yarn: deep blue #731; turquoise #728; green #550; white #005.

5-15. Pattern 8.

Color Pattern for Rows of Double Zig Zag Chain. 1st and 2nd Rows, blue; 3rd, turquoise; 4th, green; 5th, white.

Repeat the first 5 rows for desired coverage (repeated 3 times in the sample). End with 2 rows of blue to balance the beginning.

Work blue Fill-in Stitches (Fig. 5-6) down each side to form straight edges, as shown on the right side of the pattern. (The canvas can be worked in either direction if you wish to change the direction of the waves.)

REVERSED ZIG ZAGS WITH CENTER INTEREST

The next two patterns—9 and 10—show examples of design possibilities when certain of the rows of zig zags are reversed, leaving space between for "center interest." One example of the Reversed Single Zig Zag Chain and one of the Reversed Double Zig Zag Chain are presented with diagrams, and they indicate how the reversed rows are worked and how the small center motifs are placed between the rows. These are only *two* examples but many, many variations can so easily be keyed. Think of the color possibilities and how stripes can be widened by additional rows of color. Notice in Pattern 10 how the Diamond Center changes into two tiny green vertical leaves while the two horizontal stitches appear to be part of the background because they were worked in white yarn. Without a French Knot in the center the purple Diamond Center simply forms a shape. Add the French Knot and your eye tells your brain, flower! The connecting rows of Round Centers in Pattern 9 can quickly be

changed into tiny flowers by placing a French Knot in the center of each. (See Fig. 5-19.) Work the rows of Round Centers in a middle-value pink with a deep-pink French Knot in each center. Work the enclosing reverse rows in green. Add a number of white rows between as background and you end up with a creation that is all pink 'n white 'n feminine. My point is, don't stop with these two examples; they are only the beginning.

Both patterns are worked in a similar manner. Study the drawings. Notice how the zig zag rows are *reversed* at certain points to make room for the centers to be worked between them.

The stitches and motifs are worked from the top to the bottom.

The rows are worked from left to right. Different starts for rows are necessary to produce the reverse directions of the zig zags. This will become clear as the work progresses and the pattern unfolds. In both diagrams (Figs. 5-20 and 5-22), the two groupings are indicated by letters—one with Starts A and B, the other with Starts a and b.

When the enclosing reversed zig zag rows are completed (one row on each side with space left between), the instructions for the center motifs are given so that you can fill in the spaces as the work progresses.

Half motifs or Fill-in Stitches are necessary at the top and bottom of *every other* row of center motifs. The top Fill-ins are shown at the right of each diagram between the reversed rows of zig zags indicated by the small letters a and b. Reverse the top Fill-in Stitches when the lower

There are three basic shapes for center interest: Round Center, Diamond Center and French Knot Center. These are three small accent shapes with completely different personalities that can be used in numerous ways to create added excitement in design patterns. They turn up as centers of designs—centers of flowers; they fill in open spaces between reversed zig zag rows; or they sometimes become integral parts of overall patterns. All three will work overtime for you, the designer, providing that extra-special zing, if they are used as a sharp value contrast or bright color accent. The French Knot Center is three-dimensional, so that it also creates textural interest.

When working the round and diamond versions, you must keep turning the canvas so as to work each stitch in the correct direction (the arrows should point toward you). From now on you will be turning the canvas every which way. But turning will become completely automatic in a short time.

If the center motifs are far apart, it is necessary to end the yarn after working the individual center. However, if they are close together, you can easily jump under on the wrong side and come up in the correct spot to start the next motif. Catch once on the wrong side if the run is a bit long.

MECHANICS FOR THE THREE CENTERS

Round Center. See Figure 5-16. The yarn is used single strand, but can also be used single strand doubled for a heavier effect. Follow the directions of the arrows. Keep turning the canvas while working the stitches so that the arrows point *toward* you. The stitches are worked diagonally around a center hole.

1. Bring the needle up to the surface in A.

2. Work one chain stitch in each of the four diagonal directions indicated by the arrows. Turn the canvas after each stitch is completed so that it is in the correct position for the next stitch. End at B (the same hole as A).

3. Loop the yarn over the last chain as in the end of a row. End the yarn.

Diamond Center. See Figure 5-17. The yarn is used single strand, but can also be used single strand doubled for a heavier effect. Keep turning the canvas while working stitches so that the arrows point toward you. Stitches are worked out from the center hole.

1. Bring the needle up to the surface in center hole A. Work one chain stitch in a downward direction B, catching the yarn over a bar of canvas as indicated before pulling it through to the wrong side. Bring the needle back up to the surface in center hole A. (You can go down in B and up in A in one motion.)

2. Repeat single stitches in the three remaining directions. Turn the canvas each time so the arrows point toward you, bringing the needle up each time in center hole A to start the next stitch. When the fourth stitch is completed, end the yarn.

French Knot Center. See Figure 5-18. Follow the direction of the arrows. The first 4 knots are worked diagonally out from the center hole. The fifth center knot is worked from the outside hole into the center hole. The yarn is used single strand doubled, since the single strand does not properly cover the canvas. For detailed instructions for the French Knot, see Chapter 2.

1. Bring the needle up to the surface in the center hole at 1. Work a French Knot (around the needle once with heavier yarn, such as Pat Rug Yarn, but twice with lighter-weight yarn, such as Nantucket 6-Ply Cable), in an upward left diagonal direction, going over a crossbar of canvas and down in 2. This might take a bit of practice because of the single strand doubled yarn. Close the yarn slowly around the needle—not too tightly—and pull through slowly to produce a trim knot.

2. Bring the needle up to the surface in the center hole. Repeat Step 1 in the remaining three diagonal directions. When the fourth knot is completed, bring the needle up to the surface in hole A.

3. Work a French Knot around the needle once (once

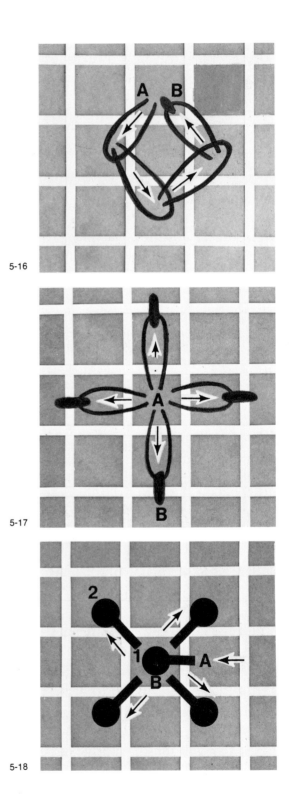

5-16

5-17

5-18

with heavy, twice with the lighter yarn), going over a bar of canvas and down in the center hole at B—right in the center of the four knots. Catch securely on the back before weaving for at least 1 in. to end the yarn. Arrange the knots neatly in place with your fingers.

Pattern 9. In this reversed Single Zig Zag Chain pattern, white center interest rests between stripes of turquoise and shocking pink with a yellow-green background. (Fig. 5-19.)

5-19. Pattern 9.

Pat Rug Yarn: green #550; turquoise #728; shocking pink #259; white #005.

Follow Figure 5-20. The center motifs are indicated by cross lines.

Color pattern for zig zag rows:

1st and 2nd Rows. Start at the upper left. The first two rows are worked in the same manner as Row A (see the grouping at the left of Fig. 5-20). Use green yarn—Start A. Work two rows (12 stitches in each row in the sample).

Note: When keying your own designs, always use an even number of stitches in the rows. Each Round Center falls within a Single Zig Zag Chain—two individual Chain Stitches—between the reversed rows. The top and bottom center motifs in rows should be the same, either completed Round Centers or two one-half centers. When keying your own designs, multiply the number of Round Centers to be used by two and you will determine how many stitches to work in the first row.

3rd Row. Use turquoise yarn—Start A.

4th Row. Use turquoise yarn—Start B. Leave one canvas hole free for center motifs to be filled in later. See Figure 5-20 for the correct hole to start B rows. The first stitch is worked in the opposite or reverse direction to that of Start A.

Round Center Motifs. Use white yarn. See the detailed directions for working Round Centers preceding this pattern. Start at the top. Follow the grouping at the left of Figure 5-20. Bring the yarn up to the surface in hole 1 between the two reverse rows of turquoise. Work four diagonal stitches to form the top Round Center. When you have completed the first motif, drop down on the

5-20

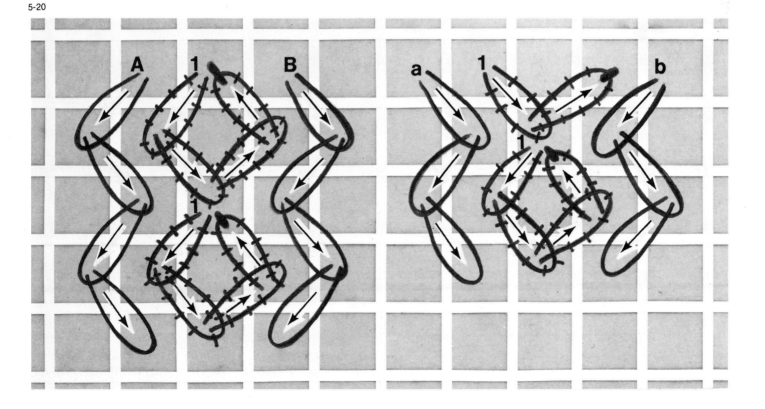

wrong side and bring your needle up to the surface in hole 1 to start the second motif (share the same hole as was used for the top motif). Repeat the first motif. Continue down to the bottom for desired coverage.

Color pattern for zig zag rows continued:

5th and 6th Rows. Use green yarn—Start B. (Follow the grouping at the right of Fig. 5-20 for the start of the seventh row.)

7th Row. Use pink yarn—Start a, which is the same as Start B.

8th Row. Use pink yarn—Start b. Count over to the right and bring your needle up to the surface in the fourth hole from the start of the seventh pink row indicated by "b" in Figure 5-20.

Round Center Motifs for Alternate Rows. Use white yarn. Follow the grouping of stitches at the right of Figure 5-20. Bring the needle up to the surface in hole 1 to the right of Row a. Work the bottom half only of the Round Center, as shown in the diagram. Drop down on the wrong side and bring your needle up to the surface in the hole under the half-motif indicated by "1." Work four diagonal stitches to form the Round Center. Continue down to the bottom for desired coverage. Reverse the half motif at the bottom to continue the pattern to the edge.

Color pattern for zig zag rows continued:

9th and 10th Rows. Use green yarn—Start b. The tenth row completes the pattern shown in the sample. It brings you up to the second group of turquoise zig zags. (Repeat the third through sixth rows to duplicate the sample.) Continue the pattern across for desired coverage.
Note: I suggest you end your pattern with the same color grouping as the first one so that there is a balance of color on each side. This is not absolutely necessary, but it creates a better design. The background stripes which are yellow-green in the sample should also be balanced on each side.

Pattern 10. A Reversed Double Zig Zag Chain with a marvelous mosaic quality has purple and white wavy stripes on a blue background. Flowerets of purple and white with yellow French Knot centers add texture and interest. (Fig. 5-21.)
Pat Rug Yarn: blue #356; purple #632; white #005; green #545; yellow #413.
Follow Figure 5-22. The center motifs are indicated by cross lines.

Color pattern for zig zag rows:

5-21. Pattern 10.

1st and 2nd Rows. Start at the upper left. The first four rows are worked in same manner as Row A (see the grouping at the left of the diagram). Use blue yarn—Start A. Work two rows of Double Zig Zag Chain (20 stitches in each row in the sample).
Note: Each Diamond Center falls within a Double Zig Zag Chain—4 individual Chain Stitches—between the reversed rows. When keying your own designs, multiply the number of Diamond Centers to be used by 4 and you will determine how many stitches to work in the first row.

3rd Row. Use purple yarn—Start A.

4th Row. Use white yarn —Start A.

5th Row. Use white yarn—Start B. See Fig. 5-22 for the correct hole to start B rows (Reverse Zig Zags). This is the same hole used for the start of the preceding A row. The space between the rows will be filled in with Diamond-Center motifs.

Diamond Center Motifs. See detailed directions for working the Diamond Center preceding Pattern 9.

Purple Motifs. Use purple yarn. Fill in the top Diamond Center motif as indicated in Figure 5-22. Work the bottom petal last. When you have completed the top motif, do not end the yarn. Drop down on the wrong side, skipping one open space formed by the Reverse Zig Zags and work the second purple motif. Continue down to the bottom, skipping one open space between purple motifs.

Green and White Motifs. The green-and-white motifs between the purple are worked so that they appear to be two small vertical leaves while the horizontal white stitches become part of the background. Use green yarn

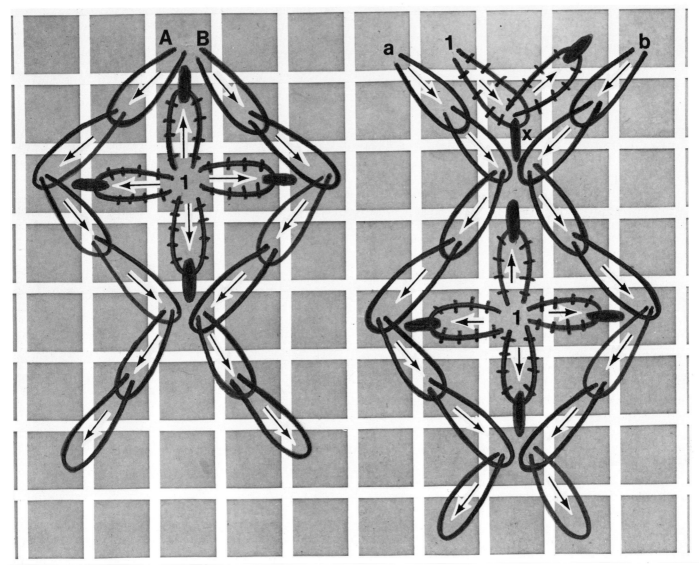

5-22

for the green leaves. Start at the top open space and work only the top and bottom vertical stitches of the Diamond Center motifs in each space. Drop down on the wrong side to the next open space until you have worked all the green leaves down to the bottom of the row.

Use white yarn for the white horizontal stitches. Start at the top and fill in the two side horizontal stitches down to the bottom.

Color pattern for zig zag rows continued:

6th Row. Use purple yarn—Start B.

7th and 8th Rows. Use blue yarn—Start B.

9th and 10th Rows. Use blue yarn—Start b. Follow the second group of stitches at the right of Figure 5-22 indicated by Rows a and b. The last row of blue worked—the eighth row—corresponds to Row a on the diagram.

Alternate Row of White Diamond Center Motifs. Use white yarn. The Fill-in Stitches at the top and bottom of the rows which are necessary to continue the pattern are a bit tricky. Follow the right grouping in Figure 5-22. Bring the needle up to surface in 1. Work two chain stitches as

indicated. When the second chain is completed, bring the needle up in the loop of the first chain. Loop the yarn over the bar of canvas (indicated by x) before dropping down on the wrong side to 1 for the start of a Diamond Center motif. This extra stitch prevents any canvas from being exposed. Continue the diamond motifs down to the bottom. Fill-in Stitches used at the top are worked in the reverse position at the bottom.

Note: Blue yarn can be substituted for the white in this alternative row of motifs. The area will then become background. The diamond motifs disappear and form a very textural effect.

French Knots. Use yellow yarn. Work a yellow French Knot (single strand—around the needle once) in the center of each purple and each white motif.

Zig Zag Rows 1 through 10—including the center motifs—complete the pattern. The pattern can be continued across the canvas for desired coverage. (Repeat Rows 3 through 8 to produce the sample shown.)

Fill-in Stitches to Even the Side Edges. See Figure 5-6. The Fill-in Stitches along the side edges are necessary because they cover exposed canvas left by the Double Zig Zags. The right side of the pattern shows an even edge.

SINGLE ZIG ZAG CHAIN
SQUARE MOTIF

In addition to walking in zig zag rows, the Single Zig Zag Chain turns corners too. Squares that grow to any size can be created, with endless pattern possibilities and color combinations.

And it turns corners with charm! Something wonderful happens when your eye is carried around by the chain with its constantly changing direction. The patterns and finished samples create delicate frames which wave around the square, growing larger and larger as the rows multiply—growing to any size you wish. If you push your Aware Button, you can easily imagine the numerous exciting patterns which can be keyed by using different sequences of color in the rows. You could substitute many of the color combinations shown for the other versions of the Chain Stitch and come up with some eye-stoppers.

First of all, you must learn to turn those corners, which is a bit tricky in the beginning. You start by working the outside row of a basic 12-stitch square (12 stitches on each side). The rows are worked in toward the center until the area within is completely covered. You can add rows around the outside so the square can grow to any size you wish. By using the basic 12-stitch starter square—working in toward the center and then out—you will eventually find it easy to key your own designs. You have more control over what will occur in the center area if you do not start the stitches way out in left field.

Note: When I first worked the Single Zig Zag Chain on the large canvas, I almost settled for the fact that it walked in one direction only—from top to bottom. How wrong I was! Somewhere along the way—with a nudge from my idea angel—I had the feeling it would also turn corners, but how? How could the rows be made to "walk" around a square? If you end a row on a zig, you must turn the corner one way—and an entirely different way if you end on a zag. Also, the two types of corners must fit closely together to properly cover the canvas. After several dismal failures, a light flashed and there was the answer: Male and female corners! Sex and the Now Needlepointer!!! I understand electricians and plumbers refer to items as "male" and "female," but whoever thought of such terms in connection with needlepoint? *Vive la différence*, for the rows fit beautifully if you alternate the corners. I refer to the two different turns in the usual manner in the directions, as Corner A and Corner B, but I thought this bit of information would lighten the serious learning process.

Pattern 11. This basic pattern for a Single Zig Zag Chain Square motif has 12 stitches on each side. (Fig. 5-23.) Size of sample: 4¼ in. square.
Nantucket 6-Ply Cable Yarn: blue #61 (deep value); shocking pink #38 (middle value); white #1 (light value).

5-23. Pattern 11.

Single Zig Zag Chain Stitches are worked from top to bottom in rows around the square. Turn the canvas 90 degrees at each corner, so you can continue to work the stitches in a downward direction. As previously explained, there are two different corners necessary because of the nature of the zig zag stitch. Carefully follow the instructions for the start of each row. Work the number of stitches indicated, use the proper corner, turn the canvas before working the next side, and the zig zag rows will fit neatly together. You start with an outline square with 12 stitches on each side and work in toward the center. See Figure 5-24 to work the two corners. The corner stitches are indicated by the heavy lines. Corners A and a are the same. Corners B and b are the same. The turns show how the first 4 rows fit together in one corner as they are worked in toward the center. Three more turns are necessary to complete each row. Follow the diagonal arrows in Figures 5-25 and 5-27 for the start of rows. It is important to start in the exact hole indicated by the arrow point. The Single Zig Zag Chain is used throughout. Please note the stitch count is given for *individual* stitches (not zig zags) to avoid confusion.

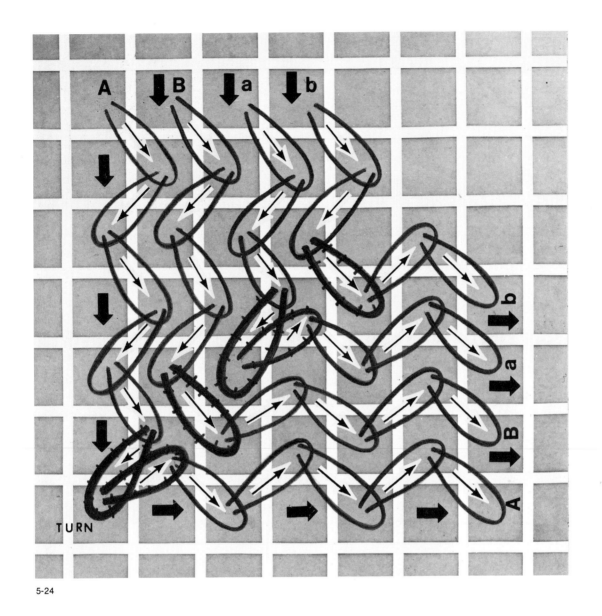

5-24

1st Row. Start in the upper left corner indicated by the outer diagonal arrow in Figure 5-25. Use the deep-value yarn—Corner A. Start with a Single Zig Chain Stitch. Work 11 more Single Zig Zag Chain stitches. Make one 90-degree turn of the canvas. Follow Figure 5-24 for Corner A. Work one Zig Chain Stitch back into the same hole used for the last two stitches of the first side. (This is a bit of a squeeze, but be certain you get back in the correct hole.) Work 11 more Single Zig Zag Chain Stitches. Make one 90-degree turn of the canvas and repeat Corner A. Continue the row around the square, turning the canvas at each corner, until the four sides are completed. End the last stitch of the fourth side in the same hole as you used for the first stitch in the row.

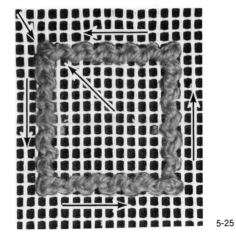

5-25

2nd Row. The inside diagonal arrow in Figure 5-25 indicates the hole for starting. Bring the needle up to the surface in the correct hole. Follow the arrows in Figure 5-26. Use the middle-value yarn—Corner B. Work one Zag Chain Stitch at the top corner. Following the zigs zags of the first row, work 8 more Single Zig Zag Stitches to bring you down to the corner. Make one 90-degree turn of the canvas. Follow Figure 5-24 for Corner B. This one is easy. Work one Zag Stitch diagonally across the corner. Work 8 more Single Zig Zag Stitches down to the next corner. Make one 90-degree turn of the canvas. Repeat Corner B. Work 8 more Single Zig Zag Chain Stitches. Continue the row around the square—turning the canvas at each corner—until you have completed the four sides and you end up in the same hole as the first stitch of the row.

5-27

5-26

3rd Row. See Figure 5-27 for your start. Bring the needle up to the surface in the corner hole indicated by the diagonal arrow. Use the light-value yarn—Corner A. Work one Zig Chain Stitch at the top corner. Work 7 more Single Zig Zag Stitches. Make one 90-degree turn of the canvas. Work Corner A (the third row is indicated by a small "a" in Figure 5-24 and is the same as Corner A). Count the last corner stitch as one. Work 8 Single Zig Zag stitches down to the next corner. Continue the row around the square, turning the canvas at each corner, until you have completed the four sides and you end up in the same hole as the first stitch of the row.

4th Row. The start is the same as with the second row. Bring the needle up to the surface in the correct hole under the top left corner of the third row. Use the middle-value yarn—Corner B. Work one Zag Chain Stitch across the corner. Work 4 more Single Zig Zag stitches. Make one 90-degree turn of the canvas. Work Corner B (the fourth row indicated by a small "b" on the diagram is the same as Corner B). Work 4 more Single Zig Zag stitches

down to the next corner. Continue the row around the square—turning the canvas at each corner—until you have completed the four sides and you end up in the same hole as the first stitch in the row.

5th Row. Start in the same manner as in the third row. Bring the needle up to the surface in the correct hole under the top left corner of the fourth row. Use the deep-value yarn—Corner A. Work one Zig Chain Stitch. Work 3 more Single Zig Zag stitches down to the corner. Make one 90-degree turn of the canvas. Work Corner A. Count the last corner stitch as one. Work 4 Single Zig Zag stitches. Continue the row around the square—turning the canvas at each corner—until you have completed the four sides and you end up in the same hole as the first stitch in the row.

Note: If necessary, use your needle and fingers to ease the corners in place. Once you tuck the stitches in next to each other, they obediently stay in place.

French Knot Center. Use the light-value yarn (single strand doubled—around the needle twice). See the detailed directions for the French Knot Center preceding Pattern 9. Place the knot in the open area in the center of the square (Fig. 5-28).

The basic 12-stitch Single Zig Zag Chain square as shown in Figure 5-23 is now complete. The directions sound complicated at first but after working a square or two, you will only need to glance at them once in a while. You shift a magic gear along the way and it all becomes automatic. To summarize: you key the outline for the 12-stitch square and then work the rows in toward the center, alternating Corners A and B. Corner A is the pointed and Corner B the diagonal version.

The basic square grows and grows to any size. To increase the size of the square, you add rows on the outside. (See Fig. 5-28.) Use the yarn color of your choice.

5-28

Start at the upper right where the diagonal arrow is pointing. The outer corners of the basic square were worked in Corner A, so we must start with Corner B. (The corner stitches in Figure 5-24 are worked in the opposite directions for the outer rows. If you should find this confusing at first, you can start the outer rows at the upper left corner—working down the left side—and follow the turns in the diagram exactly. I think it is easier to work the outside rows with the free canvas to the right and suggest you use this system after you have gotten on friendly terms with the two corners.) Work one Zig Chain Stitch across the top right corner. Follow the straight arrows in the photograph. Continue working down the right side with Single Zig Zag Chains until you reach the corner. Turn the canvas 90 degrees and work Corner B. Continue the row around the outside of the square, turning the canvas at each corner, until you have completed the four sides and you end up in the same hole as the first stitch in the row. Add as many rows as you wish for desired coverage, alternating the corners as you proceed.

ZIG ZAG CHAIN FINISHED ITEMS

A matching pincushion and pillow for the bedroom or a favorite needlework spot in the living room form a happy pair worked in Single Zig Zag Chain stitches. The related colors—gold, orange, shocking pink with crisp white—are radiant. The samples shown have dancing white bows for added interest and fancy, matching Now Needlepoint backings.

The pattern for both items is easy to work, since it consists of individual rows of Single Zig Zag Chain stitches. The top and back are worked at the same time. Start at the top and work down the necessary number of stitches for the topside; then skip under one bar of canvas—left exposed for the Braid Stitch construc-

tion—and continue the stripe down the back. Notice that there is one stripe of white in the exact center of the area, and the color pattern reverses on each side. The color pattern of the rows for the two matching items are given from left to right across the canvas. However, you can key your own color sequence by proceeding in a different manner, as will be explained. The approximate yarn count for both pincushion and pillow covers the top, back, braid and bows. If you wish to work only the top area, divide the amounts in half.

Pincushion. (Fig. 5-29.) Size of sample: 4¾ in. plus the braid.
Pat Rug Yarn: gold #421 (5 str.); orange #968 (5 str.); shocking pink #259 (5 str.); white #005 (8 str.).

Start at the upper left. Work vertical rows from left to right.

5-29

Color Pattern for rows of Single Zig Zag Chain. 1st Row, use gold yarn. Starting at the top with a zig, work down 15 Single Zig Zag Chain stitches (ending with a zig). Catch over the last stitch as at the bottom of a row but do not end the yarn. Drop under on the wrong side and bring the needle up to the surface in the proper hole (to the left) to start the first zig stitch of the backing, leaving one horizontal bar of canvas exposed. Stitches are worked on the same vertical bar as was used for the topside. Starting with a zig, work down 15 Single Zig Zag stitches (ending with a zig). The top and the back are exactly alike. Work each row similarly to the 1st Row. The color pattern for subsequent rows is: 2nd, orange; 3rd, pink; 4th, white;

5th, 6th, 7th and 8th, repeat the color pattern for the 1st through 4th Rows (the 8th Row forms the white stripe in the exact center; colors are now reversed to the right edge); 9th, pink; 10th, orange; 11th, gold; 12th, white; 13th, pink; 14th, orange; 15th gold.

Double Bow in Center of Top. Use white yarn—½ strand or 32-in. length. Thread the needle as you would for a single strand doubled. Even up the ends. Run under both sides of the center white Chain Stitch. Cut through the yarn to release the needle. Tie one regular bow, using the double strands as single strands. With white sewing thread, catch through the knot at the center of the bow several times to prevent it from untying. Catch so the stitches are invisible. Tie a knot on each of the four ends of yarn at a point which is the same distance from the center of the bow as the ends of the loops as follows: Tie one tight overhand knot. Tie a second tight overhand knot directly over the first. Cut off the ends fairly close to the knots. Spread the loops as shown in Figure 5-29.

Braid Construction. Follow the basic directions for braid construction and stuffing given for the rosebud mini pillow in Chapter 8. Use the white yarn (single strand). Work the Regular Braid Stitch—Start A.

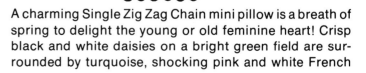

Pillow. (Fig. 5-30.) Size of sample: 9½ in. square plus the braid.
Pat Rug Yarn: gold #421 (17 str.); orange #968 (17 str.); shocking pink #259 (17 str.); white #005 (25 str.).

Start at the upper left. Work vertical rows from left to right.

5-30

Color Pattern for Rows of Single Zig Zag Chain. 1st Row, use gold yarn. Starting at the top with a zig, work down 31 Single Zig Zag Chain stitches (ending with a zig). Catch over the last stitch as at the bottom of a row but do not end the yarn. Drop under on the wrong side and bring the needle up to surface in the proper hole (to the left) to start the first zig stitch of the back, leaving one horizontal bar of canvas exposed. Stitches are worked on the same vertical bar as was used for the top. Starting with a zig, work down 31 Single Zig Zag Chain stitches (ending with a zig). The top and back are exactly alike. Work each row similarly to the 1st Row. The color pattern for subsequent rows is: 2nd, orange; 3rd, pink; 4th, white; 5th through 16th, repeat the 1st through 4th Rows three more times; (the 16th Row forms a white stripe in the exact center—colors are now reversed to the right edge); 17th, pink; 18th, orange; 19th, gold; 20th, white; 21st through 28th, repeat the 17th through 20th Rows two more times; 29th, pink; 30th, orange; 31st, gold.

Double Bows. Use white yarn—½ strand or 32-in. length. Follow the directions for tying the bow given for the matching pincushion. (Fig. 5-29.) On the second white row in from each side, place a bow on the eighth stitch down from the top, and one on the eighth stitch up from the bottom, as shown in Figure 5-30.

Braid Construction. Follow the basic directions for braid construction and stuffing given for the rosebud mini pillow in Chapter 8. Use white yarn (single strand). Work the Regular Braid Stitch—Start A.

Design Note: Notice how the three related colors, close in value, blend and form wide stripes in contrast to the narrow white ones. You can use numerous color combinations, making them blend or contrast as you wish. An easy way to key your own color pattern follows:

1. Work the first row exactly down the center (such as the white row in the sample).

2. Starting at the right side of the center row, work your rows of color pattern out to the right edge.

3. Starting at the left side of the center row, work the color pattern in reverse out to the left edge.

The area covered can grow to any size when you increase the number of stitches in the rows and work as many rows as you wish. The pincushion and pillow were worked in the Single Zig Zag Chain, but they could easily be adapted to the Double Zig Zag Chain, which would produce deeper waves. Zig Zag Fill-in Stitches along the edges would then be necessary.

A charming Single Zig Zag Chain mini pillow is a breath of spring to delight the young or old feminine heart! Crisp black and white daisies on a bright green field are surrounded by turquoise, shocking pink and white French

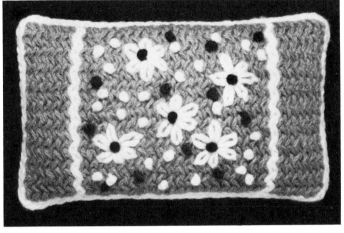

5-31

Daisies. See Chapter 2 for detailed instructions for the Lazy Daisy Stitch. Make the stitches irregular as in Figure 5-31—even more so if you wish. Use white yarn. Follow Figure 5-32 for placement. Measurements are given from the top or bottom and from the white side stripes to the center of each daisy. Start the 1st Daisy 2 in. from the left stripe—1¼ in. from the top; 2nd Daisy, 1¼ in. from the right stripe—2 in. from the top; 3rd Daisy, 1¼ in. from the left stripe—1¾ in. from the bottom; 4th Daisy, 3 in. from either stripe—2¾ in. from the bottom; 5th Daisy, 1¾ in. from the bottom—1¾ in. from the right stripe.

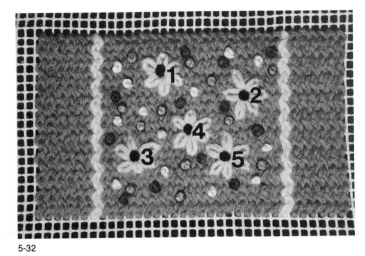

5-32

Knot buds. There is a matching Now Needlepoint backing side (without flowers) plus white yarn braid. (Fig. 5-31.) Size of sample: 6 in. × 10½ in.

Note: This sample introduces another technique which opens doors on a whole new world of possibilities. The overall area is worked first to form the background. The daisies are surface stitches worked on top of the background. The open Lazy Daisy Stitches create a lacy effect which is pleasing against the textural background. Figure 5-32 shows the topside only, but I also include directions for the matching backing, which I did as an afterthought.

Nantucket 6-Ply Cable Yarn. Background on the top: green #84 (26 str.); white #1 (2 str.). Flowers and French Knots: white #1 (3 str.); turquoise #64 (2 str.); shocking pink #38 (2 str.); black #120 (1 str.). Backing, Fill-in and Braid: green #84 (26 str.); white #1 (11 str.).

The stitches are worked from top to bottom in rows across from left to right.

Top Background and the Backing. 1st Row, use green yarn. Start at the upper left. Starting with a zig, work 20 Single Zig Zag Chain stitches (ending with a zag). Catch over the last chain as at the end of a row but do not end the yarn. Drop under to the wrong side and bring the needle up in the hole directly below, leaving one horizontal bar of canvas exposed. Starting with a zig, work 20 Single Zig Zag Chain stitches (ending with a zag). End the row. Subsequent rows are worked in the same manner: 2nd through 6th, green (first 6 rows green); 7th, white; 8th through 27th, green; 28th, white; 29th through 34th, green.

The surface stitches for the topside center panel include:

French Knots. Place one black French Knot (single strand—around the needle once) directly in the center of each daisy. Sprinkle pink, turquoise and white French Knots in among the daisies (in the center panel only).

Braid Construction. Use white yarn. Before starting the construction, work one row of Regular Fill-in Stitches (see Chapter 8) completely around each separate area. If you use heavier yarn, this step won't be necessary. Follow the basic directions for braid construction and stuffing given for the rosebud mini pillow. (Ch. 8.) Use white yarn (single strand). Work the Regular Braid Stitch—Start A.

Design Note: Press that Aware Button for this is only one example of what can be keyed by working the overall textural background and placing surface stitches on top. Keep the surface stitches open and simple so that the background peeks through and is not wasted. You can easily create the image of stems by simple straight stitches—and leaves with small chain stitches. I can't begin to point out the possibilities. Visualize an overall white textural background with multicolored flowers dancing on the surface. Make your own thumbnail sketches for placement if you are designing your own or—if you are courageous—plant the flowers and knots at random as I did with this sample. Use the Squint Test while you are planting so that you can make sure there is a balance of color and placement throughout.

▄▄▄▄▄▄

A merry little pincushion! The Single Zig Zag Chain basic square (Pattern 11—Fig. 5-23) is worked in shocking pink, yellow-green and white. There's a fancy Now Needlepoint backing, if anyone should peek. (Fig. 5-33.) Size of sample: 5 in. square including the braid.
Pat Rug Yarn: shocking pink #239 (9 str.); green #550 (5 str.); white #005 (6 str.). The yarn count includes the topside, backing and braid.

5-33

Topside of Pincushion. Follow the general directions for the basic 12-stitch Single Zig Zag square (Pattern 11), using the correct corners indicated. The pincushion design has one additional outside row around the basic square. Substitute the following color sequence:

Basic Square. 1st Row, pink, Corner A; 2nd Row, green, Corner B; 3rd Row, white, Corner A; 4th Row, green, Corner B; 5th Row, pink, Corner A.

Outside Row. Worked on the outside of the basic square, the 6th Row is pink, Corner B.

French Knot Center. Use white yarn (single strand doubled—around the needle once). Follow the directions for the French Knot Center preceding Pattern 9.

Fancy Now Needlepoint Backing. The backing is the exact size and shape as the top. The only difference is that you substitute a Round Center for the French Knot Center so that the bottom will sit flatly on a surface. See Figure 5-34. One bar of canvas (to be used for the Braid Stitch) must be left free between the top and back. Use pink yarn. The size of the square is already keyed, so start with the outside row (sixth row in the top) and work in toward the center. Bring the needle up to the surface in the correct hole under the lower left corner of the topside, leaving one bar of canvas exposed. Work the outside row around the square—use Corner B—so that it is the exact size of the topside.

Not counting the diagonal corner stitches, there will be 12 single zig zag stitches along each side. Repeat the color pattern of the first through fifth rows for the top.

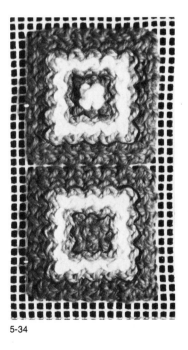

5-34

Round Center Motif. Use pink yarn (single strand). Work a Round Center motif to fill in the center. Follow the directions preceding Pattern 9.

Braid Construction. Follow the basic directions for braid construction and stuffing given for the rosebud mini pillow in Chapter 8. Use white yarn (single strand). Work the Regular Braid Stitch—Start A.

▄▄▄▄▄▄

The Single Zig Zag Chain basic square grows to a 10 in. square pillow with springlike colors green, yellow and white. (Fig. 5-35.) A fancy Now Needlepoint backing matches the front.

5-35

5-36

Pat Rug Yarn: green #559 (36 str.); yellow #413 (28 str.); white #005 (29 str.). The yarn count includes the top, backing and 13 strands of white used for the braid construction.

Topside of Pillow. Follow the general directions for the basic 12-stitch Single Zig Zag square (Pattern 11, Fig. 5-23) using the correct corners indicated. The pillow motif starts with the basic square, to which 11 outside rows are added. Use the following color sequence for the rows.

Basic Square. The rows are worked in toward the center. Letters indicate the type of corner. 1st Row, green—A; 2nd, yellow—B; 3rd, white—A; 4th, yellow—B; 5th, green—A.

Outside Rows. Rows are worked on the outside of the basic square. 6th, green—B; 7th, yellow—A; 8th, white—B; 9th, yellow—A; 10th, green—B; 11th, green—A; 12th, yellow—B; 13th, white—A; 14th, yellow—B; 15th, green—A; 16th, green—B.

French Knot Center. Use white yarn (single strand doubled—around the needle once). Follow the directions for the French Knot Center preceding Pattern 9.

Fancy Now Needlepoint backing. The back is the exact size and shape as the top. The only difference is that you substitute the Round Center for the French Knot Center. (Fig. 5-36.) One bar of canvas (to be used for the Braid Stitch) must be left free between the topside and the backing. The size of the overall square is already keyed, so start with the outside row and work rows in toward the center for the entire area. Bring your needle up to the surface in the hole under the lower left corner of the topside so that one free bar of canvas is left exposed. Use

green yarn. Work the outside row around the square (use Corner B) making it the exact size of the topside. Not counting diagonal corner stitches, there will be 32 Single Zig Zag Chain stitches along each side. Double-check the count, for this area must be identical to the top or you will have problems when you work the braid construction. Follow the exact color pattern of the top, working rows in toward the center, alternating Corners A and B. (The first outer row was worked with Corner B.)

Round Center Motif. Use green yarn. Work a Round Center motif to fill in the center. Follow directions preceding Pattern 9.

Braid Construction. Follow the basic directions for the braid construction and stuffing given for the rosebud mini pillow in Chapter 8. Use white yarn (single strand doubled). Work the Regular Braid Stitch—Start A.

You will find three additional finished items in the construction and finishing chapter. See Chapter 8 for directions for the rosebud mini pillow (Fig. 8-22), the eyeglass case (Fig. 8-37) and the black and white belt with the gold buckle (Fig. 8-43) which are worked in zig zag chain stitches.

6.

The Wonderful Wiggly Chain

The Wonderful Wiggly Chain is a completely unique concept—a kind of wayward version of the chain stitch! The chain wiggles and stretches in an irregular fashion on the canvas and produces frolicsome design motifs and overall patterns. When you have become familiar with both versions of the Single and Double Zig Zag Chain, you will easily be able to interpret on canvas the motifs for the Wiggly Chain. The individual stitches are like musical notes which are blended to produce an endless number of designs.

Personality. Read the diagrams slowly at first—then faster as you begin to "sight read." There are uniform overall repeat patterns (to cover any size area) plus a variety of individual Design Motifs to be used alone—repeated as many times as you wish—or combined to tell a story. See the little bees buzzing around the flower (Fig. 6-49), and the worm eyeing the apple (Fig. 6-47) on the pillows among the finished items. Frolicsome motifs for fun designing! They are gifts to you that you can switch and combine to tell your own story. The system for placement that is explained to you enables you to anticipate the overall visual effect of the finished item and to determine the exact spot in which to start each motif. Many of the design motifs are worked entirely in different versions of the Chain Stitch. Some include touches of a variety of stitches. The individual motifs are combined with backgrounds worked in straight rows, or in rows around the square or rectangle. There are no set rules; the primary purpose is to show you how easy it is to be creative with the helpful vocabulary of patterns and design motifs.

Will Travel. The stitch travels in every direction—up, down, sideways, diagonally; it stretches, shrinks and even stands on its head. Not only does the stitch travel but the canvas travels too. You turn it in all directions. About

the only thing which stays right side up is *you!* Some of you might have to make friends slowly with this different way of working Now Needlepoint. For many of us, new methods are startling until we master them. "Wow, they can't mean it!" is the initial reaction. But then something clicks along the way and the very thing which rattled us becomes fascinating enjoyment. You will not give much thought to the turns and twists of the canvas once the textural effects and patterns of the Wiggly Chain start to emerge.

There are no actual mechanics to master for the Wiggly Chain. You are already familiar with the basic Chain Stitch. The stitches are worked in rows indicated by the numbers on the diagrams. The diagrams show you exactly how to "walk" the stitches around, over and into the holes of canvas. Sometimes, individual stitches are stretched over several bars of canvas, sometimes over only one bar. The Chain Stitch is always worked *toward you.* The canvas must be turned so that the arrow in each individual stitch is pointing downward toward you. You must read the diagrams carefully and follow the direction of the arrows and the size of stitches. As when you learned to read, talk out loud to yourself at first. Think of the stitches in groupings such as "one downward-left diagonal," "three straight down," "three Single Zig Zags." Notice whether there is an extra stretch to a stitch—just how many bars of canvas it jumps over. In a short time and with a little practice, you will develop the ability to quickly "read" the diagrams, and the talking out loud and written instructions will not be necessary. You will automatically interpret the diagrams with yarn and canvas.

The freedom with which the Wiggly Chain can be worked softens edges so that you can simulate curves and form circles, thereby eliminating the rigid, squared-off

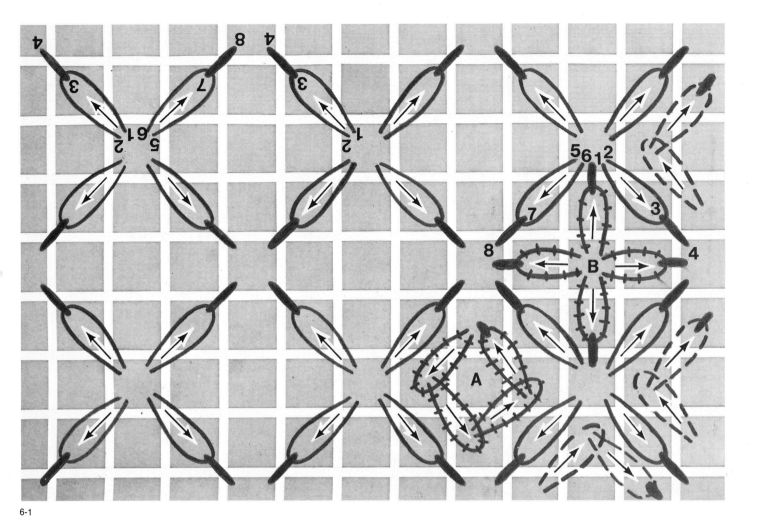

6-1

look which is so exaggerated in most large needlepoint. For geometric designs the squared look is an asset, but I felt the need of softer lines and edges for many design interpretations. Consequently, the Wiggly Chain was born, and, like a young child darting in all directions, it tries your patience at times but it ends up being an expression of fun and joy.

WIGGLY CHAIN LATTICE PATTERNS

The chain truly wiggles in the first three overall patterns. Although the three patterns appear entirely different to the eye, they all have the same mother. A basic, open lattice-type of design is worked in the same manner in each pattern. (See Fig. 6-1.) The open spaces of the lattice are filled in either with the Round Center or the Diamond Center. Pattern 1 (Fig. 6-2) shows the delightful result when the Round Center is used throughout. Pattern 2 (Fig. 6-3) takes on an entirely different personality merely by using Diamond Centers instead. Pattern 3 (Fig. 6-4) incorporates both types of centers. (Alternate rows of Round Centers produce a background area when worked in the same color as the basic lattice.) You can completely change the visual effect by switching the types of centers and using different color combinations.

Basic Lattice Overall Pattern. The basic lattice can be worked in a number of ways. The directions represent the system I found to be the easiest and which I strongly suggest you follow in the beginning. You might wish to change the working order when you are familiar with the mechanics. As shown in Figure 6-1, the lattice is formed by working four diagonal chain stitches out of the same hole of canvas—two in the upward direction and two in the downward direction. You start by turning the canvas and the diagram upside down. Remember, the chain stitches are always worked with the arrows pointing toward you. With the canvas in this position, work the entire row of *pairs of stitches* across from right to left, jumping under on the wrong side and bringing the needle up to the surface in the correct hole to start the next pair. Then turn the canvas and the diagram right-side up. Using the same center hole as you did in the first row, work the bottom pairs of stitches across from right to left. Continue working the rows, turning the canvas after you complete each row.

For the detailed directions, follow Figure 6-1. Remember to place a yarn tie marker at the top of the canvas. Use the yarn color indicated in the pattern directions or substitute a color of your own choice. Turn the canvas and Figure 6-1 upside down.

1st Row. Work from right to left. Start the first stitch in what has now become the lower right corner. The crossbar of canvas at 4 will be the corner of the Now Needlepoint area. Bring your needle up in the correct hole for starting designated by 1. Leave a 6 in. tail on the wrong side, to be woven in later. Work the first chain in a zig direction. Place the needle down in 2 and up in 3. Place the needle down in 4, catching over the chain loop and the crossbar of canvas. Bring the needle up in 5 (same hole as 1) and work the Chain Stitch in a zag direction, catching over the chain loop and the crossbar of canvas, going down in 8 and bringing the needle up in 1 in the next group to the left. Repeat the first pair of stitches. Continue across to the left for desired coverage. Do not end the yarn.

Turn the canvas and the diagram right side up.

2nd Row. Bring the needle up in the same center hole used for the last two stitches in the first row (indicated to the right of the diagram). Work one chain in a zig direction and one chain in a zag direction—using the same center hole as indicated—going down in 8 and bringing the needle up in the center hole in the next grouping to the left. Continue across to the left for desired coverage. Do not end the yarn.

Turn the canvas and diagram upside down.

3rd Row. Repeat the first row. Notice how the end loops on the chains share holes with the preceding row and the neighbors on each side. Your own system of finding the correct hole for the starts will quickly materialize. I do it by walking my fingers along the canvas holes. The centers are the same distance apart both vertically and horizontally.

Turn the canvas and diagram right side up.

4th Row. Repeat the second row. Repeat the first and second rows for desired coverage, inverting the canvas at the end of each row.

Note: If you wish the top and bottom to be identical, you must work an even number of rows in the basic lattice.

🠲🠲🠲🠲🠲

Pattern 1. A lattice chain with Round Centers is turquoise and white and textural. (Fig. 6-2.) Size of pattern: 3½ in. × 6 in.

6-2. Pattern 1.

Pat Rug Yarn: turquoise #738; white #005.
Follow Figure 6-1.

1. Use white yarn. Work the basic lattice pattern for desired coverage. The sample shown has five groupings of 4 stitches across—three groupings of 4 stitches from the top to bottom.

2. Use turquoise yarn. Fill in each open area in the lattice with Round Centers, indicated by A in Figure 6-1. (See the detailed directions for Round Centers in the preceding chapter.) Skip under on the wrong side to the next closest opening after each Round Center is completed. Edges are filled in with the lattice color.

3. Use white yarn. Work Fill-in Stitches along all edges as indicated at the right of the diagram.

🠲🠲🠲🠲🠲

Pattern 2. A lattice chain with Diamond Centers has connecting diamonds of shocking pink with a crisp white background. (Fig. 6-3.) Size of sample: 3½ in. × 6 in.
Pat Rug Yarn: shocking pink #259; white #005.
Follow Figure 6-1.

6-3. Pattern 2.

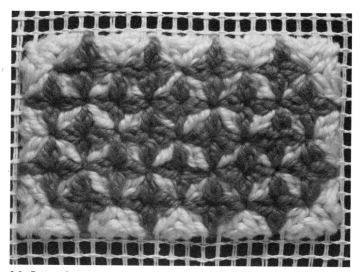

1. Use white yarn. Work a basic lattice pattern for desired coverage. The sample shown has five groupings of 4 stitches across—three groupings of 4 stitches from top to bottom.

2. Use pink yarn. Fill in each open area in the lattice with Diamond Centers, indicated by B on the diagram. (See detailed directions for Diamond Centers in the preceding chapter. Skip under on the wrong side to the next closest opening after each Diamond Center is completed. Fill in the edges with the lattice color.

3. Use white yarn. Work Fill-in Stitches along all edges as indicated at the right of the diagram.

🠲🠲🠲🠲🠲

Pattern 3. A lattice chain has alternating rows of Round and Diamond Centers in yellow-green with white. The

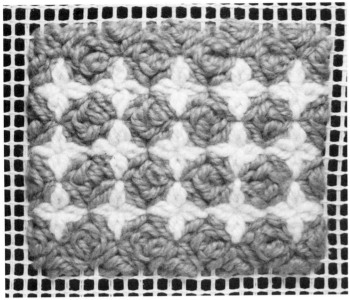
6-4. Pattern 3.

split personality creates a charming effect. (Fig. 6-4.) Size of pattern: 4¾ in. × 6 in.

Pat Rug Yarn: green #550; white #005.

Follow Figure 6-1.

1. Use green yarn. Work a basic lattice pattern for desired coverage. The sample shown has five groupings of 4 stitches across—four groupings of 4 stitches from top to bottom.

2. Starting with the top horizontal row of open areas in the lattice, fill in as follows: 1st Row, green, work Round Centers (A on the diagram); 2nd Row, white, work Diamond Centers (B on the diagram); repeat 1st and 2nd Rows for desired coverage. The pattern shown repeats two more times, plus an extra 1st Row along the bottom.

3. Use green yarn. Work Fill-in Stitches along the edges as indicated at the right of the diagram.

Design Note for all Lattice Patterns: Strange but exciting things can happen when you combine the basic lattice with the two centers. Notice how the centers or side Fill-in Stitches become an integral part of the background when worked in the same color as the lattice. Only two colors have been used for the samples, but you do not have to adhere to this formula. There are so many possibilities! The center motifs can easily be transformed into rows of small flowers by placing a French Knot in the center of each and using color in some interesting way. The textural look of these patterns is their outstanding trait and is especially pleasing. With the proper control of color, they would be suitable for many different types of décor for texture is a happy addition anywhere.

WIGGLY CHAIN DESIGN MOTIFS

In the following vocabulary of Design Motifs, the simple ones—easiest to follow—are listed first and then gradually the more advanced. Practice with the less complicated motifs until you get the feel of this new Now Needlepoint language and can interpret the diagrams easily.

Rows and Color Changes. The numerical sequence of the rows is indicated on the diagrams and color changes are given in the written instructions. Certain of the rows wiggle, twist and turn while traveling, the last stitch sometimes ending up in the same hole as the first stitch in the row. Many arrows dutifully point out the changes in direction. To produce certain of the motifs you start with the outside row and work in toward the center. With others, you start in the center and work out. The first row usually keys the overall contour of the form. In many instances, the start of a new row is so close—planned this way on purpose—that it is not necessary to end and start yarn. Simply pull the needle through to the wrong side and bring it up to the surface in the correct spot to start the next row. This is not possible if there is a change of color indicated.

Stitches. You will find many unusual versions of the chain stitch mixed together in one motif. Carefully follow the stitch nuances as shown in the diagrams. Stitches stretch over several bars of canvas, shrink to squeeze into the next hole. There are short runs of Single Zig Zags, Double Zig Zags, straight runs of Chain Stitches, pairs of chains (one worked directly around another) . . . Anything goes! Like a joyous adventure!

Turning of Canvas. The chain stitches are worked so the arrows in the diagram *point in a downward direction toward you*. The canvas must be turned as many times as necessary so the stitches are always worked toward you. The turning of the canvas quickly becomes automatic. There are times when it is helpful to turn the diagram too—especially in the beginning—so that the position of both the diagram and the canvas correspond, making it easier for you to follow the changes in direction.

Learning Procedure. The early motifs include considerable explanations to help you get started in this new Now Needlepoint language. The words become less important as you advance. Eventually you will need only the diagrams and color indications for the rows.

Don't be concerned with the color of the yarn. Any color will do for your first attempts. Concentrate on following the diagrams and instructions. Do not pull the individual stitches tight or they will appear tortured and fail to cover the canvas properly. Let the wool live in a relaxed state —but not *too* loose—so that the interesting textural quality is produced.

Creative Designing with Wiggly Chain Motifs. Many of the motifs are statements in themselves and can be used alone on a solid color background, especially for small finished items. But this is your chance, a golden opportunity for you to create designs of your own by combining the motifs presented in any way you wish. You can repeat them in vertical rows—horizontal rows—place them around a square. Designs can be made up of all flowers and leaves, all strawberries, all bees—or combinations such as the apple and worm used for the small pillow. (Fig. 6-47.) Backgrounds are usually worked in a solid color, but they can be patterned if you wish. You work the individual motifs first and then fill in the background. The finished design must have pleasing balance, so proper placement of the motif or motifs is an important factor. You can eliminate guessing and determine the exact placement for an individual motif or a combination of several motifs if you use my system.

Working Samples of Wiggly Chain Design Motifs. The trick I use to arrive at proper placement is to make up working samples of the motif or motifs I intend to use in keying a design. It involves the following steps:

1. Duplicate the sample motif or motifs on a piece of canvas, leaving enough canvas surrounding each motif so it can be cut out separately with three bars of canvas left free on all sides, exactly as in the samples shown.

2. Before cutting out the individual motifs, either machine zig zag twice around each motif on the third bar out from the design motif—or squeeze Elmer's or Sobo glue along the same bars, letting it dry thoroughly. Either process prevents unraveling.

3. Cut out the individual motifs directly outside of the machine zig zagging or the glued bars.

Note: Don't use masking tape, since it will be necessary to see through and match the canvas holes while you key the designs.

Using the Working Samples for Designing. Figures 6-39 and 6-40 show the steps involved in keying the worm eyeing the apple on the mini pillow. By overlapping the two small working samples on a flat surface, then moving them around for desired effect, you can determine the placement you wish and somewhat visualize what the finished item will be like. In the next step, you place the blank canvas on which you will work the finished design on top of the combined working samples. You can see through the top canvas, thus making it possible for you to mark with yarn ties the exact spots where the motifs will be started (indicated by No. 1 on the individual motif diagrams). After you have worked the first motif, it is a good idea to double-check the placement of the remaining yarn ties to make certain they are in the proper spots for correct starts.

The working samples are valuable aids in designing. Most importantly, they tell you in a flash the exact size of the motif or motifs involved, giving you a quick gauge for spacing and placement. The ideal situation would be to go through the entire lot and make up working samples in advance for future reference. Because of the variety of yarn colors involved, this is not always feasible. Temporary working samples can, of course, be made in any color yarn available. These would key the exact size and help with placement and also give you practice in reading the diagrams. You can make samples with the correct colors after you have purchased the yarn for a specific item. You can easily purchase the necessary yarn and canvas for the item you have in mind, since the yarn colors used for each motif are given. It is best to make up a working sample in the exact colors you intend to use for each motif before you start work on the actual finished item. By following this procedure you iron out any kinks in advance and end up with a variety of delightful working samples which can be placed in your creative file and used for future designing.

Repeat Patterns. When you key designs which involve repeat patterns of the Wiggly Chain Design Motifs, experiment a bit. Make up a number of very rough, quick thumbnail sketches, trying out placement possibilities, and choose the most successful. After you have purchased the necessary yarn and canvas, make up a working sample of the motif to be used. The next step would depend on the design involved, so it is difficult to give specific instructions. Sometimes it is best to start a row of motifs with a corner motif—I would say this is the usual procedure—but there are times when the center motif in a row should be worked first and the row continued out to each side. Once you have worked a repeat pattern, the steps involved will become obvious and you will choose the best way to proceed. The specific instructions outlined for the finished items involving repeat motifs might be helpful for reference in the beginning. An important point to remember in keying repeat patterns is that the motifs must be equidistant. Therefore, a little careful planning is necessary.

1st Row of Motifs. To establish the proper spot to start the first motif, place the working sample (you'll be lost without it) under the canvas on which the item will be worked. Gauge the placement with your eye, taking into consideration the space necessary for the background area and the excess canvas edge. In addition to the 3-bar excess, it is advisable to allow a number of extra bars of canvas along all sides when you are creating a design, for you might wish to add an extra row or two of background as an afterthought. When the first motif is completed, place the working sample under the canvas, moving it around until you find the proper placement for the second motif. This establishes the distance between motifs. Take a little time at this point, since this placement keys the spacing for all of the repeats throughout the design. Place a yarn tie marker indicating the exact spot where the first stitch of the second motif will be worked (No. 1 in the motif diagram). This must be exact in order to get the motifs to fall in an even row. Finding that starting spot is tricky at first, but you can easily develop a system of your own for counting the canvas holes across or down, depending on the design. Work the first row only of the second motif and then quickly double-check the placement before you proceed. Using the diagram and working sample as aids, count up and down to make certain the motif will fall in exact alignment with the first motif. (I use this quick double-check for each motif. The first row can easily be pulled out and corrected if you have missed the start.) With the completion of the second motif, the distance between the motifs is established and you can carefully tie yarn markers across the canvas to mark the starts for the other motifs in the first row. Make certain there is the same number of holes or bars between the markers. If not, something is off. Complete the motifs in the first row.

2nd Row of Motifs. If your design calls for additional repeat rows of motifs, place the working sample under the canvas for placement of the second row. The motifs can be worked directly under those in the first row or can be dropped down and appear halfway between as in the large strawberry pillow. (See Fig. 6-55.) Use your eye as a judge and the Squint Test. Find the spot where the motif appears to be equidistant from the motifs in the first row by moving the working sample around under the canvas. The distance from side to side and the distance from top to bottom should appear to be equal. I use the word "appear," because you must take into consideration the overall bulk shape of the motif which sometimes minimizes stems or bug legs or antennae. Mark the exact spot for the start of the first motif in the second row with a yarn tie marker. Complete the motif. Mark the exact starts for the remaining motifs with yarn tie markers. Complete the motifs across the second row. (If the motifs in the second row are halfway between those in the first row, as in the strawberry pillow, the subsequent rows must be alternated.) Continue repeating the rows for desired coverage. With a little practice and the help of "walking fingers" for counting the holes or bars of canvas, you will become adept at figuring out the correct starting spots. It's all in the doing!

Backgrounds. Backgrounds in the finished items are worked in the Orr Weave Stitch in vertical rows, in horizontal rows, or in rows around the square or rectangle, depending on the design. It will therefore be necessary to read ahead and familiarize yourself with Chapter 7, The Orr Weave: A New Textural Stitch for Designs and Backgrounds, and master the stitch mechanics before you can work the backgrounds for the Wiggly Chain Design Motifs.

The Orr Weave has a definite textural quality but it is not too busy and so does not detract from the design motifs. The backgrounds are mostly solid colors, but a pattern can be introduced. (See the strawberry pillow, Fig. 6-55.)

Proceed with caution when using patterned backgrounds for the motif or motifs must stand out clearly if the design is to be successful. The Orr Weave Stitches are worked closely around the motifs so as to leave no canvas exposed. Keep the tension on the stitches relaxed so the wool can puff up around the motifs—but not too loose or the formation of the weave will be destroyed. I even push back motif stitches to work a background stitch under the motif if this is necessary to prevent the canvas from peeking through. If the motifs are fairly small, work up to them—drop underneath on the wrong side—and bring the needle up to the surface on the other side to complete the row.

The Orr Weave is worked in rows across the canvas from right to left. If you wish vertical rows, you simply turn the canvas 90 degrees while working the background and work the rows in the normal manner. If you wish rows that are worked around the square or rectangle, start with the outer row first and work in toward the center. The outer square or rectangular row of stitches must appear to be equidistant from the central motif on all sides (usually the same number of bars between the center design area and the initial outside row on all sides). Double-check with your eye when the row is completed for this row keys all of the rows which are worked in toward the center. This system is not feasible for all designs but can be used when motifs are placed to form a symmetrical pattern, as in the finished bee pillow. (Fig. 6-49.) For the most part, straight vertical or horizontal rows are used for backgrounds.

How much background to work around a design motif becomes an easier and easier question to answer as you gain familiarity with the basic problems involved. The surrounding background area acts much like a mat on a painting and can vary in size. It literally frames the central design motif, so that it stands out in your eye. Allow enough solid area around the outside—I call it "air"—for the main design to breathe and not appear to be squeezed in too small a space. Don't be skimpy when you are keying the background area, since the proper ratio or proportion can do much to enhance the overall design. Keep in mind that allowance must be made for the "roll-back" on all sides of knife-edge pillows so that the design motifs can remain in the top central area and not appear to be sliding off the edges.

Use yarn tie markers for all types of backgrounds to let you know when you have reached edges and corners. When the background is completed, use a needle and pull the motif stitches to the surface up over the background stitches where necessary. The stitches sometimes get tucked underneath. Bringing the motifs forward from the background helps to create a dimensional effect.

Note: It is best to work all the background stitches in continuous rows so as not to interrupt the weave appearance. However, in an emergency, individual stitches can be worked close to the motifs if pesky spots of canvas peek through after the background has been completed.

Stitch Mechanics for Two Versions of the Stem Stitch Used in Wiggly Chain Motifs. Both versions of the stitch are sometimes used in a single stem; you switch from one to the other to produce a curved effect.

In example 1, the Stem Stitch is worked over a single bar of canvas, as with the Regular Fill-in Stitch used around the outside edges before construction. The stitches are worked from left to right. Turn the canvas when necessary in order to work the stitches in this direction. (Fig. 6-5.)

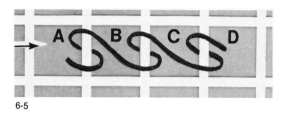

6-5

1. Bring the needle up to the surface in A. Go over one bar of canvas. Place the needle down in B and up in A in one motion.

2. Go over two bars of canvas. Place the needle down in C and up in B in one motion.

3. Go over two bars of canvas. Place the needle down in D and up in C in one motion.

Continue for the desired length, following the motif diagram.

In Example 2, the Stem Stitch is worked over a crossbar of canvas. The stitches are worked from left to right. Turn the canvas when necessary in order to work the stitches in this direction. (Fig. 6-6.)

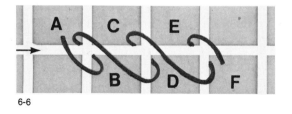

6-6

1. Bring the needle up to the surface in A. Go over a crossbar in a downward right, diagonal direction. Place the needle down in B and up in A in one motion.

2. Move to the next free crossbar of canvas to the right. Place the needle down in D and up in C in one motion.

3. Move to the next free crossbar of canvas to the right. Place the needle down in F and up in E in one motion.

Continue for the desired length, following the motif diagram.

WIGGLY CHAIN DESIGN MOTIFS

The motifs are worked on 3 to the inch canvas.

General Note: To start and end yarn in small-size motifs, leave 6 in. tails on the wrong side if there is not sufficient worked area close at hand to weave under for at least 1 in. The tails can be woven in after the background is completed.

Motifs 1A, 1B and 1C depict three small flowers. Use yellow yarn for flowers, black for the centers.

Flower 1A. (Fig. 6-7.) Pat Rug Yarn: yellow #413.

1. Working out from center hole, make 4 diagonal chain stitches as shown at the left of Figure 6-8. Catch over the crossbars of canvas at the outer ends as indicated.

Flower 1B. (Fig. 6-9.) Pat Rug Yarn: yellow #441; black #050.

1. Work Step 1 in Flower 1A.

2. Using the same center hole as in Step 1, work 4 straight chain stitches in the spaces between the diagonal chains. Catch over canvas bars at the outer ends as indicated at the right of Figure 6-8.

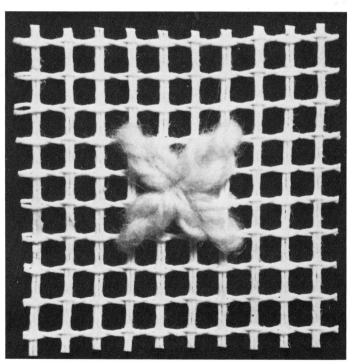

6-7. Motif 1

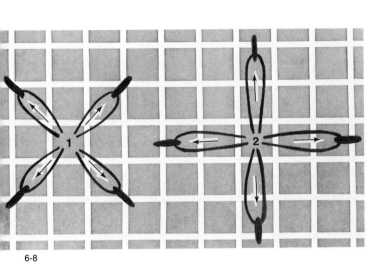

6-8

6-10. Motif 1C.

2. Using the same center hole, work 4 diagonal chain stitches *around* each of the chain stitches. (Fig. 6-11.) Notice that the needle is placed back in the same hole when you catch over the end of the outer chain. (The needle does not loop over the canvas.)

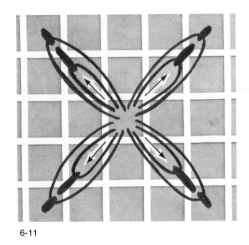

6-11

Motif 2. Willie the Worm. (Fig. 6-12.)
Pat Rug Yarn: green #550; black #050.

6-12. Motif 2.

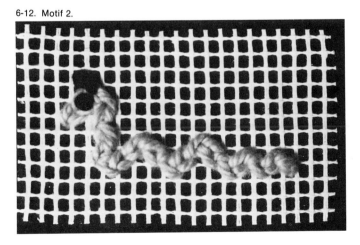

6-9. Motif 1B.

Flower 1O. (Fig. 6-10.) Pat Rug Yarn: yellow #441; black #050.

1. Work the inner chain stitches first (same as Step 1 in Flower 1A).

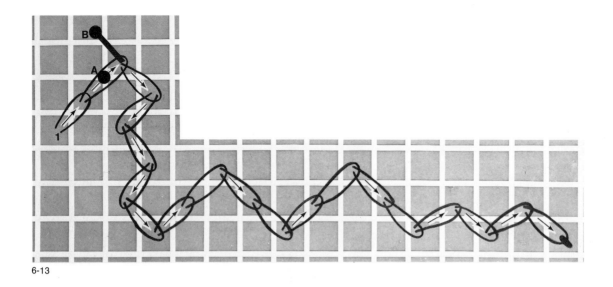

6-13

Head and Body. Use green yarn. Start at the head. Bring the needle up in 1. Follow Figure 6-13 for the zig zag changes. Turn the canvas when necessary. The entire worm is made up of Single Zig Zag Chains and Double Zig Zag Chains.

French Knot Eye and Antenna. Use black yarn. *Eye:* Work the French Knot (single strand—around the needle once) in the spot on the head indicated by A. *Antenna:* Bring the needle up to the surface in the chain loop at the top of the head (see Fig. 6-13) and work the French Knot, going over a crossbar of canvas and down in B.

Motif 3. A luscious shocking pink strawberry. (Fig. 6-14.) Pat Rug Yarn: shocking pink #259; green #545.

The strawberry is formed by working a diamond shape at the top (2 stitches on each side) with 2 rows of stitches tapering in toward the bottom. The green leaves and seeds are worked last since some of the green stitches are worked on top of the pink.

When you complete each pink row of the strawberry, do not end the yarn; pull it through to the wrong side and bring the needle up to the surface in the correct place for starting the next row. The stops and starts are close enough to make this possible.

1st Row. Use pink yarn. Bring the needle up to the surface in 1. Work the first row as indicated in Figure 6-15, ending back in hole 1 (2 diagonal Chain Stitches in each direction).

2nd Row. Bring the needle up to the surface in 2. Work a 4-stitch Round Center as indicated, ending back in hole 2.

3rd Row. Drop down on the wrong side and bring the needle up to the left in 3. (Now you must carefully watch for changes in the length of the Chain Stitches. The third row has stitches which are stretched at either end. Notice also how the row starts and stops in holes shared with the first row.) Work the third row under the first row as indicated.

4th Row. Drop down on the wrong side and bring the needle up in 4. Work the 2 stretched diagonal stitches as indicated. End the yarn under the worked area.

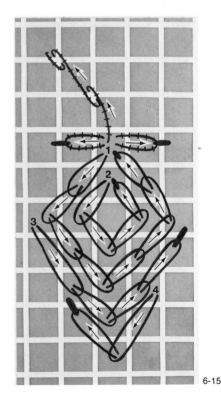

6-14. Motif 3.

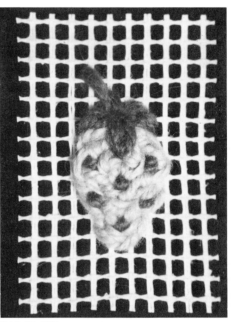

6-15

The stems, leaves and seeds use green yarn. *Stem:* Bring the needle up to the surface in 1 (same hole where the first row started and ended). Work a stem stitch over the crossbars, carefully following the top patterned stitches in the direction of the arrows. Pull the yarn through to the back, but do not end it. *Leaves:* Bring the needle up to the surface in the same hole 1 and work a single chain stitch in a straight direction on each side as indicated in the diagram. See Figure 6-14: The following is not shown in the diagram. Bring the needle back up in the same hole 1 and work one chain in a straight downward direction (on top of the stitches in the strawberry) approximately the same size as the 2 side leaves. Pull the yarn through to the back, but do not end it. *Seeds:* Use simple straight stitches (known as seed stitches in crewel embroidery). Follow the approximate placement of the 6 seeds in the photograph. Bring the needle up to the surface in the correct spot. Go over a strip of yarn and down to the wrong side, so that a small dot of green shows on the surface to simulate a seed. If possible, catch your stitch over a bar of canvas to prevent it from slipping under to the wrong side. Repeat this until the 6 seeds are completed. When necessary, use the needle to keep the seed stitches up on the surface.

Motif 4. A cool slice of fresh lime. (Fig. 6-16.)
Pat Rug Yarn: deep green #545; pale green #565; white #005.

The rows are worked from the outside in toward the center.

1st Row. Use deep green yarn. Bring the needle up to the surface in 1. (Fig. 6-17.) Work the row completely around, ending up in the same hole as the first stitch. End the yarn.

6-16. Motif 4.

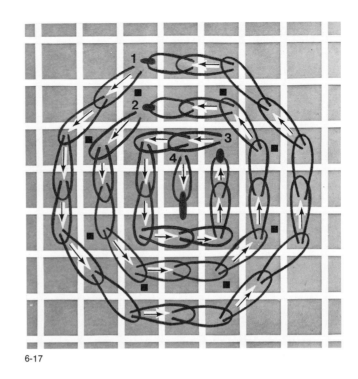

6-17.

2nd Row. Use pale green yarn. Bring the needle up to the surface in 2. Work the row around, ending up in the same hole 2. Do not end the yarn.

3rd Row. Drop under on the wrong side and bring the needle up to the surface in 3. Work the row around, ending up in hole 3. Do not end the yarn. Bring the needle up in 4 and work a single stitch as indicated to close the center. End the yarn.

White Sections. Use white yarn. Bring the needle up in the exact center each time. Place the needle down in the 8 spots between the first row and second row indicated by the small squares. This divides the pale green center area into 8 sections. Connect the outer points of sections by working the straight stitches to form a continuous line between the first and second row as portrayed in Figure 6-16.

Motif 5. Shocking pink and white peppermint candy cane. (Fig. 6-18.)
Pat Rug Yarn: shocking pink #239; white #005.

Turn both the canvas and the diagram upside down to start.

6-18. Motif 5.

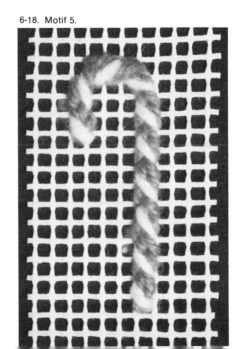

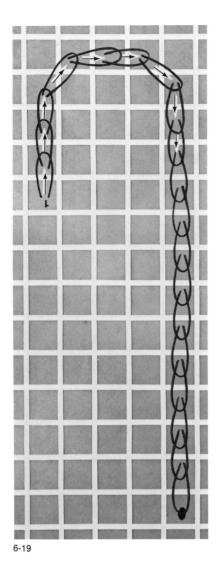

6-19

6-20. Motif 6.

The flower is worked in the following order: 4 pink petals, 4 green leaves, purple center. The 4 petals and center are Round Centers. (See the detailed directions preceding Pattern 9 in the previous chapter.)

4 Pink Petals. Use pink yarn. Start with the canvas and diagram upside down. Bring your needle up to the surface in 1. (Fig. 6-21.) Work one Round Center. Do not end the yarn. Turn the canvas 90 degrees in a clockwise direc-

Candy Cane. Use pink yarn for the candy cane. Bring the needle up to the surface in 1. (Fig. 6-19.) Work the Chain Stitches as indicated, turning the canvas and diagram when necessary so that the directional arrows point down toward you. The length of the cane can be changed as desired. To duplicate the sample, work 12 chain stitches down after you have completed the second diagonal chain. End the yarn.

Surface Whipping for a Spiral Effect. Use white yarn. Turn the canvas upside down. Bring the needle up in 1. Surface whip every other Chain Stitch for the entire length of the cane, turning the canvas when necessary. Straight stitches are used for the cane, but whipping is done in the same manner as for the Single Zig Zag Chain. (See Pattern 1A, Figs. 5-7 and 5-8.)

Note: When you work the Orr Weave background around a cane motif, push back the cane stitches with your left hand and cover the canvas bars close along each side of the cane. This maneuver is a bit of a squeeze, but it causes the cane to pop out in a three-dimensional effect, so it is worth the extra effort.

Motif 6. A shocking pink flower with a purple center and green leaves. (Fig. 6-20.)
Pat Rug Yarn: shocking pink #259; purple #632; green #545.

6-21

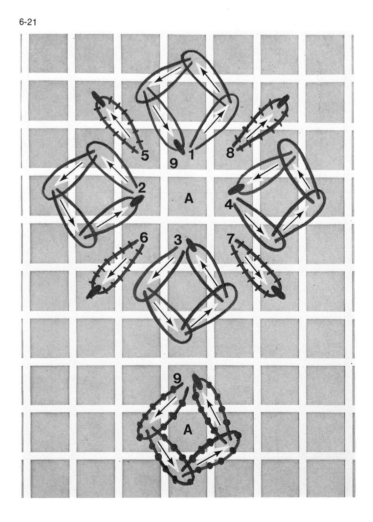

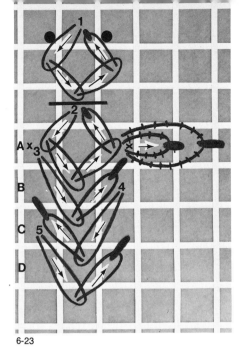

6-23

tion. Drop under on the wrong side and bring the needle up to the surface in 2. Work a second Round Center. Continue around, bringing the needle up in the correct holes to work the third and fourth petals and turning the canvas when necessary. End the yarn.

Green Leaves. Use green yarn. Turn the canvas to the correct position when necessary. Bring the needle up to the surface in 5. Work one diagonal Chain Stitch between the two petals as indicated in the diagram. Do not end the yarn. Drop under on the wrong side and bring the needle up in 6 and work a diagonal chain. Repeat this in 7 and 8, working a leaf between each of the four petals. End the yarn.

Purple Center. Use purple yarn. Bring your needle up to the surface in 9 (same hole as 1). Work a Round Center around hole A as indicated by the small diagram at the bottom of Figure 6-21. This is worked directly in the center of the flower. End the yarn.

Motif 7. Busy little bee. (Fig. 6-22.)
Pat Rug Yarn: black #050, yellow #443.

The bee is worked in the following order: Head, body, yellow surface stripes on top of the body, wings, eyes.

Use black yarn for the head.

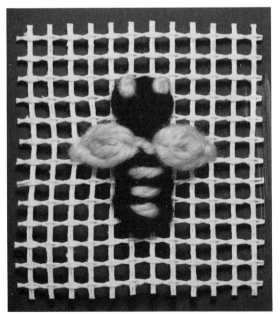

6-22. Motif 7.

1st Row. Bring the needle up to the surface in 1. (Fig. 6-23.) Work one Round Center (see the detailed directions preceding Pattern 9 in the previous chapter) ending back in 1. Do not end the yarn.

Use black yarn for the body.

2nd Row. Bring the needle up to the surface in 2 (sharing the hole used in first row). Work one Round Center, ending back in hole 2. Do not end the yarn.

3rd Row. Bring the needle up in 3. Work two diagonal Chain Stitches. Notice how the start and end share holes with the second row. Do not end the yarn.

Note: Stretch stitches in third, fourth and fifth rows to conform exactly with the diagram.

4th Row. Drop down to the hole directly below and bring the needle up in 4. Work two diagonal Chain Stitches. Do not end the yarn.

5th Row. Drop down and bring the needle up in 5. Work two diagonal Chain Stitches. Do not end the yarn.

Black Band between the Head and Body. Catch the yarn under stitches on the wrong side and bring the needle up in the hole to the left of 2 (see straight black line in the diagram). Work one Straight Stitch across, going down and through to the back in the hole to the right of 2. End the yarn. This extra stitch is not visible in the photographs but it defines the head and body.

Yellow Stripes. Use yellow yarn. There are 4 stripes. Their placement is indicated by the letters A through D down the left side of diagram. The stripes are Straight Stitches similar to the band between the neck and head except that you bring the needle up in the center of the Chain Stitch on the left, go over the center hole and place the needle down in the center of the Chain Stitch on the right. This leaves a little black border around the body of the bee. Work 4 Straight Stitches. Do not end the yarn.

Yellow Wings. Use yellow yarn. *Right wing:* Bring the needle up in X on the right side. The wings are worked at right and left ends of the top stripe. Bring the needle up in the same side spots used for the top stripe in the center of the chain. The wings and stripe make one continuous pattern of yellow. Work a small center Chain Stitch as indicated in the diagram. Bring the needle up in the same spot and work one second, larger chain around the first.

Do not end yarn. *Left wing:* Drop under on the wrong side and bring the needle up in X on the left side. Repeat the right wing in a reverse direction. Do not end the yarn.

French Knot Eyes. Use yellow yarn. Catch the yellow yarn on the wrong side under the body stitches and bring it up on the surface in the correct spot on the head for working the eye. (Bring the needle up in the center of the diagonal chain.) Work one French Knot (single strand—around the needle once). Catch over a bar of canvas so that the knot will not slip through to the wrong side. Repeat this for the second eye on the opposite side. End the yarn.

Background. When working the Orr Weave background around the bee motif, push back the wings and work the stitches underneath. Pull the wings to the surface with your needle after working the background and they will stand out in three dimensions.

Motif 8. Different versions of green leaves will lend themselves to creative use. Combine them with flowers or fruit. There are individual leaves, a pair of leaves and a grouping of leaves. (Fig. 6-24.)
Pat Rug Yarn: green #550.

The samples shown were worked on a single piece of canvas. It is helpful for designing purposes to work the different versions on individual pieces of canvas. You can then easily gauge how much canvas should be left free to accommodate leaves around or between flower or fruit motifs. Use green yarn.

A and B. These are two sizes of diagonal leaves. (Fig. 6-25.) The inner chain (1) is worked first in A—the outer second chain (2) is worked around the first stitch. In B the diagonal chain is worked over the crossbar only to produce the small leaf.

C. The pair of leaves is worked out of the same hole. The inner chain is worked first.

D. A grouping of three leaves is shown with a connecting stem. Two diagonal leaves (1 and 2) are worked first. Drop down on the wrong side and work the bottom straight leaf (3). Bring the needle up at the top of the bottom leaf. Turn the canvas and work the stem (4) in the direction indicated by the arrows.

Note: The bottom straight vertical leaf can be worked individually—also in horizontal pairs by bringing the needle up to the surface in the same hole and working each leaf in the opposite direction as was used for the apple in Motif 9.

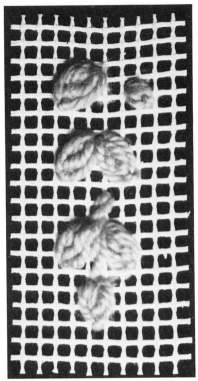
6-24. Motif 8.

6-25
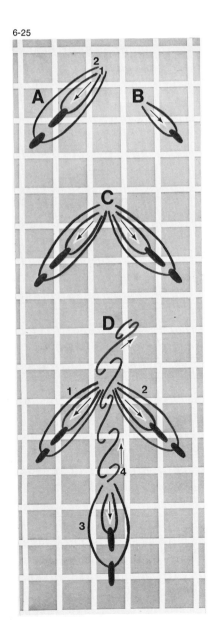

124

Motif 9. Luscious red apple. (Fig. 6-26.)
Pat Rug Yarn: red #237; green #545.

The top of the apple is formed by first working a figure 8 shape and then filling in two open centers. Rows of Zig Zag Chain Stitches are worked under the top shape down to the bottom of the apple. The green stem and leaves are worked last.

Apple. Use red yarn.

1st Row. Start in the center hole at the top of the apple. (Fig. 6-27.) Bring the needle up to the surface in 1. Work Chain Stitches following the direction of the arrows in the diagram. When the left side is completed, continue working in diagonal stitches up to the top right side of the apple. Follow the arrows around the right side and end in the same hole where you started. Do not end the yarn.

2nd Row. Drop under on the wrong side. Bring the needle up to the surface in 2 (the opening on the right side in the figure 8). Work a Round Center (see the detailed directions preceding Pattern 9 in Chapter 5), ending back in hole 2. Do not end the yarn.

3rd Row. Drop under on the wrong side. Bring the needle up in 3 (the opening on the left side in the figure 8) and work a Round Center, ending back in hole 3. Do not end the yarn.

Note: The remaining rows are worked in zig zag chain stitches. The first and last stitch in each row are stretched to form the round shape of the apple. Follow the diagram carefully. The canvas is reversed after each row so that the arrows in the diagram for the next row point in the downward diagonal directions.

4th, 5th, 6th and 7th Rows. Drop under on the wrong side. Bring the needle up in 4. Work the fourth row. Do not end the yarn. Drop under and bring the needle up in 5. Reverse the canvas. Work the fifth row. Do not end the yarn. Repeat this through the seventh row. Do not end the yarn.

8th Row. Drop under on the wrong side, catching once under the yarn. Bring your needle up in 8. Work the two stretched diagonal Chain Stitches to fill in the bottom center area. End the yarn.

Stem and Leaves. Use green yarn. *Stem:* Bring the needle up to the surface in 1 (top center hole—same as start for the first row). Turn the canvas so that you can work the stem stitches in a left-to-right direction. Skip over bars of canvas as indicated in the diagram and work the stem. Do not end the yarn. *Leaves:* Drop under on the wrong side and bring the needle up in the correct hole to work a straight leaf. Work the small inside chain first, then

6-26. Motif 9.

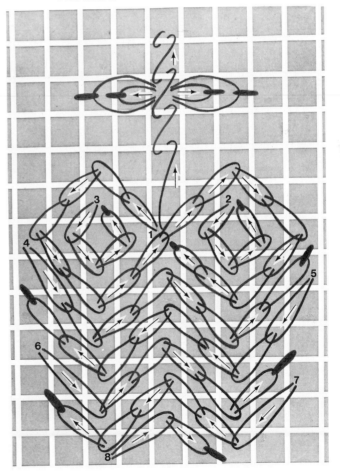

6-27

the large outside chain around the smaller one. Bring the needle up in the same hole on the opposite side of the stem and repeat a leaf on the other side. End the yarn.

Motif 10. The cherries are ripe—a shocking pink cherry with green leaves. (Fig. 6-28.)
Pat Rug Yarn: shocking pink #259; green #545.

Cherry. Use pink yarn. Bring the needle up to the surface in A. (Fig. 6-29.) Work one Round Center (see the detailed directions preceding Pattern 9 in Chapter 5).

Stem and Leaves. Use green yarn. *Stem:* Bring the needle up to the surface in A. Work the stem as indicated in the diagram. Do not end the yarn. *Leaves:* Drop under on the wrong side and bring the needle up in B. Work the first leaf. Do not end the yarn. Bring the needle up in C and work the second leaf on the opposite side. End the yarn.

6-28. Motif 10.

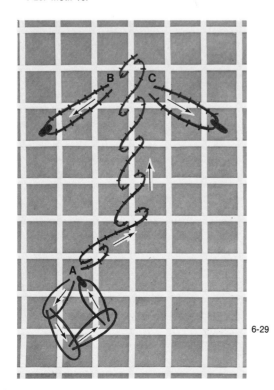

6-29

Motif 11. A Butterfly complements the flowers. (Fig. 6-30.)
Pat Rug Yarn: yellow #413.

Note: Figure 6-30 does not include the body of the butterfly, nor the antennae. Figure 6-57 shows the finished version of the two-color butterfly. The body is worked after the wings are completed. The antennae are worked on top of the background stitches.

Butterfly. Use yellow yarn. *Two small bottom sections:* Bring the needle up to the surface in A. Work one diagonal bottom section following Figure 6-31. The small inside chain is worked first—the outside larger chain around the small chain. Drop under on the wrong side and bring your needle up in A. Repeat this section on the opposite side. Do not end the yarn. *Two large upper sections:* Bring the needle up to the surface in B (the hole directly above A). Follow the direction of the arrows and work the outside row of wings in one continuous row, ending up in the center hole B and forming a figure 8. Do not end the yarn. Bring the needle up to the surface on the right side of the figure 8, in opening C. Work one Round Center (see the detailed directions preceding Pattern 9 in Chapter 5). Do not end the yarn. Drop under on the wrong side—catch once under the yarn—and bring the needle up to the surface on the left side of figure 8, in opening D. Work one Round Center. End the yarn.

Body. Use contrasting color yarn. The body is worked on top of the butterfly. Catch the yarn securely on the wrong side. Bring the needle up to the surface in 1. Go over the worked stitches and down in 2. Catch on the back but do not end the yarn. Bring the needle up in 1. Going under the surface stitch only, whip over and over again until the center surface stitch is solidly covered with whipped stitches. Work them tightly together and the body will stand out in three dimensions.

Antennae. Use a yarn of contrasting color which will show up on the background. Work the background first. Antennae are worked on top of the background stitches. Work two straight stitches in the form of V as follows. Bring the needle up in B (at the top of the body). Go up in a diagonal direction—over about 3 bars of canvas—and down to the wrong side. Bring the needle up in B and repeat the diagonal stitch on the other side. Bring the needle up at the top of the first stitch and work a French Knot (single strand—around the needle once). Repeat this on the second stitch. End the yarn.

Two-Color Butterfly. A two-color butterfly can be produced by using contrasting colors:

Color 1. Work the inside chain stitches of the bottom sections.

Color 2. Work the outside stitches of the bottom sections.

6-30. Motif 11.

6-31

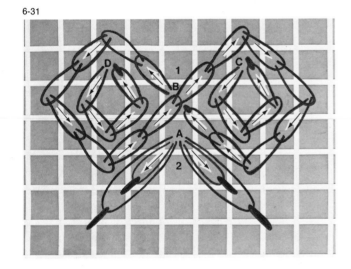

6-32. Motif 12.

2nd Row. Use white yarn. Bring the needle up in 2. Work a square of straight Chain Stitches, ending back in hole 2. End the yarn. Use pink yarn for the *French Knot in the center.* Work one French Knot (single strand—around the needle once).

Jelly Bean (B). Use pink yarn. Jelly beans can be scattered on a background or piled high close together in a candy dish or in the outline of a jar. Bring your needle up to the surface in 1. Work 2 diagonal chain stitches. Skip under on the wrong side to a spot where the next jelly bean is to be worked and bring the needle up to the surface. The canvas can be turned in order to work the jelly beans in different directions.

Striped Peppermint Candy (C).

1. Work pink stripes across (follow the solid black lines on the diagram). Use pink yarn. Bring the needle up to the surface in 1. Go over 3 bars of canvas and place the needle down in 2 and up in 3 in one motion (3 is the same hole as 1). Place the needle down in 4 and up in 5 in one motion. Continue until there are 6 pink stitches (2 in each hole). End the yarn.

2. Use white yarn. Follow the patterned lines in the diagram. Work white stripes between each set of 2 pink stitches. Bring the needle up to the surface in "a." Place the needle down in "b" and up in "c" in one motion. Continue until the 3 white stripes are completed.

Pink Hard Candy (D). Use pink yarn. Work the small diagonal inner chain first. Using the same hole to start, work 2 larger diagonal chains—the second chain around the first and the third chain around the second—stretching them as indicated in the diagram. End the yarn.

Small, Round, Pink, Hard Candy (E). Use pink yarn. Bring the needle up to the surface in 1. Work 4 small, straight Chain Stitches, ending back in hole 1.

Color 2. Work the outside row of the top wings.

Color 1. Work the inside sections of the top wings (two Round Centers).

Motif 12. Old-fashioned hard candy and a jelly bean make a tasty ensemble. (Fig. 6-32.)

Pat Rug Yarn: shocking pink #239; white #005.

Note: Leave 6 in. tails of yarn at the start and end of very small motifs for weaving in after the background is completed.

Fancy Old-Fashioned Hard Candy (A). 1st Row. Use pink yarn. Bring the needle up to the surface in 1. (Fig. 6-33, p.128.) Work a row around, following the direction of the arrows and ending back in hole 1. End the yarn.

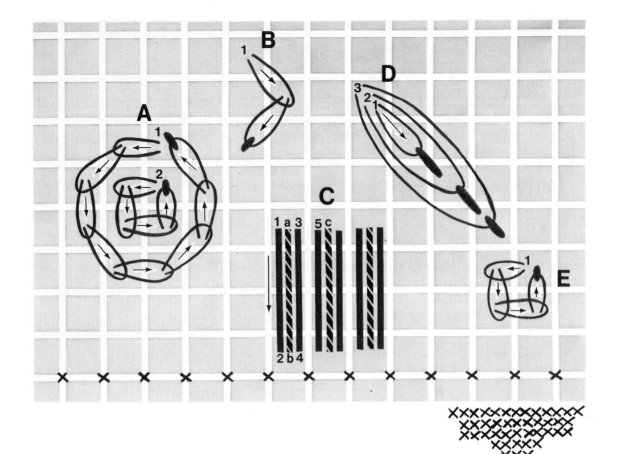

Design Note: If you follow the exact placement of the diagram (same spaces between candies), you can use the little key at the bottom and work a candy dish in the Orr Weave Stitch. The row of small X's under the candies show the exact placement for the dish. Work the top row of the dish on those crossbars of canvas. Then work the rows down until the shape of the dish is completed. See Figure 6-59, the mini pillow with the candy dish piled high, plus a sprightly candy cane on each side. I filled the candy dish with a sprinkling of jelly beans and small round shapes in a variety of colors after working the basic candies in the exact placement shown. You can easily design a different shape for a candy dish and pile the candies on top in your own fashion. Make a rough thumbnail sketch outlining the shape of the dish on graph paper (use X's as in the design shown) and work that first. In this way, you can pile your candy on top, so that it does not spill over. You can always think up some new candy shapes too! For a completely different effect, you could easily create a delightful design by keying straight rows of several different types of candy motifs.

Motif 13. A large decorative yellow tulip with fresh green leaves brings a breath of spring. (Fig. 6-34.)
Pat Rug Yarn: yellow #441; green #550.

Basic Yellow Tulip. Use yellow yarn. Follow Figure 6-35. The outside row is worked first. Subsequent rows are worked in toward the center.

1st Row. Bring the needle up to the surface in 1. Work the row completely around, turning the canvas when necessary. This first row keys the outside shape. The top outside points are a bit tricky to work, so follow the diagram carefully. Do not end the yarn.

6-34. Motif 13.

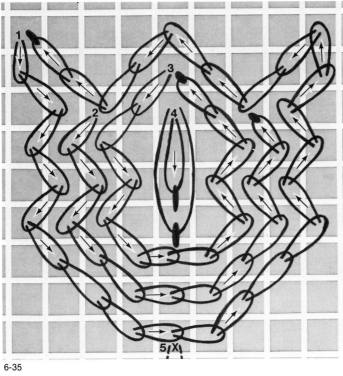

6-35

6-36

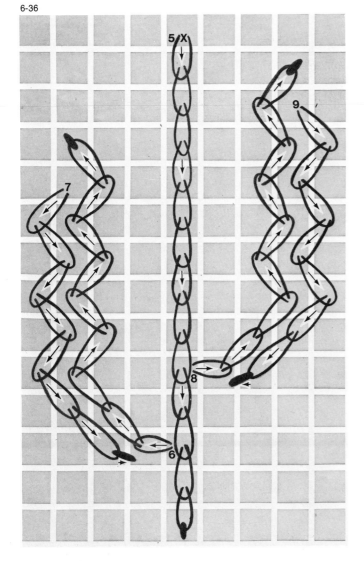

2nd Row. Drop under on the wrong side. Bring the needle up in 2. Work a row around, ending up on the right side. Do not end the yarn.

3rd Row. Drop under on the wrong side. Bring the needle up in 3. Work a row around, ending in the same hole 3. Do not end the yarn.

4th Row. Drop down one hole and bring the needle up in 4. Work the smaller center chain. Using the same hole, work the larger chain around the smaller chain. Push the yarn back to hook over the bottom bar. End the yarn.

Green Stem and Leaves. Use green yarn. The start of the stem is indicated in Figure 6-35 by X at the center bottom. Bring the needle up to the surface at this center point and follow Figure 6-36 for the stem and leaves.

5th Row. Bring the needle up in 5. Work down 13 straight Chain Stitches. Do not end the yarn.

6th Row. Bring the needle up in 6. At this point, start to turn the canvas—and the diagram too—upside down so that the arrows point in a downward direction toward you. Reverse the canvas and diagram at the top of each leaf to start the next row and you will find the diagram easy to follow. Complete the sixth row as indicated. Do not end the yarn.

7th Row. Bring the needle up in 7 and complete the row, ending in the hole indicated. Notice it is the same hole that was used in the sixth row.

8th Row. Drop under and bring your needle up on the right side of the stem at 8. Work the row. Do not end the yarn.

9th Row. Bring the needle up in 9. Work the row, ending in the same hole as was used for the eighth row as on the left leaf. End the yarn.

Surface Whipping on the Stem. Use Green yarn. Bring the needle up to the surface in X at the top of the stem. Surface whip every other chain stitch down to the bottom. End the yarn. See the directions with Figure 5-8 for a Zig Zag Chain. The whipping here is worked in the same manner except that the tulip stem has straight stitches.

Motif 14. Ladybug, ladybug, fly away home! An oversized perky ladybug in shocking pink, red and black holds appeal for all ages. (Fig. 6-37.) Three or four worked across a pillow could create a real eye-stopper.
Pat Rug Yarn: black #050; red #237; shocking pink #259.

The head is worked first—then the body. The finishing touches are worked in the order outlined.

Head. Use black yarn. Turn the canvas and Figure 6-38 upside down to start. Reverse the position of both at the end of each row for starts, so that the arrows point down toward you.

1st Row. Bring the needle up to the surface in 1. Work one Round Center, ending back in hole 1. Do not end the yarn.

2nd Row. Drop under and bring the needle up in hole 2. Work 2 diagonal Chain Stitches. Do not end the yarn.

3rd, 4th and 5th Rows. Continue to follow the diagram, dropping under to reach the correct spot for the start of the next row. When the fifth row is completed, end the yarn.

Body. Use red yarn. Starts for all the rows in the body are made with the canvas right side up. Turn the canvas when necessary for the correct position to work the stitches as each row progresses.

6th Row. Bring the needle up in 6 (the same hole as was used for the start of the fifth row). Work the outside row around, carefully following the turns on the diagram. The row ends on the right side of the head, in the same hole as was used for the start of the third row. This keys the outside shape of the body. Subsequent rows are worked in toward the center.

7th, 8th and 9th Rows. Work the rows around. Notice that the eighth and ninth rows end in the same holes as where they began.

10th Row. Work 2 straight Chain Stitches to close in the center. Push the yarn back to find the canvas bars if necessary.

Decorative Shocking Pink Necklace and French Knot on the Bottom. Use pink yarn. *Necklace:* Follow the patterned bars separating the head and body in the diagram. Catch securely on the wrong side before you bring the needle up to the surface in the center hole (same hole as 1 and 8). Go over the bars of canvas to the right side as indicated. Place the needle down at the right side and up in the center hole. Go over the bars of canvas and place the needle down at the left side. Catch securely on the wrong side but do not end the yarn. This creates 2 straight

6-37. Motif 14.

stitches across the neck. *Surface whipping:* Bring the needle up to the surface at the left side of the straight stitches. Turn the canvas 90 degrees so that the straight stitches are in a vertical position. Whip over the two stitches as many times as necessary to form a solid, tight row. Continue over the middle break and it will not be noticeable. The whipping should be tight to resemble cording. Do not end the yarn. The next step is simply a fun touch of whimsy! *Bottom French Knot:* Run the yarn down, catching on the wrong side and place a French Knot (single strand—around the needle twice) in the center bottom. End the yarn.

Note: Catch all French Knots over worked yarn or, whenever possible, over a canvas bar to prevent them from slipping through to the wrong side.

Eyes. Use red yarn. Work 2 French Knots (single strand—around the needle twice) in those spots on the head indicated by the black dots on the diagram.

Black Decorative French Knots on the Body. Use black yarn. Work the black French Knots (single strand— around the needle once) on the body approximately following their placement in the photograph. I left some plain area down the middle to suggest separate wings.

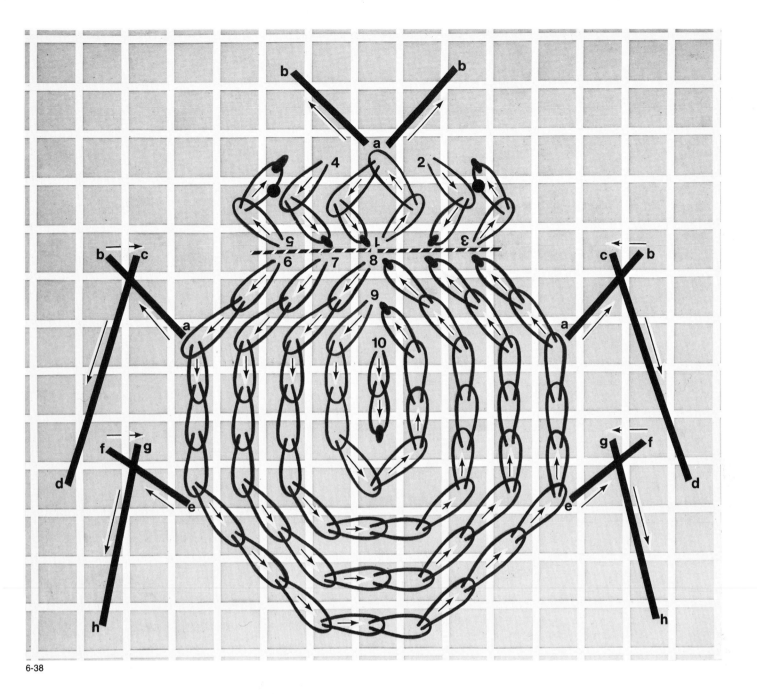

6-38

Antennae and Legs. Both the antennae and the legs are worked on the surface *after the background has been worked.* You have to hunt a bit for the correct holes, but the background Orr Weave Stitches stand out individually, so you can determine where the needle should go down and up. The important point is to have them identical on each side. I hooked the legs around the bars of canvas to simulate the scratchy look of bug legs. *Antennae:* Use black yarn. Bring the needle up to the surface at top of the head in "a". Place the needle down in "b" to the left and up in "a". Place the needle down in "b" to the right. Do not end the yarn. *Legs:* Run the yarn under on the wrong side. Bring the needle up to the surface in

"a" at the upper leg on the left side. Place the needle down in "b". Hooking the needle around the canvas bar, as shown in the diagram, bring it up to the surface in "c". Place the needle down in "d". Drop under on the wrong side to start of the bottom leg and bring the needle up in "e". Work the lower leg following the diagram for placement. When you have completed the 2 left legs, do not end the yarn. Run under the body on the wrong side and bring the needle up in "a" at the upper leg on the right side. Follow the directions of the arrows in repeating the legs on the right side. Hook the yarn around the canvas in a reverse direction.

Keying Designs with Wiggly Chain Design Motifs. This can be a joyous, creative adventure! You need not start from scratch since you have helpful aids in the form of the already designed individual motifs. By combining or repeating the individual motifs, you can create your own designs and quickly produce professional-looking finished items. As an example, I will go through the steps which would lead you up to the apple and worm pillow. (See Fig. 6-47.) You can use the same method to produce many combinations if you make up working samples as suggested.

1. Figure 6-39 shows the two Design Motifs. They are completely different shapes, so you must give thought to their placement in order to achieve asymmetric balance and please the eye. A few rough thumbnail sketches help to pull your creative thoughts into focus. An easy way to arrive at the best placement is to move the two samples around, overlapping them, switching them around, using the Squint Test—until your eye is satisfied. (Fig. 6-40.) Try to visualize the background area. Using four pieces of plain white paper as suggested in Step 3 can be of great assistance at this point too.

2. When you have decided on the placement, you must then determine the correct spot to start each motif by referring to the motif diagrams. Place the canvas on which the finished design is to be worked on top of the two overlapping motifs (you can see right through it). Place yarn tie markers on the exact spots where the two motifs are to be started. The starts are indicated by 1 on each of the motif diagrams. I worked the apple first in this design. When the apple motif is completed, double-check the correct spot for the start of the worm. When one motif is completed, it is much easier to determine the correct spot to start the second motif. Complete the worm.

3. Determine how much background area you wish and place a yarn tie marker in each of the four corners as guides. The background should appear to be even all around. This does not always mean that there is an equal number of rows or stitches on each side or on the top and bottom. If completely different shapes are involved—as with the apple and worm—you must arrive at the best proportions for the design which appear even, as shown in the finished sample. A good trick, used by many artists in cropping a drawing or painting, is to place pieces of plain paper on all four sides of your design—overlapping them to form a mat which frames the area. Keep moving them slightly until you determine the desired area. Use the Squint Test again. Then place the four yarn tie markers in the corners. Remember to allow space for the roll along the edge of a knife-edge pillow or pincushion. I can state that without exception designs keyed with the individual motifs need ample background around them to set them off properly. If you key your designs so that the motifs are close to the edges, they will look as if they are sliding off the top or moving around to the back. After

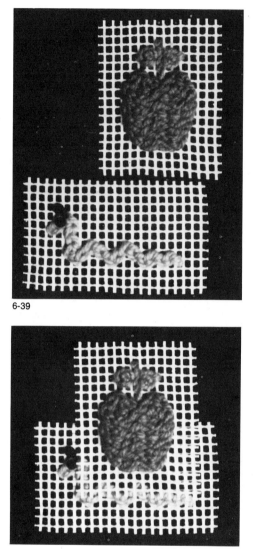

6-39

6-40

having worked the Design Motifs on the canvas, I often place the canvas on top of any pillow to see what will happen when the design rolls back around the pillow stuffing. This helps you decide how much surrounding area is needed.

Repeat motifs used for symmetric designs are keyed in a different manner. I make a number of rough thumbnail sketches and try different arrangements to establish the number of motifs across, the number of motifs down. Should they be in rows or a border around? Always keep in mind the size of the repeat motif and how large an area you wish to cover. Prepare your canvas and work one motif. You must decide which is the best spot to start the first motif. It is impossible to give you a rule for this; it depends so much on the type of design you are keying. Repeat motifs must be equidistant in most designs. Many times it is best to start in a corner and work across.

Work the first motif. Then place your working sample underneath the canvas on which the design is being worked and determine the distance you wish between the motifs. Place a yarn tie marker in the exact spot where the second motif will be started. If there are many repeats in your design, you can devise a little formula for determining the proper spots for starts. For example: so many bars (or holes) over from the side of the last worked motif—so many bars (or holes) down from the top. You can mark the starts for the entire first row if you wish. When the first row is completed, place the working sample underneath and again move it around for placement of the motifs in the second row. The motifs can be worked directly under those in the first row and this forms vertical stripes if placed close together, or else, place them down a bit and halfway between those in the first row, as in the large strawberry pillow. (See Fig. 6-55.)

I suggest you complete a finished item involving only one or two Design Motifs before you attempt to combine a large grouping. Once you understand the techniques, you can then easily key many variations of combinations that involve any number of motifs. Vertical or horizontal rows or stripes of motifs can produce delightful eye-catching patterns, such as rows of several different fruits, rows of flowers, alternating rows of flowers and bees or rows of flowers with green leaves interspersed. Press the Aware Button and do your own thing!

WIGGLY CHAIN FINISHED ITEMS

Shocking pink and purple posies form a charming border design for a dainty-size pillow. (Fig. 6-41.) Size of sample: 9¼ in. × 11½ in. The pillow has shocking pink velvet backing and cording.
Pat Rug Yarn: shocking pink #259 (5 str.); purple #632 (2 str.); green #545 (6 str.); white #005 (33 str.).

The floral border design is made up of 10 repeats of Motif 6 (Fig. 6-21). Follow the instructions given for working the individual motifs. Figure 6-42 shows the placement: 4 motifs across, 3 up and down, with one row of background stitches between the petals of adjoining motifs. The pillow top is worked in the following order: 1. Work all of the pink petals around the border. 2. Work all of the green leaves between petals. (The French Knots are worked after the background is completed.) 3. Work all of the purple centers. 4. Work the white background. 5. Work the green French Knots.

Note: Drop under on the wrong side from one motif to the next until the yarn runs out when you work different colors in the motifs. Start with the motif in the upper left corner, so that at least 10 horizontal and 10 vertical bars of canvas will be left free on top and to the left side of the motif when it is completed. This allows 6 bars for the surrounding white background, plus 4 extra ones along the edges. (If it is available, place a working sample

6-41

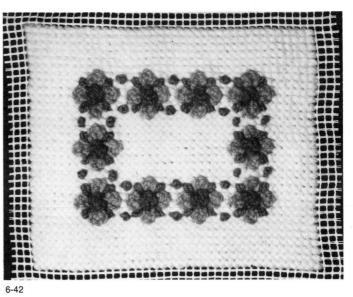

6-42

underneath the canvas to determine the correct spot to start.)

Pink Petals. Use pink yarn. Follow Figure 6-42 for placement. Using the correct spot to start, work 4 petals of the first motif. Do not end the yarn. Drop under on the wrong side and bring your needle up in the correct spot to start the second motif (to the right), leaving one free bar of canvas between the 2 motifs. The second motif must be in exact alignment with the first. Work 4 petals of the second motif. Do not end the yarn. Continue across to the right until there are 4 sets of petals, with one free bar between each set. The next 2 sets of petals are worked directly under the fourth. Continue around the 4 sides of the rectangle, working all 10 sets of pink petals with the one free bar between each grouping. End the yarn.

Green Leaves. Use green yarn. Work 4 green leaves between the petals of each of the 10 sets. Drop under on the wrong side to move to the next set.

Purple Centers. Use purple yarn. Work a purple center in the middle of each flower motif. Drop under on the wrong side to move to the next flower.

Background. See Chapter 7 for Orr Weave Stitch directions and information on backgrounds. Follow Figure 6-42. The central overall design area of 10 flower motifs is surrounded on all sides by a background area that is 6 stitches deep. Mark the 4 corners as follows. Start with any one of the 4 corner motifs. Using the *2 pink outer-corner petals* as guides, place a finger from each hand on the sixth free canvas bar in the 2 outward directions. Run your fingers along the 2 bars toward the corner. Tie a yarn marker diagonally over the crossbar where they meet. Repeat this at all four corners. The corner stitches will be worked over the crossbars of canvas on which the markers have been placed. Use white yarn. The Orr Weave Stitch is worked from right to left across the canvas. The first stitch is worked over the crossbar of canvas indicated by the yarn marker. Remove the markers immediately before working the corner stitches.

1st Row. Work one row completely across the top, from the right yarn marker to the left. End the yarn. Double-check the canvas bar count on top and the 2 sides since this first row keys the background area.

2nd Row. Start at the right, directly under the preceding row and work the second row.

3rd, 4th, 5th and 6th Rows. Work them the same way as the second row.

7th Row. Start at the right side as in the previous rows. Drop underneath the motifs as you reach them, filling in the stitches between. Complete the row to the left edge. Catch the yarn once on the wrong side under the motifs to help keep the stitches even around the motifs. Do not pull the yarn tight around the motifs. Let the yarn "live" and work as many stitches as necessary to prevent the canvas from peeking through.

Continue working the remaining rows down to and including the bottom bar on which the yarn markers are tied. Rows of stitches are continued across the central area when that is reached.

Green French Knots. Use green yarn. Follow Figure 6-42 for placement. Work French Knots (single strand—around the needle twice) on top of the background halfway between the ends of green leaves. Notice the placement at the inside corners. Catch over the bars of canvas so that the knots will not pull through to the back. This added note of color pulls the motifs together to unify the border design effect. Use white yarn. Work one row of Regular Fill-in Stitches (see Chapter 8) around the

background area when it is completed. This row will be cropped during construction.

See Chapter 8 for directions for attaching material backing and cording.

Design Note: This border design can be worked in a variety of sizes by increasing or decreasing the number of motifs in each direction. If you wish a square shape instead of a rectangle, work an even number of motifs on all sides.

A decorative pink and red and black ladybug on a pincushion or mini pillow charms the eye. (Fig. 6-43.) Size of sample: 5¾ in. square. Add a fancy Now Needlepoint backing.
Pat Rug Yarn: black #050 (3 str.); red #237 (10 str.); shocking pink #259 (10 str.); white #005 (9 str.).

6-43

Ladybug Design Motif. Follow the directions under Motif 14. (See Fig. 6-38.) Work the head, body, decorative necklace and all the French Knots. Follow the colors indicated. Do not work the antennae and legs.

Background. Use white yarn. The Orr Weave Stitch runs in vertical rows from top to bottom. Place yarn tie markers in each corner as follows. *Two top corners:* Place a finger of one hand on the fifth canvas bar up from the top of the head. Place a finger of the other hand on the fifth bar of canvas out to one side of widest part of the red body. Run your fingers along bars toward the corner and tie markers diagonally over the crossbar where they meet. Repeat this procedure for the opposite top corner. *Two bottom corners:* Run a finger horizontally along the third bar down from the bottom of the body and tie yarn markers over crossbars in alignment with the top 2 corner markers. The corner stitches will be worked over the 4 crossbars indicated by the markers. Remove the markers just before working the stitches. Double-check your count—5 free bars each on the top and two sides, 3 bars on the bottom (18-stitch square). *To start:* Turn the canvas 90 degrees so that the head is on the right side. With the canvas in this position, start at the top right. Work stitches in horizontal rows from right to left until the 18-stitch square of white background is formed. When you reach the ladybug motif, work the area along the top of the motif, then along the bottom; then resume the longer straight runs along the side. The bug is too large to skip under. When working the short runs at the top and bottom, I wove back under the completed short row on the wrong side to the correct position to start the next short row rather than start and end the yarn each time.

Antennae and Legs. Use black yarn. Work antennae and legs as instructed for Motif 14 on the surface of the background.

6-44

Now Needlepoint Backing. See Figure 6-44. The backing is worked in rows around the square. Start under the lower right corner of the topside. Use red yarn. Leave one free bar of canvas between areas (for braid stitch construction). Work 18 stitches from right to left, turning the canvas at corners until an 18-stitch square outline is completed. Use Corner A (directions in Chapter 7). The backing is worked in rows from the outside in toward the middle in the following color pattern: 1st and 2nd Rows, red; 3rd Row, pink; 4th Row, red; 5th Row, pink; 6th and 7th Rows, red; 8th and 9th Rows, pink (these last two form the square in the center).

Follow the basic directions for the braid construction and stuffing given for the rosebud mini pillow in Chapter 8. Use pink yarn (single strand). Work the Regular Braid Stitch—Start A.

Fresh lime slices combined with candy sticks create a pillow with quiet charm. (Fig. 6-45.) Size of sample: 8½ in. × 10½ in. Shiny white embroidery floss adds a decorative touch. Add green velvet cording and backing.
Pat Rug Yarn: deep green #550 (8 str.); pale green #580 (7 str.); white #005 (24 str.). DMC Perle Cotton #3, white (approximately 25 yds.).

Follow the detailed directions for the Lime Design Motif 4 (Fig. 6-17) using the colors listed here. Lighter values of green were used for the pillow to create a pastel effect. Follow Figure 6-46 for the placement of lime slices and candy sticks. Use deep green yarn. Start at the top left corner and work the outer first row of corner lime slice, leaving at least 8 free bars of canvas on top and 8 free bars to the left side. Work the outer rows of all 3 limes in the first vertical row—one directly under the other—leaving one free horizontal bar of canvas between motifs. (This

6-45

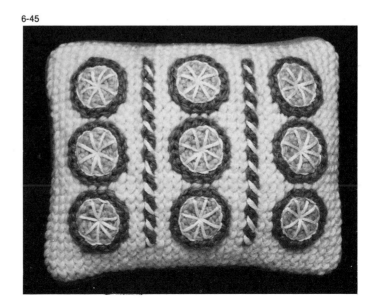

135

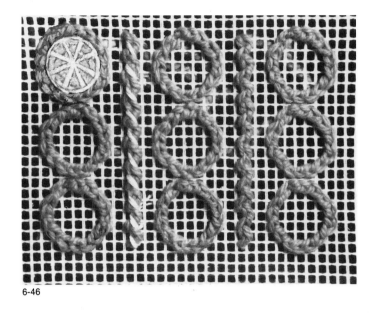

6-46

bar is not visible in some spots in Fig. 6-46.) The centers will be filled in later. Use deep green yarn. Start at the top. Move to the right on the top horizontal bar used for lime so that there are 2 vertical bars left free and work 20 Single Zig Zag Chain Stitches down to the horizontal bar that is even with the bottom lime. End the yarn. Work outlines of the second row of limes so that there are 2 vertical bars left free between the limes and row of Single Zig Zags. Continue across, following the photograph and completing 3 rows of lime slices with the two candy sticks between them. Fill in the centers of limes with pale green yarn as instructed for Motif 4.

White Surface Stitches on Lime Slices. Use white DMC Perle Cotton #3 (single strand doubled). Follow the directions for dividing centers into sections. Because the embroidery cotton is finer than the rug yarn, I worked a Stem Stitch between the first and second rows for the continuous white line around.

White Surface Whipping on the Candy Sticks. Use white DMC Perle Cotton #3 (double strand doubled—4 strands). Start at the top of the candy sticks and surface whip every other Chain Stitch down to the bottom. (See Pattern 1A in Ch. 5 and Fig. 5-8.)

Background. Place yarn tie markers in the corner as follows: Using a corner lime motif as a guide, count 4 canvas bars in the 2 outward directions. Run your fingers along the bars and tie a yarn marker diagonally over the crossbar where they meet. Repeat this procedure in the 4 corners. The corner stitches will be worked over the crossbars indicated by the markers. Remove the markers just before working the stitches. The background is worked in the Orr Weave Stitch in vertical rows from the

top to bottom. Use white yarn. Turn the canvas 90 degrees so that the rows of limes and candy sticks run in a horizontal direction. With the canvas in this position, start at the top right and work stitches from right to left. Fill in the background indicated by the markers. The lime motifs are small, so you can drop under on the wrong side and continue the rows across without ending the yarn. Remember to work the single background stitches *between* the lime motifs. The surrounding background area should be 4 stitches deep on all sides. Use white yarn. Work one row of Regular Fill-in Stitches around the background area where it is completed. This will be cropped when construction takes place.

See Chapter 8 for directions for attaching material backing and cording.

Kooky purple worm eyes a luscious red apple in a fun mini pillow or extra-large pincushion. (Fig. 6-47.) Size of sample: 6½ in. square. Add a background of yellow-green, with matching velvet cording and backing.
Pat Rug Yarn: purple #632 (1 str.); dark green #528 (1 str.); red #237 (3 str.); light green #565 (17 str.).

Note: The designing steps are explained in detail under Figures 6-39 and 6-40.

6-47

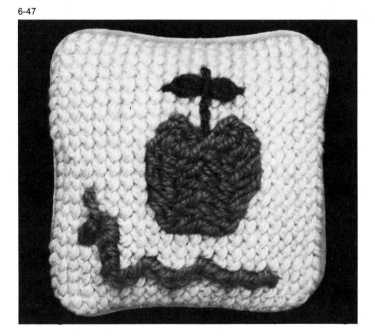

Red Apple. Follow the instructions for Motif 9 (Fig. 6-27) using the colors listed here.

1. Use red yarn. Start by bringing the needle up to the surface in the correct hole, indicated by 1 at the top center of the apple (see Fig. 6-27) so that there are at least 17 bars of canvas to the left of the start and 14 bars on top. Work the basic shape of the apple.

2. Use dark green yarn. Work the stem and leaves.

Purple Worm. Use purple yarn. Follow the directions for Motif 2 (Fig. 6-13) using the colors listed here. The worm should be placed so that there are the same number of background stitches (or bars of canvas at this point) between the apple and worm as in the sample. This is where your working sample will come in handy if you have one. Simply place it underneath, moving it to the correct place, and you can easily determine the exact spot to start the head. Complete the body of the worm.

Antennae. Use purple yarn. Work the antennae on top of the worm's head.

Eye. Use red yarn. Work one French Knot (single strand—around the needle once) in the correct spot for the eye.

Background. Use light green yarn. The Orr Weave background stitches run in vertical rows from top to bottom. Mark the 4 corners with yarn tie markers as follows. Count up 3 bars of canvas from the top of the green stem. Count out 3 bars to the left of the worm's nose. Run your fingers along the bars toward the top left corner and place a yarn marker diagonally over the crossbar where they meet.

6-48

Count down 3 bars from the bottom points of the worm. Count out 3 bars to the left of the nose. Run your fingers along the bars toward the lower left corner and place markers over the crossbar where they meet. The right 2 corner markers are placed on the fourth bar to the right of the worm's tail at the 2 points where it crosses the top and bottom horizontal bars indicated by the markers at the left corners. Double-check the stitch count. The

background area should form a square with equal number of stitches on each side. (The sample has 22 stitches.) Adjust the corner markers at this point if necessary. Make certain motifs appear to be centered in the area. To start, turn the canvas 90 degrees so the worm is on the left side. With the canvas in this position, start at the top right and work the background stitches in horizontal rows from right to left. Markers indicate where the corner stitches will be worked. Remove them just before working the stitches. When you reach the motifs, skip under on the wrong side and continue the row to the edge. I caught the yarn once on each skip under the apple since it is rather a long run. Work the stitches around the motifs so that no canvas peeks through. Work one row of Regular Fill-in Stitches (see Chapter 8) around the background area when it is completed. This row will be cropped during construction.

See Chapter 8 for directions for attaching material backing and cording.

⬤⬤⬤⬤⬤⬤

Honey bees and flowers combine to create charm for a pillow top. Orange, yellow, black and touches of green create a sparkling effect on a white background. (Fig. 6-49.) Size of sample: 9 in. square. Add a gold velvet cording and backing.
Pat Rug Yarn: orange #421 (6 str.); green #545 (1 str.); black #050 (6 str.); yellow #413 (2 str.); white #005 (28 str.).

6-49

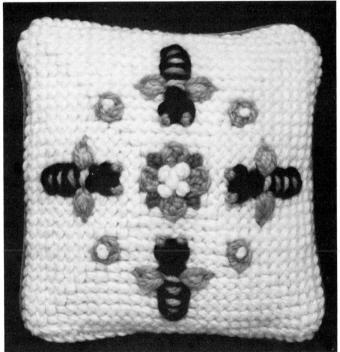

Figure 6-50 shows placement of the motifs before the background was completed. Motifs are worked in the following order: Center flower, 4 bees, 4 small flowers between bees.

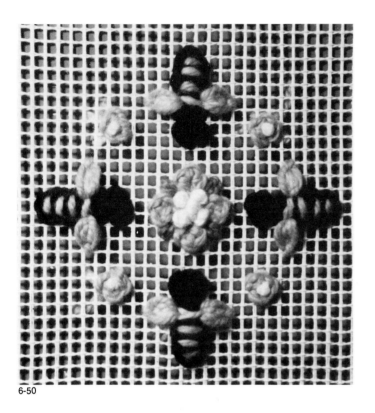

6-50

Center Flower. Follow the directions for Motif 6 (Fig. 6-21), substituting the colors indicated and the French Knot Center. The color pattern is: 4 petals, orange; 4 leaves, green. In the center of the flowers, substitute the French Knot Center. (See the directions under Fig. 5-18.) Use white yarn (single strand doubled—around the needle once).

Four Bees. Follow the directions for Motif 7 (Fig. 6-23), substituting the colors indicated. Individual bees are placed directly opposite the 4 petals so that there are 2 free bars of canvas between the outer point of each petal and bee. Use black yarn for the heads and bodies. Work the head and body of each bee as directed. The color pattern for the stripes, wings and eyes follow. *Stripes:* Start at the top with a yellow stripe. A-yellow; B-orange; C-yellow; D-orange. *Wings:* small inner Chain Stitch yellow, outer Chain Stitch orange. *Eyes:* orange.

Small Flowers between Bees. See instructions for the Round Center under Figure 5-16. Use orange yarn. Work 4 Round Centers halfway between each pair of bees as shown in Figure 6-50. Place them carefully so that the color pattern of wings and small flowers runs around the

design to form a circle of color. Place a white French Knot (single strand—around the needle once) in each center. Catch over the yarn so that they do not slip through to the back.

Background. Use the Orr Weave Stitch. Mark the 4 corners with yarn ties as follows. Count 3 bars of canvas out from the bottom of a bee. Count 3 bars out from the bottom of a bee to one side. Run your fingers along the bars toward the corner and tie a yarn marker diagonally over the crossbar where they meet. Continue until the 4 corners are marked. The corner background stitches will be worked over the crossbars indicated by the markers. Remove the markers just before working the stitches. The background is worked so that there are 3 rows beyond the bottom of each of the 4 bees. Start at any corner. Use white yarn. Work stitches from right to left. Use the yarn markers as guides. Work the outer row of background stitches around the square, using Corner A. Subsequent rows are worked in toward the center, using the previous row as a guide. Drop under on the wrong side when you reach the motifs and continue the row of background stitches on the other side. Work stitches close to the motifs in order to cover the canvas. Push the wings on the bees over and work the background stitches underneath to give the appearance of dimension. Continue working the rows around the square in toward the center, ending with the last row of stitches around the leaves between the petals of the center flower.

Work one row of Regular Fill-in Stitches (see Ch. 8) completely around the background area when it is completed. This row will be cropped during construction. Pull the motifs on top of the background with your needle where necessary.

See Chapter 8 for directions for attaching velvet cording and backing.

A strawberry delight pincushion with fancy Now Needlepoint backing can be made in a twinkling! A combination of deep shocking pink, pale pink, yellow-green and white evokes thoughts of strawberries and cream. (Fig. 6-51.) Size of sample: 5 in. square.
Pat Rug Yarn: deep shocking pink #259 (12 str.); green #545 (2 str.); pale shocking pink #831 (5 str.); white #005 (8 str.).

Work Strawberry Motif 3 (Fig. 6-15) in the topside center area as follows:

Strawberry. Start at the upper left corner of the canvas. Count 14 bars of canvas across from left to right. Hold your finger on this bar and, counting the top bar as one, count down 11 bars. The strawberry motif is started in the hole which is in a downward right diagonal direction from the eleventh crossbar. Work Motif 3 as directed, including the green leaves and seeds.

6-51

Frame. The outer frame of deep shocking pink and pale pink is worked next in rows around the square. Start in the upper right corner. To find the correct spot to start, count up 5 bars from the top of the right green leaf. Hold the finger of your left hand on this bar. Count out 6 bars to

6-52

the right of the widest part of the strawberry. Hold the finger of your right hand on this bar. Run your fingers along the 2 bars toward the upper right corner. Place a yarn tie marker diagonally over the crossbar where they meet.

1st Row. Use deep shocking pink yarn. Start on the crossbar where the marker is tied (remove it before starting the first stitch). Work 16 Orr Weave Stitches in a right-to-left direction, turning the corner after the sixteenth stitch. Use Corner A for working rows in toward the center. Complete the row around, turning the canvas when necessary, so that there are 16 stitches on each side of square. End the yarn.

2nd Row. Use pale pink yarn. Work one row of Orr Weave Stitches around the square directly inside the first row. End the yarn.

White Background. Turn the canvas 90 degrees so that the top becomes the right side. Use white yarn. With the canvas in this position, start at the upper right (inside frame) and work 12 stitches from right to left. End the yarn and start the second row at the right directly under the first white row. Continue working the rows—one under the other—until the exposed canvas in the center area is completely filled with white stitches. When you reach the area where the strawberry is worked, skip under on the wrong side and bring the needle up to the surface at the other end to continue the row. Be certain to work sufficient background stitches close to the outside edges of the motif so that the canvas is properly covered.

Corner Leaves and French Knots. *Leaves:* Use green yarn. Bring the needle up to the surface in the corner of the white background, diagonally in toward the center so that one white corner stitch is left exposed. Follow Figure 6-52. Work one small Lazy Daisy Stitch (about the depth of one Orr Weave Stitch) in a vertical direction and then, bringing the needle back up to the surface in the same spot, work one Lazy Daisy Stitch in a horizontal direction. The Lazy Daisy Stitches should follow the contour of the outer frame. Repeat the same process in the 4 corners. *French Knots:* Use deep shocking pink yarn. Work one French Knot (single strand—around the needle twice) in the same spot where the needle was brought to the surface between each pair of green leaves.

Fancy Backing. The backing is worked directly under the top, leaving one free bar of exposed canvas between as shown in Figure 6-52. Stitches are worked in rows around the square.

1st Row. Leave one free bar between. Start under the bottom right corner of the top. Use deep shocking pink yarn. Work Orr Weave Stitches from right to left. Complete the row around the square, turning the canvas when necessary, so that there are 16 stitches on each side duplicating the exact area of the top. End the yarn.

Subsequent Rows: Work them in toward the center in the following colors. 2nd Row, pale pink; 3rd Row, white; 4th, deep shocking pink; 5th, pale pink; 6th, white; 7th, deep shocking pink. *Center:* Use deep shocking pink yarn. Work a Round Center following the directions under Figure 5-16. *Braid construction:* Follow the basic directions for braid construction and stuffing given for the rosebud mini pillow in Chapter 8. Use deep shocking pink yarn (single strand). Work the Regular Braid Stitch—Start A.

━━●●●●●●━━

A pillow to brighten any décor. Crisp white tulips on a green background shout spring! Saucy French Knots and leaves of brilliant yellow add decorative touches. (Fig. 6-53.) Size of sample: 9 in. × 12½ in. Add velvet cording and backing.
Pat Rug Yarn: White #005 (8 str.); yellow #413 (8 str.); green #545 (33 str.).

Follow the directions for Motif 13 (Figs. 6-35 and 6-36) using the colors listed here.

6-53

Tulips. Use white yarn. Start with the center tulip. Find the center of the canvas by folding it in half vertically. Count down at least 11 bars of canvas from the top. Counting the center hole as one, move to the left and bring the needle up to the surface in the fifth hole to the left of center. This is the correct hole to start the first tulip motif so that it will be centered in the design. Work the first tulip motif (without stems and leaves). Work 2 side motifs, leaving 4 free bars of canvas between each and the center motif. A working sample is helpful at this point. The right motif is easy to start. The left takes a bit of figuring—4 bars to be left free for background plus 8 for the tulip motif. Count to

the left. Bring the needle up to the surface in the hole to the left of the twelfth vertical bar from the top left point of the center motif and you are ready to start the left motif.

Yellow Stems and Leaves. Use yellow yarn. Work stems and leaves on the 3 motifs. (The French Knots are worked after the background is completed.)

Background. Tie yarn markers in the corners as follows. Use the sides as guides. Count up 7 bars of canvas above the top side points of the tulip. Count out 6 bars from the side of the tulip. Run your fingers along the bars toward a top corner and tie a marker diagonally over the crossbar of canvas where they meet. Repeat this for the opposite top corner. Count down 2 bars from the bottom of the stem. Count out 6 bars from the side of an outside leaf.

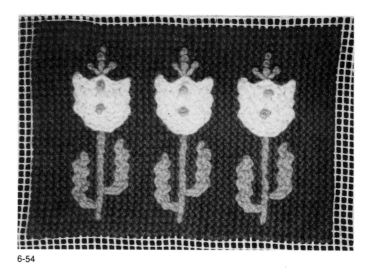

6-54

Run your fingers along the bars toward a bottom corner and tie a yarn marker diagonally over the crossbar where they meet (it should be in line with the top corner marker). Repeat this procedure for the opposite bottom corner. The background is worked in the Orr Weave Stitch. Rows run vertically from top to bottom. Use green yarn. Turn the canvas 90 degrees so that the white tulips are on the right. With the canvas in this position and using the yarn tie markers as guides for the corners, start at the top right and work the first row across from right to left. Continue working rows, one under the other, skipping under the motifs on the wrong side (catch once on long runs) until the background area is completed.

Note: When working background along the sides of stems, push back the yellow yarn to cover bars of canvas which are slightly hidden underneath. It is a squeeze but will produce a three-dimensional look. Pull the motifs to the surface with a needle when necessary after the background is completed so that they appear to be on top of the background.

140

Work one row of Regular Fill-in Stitches (see Chapter 8) around the background area. This row will be cropped during construction.

Decorative Yellow French Knots. Use yellow yarn (single strand—around the needle twice) for all knots. See Figure 6-54. Place 2 French Knots in the center of each white tulip (approximate placement—top and bottom of the fourth row of the motif). Work over a bar of canvas so that they do not slip through to the back. Bring the yarn up to the surface in the hole used for the top center point of the tulip. Work 3 French Knots—one on top of the other—catching each over a bar of canvas. Bring the needle up to the surface at the top of the center point of the tulip, directly under the three knots. Work one Straight Stitch ½ in. in length in an upward right diagonal direction. Bring the needle up in the same spot at the center point of the tulip and work a matching upward diagonal Straight Stitch on the left. Work a French Knot at the end of each stitch. Repeat this on all 3 tulips.

See Chapter 8 for the directions for attaching material backing and cording.

ᗢᗢᗢᗢᗢ

A feast for the eyes! A strawberry festival on a maxi pillow is this repeat pattern of shocking pink strawberries. (Fig. 6-55.) The purple and white striped background is framed with a pink border. Add a matching velvet backing. Size of sample: 11½ in. × 17½ in.
Pat Rug Yarn: shocking pink #259 (26 str.); green #545 (5 str.); white #005 (33 str.); purple #632 (15 str.).

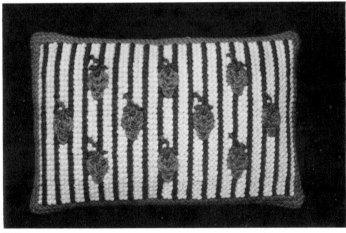

6-55

Note: The background area within the pink border can be worked in solid white to create an equally attractive effect. The purple strand count should then be added to the white.

The design is worked in the following order: strawberries in horizontal rows, purple and white striped background and then the pink border.

Strawberries. Follow the directions for Motif 3 (Fig. 6-15) including the color pattern. The strawberries are worked in horizontal rows from top to bottom.

1st Row, Three Motifs. Start with the middle strawberry in the top row. Find the exact middle of the canvas by folding it in half vertically. Count down at least 13 bars from the top edge of the canvas. Bring the needle up to the surface in the center hole directly under the thirteenth bar for the start of the first strawberry. Complete the center strawberry. At this point a working sample is extremely helpful. Slip it underneath, count bars between and you will easily determine the correct spots to start the subsequent strawberries. Work the 2 side strawberries in exact alignment with the first. Work them so that there are 10 free bars of canvas (at the widest part of the strawberry) between each side strawberry and the center motif. (Use the widest part of the strawberry as the guide throughout.)

2nd Row, Four Motifs. Notice that the second row is dropped down and the motifs (Fig. 6-56) are worked so that they fall halfway between those in the top row. Start with either of the motifs closest to the center. Find the center row of holes between 2 of the top motifs (5 bars on each side using the widest part of the strawberry as guide). Drop down and bring your needle up to the surface in the correct hole to start the strawberry so it will be placed exactly as shown in the photograph. (The top of the stem falls on the same horizontal bar used for the bottoms of the top strawberries.) Complete the strawberry. Repeat the second center strawberry on the opposite side, leaving 10 free vertical bars between the 2 motifs. Work the 2 side motifs, lining them up exactly and leaving 10 free bars between motifs.

3rd Row. This row is exactly the same as the first row and is worked directly under the top 3 motifs (down and halfway between those worked in the second row). Work them so that the top of each stem falls on the same horizontal bar used for the bottoms of strawberries in the second row.

Striped Background Area. This is a case where the surrounding background area must be worked to look even. Four bars of canvas are used for background at the bottom and 2 sides but only 3 above the stems on the top. It is necessary to make allowances for the extra background area around the thin stems to equalize the eye's perception of the overall surrounding area. This is an important point to keep in mind when you are keying your own designs. The background is worked in the Orr Weave Stitch in vertical rows which run from top to bottom. Use white yarn. The 2 *center* rows of white are worked first. These 2 center rows form the white stripe which runs

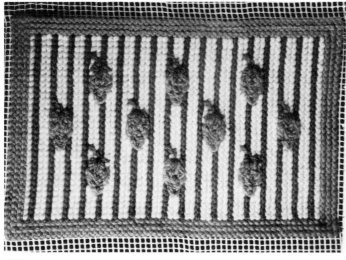

6-56

pink yarn. Start in the lower right corner. Work the stitches from right to left, turning the canvas when you reach the corners. Work one row completely around the striped area. Continue working rows, one outside the other, until there are 3 rows of pink.

Work one row of Regular Fill-in Stitches (see Chapter 8) around the entire area. This row will be cropped during construction.

See Chapter 8 for directions for attaching material backing. Cording is not necessary since the 3 outside pink rows create a frame.

━━━━━

Petite flowers and decorative butterfly become delightful companions in a pincushion of blue, purple and white with Now Needlepoint backing. (Fig. 6-57.) Size of sample: 3½ in. × 7½ in.

Pat Rug Yarn: blue #760 (13 str.); purple #632 (3 str.); white #005 (10 str.).

Note: This little item can be made in a flash in endless color combinations and can be a charming gift for

directly through the exact centers of the 2 middle motifs in the first row and third row. (Fig. 6-56.) Subsequent rows are worked out from this center stripe in two directions. Turn the canvas 90 degrees so that the stems are on the right. Start at the right. Count 3 bars out to the right from the bar of canvas used for the top of the stem of the center motif. Start the first stitch on the correct bar which will run through the middle of the motif (forming one half of the white stripe). Work the row from right to left, dropping under to the wrong side when you reach the motifs. End the row with 4 white stitches after skipping under the second motif. Work the second row to form the other half of the white stripe. Now double-check! Using the bottoms of the strawberries as guides, be certain the white stripe is directly in the center as shown in Figure 6-56. The first stripe must be correct or the symmetry of the overall effect will be destroyed. *Color pattern:* 2 rows, white; one row, purple. Holding the canvas so that the stems are on the right, work the rows under the center white stripe in a downward direction. Follow the color pattern until there are 9 purple stripes. Work one row white. Constantly check Figure 6-56 where the rows are easily distinguishable. Still holding the canvas so that the stems are on the right, work rows on top of the center white stripe in an upward direction. Follow the color pattern until there are 9 purple stripes above the center white stripe. Work one row white. This completes the striped area (total: 18 purple stripes).

Note: For a solid-colored background, use white yarn throughout, covering the same overall area.

Pink Border. The pink border is worked in the Orr Weave Stitch in rows around the rectangle, using Corner B. Use

6-57

numerous occasions. The butterfly is worked first, then the petite flowers on each side.

Two-Toned Blue and Purple Butterfly Motif. Follow the basic directions for Motif 11 (Fig. 6-31) using the color changes that are listed here. Fold the canvas in half vertically to determine the middle. Count down 10 horizontal bars of canvas. Bring the needle up to the surface in the center hole under the tenth bar. This is the hole in which to start the butterfly motif (A on Fig. 6-31). Bottom sections are worked first. Use blue yarn. Work the 2 *inside* chain stitches only of the bottom sections. (Leave 6 in. tails of yarn to be woven in later.) Use purple yarn. Bring the needle up in the same hole A and work the 2 *outside* large chains around the 2 blue stitches. Do not end the yarn. Drop under on the wrong side and bring the needle up to the surface in B. Work the outside figure 8 around the top. End the yarn. Use blue yarn. Work the 2 middle sections C and D. Do not end the yarn. Bring the needle up to the surface in B to start the body. Work the body in blue yarn.

Note: The antennae are worked after the background is completed.

Petite Side Flowers. Follow the instructions under Motif 1A (Fig. 6-8) to produce the 4-petaled single flower. Use purple yarn. Work a small flower on each side of the butterfly. (See Fig. 6-58.) There is one free vertical bar between the widest portion of each wing and the bars on each side used for flower petal points. The bottom points of the flowers are one bar up from the bar used for the bottom of the butterfly.

Background. Work Orr Weave Stitches from right to left in horizontal rows from top to bottom. Mark corners with yarn ties as follows. *Two top corners:* Count up 3 bars from the top point of the wing. Count out to the side 3 bars from the bars used for the outer points of the flower. Run your fingers along the bars toward the corner and tie a yarn marker diagonally over the crossbar where they meet. Repeat this on the other side. *Two bottom corners:*

6-58

Count down 2 bars below the bar used for the bottom points of the butterfly. Count out to the side 3 bars from the bar used for the point of the flower (same bar as for the top corner). Run your fingers along the bars toward the corner and tie a yarn marker diagonally over the crossbar where they meet. Repeat this on the other side. Use white yarn. Start at the upper right. The markers

indicate where the corner stitches will be worked. Remove them just before working the stitches. Work the top row across from right to left. Continue working the rows down to the bottom, skipping under the motifs on the wrong side when you reach them.

Butterfly Antennae. Use purple yarn. Bring the needle up to the surface in B. (See Fig. 6-31.) Work 2 diagonal stitches up from B in the form of a V, placing the needle down between the top and the second rows. This leaves one horizontal row of background stitches free along the top. (See Fig. 6-58. The antennae stitches are not shown in Fig. 6-31.)

French Knots. Use blue yarn. All the knots are worked single strand—around the needle once. Work a French Knot at the 2 top points of the purple antennae. Do not end the yarn. Drop under on the wrong side—catch once under the yarn—and bring the needle up in the center of the side flower. Work a French Knot in the center and work 4 knots around the flower between the petals as shown in Figure 6-58. Drop under on the wrong side—catch the yarn once under the butterfly—and repeat this for the second flower.

Now Needlepoint Backing. The Orr Weave Stitch is worked in rows around the rectangle. Use Corner A. The backing is blue, with one stripe of white for interest as shown in Figure 6-58. Start with the outside row.

1st Row. Use blue yarn. Leave one bar of canvas free between areas. Start at the right under the worked top-side area. Work 24 stitches from right to left. Turn at the corner. Work a row around, completing the rectangle so that there are 24 stitches on the long sides and 11 stitches on the short sides duplicating the topside area. Continue working rows in toward the center in the following color pattern: 2nd and 3rd Rows, blue; 4th, white; 5th and 6th, blue. The last row closes in the center and is worked in one single straight row from right to left.

Follow the basic directions for the braid construction and stuffing given for the rosebud mini pillow in Chapter 8. Use blue yarn (single strand). Work the Regular Braid Stitch—Start A.

A decorative shocking pink dish is piled high with colorful old-fashioned hard candy. A sprightly candy cane dances on each side. (Fig. 6-59.) Size of sample: 7 in. × 10½ in. There's a peppermint-striped Now Needlepoint backing if anyone should peek.

Note: This finished item is a creative challenge—a fun one! I help by providing the motifs, color pattern and key for the candy dish. *You* must improvise and fill in some small candies. You also must reverse one candy cane to

6-59

Motif E. Yellow.

Fill in the spaces between candies after working the dish.

Candy Dish. Follow the key at the bottom of Figure 6-33. The dish is worked in horizontal rows of the Orr Weave Stitch from right to left. Start with the top row and work down. Use pink yarn. The small X's at the bottom of the motif diagram indicate placement of the top row of the candy dish. Start at the right. Drop down one bar of canvas, leaving one bar of canvas free between the bottom of Motif C and the top row of the dish. Work the top row across to the left (13 stitches). Make certain the candy motifs are within the side points of the dish. Starting at the right each time, continue working down in rows, following the dish key in the diagram. (*Note:* Do not end and start the yarn on short runs. Catch it once on the wrong side and bring the needle up in the correct place to start the new row.)

Back to Hard Candy. Now you must improvise! The object is to fill in solidly the areas between the basic motifs with tiny candies, so that no canvas is exposed. I used Motif B (jelly bean) and Motif E (small round candy) plus single diagonal Chain Stitches for the fill-in candies. Study Figure 6-60 to see how tiny candies are squeezed between the basic shapes. Keep within the side points of the dish. Complete one color at a time, skipping to the next spot on the wrong side and repeating it in approximately 5 or 6 spots. Try to create a balance of color and shapes. Repeat the colors used in the basic motifs. I also used white here and there but always *in* from the edges, since it would be lost against the white background. Single chains of deep-purple value were also introduced. The touches of white and purple produce an extra sparkle. (See Fig. C-105 in the color section.) Have fun filling the dish and don't be in the least concerned if your design does not look exactly like the sample shown. Keep giving it the Squint Test for color and value balance.

Candy Canes. Place the canes so that the bottom points cover the same horizontal bar used for the bottom of the dish, with 3 free vertical bars between each cane and the top widest points of the dish. (Count the bar which runs down the side of the cane and is partly hidden as one of the free bars.) Use pink yarn. Follow the directions for Motif 5. (See Fig. 6-19.) Work the left cane first. The start is a bit tricky. You simply have to count bars to find the proper spot to start. Using the widest point on the dish as a guide, I counted out to the left and placed my finger on the fourth vertical bar, ran it down to the horizontal bar on which the bottom row of the dish is worked and placed a yarn tie marker diagonally over the crossbar where they meet. This indicates the bottom of the cane. Then, starting at this point (following the cane diagram), I counted

create happy eye entertainment. Once you complete this suggested design, there is nothing to stop you from creating numerous candy dishes and candy shapes of your own. If you are not partial to peppermint, you might wish to substitute your favorite flavor color.

Pat Rug Yarn: green #550 (1 str.); yellow #443 (1 str.); purple #632 (1 str.); lavender #672 (1 str.); shocking pink #259 (24 str.); white #005 (31 str.).

Hard Candy and Candy Dish. Follow the directions for Motif 12. (See Fig. 6-33.) First work the various hard candy motifs in the placement shown using the colors to be listed. The candy dish is then worked underneath. The spaces around the 5 candy motifs and above the dish are filled in with small motifs of various colors so that the dish appears to be piled high with candy.

Hard Candy. Follow the *exact* placement for the hard candies in Figure 6-33, using the colors indicated here. Leave 6 in. tails on the small motifs to be woven in later.

Motif A. To start, bring the needle up in 1, so that there are 11 free bars on top and 18 free bars to the left side. The first row is green, the second row, white. Work a green French Knot in the center (single strand—around the needle once).

Motif B. Yellow.

Motif C.
1, pink; 2, white.

Motif D. 1, 2 and 3, lavender.

bars up, then over to the left and down to 1, where you bring the needle to the surface to start the cane. Complete the left cane. Keep loose. Pull out the cane and correct the start if your first attempt is off. The Chain Stitch pulls out easily. Repeat this procedure but reverse the position of the cane on the right side. Figure 6-60 is a helpful guide for your start. Better still, if you have a working sample of the cane made up, flop it so the wrong side is up and the cane's position is reversed. You still have to count stitches and pinpoint the start, but it helps to have the cane in the reverse position. Use white yarn. Surface whip every other stitch the entire length of each cane. (See Fig. 5-8.)

Background. Work vertical rows of the Orr Weave Stitch. Tie yarn markers at the corners as follows. *Two top corners:* Use the top yellow jelly bean as guide (Motif B in Fig. 6-33). Count up 4 horizontal bars of canvas. Count out to the side 4 vertical bars, using the outer short side of the cane as a guide. (Include in your count the bar which is partly hidden under the side of the hook). Run your fingers along the bars toward the corner and tie a yarn marker diagonally over the crossbar where they meet. Repeat this at the opposite top corner. *Two bottom corners:* Use the bottom of the cane as the guide. Count down 4 bars. Count out to the side 4 vertical bars (the same bar as for the top corner). Run your fingers along the bars toward the corner and tie a yarn marker diagonally over the crossbar where they meet. Repeat this at the opposite corner. Turn the canvas 90 degrees so that the tops of the canes are on the right. Use white yarn. With the canvas in this position, start at the upper right and work the Orr Weave Stitch from right to left in horizontal rows down to the bottom. Drop under on the wrong side when you reach the curved hooks of the cane motifs. Remember to push back the cane stitches and to cover the canvas bars along each side of the cane. The candy dish covers a large area, so I suggest you fill in the top and bottom areas separately. When you reach the candy area at the top, do not end the yarn, but drop under to the wrong side, weave once under the top background area and bring the needle up on the edge for the start of the next short row. The same system can be used for the bottom of the dish. Remember to work all the rows from right to left in order to maintain the pattern of the weave.

Peppermint Backing. See Figure 6-61, which shows a small section of the backing at the bottom. There is one wide stripe of pink down the center with alternating single rows of pink and white stripes to each side. The backing is worked the same way as the topside—in vertical rows—leaving one free bar of canvas between the areas for the braid stitch construction. Turn the canvas 90 degrees so that the tops of the canes are on the right. Start at the upper right. Work from right to left so that

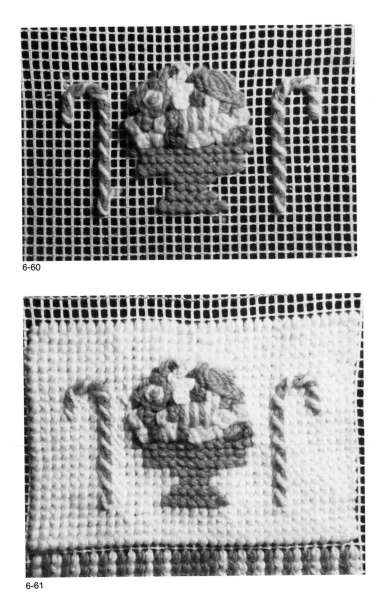

6-60

6-61

there are 23 stitches in each row (as in the topside area) in the following color pattern: 1st Row, white; 2nd Row, pink; 3rd through 15th Rows, repeat the 1st and 2nd Rows until there are 7 rows of pink and 8 rows of white; 16th through 20th Rows, pink; 21st Row, white; 22nd Row, pink; 23rd through 35th Rows, repeat the 21st and 22nd Rows until there are 7 rows of pink and 8 rows of white.

Follow the basic directions for the braid construction and stuffing given for the rosebud mini pillow in Chapter 8. Use pink yarn (single strand). Work the Regular Braid Stitch—Start A.

7.

The Orr Weave: A New Textural Stitch for Designs and Backgrounds

Personality. A delightful woven effect is created by a twist to the age-old Cross-stitch! Like a child, it has many of the characteristics of its parent, but something new has been added which gives it a distinctive personality of its own. The secret lies in the order and direction in which the stitches are worked. Each stitch is worked over one crossbar of canvas and is completed before proceeding to the next. Carefully follow the sequence of steps outlined in the directions and the two legs of each stitch will cross in an unusual way which happily produces the woven effect, quite different from the individual rigid squares of the traditional version of the Cross-stitch known to us all. While the visual effect is uneven and textural, the cross tension pull of the stitches remains even. When you complete an article, a few diagonal cross pulls of the canvas with the hands will suffice in most cases to square off edges before you start construction.

Will Travel. Stitches are normally worked from right to left in horizontal rows. Rows are normally worked from top to bottom. The textural quality is created by systematically working the stitches and rows in the normal directions. However, the rows can be worked one on top of the other without destroying the woven pattern. I use the top-to-bottom direction whenever possible for I find it faster and easier to work the stitches when the free canvas is on the bottom. If you wish the rows to appear to run vertically in the design, simply turn the canvas 90 degrees to the right (the top becomes the right side) and follow the normal procedure. The individual stitches can also be made to walk in the following directions: straight downward direction (one stitch directly under the other); left and right downward diagonal direction; and left and right upward diagonal directions by turning the canvas upside

7-1. The Orr Weave.

down while you work the stitches. Stitches can also be worked in rows around a square or rectangle as they dutifully turn corners with ease.

Note: The Orr Weave Stitches will not walk in a straight upward direction or horizontally from left to right. The normal procedure of working from right to left must be followed to maintain the woven effect. When the ritual of working from right to left is interrupted, the stitches appear in the traditional form of the Cross-stitch rigid squares and the woven quality is lost. However, when used sparingly in very small design areas, the change is hardly detectable since the woven look predominates throughout in the larger design areas and background stitches.

Design and Color Potentials. *Backgrounds:* The Orr Weave can be used for backgrounds in combination with design motifs worked in various other stitches. Each stitch is worked over a single crossbar of canvas and is completed before proceeding to the next, making it a natural for use in backgrounds. Its personality is such that it creates a subtle textural entertainment for the eye when worked in solid areas of one color, but it does not detract from the specific design motif or overall theme. If you wish to enliven the background, you can easily introduce stripes or patterns—subtle or startling ones. An example of a striped background is the strawberry pillow in the previous chapter. (See Fig. 6-55.) However, use caution in this area so that the background does not end up fighting the main design or motif but enhances it. Interesting, offbeat effects of pattern on pattern—used so much in contemporary décor— can easily be introduced. Stripes can be made to run around the square or rectangle. A polka-dot effect can be achieved by skipping under a crossbar of canvas at even intervals and later filling in the single stitch in a contrasting color.

As pointed out, the woven pattern can be worked to run horizontally, or vertically or in rows around the square. The choice of direction is yours and the correct decision depends on the type of design involved and the basic shape of the area. It is best to work the central design or motif and then decide on the proper direction for the background weave. Here is a trick I use: When the design motif is completed, place several strands of the background yarn color you have chosen on the item, holding the strands parallel to one another. Try several different directions, giving each the Squint Test before you make your final decision. Many times the design is such that any direction would be equally as pleasing, but since there are certain designs which seem to demand one direction over the others, it is worth doing the test to determine the one which will best enhance the item.

The correct choice of color for backgrounds is important. Unless there is sufficient light-and-dark contrast between the design motif or motifs and the background color, the edges will blend in the eye, causing the design to be lost. Remember that the textural quality of the background diminishes in relation to how deep a color you use. The deeper the color, the less the eye can distinguish the construction of the individual stitches. There are many exceptions, but it is usually best to key designs with the accents of deeper values used in the design theme and the lighter values reserved for backgrounds. It is not necessary to have extreme contrasts in value, but there must be enough to allow the background to become a separate area around and between the design motifs. The design and color possibilities for backgrounds are endless and can be as simple or as busy as you wish.

Overall Designs: The Orr Weave is worked in straight rows so that numerous versions of stripes of various widths can easily be keyed. Let color assist you by creating startling contrast or subtle blending in the eye. Increase the width of a stripe by working a number of rows in the same-color yarn. Many of the color combinations for zig zag patterns can be adapted to the straight stripes created by the rows of Orr Weave. As explained, the stripes can be made to run vertically or horizontally depending on how you hold the canvas while you work the stitches.

Keep in mind that the Orr Weave walks around a square or rectangle, so that any of the *bull's-eye type of designs* can be adapted. You form a basic square by working an outline row and then working rows in toward the center. You work any number of additional rows around the basic square to increase the size. The inside and outside rows involve two different turns for corners. In this type of design, your eye is carried directly to the center, so you must have extra interest and entertainment in that spot, such as a textural bunch of French Knots.

Repeat Patterns: Interesting repeat patterns can be keyed when you skip under on the wrong side, leaving crossbars free to be filled in later with a contrasting color. Press that Aware Button, since the patterns included in this chapter represent only a tiny sample of the possibilities for repeat designs with this stitch. Experiment with thumbnail sketches that use X's to indicate stitches (graph paper is a great help). Inspiration is all around you. Marvelous borders for use around a square or a rectangle can be keyed. A glance at a good book on design should leave your head spinning with ideas.

Possible Uses. Since the Orr Weave produces a closely woven stitch with a thick backing, it is suitable for the complete gamut of finished items: pillows, pincushions, bench tops, seat pads, wall hangings—even rugs.

MECHANICS FOR THE ORR AND DOUBLE ORR WEAVE

The stitch is worked on 3 to the inch canvas.

Detailed directions for two versions of the stitch are included. The Orr Weave is the normal version of the stitch for use with yarns comparable in weight—or heavier—to Pat Rug Yarn. The Double Orr Weave should be used with lighter-weight yarn comparable to the Nantucket 6-Ply Cable. If the yarn does not properly cover the canvas when you follow the normal procedure, the Double Orr Weave provides an extra step which spreads the yarn to hide the canvas but does not destroy the textural woven look. *All general directions are the same for both versions.* Keep the tension of the yarn relaxed while you work the stitches. Let it live—not too tight or the canvas will peek through, but not too loose or the woven pattern will be destroyed. You will quickly develop even tension.

Let your eye be the judge. Special Fill-in Stitches are not necessary since the stitches create even edges at the top and bottom of the rows and along the sides.

The stitches are worked in horizontal rows from right to left.

The rows are normally worked from top to bottom. Rows can also be worked in an upward direction—one on top of the other—if this is more convenient for a specific design. Follow the normal procedure whenever possible since it is quicker and easier to work the individual stitches when the free canvas is on the bottom.

Follow Figure 7-2 for the Orr Weave.

1. Start at the upper right. Work the stitches from right to left. Bring the needle up to the surface in hole 1, leaving a 6 in. tail in the back to be woven in later.

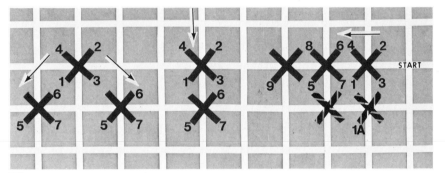

7-2

2. Place the needle down in 2 and up in 3 in one motion, going under a horizontal bar of canvas. See Figure 7-3.

3. Place the needle down in 4 and up in 5 in one motion, going under a crossbar of canvas. See Figure 7-4.

4. Place the needle down in 6 and up in 7 in one motion. See Figure 7-5.

5. Place the needle down in 8 and up in 9 in one motion. See Figure 7-6.

Repeat these steps across to the left until the row is completed.

End of Row. When you reach the end of the row, complete the upward left diagonal cross of the last stitch, pulling the yarn through to the back. Run the yarn under at least 1 in. of worked area away from the edge. Snip it off, leaving a ½ in. tail.

To End a Strand. If you use up a strand of yarn before the end of a row, follow this procedure to prevent the woven pattern from being interrupted. End the strand on the upward right diagonal cross. As an example, see the top right stitch in Figure 7-2. The yarn is up in 1. Go down in 2 and pull the yarn through to the back. Run the yarn under at least 1 in. of worked area. Snip it off, leaving a ½ in. tail.

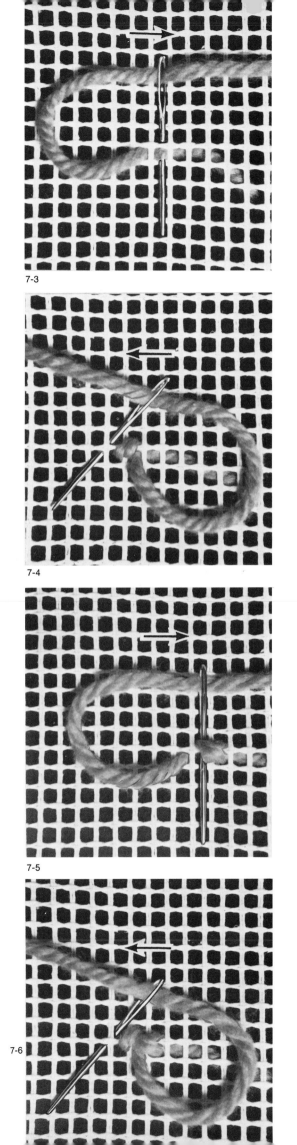

7-3

7-4

7-5

7-6

To Start a Strand. Run under at least 1 in. of worked area. Bring the needle up to the surface in 3 and follow the normal procedure (down in 4 and up in 5, and so on).

Second Row. The second row, which is worked directly under the first, is indicated by the patterned crosses at the right of Figure 7-2. Start at the right. Bring the needle up in the correct place to start, as indicated by 1A. Continue across from right to left in the same manner as in the first row.

Note: When you have completed several rows, flatten the stitches by running your thumb over them in the direction they were worked. Notice how happily they spread out next to each other to form the woven appearance.

Straight Downward Direction. Follow the stitches in the center of Figure 7-2. The stitches can be worked one directly under the other as follows. Work a stitch to the point where the needle is brought up to the surface in 3. Place the needle down in 4, going under two canvas bars as indicated and bring the needle up to the surface in 5. See Figure 7-7. Repeat the steps for as many stitches as desired, skipping under the two bars of canvas to bring the needle up to the surface in the correct place to start the next stitch.

Left and Right Downward Diagonal Directions. Follow the stitches at the left of Figure 7-2. *Left downward diagonal direction:* Work a stitch to the point where the needle is brought to the surface in 3. Follow the left diagonal arrow. Place the needle down in 4 and up in 5, skipping under on the wrong side to bring the needle up to the surface in the correct hole to start the next stitch. See Figure 7-8. Repeat these steps for as many stitches as desired. *Right downward diagonal direction:* Work a stitch to the point where the needle is brought to the surface in 3. Follow the right diagonal arrow. Place the needle down in 4 and up in 5, skipping under on the wrong side to bring the needle up to the surface in the correct hole to start the next stitch. See Figure 7-9. Repeat these steps for as many stitches as desired.

Note: A good trick is to place a finger on the crossbar of canvas over which the next stitch will be worked (down one and over one crossbar to the left or right in a diagonal direction from the preceding stitch). After a bit of practice, you can quickly determine the correct hole to use when the needle is brought to the surface.

Upward Left and Right Diagonal Directions. Reverse the canvas—turn it completely upside down. Follow the directions for downward diagonal directions. Crosses will be consistent throughout even though they are worked in the upside down manner.

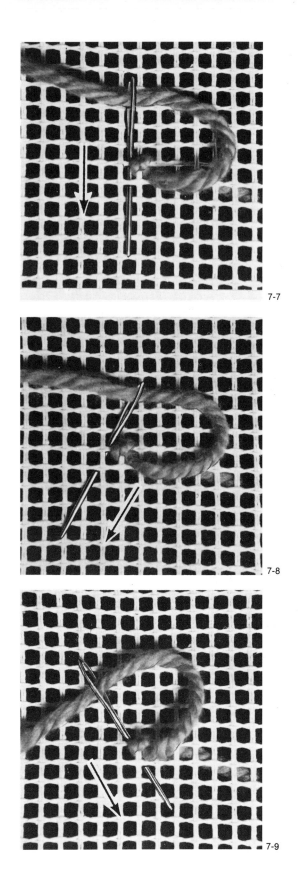

7-7

7-8

7-9

Alternate corners are used when working rows around the square or rectangle.

Corner A. Use this corner when the outside row is worked first and subsequent rows are worked in toward the center.

1st Row. Start the outside row of the square at the upper right. Work the desired number of stitches in a normal manner from right to left. When you reach a corner, follow

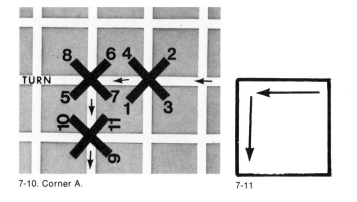

7-10. Corner A.

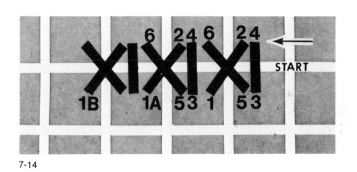

7-11

Figure 7-10 up to the point where the needle is brought to the surface in 7. Place the needle down in 8 and pull the yarn through to the back. Turn the canvas 90 degrees so that the top becomes the right side. Turn the diagram too. Bring needle up to the surface in 9. *Note:* The needle can easily be placed down in 8 and up in 9 in one motion after you are familiar with the turning process. Place the needle down in 10 and up in 11 in one motion. Continue across from right to left until there are the same number of stitches as in the first side. Work the second and third corners in the same manner and turn the canvas as directed. Continue working stitches along the fourth side until you reach the original start which closes the square. Do not end the yarn unless there is a change in color for the second row.

2nd Row. Start at the top right corner directly *inside* the first row of stitches. Work across from right to left, turning the corners as directed. Continue working the rows in toward the center—making color changes when necessary—until the inside area is covered. Rows become smaller and smaller as work progresses. The small space in the center of the area can be used for special center interest.

Corner B. Use this corner when additional rows are to be added around the already worked central square or rectangle.

1st Row. Start directly under the lower right corner stitch of the already worked square or rectangle. Work stitches in the normal manner, from right to left. Follow Figure 7-12. When you reach the corner, work one additional stitch to the left beyond the worked area up to the point where the needle is brought to the surface in 7. Place the needle down in 8 and pull the yarn through to the back.

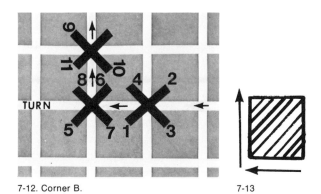

7-12. Corner B.

7-13

Turn the canvas 90 degrees so that the bottom becomes the right side. Bring the needle up to the surface in 9. (The needle can go down in 8 and up in 9 in one motion after you are familiar with the turning process.) Place the needle down in 10 and up in 11 in one motion. Continue across from right to left—turning corners as directed—until all four sides are completed. Do not end the yarn unless there is a change in color for the second row.

2nd Row. Start at the lower right directly under the corner stitch of the first row. Work the second row directly outside the first row, turning the corners as directed. Continue working the rows out toward the edges for desired coverage, making color changes when necessary. The rows become larger and larger as the work progresses.

Double Orr Weave. As explained previously, the extra step for the Double Orr Weave does not destroy the stitch's woven appearance but merely spreads the yarn to prevent any canvas from peeking through. The procedure becomes completely automatic in a short time.

Follow Figure 7-14.

![7-14 diagram showing stitch numbering 6 24 6 24 START, 1B 1A 53 1 53]

7-14

1. Start at the upper right. Work stitches from right to left. Bring the needle up to the surface in hole 1, leaving a 6 in. tail to be woven in later.

2. Place the needle down in 2 and up in 3 in one motion.

3. This is the extra step. Place the needle down in 4 and up in 5 in one motion.

4. Place the needle down in 6 and up in 1A (to the left) in one motion. You are now ready to start the second stitch. The start of the third stitch is indicated by 1B. Continue across from right to left for desired coverage.

The stitches for the Double Orr Weave can be made to walk in the various directions just as with the Orr Weave and the corners are turned in the same manner, *after the extra step is worked in each stitch.*

ORR WEAVE PATTERNS

Orr Weave horizontal stripes are produced by working stitches in the normal manner from right to left in rows

7-16. Pattern 2.

from top to bottom. There are certain times when you might wish to work rows one on top of the other to key a design, but follow the normal procedure whenever possible.

Turn the canvas 90 degrees while working the stitches to produce *Orr Weave vertical stripes.* With the canvas in this position, work the stitches in the normal manner.

Pattern 1. Startling vertical black and white stripes are combined with turquoise. (Fig. 7-15.)
Pat Rug Yarn: turquoise #738; white #005; black #050.

Turn the canvas 90 degrees so that the top becomes the right side. With the canvas in this position, work Orr Weave stitches in a normal manner from right to left. Start at the upper right and work the stitches in rows of the desired length from the top to the bottom in the following color pattern. (There are 11 stitches in each row in the pattern shown.) 1st and 2nd Rows, turquoise; 3rd Row, white; 4th Row, black; 5th Row, white. Repeat the first through fifth rows as many times as necessary for desired coverage. The pattern is repeated 3 times in the sample. Work 2 rows of turquoise at the end to balance the beginning. The black and white rows appear as stripes on a turquoise background.

7-15. Pattern 1.

Pattern 2. Vertical stripes in deep yellow-green, pink and white harmonize to produce a pleasing combination. (Fig. 7-16.)
Pat Rug Yarn: green #545; pink #831; white #005.

Turn the canvas 90 degrees so that the top becomes the right side. With the canvas in this position, work Orr Weave stitches in a normal manner from right to left. Start at the upper right and work the stitches in rows of desired length from the top to the bottom in the following color pattern. (There are 12 stitches in each row in the pattern shown.) 1st Row, green; 2nd Row, pink; 3rd Row, white.

Repeat the first through third rows as many times as necessary for desired coverage. The pattern is repeated 5 times in the sample. Work one row of green at the end to balance the beginning. Notice how the eye singles out the deep green row. The 2 rows of lighter value blend into one wider stripe, producing a contrast of narrow and wide. The overall appearance of the pattern is entirely controlled by the choice of color.

Design Notes for Orr Weave Stripes. A novice can produce professional-looking designs like magic by varying the color and the width of the stripes. Practice the stitch until you have thoroughly mastered the mechanics. Read Chapter 1 on design and color. You can literally make color work for you and produce whatever effect you desire. It can cause a pattern to stand out boldly or blend harmoniously in your eye. You can use as many colors as you wish. Key wide stripes by working several rows of one color or narrow stripes by working single rows. The possibilities are so obvious and so easily visualized that I limited the number of sample patterns. Any of the color patterns for the Single and Double Zig Zag Chain can easily be adapted to the straight stripes produced by the Orr Weave. Areas of solid color can be worked at the beginning and end to create a background area which centers the stripes.

You start out with a plus—the stitch itself with its textural quality. Do the rest with color. Make it work for you. And remember the lovable friend to all colors: white. Drop white stripes in here and there and produce that extra sparkle which gives the design zing!

Pattern 3. Interrupted and solid horizontal stripes produce a sparkling green and white design that is quickly keyed and easy to work. (Fig. 7-17.) Size of pattern: 4½ in. × 6 in.
Pat Rug Yarn: white #005; green #559.

Start at the upper right and work the Orr Weave stitches in the normal manner from right to left. Rows of desired length are worked from top to bottom in the following color pattern. (There are 20 stitches in each row in the pattern shown.)

7-17. Pattern 3.

1st Row. Use white yarn. Work 20 stitches.

2nd Row. The interrupted pattern is formed with 2 white stitches and 4 green stitches. Repeat the stitches for desired coverage.

1. Start at the right. Use green yarn. Leave 2 crossbars of canvas free to be filled in later in white. Start directly under the third stitch in from right edge in the top row and work 4 green stitches (toward the left). When you have completed the fourth stitch, skip under on the wrong side and bring the needle up to the surface, leaving 2 crossbars of canvas free for 2 white stitches. (You must jump to the left of the crossbar on which the green stitch will be worked.) Repeat this across to the left for desired coverage. Leave 2 free crossbars at the end of the row to balance the beginning. (The sample repeats the green pattern 3 times, leaving 2 free crossbars for white stitches.)

2. Start at the right in the *same* row where the green stitches were worked. Use white yarn. Work 2 white stitches. Skip under the 4 green stitches already worked and work 2 white stitches. Continue across the row, ending with 2 white stitches at the left edge for balance.

3rd Row. Use white yarn. Work one solid white row.

4th Row. Use green yarn. Work one solid green row. Repeat the first through fourth rows as many times as necessary for desired coverage. (The pattern is repeated 3 times in the sample plus the first through third rows to balance the top.)

Design Note: The interrupted stripe makes keying designs easy—even for the novice. Any number of stitches can be keyed in the groupings and any number of rows can be used in the pattern. You will be overwhelmed with the possibilities when you press the Aware Button. Patterns and designs start to unfold like magic. Make thumbnail sketches of them.

Extended Coverage. The basic pattern can be repeated many times but there are a few important points to remember regarding the size of the area to be covered. The top and bottom outside edges should be the same and balance, as in the sample. The right and left sides should also balance. Notice how the 2 white stitches are balanced at each side in the interrupted stripe rows. Here a preliminary Think Plan can be helpful. If you wish to end up with specific outside measurements, you must count crossbars of canvas for proper coverage as follows: 1. The number of stitches in the interrupted stripe horizontal rows must be divisible by 6 in the pattern shown (2 white plus 4 green or a total of 6 stitches are involved in the repeat pattern) plus 2 for balance at the end of the row. There are 20 stitches in the sample. 2. The rows from top to bottom must be divisible by 4 for the pattern shown (4 rows are involved in the repeat pattern) plus 3 for balance at the bottom. There are 15 rows in the sample.

It is usually not necessary to adhere to exact measurements since most designs can easily be keyed to approximate sizes. However, there are times when it is a great designing asset to be able to manipulate a pattern to fit a specific shape (such as for a bench top, window-seat pad and other items). The pattern in Figure 7-17 starts with a white stripe, but it could easily be keyed with a green stripe along the top and bottom. Place yarn tie markers at the corners of the area to be covered and check your count of crossbars to determine whether you have the correct number for the interrupted pattern row and for the repeat rows of pattern from top to bottom. By making up a little working sample of the pattern, you can juggle the pattern until it fits into the area to be covered. Remember that the outside edges must balance. For example, you can add 2 single rows of white—one at the top and one at the bottom (you must have 2 for balance). The same is true for the sides. There could be 3 white stitches at both the beginning and end of the interrupted stripe rows instead of 2. Or you could start with the green stitches and eliminate the white along the 2 sides. Keep elastic and flexible so that your creative ideas will flow. Some preliminary planning and counting is necessary to adapt designs to specific areas, but remember, the result can fill you with the joy of accomplishment when you see a custom-fitted item (at no extra charge) that is your own stunning creation!

Pattern 4. Bright green surface whipping transforms a solid white Orr Weave background into a textured barberpole striped design. (Fig. 7-18.)
Pat Rug Yarn: white #005; green #569.

Turn the canvas 90 degrees so that the top becomes the right side. Work white background stitches in the normal manner from right to left.

Background. Use white yarn. Start at the upper right and work rows of desired length. (There are 13 stitches in the pattern sample.) The surface whipping in this pattern is worked on every third row of the white background. Therefore, the number of rows of background used must be divisible by 3 plus 2 extra so that the right side is similar to the left in appearance. (There is a total of 17 rows in the

7-18. Pattern 4.

pattern sample.) Accordingly, if the surface whipping is worked on every fourth row (for wider spaces between the stripes), the number of background rows would then have to be divisible by 4, plus 3 extra rows at the right side to balance the left side.

Surface Whipping. Use green yarn. Surface whip every third row across as follows. (Figure 7-19.) The whipping is worked with the canvas in the normal position (the yarn tie marker is on top). Bring the needle up to the surface at the top of the row to the right of the vertical canvas bar. Whip through the first stitch in the row, catching under the top cross of the stitch only in a right-to-left direction. Pull the yarn through slowly until it forms a gentle curve. Skip one stitch and repeat this on the third stitch down from the top. Continue down to the bottom, whipping every other stitch in the row. Carefully regulate the tension—not too loose but not too tight—so that the twisted pattern is properly formed. Skip 2 rows and repeat the process. Continue across to the right side.

7-19

Pattern 5. Covered all over with stripes of rosebuds and tiny green leaves! Double surface whipping topped by perky French Knots weaves a charming feminine spell. (Fig. 7-20.) Size of sample: 5½ in. × 4¾ in.
Pat Rug Yarn: white #005; green #510; light shocking pink #279; deep shocking pink #239.

7-20. Pattern 5.

Orr Weave Background. The Orr Weave runs in vertical rows in the sample. Turn the canvas 90 degrees while you work the stitches so that the top becomes the right side. With the canvas in this position, start the first row at the upper right, working the stitches from right to left and the rows from top to bottom.

1. Work 3 rows in white yarn. (There are 13 stitches in each row in the sample.)

2. Work 1 row in green yarn. (Underneath the rosebud stripe is a row of green Orr Weave stitches.) Repeat from Steps 1 and 2 for desired coverage. Add 3 white rows at the end to balance the beginning. (The sample repeats the pattern 4 times, plus 3 white rows at the end.)

Note: The entire background can be completed before you add the surface whipping and French Knots. If you wish to add the decorative touches as the work progresses (I can never wait until the end), work at least one row of white beyond each green row before working the surface stitching. Otherwise you might have difficulty working the background under the surface loops.

Surface Whipping. Turn the canvas to the normal position so that the green stripes are in a vertical position. Use light shocking pink yarn.

1. Bring the needle to the surface to the right of the vertical canvas bar on which the green stitches are worked. Place the needle through the top cross of the first Orr Weave Stitch in a right-to-left direction.

154

2. Skip one top cross and place the needle through the top cross on the third stitch down from the top in a left-to-right direction (the same direction that is shown in Figure 7-21), leaving a decorative loop.

3. Skip one top cross and place the needle through the top cross in a right-to-left direction (the same direction that is shown in Figure 7-22), leaving a decorative loop on the opposite side. Continue down to the bottom of the row, whipping through every other green Orr Weave Stitch and alternating the directions as outlined in Steps 2 and 3.

4. Reverse the canvas so that the top becomes the bottom. (Fig. 7-23.) Place the needle through the *same* top cross that was used for single whipping in the opposite direction. The loops will be formed on the opposite side of those worked in the single whipping. Control the size of the loops to make them uniform throughout. Continue to the end of the row.

French Knots. Use deep shocking pink yarn. Work a French Knot (single strand—around the needle twice) in the center of each pair of loops, as shown in the pattern. Catch the yarn over the canvas bar as you are working the knot or it will slip through to the back.

Design Note: You can substitute two values of the color of your choice for the rosebuds. The background area between the stripes and at the sides can be increased by adding additional rows of Orr Weave stitches. The pattern shows the stripes in a vertical position. They can be made to run horizontally across an item if you work the rows of Orr Weave in the normal manner, from right to left. It is necessary to do a little advance figuring for the length of the background rows. For each row, allow 2 bars of canvas for each rosebud plus one extra. The sample has 6 rosebuds in each stripe, so I had to work 13 stitches in each of the background rows.

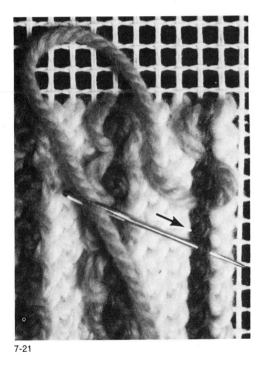

7-21

7-22

7-23

Pattern 6. A square bull's-eye in deep shocking pink and white attracts the eye. (Fig. 7-24.) Size of sample: 3½ in. square.

Pat Rug Yarn: white #005; shocking pink #239.

The outside row around the square is worked first. Subsequent rows are worked in toward the middle. Use Corner A for turning corners. There are 12 stitches on each side in the outside row. Remember to include corner stitches in your count for each side. The number of stitches on the sides is reduced by 2 in each row. The rows are worked one inside the other in the following color pattern.

7-24. Pattern 6.

1st Row. Use white yarn. Start at the upper right corner of the area where the square is to be worked. Work stitches in the normal manner from right to left until there are 12 stitches. Turn the corner on the twelfth stitch (Corner A). Continue around until you have completed the 4 sides of the 12-stitch square, turning the corners when necessary.

2nd Row. Use shocking pink yarn. Start at the upper right corner directly inside the first row. Work 4 sides until the row is completed. Do not end the yarn.

Subsequent Rows. Work them in the same manner in the following color pattern: 3rd, shocking pink; 4th, white; 5th, shocking pink. Leave the center hole of the canvas exposed.

Round Center. Use white yarn (single strand). Work a Round Center (see the directions preceding Pattern 9 in Chapter 5) around the center hole of the canvas. (The yarn can be worked single strand doubled if you want a thicker-looking center.) *French Knot:* Use shocking pink yarn. Work one French Knot (single strand—around the

needle once) directly in the center. Catch over the yarn in the Round Center so that the knot does not slip through to the back.

Design Note: This basic pattern can work overtime for you. The square as shown can be repeated as many times as you wish to form larger overall square areas, rectangles or long, skinny areas for bellpulls. You can place it directly in the center of an area and let it grow to any size by adding additional rows around it (using Corner B for the outside rows). You can alternate it with solid color squares of the same size and create a completely different image. If you leave one free bar of canvas exposed on all sides when you work the squares next to each other (to be filled in later with shocking pink), the outside white row of each square will form a frame. If you work them side by side, the white outside rows blend in the eye, and presto—there are shocking pink squares surrounded by white background. I would definitely suggest that you make up a working sample pattern of this basic square to help you visualize the potentials. You can change the color pattern of the rows and create some delightful combinations of your own with a completely different point of interest in the center. I feel strongly that the bull's-eye type of design must have center interest —some little special note to satisfy the eye. The design itself is a target type, so your eye is directed to the center. How disappointing if your eye travels there to find there is nothing special to see. There is no limit to the use of color combinations or the number of colors which can be used. One point to remember: there should be a definite and strong value contrast—light and dark—between at least two of the colors or the effect of the bull's-eye design will be lost.

The next two patterns show different interpretations of a flower in the square.

Pattern 7. A sprightly white daisy dominates a solid yellow-green background. (Fig. 7-25.) Size of pattern: 3½ in. square.

Pat Rug Yarn: green #545; white #005; orange #421.

The outside row of the green square is worked first. The subsequent rows are worked in toward the center. The orange center is worked next. Then white petals are worked on top of the green stitches. Use Corner A for turning corners. There are 12 stitches on each side in the outside row. (Include the corner stitches in your count for each side.) The number of stitches on the sides is reduced by 2 in each row. The rows are worked one inside the other as follows. Use green yarn for all rows of the basic square.

1st Row. Start at the upper right of the area where the square is to be worked. Work stitches in the normal manner from right to left until there are 12 stitches. Turn a

7-25. Pattern 7.

corner on the twelfth stitch (Corner A). Continue until the 4 sides of the 12-stitch square are completed, turning corners when necessary. Do not end the yarn. The background of the square is solid green, so skip under on the wrong side and bring your needle to the surface for the start of each subsequent row.

2nd, 3rd, 4th and 5th Rows. Continue working the rows—one inside the other—until the basic green square is completed. Leave the center hole of canvas exposed.

Round Center. Use orange yarn (single strand doubled). Work a Round Center (see p. 100) around the exposed canvas hole in the center of the square.

Daisy Petals. The rows of green background stitches running around the square make comforting guides for gauging the length and placement of the white Lazy Daisy petals. It is not necessary to have the petals rigidly uniform. As in nature, there can be slight variations, but a reasonable degree of symmetry is pleasing to the eye. Try this procedure and you will find it easy to produce the desired effect: Use white yarn (single strand). To start all the petals, bring the needle up to the surface in the correct spot between the background and the orange center motif. Do not pull too tight. Allow some of the green background to show through at the outer ends.

1. Work 4 petals straight out from the center round motif to the middle of each side. Use the middle spot between the first row (outer row) and the second row on each of the 4 sides as guides for the small tie-down stitches.

2. Work 4 stitches diagonally out from the round motif to the corners. Use the spot between the second and third rows in each corner as your guide for the small tie-down stitches (2 rows in from the corners).

3. Work one stitch of similar length between each of the existing 8 petals (total 16 petals).

Note: You can work more or less petals if you wish. By following the above directions you produce a daisy with petals close together around the center but open and lacy looking at the outer ends. Quite charming!

Pattern 8. You create a completely different effect when you add a frame around the square. An orange posy with a startling black center gracefully fills the white square framed in green. Green French Knots produce interest accents. (Fig. 7-26.) Size of pattern: 3½ in. square.
Pat Rug Yarn: green #545; white #005; orange #421; black #050.

The outside green row of the square is worked first. Subsequent white rows are worked in toward the center. The orange petals are worked on top of the white stitches. Use Corner A for turning corners. There are 12 stitches on each side in the outside row. (Include the corner stitches in your count for each side.) The number of stitches on the sides are reduced by 2 in each row. The rows are worked one inside the other as follows.

7-26. Pattern 8.

1st Row. Use green yarn. Start at the upper right area where the square is to be worked. Work stitches in the normal manner from right to left until there are 12 stitches. Turn the corner on the twelfth stitch (Corner A). Continue until the 4 sides of the 12-stitch square are completed, turning corners when necessary. End the yarn.

2nd, 3rd, 4th and 5th Rows. Use white yarn. Start each row at the upper right directly inside the previously worked row. Continue working the rows until the inside white square is completed. Leave the center hole of the canvas exposed. Skip under on the wrong side after you complete each row and bring the needle to the surface for the start of each subsequent white row.

Round Center. Use black yarn (single strand doubled). Work a Round Center (see p. 100) around the exposed hole in the center of the square.

Four Orange Petals. The rows of background stitches running around the square form guides for gauging the length and placement of the three Lazy Daisy Stitches in each petal which are worked one outside the other. In this pattern, the 4 petals must be symmetric to achieve the desired effect. Use orange yarn (single strand). To start all petals, bring the needle to the surface in the correct spot between the background and the black center motif. Follow the directions in Chapter 2 for the basic Lazy Daisy Stitch. Turn the basic square so one corner is pointing directly toward you. Bring the needle up to the surface between the black center and the white background in a direct diagonal line with the corner. Each petal is worked as follows. (The small inner Chain Stitch is worked first.)

1. *Inner stitch:* Work the chain in a diagonal line out toward the corner, using the spot between the fourth and fifth row as your guide for the small tie-down stitch.

2. *Middle stitch:* Bring the needle up to the surface to the left of the first stitch. Place the needle down to the right of the first stitch and work the second stitch around the first, using the spot between the third and fourth row as a guide for the small tie-down stitch.

3. *Outer stitch:* Work the chain around the second stitch, using the spot between the second and third rows as a guide for the small tie-down stitch.

Repeat the petal in each of the four diagonal directions.

French Knots. Use green yarn. Place a French Knot (single strand—around the needle twice) between the petals on each of the 4 sides in the spot between the second and third rows—halfway between the petals.

Design Note for Orr Weave Squares: There are moments when a large blank space can overwhelm the most experienced professional designer. Where to start? How to repeat colors for proper balance? How large to make each motif? Where to place them? The answer to such design problems can be joyfully and easily solved if you use small square patterns. The designer proceeds by enjoying the comfort of dealing with one small area at a time, working each square independently of the others. The squares are extremely obliging and can produce miracles for the designer. Endless combinations make it possible to produce professional-looking items so easily. You need only press your Aware Button and read on! Make some rough thumbnail sketches of some of the ideas. For example, let's start with the sprightly daisy on the solid green square background. Place the squares side by side, touching each other (perhaps 3 across) and run a number of white rows around the 3 center motifs —and behold, a charming pillow design. To produce the long, skinny-shaped pillow, 4 motifs were used and framed by the stripes running around the central design area (see Fig. 7-33). The overall shape of the area is controlled by the placement and number of squares. Three

across and 3 down would key a large overall square shape. The individual squares can be separated by as many rows of contrasting color as you wish. For an easily keyed bellpull, repeat a square motif—one under the other— as many times as you like for the desired length. Alternate solid-colored squares with design-motif squares and create a large checkerboard effect. (The center in the solid square can be filled in with Orr Weave Stitches or a Round Center in matching color.)

Square daisy motifs would be stunning worked on white basic squares in various multicolored combinations. You could work the individual daisies in pinks, blues, yellows—very soft colors which would produce a delicate ice cream effect. Work the daisies in deep startling colors such as purples, reds, shocking pinks and the effect could be wild and exciting! Remember that there should be enough value contrast so that your eye can easily separate the motifs from the background areas or the overall effect will suffer. You can switch and change both the flower designs and the square bull's-eye pattern to your heart's content. Make them work for you. With their help you can design like an expert. In due time, I hope you will design some square motifs of your own. In the meantime, have fun with these!

Pattern 9. Maxi turquoise polka dots stand out against a white background. (Fig. 7-27.) Size of pattern: 4¼ in. × 6½ in.
Pat Rug Yarn: turquoise #728; white #005.

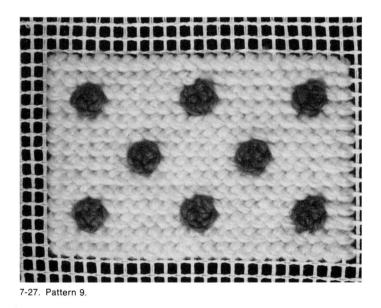

7-27. Pattern 9.

Polka Dots. Work Round Centers (see p.100). Use turquoise yarn (single strand). (Single strand doubled can also be used if you want thicker dots.) The polka dots are worked in horizontal rows.

1st Row. Start at the left corner of the canvas. Count down along the left edge at least 7 horizontal bars of canvas from the top. Place a finger on this bar and then count along it at least 7 vertical bars in toward the center. Place a yarn tie marker over the seventh crossbar. To start the first Round Center, bring your needle up to the surface in the hole diagonally down to the right from the marker. Remove the marker and work one Round Center. Pull your needle and yarn through to the wrong side but do not end the yarn. Not counting the hole of canvas in which the first Round Center started and ended, count over to the right and bring the needle up to the surface in the eighth hole. Work the second Round Center in exact horizontal alignment with the first Round Center. Continue working across to the right, repeating the dot as many times as necessary for desired coverage and leaving the same distance between dots. (There are 3 polka dots across in the sample shown.) Do not pull the yarn too tight when you skip under on the wrong side or the canvas will be tortured.

2nd Row. Place your finger on the hole directly in the middle of 2 of the top dots in the same horizontal row of holes where the top motifs are started and ended. Counting that hole as one, count down and bring the needle up to the surface in the fifth hole. Work one Round Center. This dot should be halfway between the top 2 dots and placed so that 2 horizontal rows of white background stitches can be worked between the top and second row of dots. Repeat this procedure across the second row as many times as necessary for desired coverage.

3rd Row. Repeat the first row. Drop down so that space is left for the 2 horizontal rows of background to be worked between the second and third rows of dots.

Repeat the polka dot pattern for desired coverage. The basic idea is to make the polka dots equidistant. There can be more or less space between dots if you wish.

Background. Work the Orr Weave Stitch in white yarn. The white background in the sample has a plain area surrounding the dots on the outside edges that consists of 2 stitches on both the right and left sides and 2 rows of stitches on both the top and bottom. This area can easily be increased if you wish by adding stitches on the 2 sides and additional rows on the top and bottom. The increase in background area must be anticipated before you start to work the first dot so it can be correctly placed to allow for the increase. Start at the top right. Work rows of background from right to left in the normal manner. When you reach the dots, skip under on the wrong side and continue the background row on the opposite side of the dot.

Color Note: You can substitute any number of color combinations. Keep in mind that you must have definite value contrast so that the dots will stand out against the background. The polka dots should startle the eye.

Pattern 10. Oversized turquoise French Knots on a white background create polka dots with dimension. (Fig. 7-28.) Size of pattern: 3¼ in. × 4½ in.
Pat Rug Yarn: turquoise #728; white #005.

Work the background first, leaving space for the French Knots to be worked later.

7-28. Pattern 10.

Background. Use white yarn. Start at the upper right. Work stitches from right to left and rows from top to bottom.

1st Row. Work 15 Orr Weave Stitches from right to left. (There are 15 stitches in the pattern. If you wish to increase the area coverage, the number of stitches must be divisible by 4, plus 3 stitches for balance at the end of the row.)

2nd Row. Work 3 stitches, skipping under on the wrong side when you work the last step of the third stitch so that one crossbar of canvas is left free. (The French Knots are to be worked later.) Bring the needle to the surface in the correct spot to the left for starting the next group of 3 stitches. Continue across to the left, leaving one free crossbar of canvas between each group of 3 stitches. End with 3 stitches to balance the beginning.

3rd Row. Work one solid row of stitches.

4th Row. Work one stitch. Skip under on the wrong side, leaving one free crossbar of canvas. Work 3 stitches. Skip under on the wrong side, leaving one free crossbar of canvas. Continue across to the left, leaving one free crossbar of canvas between each group of 3 stitches. End with one stitch to balance the beginning of the row. The fourth row completes the pattern for the polka dots. Notice how the spaces for the second row of dots fall halfway between the first row of spaces. Repeat the first through fourth rows as many times as necessary for desired coverage. (The pattern is repeated twice in the sample plus the first and second rows at the bottom for balance.) The best design is produced by ending with a row of polka dots which repeats the placement of those in the first row. Then add one solid row of background and your design will be in perfect balance.

French Knots. Use turquoise yarn. Start at the upper left. Bring the needle up to the surface close to a free crossbar of canvas. Work a large French Knot (single strand doubled—around the needle twice) over the free crossbar, placing the needle down in the hole diagonally opposite. By following this process the knot will dutifully stay in place over the crossbar. A bit of help from your fingers is sometimes necessary after you close the knot. Complete the first knot and skip under on the wrong side to bring the needle up to the surface in the next free spot for starting the second knot. Work all the knots throughout in the same diagonal direction over the crossbars so that they will appear uniform. Continue until you have covered all the free crossbars with the large textural knots.

Design Note: As in the preceding polka dot pattern, any number of color combinations can be substituted. The dots can also be placed farther apart if you wish.

Pattern 11. These bold maxi checks come in three colors: deep blue, yellow-green and bright white. (Fig. 7-29.) Size of pattern: 3 in. × 6½ in.
Pat Rug Yarn: green #550; blue #731; white #005.

The squares in the pattern have 2 stitches on each side. The size of the individual squares can be increased as desired. Stitches are worked from right to left and rows from top to bottom.

7-29. Pattern 11.

1st Row.

1. Use green yarn. Start at the upper right. Work 2 Orr Weave Stitches. When completing the second stitch, skip under on the wrong side and bring the needle up to the surface in the correct spot to the left so that 2 crossbars of canvas will be left free. (Blue stitches will be filled in later.) Work 2 stitches. Skip under 2 crossbars and work 2 stitches. Continue across to the left side for desired coverage, leaving 2 free crossbars between each group of 2 stitches. (There are 6 groups in the sample).

2. Use blue yarn. Fill in 2 blue stitches between each grouping of green stitches, skipping under on the wrong side when necessary.

2nd Row. Repeat Steps 1 and 2 as instructed for the first row.

3rd Row.

1. Use white yarn. (Use the second row as a helpful guide.) Start at the right. Work groups of 2 white stitches under the green stitches in the previous row, skipping under on the wrong side when necessary. Leave the crossbars under the blue stitches free.

2. Use green yarn. Start at the right. Work 2 green stitches under each group of blue stitches in the previous row.

4th Row. Repeat Steps 1 and 2 as instructed for the third row. This completes the pattern of squares with 2 stitches on each side. Repeat the first through fourth rows as many times as necessary for desired coverage. (The pattern is repeated twice in the sample plus the first and second rows to balance the top.) When you increase the size of the area, the number of stitches in each row must be divisible by 4 plus 2. The number of rows should also be divisible by 4 plus 2 for balance. This ensures design balance at the top and bottom and along both sides.

Design Note: The size of the individual squares can be increased. For example, you can increase the number of stitches across to 3, but you must then also increase the number of repeat rows to 3 to produce a square pattern. Numerous color combinations can be used successfully. To create a zestful impact, there should be one deep-value color, one middle-value color, and one very pale value (white or almost white).

Pattern 12. These single-stitch mini checks come in three colors: deep blue, yellow-green and bright white. (Fig. 7-30.) Size of pattern: 2¾ in. × 5 in.
Pat Rug Yarn: green #550; blue #731; white #005.

The stitches are worked from right to left and the rows from top to bottom.

1st Row.

1. Use green yarn. Start at the upper right. Work one Orr

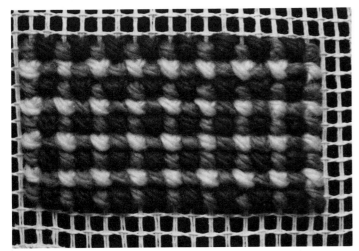

7-30. Pattern 12.

7-31. Pattern 13.

Weave stitch. Skip under on the wrong side and bring the needle up to the surface in the correct spot to the left so that one crossbar of canvas is left free (to be filled in with blue later). This can be done in one motion when you are familiar with the pattern. Work one stitch. Skip under one crossbar and work one stitch. Continue across to the left for desired coverage, leaving one free crossbar between single green stitches. (There are 9 green stitches in the sample.)

2. Use blue yarn. Start at the right. Fill in single blue stitches between green stitches. Skip under on the wrong side between stitches.

2nd Row.

1. Use white yarn. (Use the first row as a helpful guide.) Start at the right. Work one white stitch under each green stitch in the previous row. Skip under on the wrong side between stitches.

2. Use green yarn. Start at the right. Work one green stitch under each blue stitch in the previous row. Skip under on the wrong side between stitches. This completes the single-stitch checked pattern.

Repeat the first and second rows as many times as necessary for desired coverage. (The sample repeats the pattern 4 times plus the first row for balance.) When you increase the size of the area, the number of stitches in each row must be divisible by 2 plus one. The number of rows should also be divisible by 2 plus one for balance. This ensures design balance at the top and bottom and along both sides.

Design Note: This is a mini version of the bold checks in the previous pattern. Combining both versions in the same item could lead to interesting results. Note the color suggestions for the bold pattern. Value contrast is necessary for the mini pattern too.

Pattern 13. A purple and white Greek Key square produces a classic design. (Fig. 7-31.) Size of sample: 4 in. square.
Pat Rug Yarn: purple #632; white #005.

The stitches are worked in 2 continuous rows around the square. Use Corner A for turns throughout.

1st Row. Use purple yarn. Find the exact center crossbar of the canvas (or the center crossbar of the area to be covered by the 13-stitch square pattern). This can easily be determined by making one vertical fold in the canvas—then one horizontal fold. Start the first stitch on the center crossbar. Work Orr Weave Stitches from right to left in the following steps. 1. Work 3 stitches and turn the canvas 90 degrees (the top becomes the right side). Repeat the 90-degree turn throughout. 2. Work 2 stitches, turn. 3. Work 4 stitches, turn. 4. Work 4 stitches, turn. 5. Work 6 stitches, turn. 6. Work 6 stitches, turn. 7. Work 8 stitches, turn. 8. Work 8 stitches, turn. 9. Work 10 stitches, turn. (Skip under the ninth crossbar of canvas if you wish to close the outside white row. See the upper left corner of Fig. 7-31.) 10. Work 10 stitches, turn. 11. Work 12 stitches, turn. 12. Work 12 stitches, turn. 13. Work 12 stitches, turn. 14. Work one stitch to complete the outside row. (There are 13 stitches on each side of the square.)

2nd Row. Use white yarn. Turn the canvas in order to start the white row of stitches in a right-to-left direction. (The canvas is turned completely upside down compared to the start of the purple row.) Work a row of white stitches between the purple stitches, working from the center out, making turns when necessary. (Fill in one stitch at the end to close the white outside row if it was left exposed for this purpose.)

Design Note: The square key pattern shown can be repeated as many times as you wish. It can be placed side by side to form one row or a large 12 in. square can be formed by placing 3 in each direction for a total of 9. You can alternate plain-colored squares with Greek Key patterns to create a checkerboard effect. You can make the Greek Key design grow and grow if you continue the purple row around and around, leaving one row of exposed canvas in between, to be filled in later in white. Watch the turns at the corners. Make certain you go far enough before the turn to leave space for the white row of stitches in between. The pattern can be flopped and adapted to create charming companion pieces such as the 2 green-and-white pillows in Figures 7-35 and 7-37. This is only one example of the Greek Key design. Check the books on design for there are many variations which you can work out once you learn how the pattern is formed. Figure out the pattern on graph paper before you start the stitches. It takes a bit of work, but the results can be delightful and rewarding. You can substitute any number of color combinations with sharp enough value contrast to clearly define the design.

Pattern 14. The Orr Weave carnival creates twelve inches of fun! Shocking pink, turquoise, yellow green, purple and white combine in a shower of confetti. (Fig. 7-32.) Size of pattern: 5 in. × 12 in.

Only the Orr Weave stitch is used to create the busy textural effect. This pattern, which can be quickly and easily worked, will please all who are young at heart. Pat Rug Yarn: shocking pink #259; turquoise #738; green #550; purple #632; white #005.

7-32. Pattern 14.

Turn the canvas 90 degrees so that the top becomes the right side. With the canvas in this position, start at the upper right and work the stitches in a normal manner from right to left. The rows are worked from top to bottom.

Note: There are no repeat patterns involved except for the 2 pink and white borders at the beginning and end. Each row is listed separately. In rows where 2 colors are involved, work one color completely across the row. Skip under on the wrong side to leave space between the stitches for the second color. Then work the second color, skipping under the already worked stitches. See directions for surface whipping under Pattern 4 (Fig. 7-18). When surface whipping is indicated, work one additional row of stitches (following the color pattern for the rows) and then go back and add surface whipping.

The pattern shown has 17 stitches in each row. Here we go. Have fun! Work the rows in solid color (unless stitch pattern or whipping is indicated) as follows: 1st Row, pink; 2nd, white; 3rd, stitch pattern, 2 white and 1 pink; 4th, white; 5th, pink; 6th, green; 7th, stitch pattern, 1 pink and 1 purple; 8th, turquoise; 9th, purple (surface whip in white); 10th, pink; 11th, pink; 12th, white; 13th, stitch pattern, 1 green and 1 turquoise; 14th, purple; 15th, pink (surface whip in white); 16th, turquoise; 17th, white; 18th, pink; 19th, stitch pattern, 1 green and 1 purple; 20th, white (surface whip in pink); 21st, purple; 22nd, white; 23rd, turquoise; 24th, stitch pattern, 1 green and 1 pink; 25th, stitch pattern, 1 pink and 1 green; 26th, purple (surface whip in white); 27th, pink; 28th, white; 29th,

green; 30th, turquoise; 31st, stitch pattern, 1 pink and 1 white; 32nd, purple; 33rd, white (surface whip in turquoise); 34th, pink; 35th, stitch pattern, 1 turquoise and 1 purple; 36th, green; 37th, pink; 38th, white; 39th, stitch pattern, 2 white and 1 pink; 40th, white; 41st, pink.

Design Note: You can easily manipulate this pattern in a number of ways. The border along the sides can be completely eliminated by starting with the fifth row and ending with the thirty-seventh row. The pattern can be ended anywhere along the way. If you are using the 2 borders, do not end the pattern with a pink row before you work the border or it will cause an imbalance by blending into the pattern. The border pattern (the first through fifth rows) can be inserted in the pattern at *even* intervals or directly in the center. Again, be certain it is surrounded by colors other than pink. Because the border produces a separate wide stripe, it must be used in a symmetric fashion to please the eye. The overall pattern can be stopped, repeated, reversed at almost any point. It is dutifully elastic. There is a trick you can use when a large area such as a bench top or window seat is involved. You can literally stretch the pattern to any size and end up with perfect balance. All in knowing how!

The *Stretch Trick* can be made to work with or without the border pattern. Measure off on the canvas the exact area you wish to cover. Place yarn tie markers in each of the 4 corner points. (Allow extra for cropping in construction if material backing is to be used.) Place a yarn tie marker on the vertical bar of canvas in the exact center of the area to be worked. Work the pattern toward the center marker, stopping at green thirty-sixth row. If the area is very large, go back and start the pattern again at the sixth row (eliminating the border pattern this time). Repeat the rows until you reach the center bar of canvas on which you placed the yarn tie marker. Remove the marker and work the center row in the color (or colors) indicated. Here is the wonderful trick! Forget about the written pattern instructions. From here on the area you have already worked will become your only guide. Place a yarn tie marker at each end of the completed center row. This is the center row of the area you wish to cover. Using the area already worked as your guide, simply *reverse the sequence of rows of colors and patterns* away from the center row. End with the border pattern if you started with it. If you use the border pattern, it is necessary to do a bit of figuring in advance so that the center row of pink dots is balanced at the beginning and end of the row. The number of stitches in the rows should be divisible by 3 (2 white and one pink) plus 2 white for balance at the end. If exact measurement is a factor and you wish to use the border, you can work the center row of border in a stitch pattern of one white and one pink. When you place the pink dots closer together, you need not be concerned with starting and ending the row with the same color. With the dots close together, your eye does not call attention to the difference. These little tricks are extremely useful when you are rescaling the pattern; they help produce a professional-looking finished item. You can also substitute a completely different color scheme. Notice the values used in the color pattern: one deep-value color (purple), 3 middle-value colors (green, turquoise and pink) plus white. A smashing new impact can be created by substituting other colors. Do include white as one color, since it adds a wonderful sparkle. You can readily make up your own pattern for a particular item as I did with the book jacket. This type of pattern is marvelous for using up odds and ends of yarn left over from other projects. Dream up your own shower of confetti!

ORR WEAVE FINISHED ITEMS

Four sprightly daisies in a row shout spring in an unusually long pillow of green, white and pale orange with self-yarn braiding and velvet backing. (Fig. 7-33.) This pillow is especially appropriate for use on beds because of its long shape. Smaller and equally attractive pillows can be worked with only two or three daisies in a row. Size of sample: 8½ in. × 20 in.

Pat Rug Yarn: green #545 (38 str.); orange #421 (7 str.); white #005 (24 str.). The green strands include yarn for Fill-in Stitches and the braid.

7-33

The four daisy squares are worked first. The surrounding stripes are worked in rows from the center to the outside edges. Find the center crossbar by folding the canvas in half in a vertical direction and then in half in a horizontal direction. Indicate the spot by a yarn tie marker.

See Pattern 7 (Fig. 7-25) for directions for the sprightly Daisy Stitch Square.

Daisy Squares. See Figure 7-34 for the order in which to work the squares.

Square 1. Counting the crossbar on which the center marker is tied as one, count up 6 horizontal bars. Move to the left one vertical bar. Start the background of the

7-34

square at this point. (The center vertical bar is left free to be filled in with a row of white later.) Complete the first daisy square motif following the directions and colors given for Pattern 7.

Square 2. Complete Square 2 to the left of the first square, leaving one vertical bar of canvas free between the squares.

Square 3. Square 3 is worked to the right of Square 1, leaving one center vertical bar of canvas free. *Helpful Note:* The green background of the daisy square can be started at any corner. To save you from having to count over to the right for the correct start, turn the canvas 90 degrees (the top becomes the right side). With the canvas in this position, you can then start Square 3 directly under Square 1. Remember to leave one free bar between the squares.

Square 4 (not shown in Fig. 7-34). Work to the right of Square 3. Leave one free bar of canvas between the squares. The same method of turning the canvas that was used for Square 3 can be applied to start this square.

White Stripes Between Squares. Use white yarn. Turn the canvas 90 degrees (the top becomes the right side) and work 3 single rows, 12 stitches each, between squares.

Surrounding Stripe Pattern. Use Corner B for turning all corners. The stripes are worked in rows around the central design rectangle from the center out to the edges in the color pattern to be indicated. Start at the lower right corner of the right daisy square. Work the rows completely around all 4 center daisy motifs, turning the canvas when necessary. 1st and 2nd Rows, white; 3rd, orange; 4th, white; 5th, green; 6th, white; 7th, green. This completes the rows of Orr Weave Stitches. Even if you plan to eliminate the yarn braid cording and use a material backing (with or without material cording), I suggest you work one row of green Regular Fill-in Stitches (see Chapter 8) around the entire area. This row is cropped during construction but prevents the canvas from peeking through along the edges.

Green Braid Edging. To duplicate the edging shown in the sample requires some tight working. I particularly like a thick, firm edging. Somehow it makes for a trimmer overall appearance which I find pleasing. The row of Regular Fill-in Stitches can easily be eliminated if you wish less bulk along the edges.

Specific directions for working self-yarn braid to be used with material backing are given in Chapter 8 for the purple and white zig zag pillow. The same process can be followed for this pillow edging.

1. Use green yarn. Work one row of Regular Fill-in Stitches around the entire area. The stitch is worked between the last row of Orr Weave Stitches and the next outer bar of canvas on which the Braid Stitch will be worked. (This is the row which can be eliminated for less bulk if you wish.)

2. Use green yarn (single strand). Work one row of Regular Braid Stitch, Start A (see Chapter 8), turning corners when necessary.

3. Work one row of Regular Fill-in Stitches around between the braid stitch and the next outer bars of canvas. The working is rather tight but this row is necessary since it is the one which is cropped in construction and prevents the canvas from peeking through.

See Chapter 8 for directions for attaching material backing with yarn cording. Remember to crop the outside row of Regular Fill-in Stitches when you attach material backing.

A pair of charmers are the next two items! Sparkling green and white Greek Key designs on companion pillows excite the eye when the colors are reversed. The samples are both 14½ in. squares and have green felt backing.

Note: Before you attempt to work these designs, I strongly suggest that you make up a working sample following the directions for Pattern 13, leaving the white row open as in Figure 7-31. In order to form the interesting symmetric arrangement of Greek Key designs, it is necessary to flop the basic pattern, thus repeating it in reverse. The important thing is to start each individual square in the correct spot and follow the arrows carefully, since the first row jells the pattern. The working sample can literally be flopped so the wrong side is up, making it possible for you to clearly see the pattern in reverse. You can use any 2 contrasting colors to make up the working sample. When these projects are completed, place them in your design file for future reference.

The squares are worked in the order indicated by the numbers in Figure 7-36. Turn the canvas and the photograph so that the *numbers are in the correct readable position* before starting the first 3 stitches of each square. Two different turns are used for the corners. The correct turn for each square is indicated by the letters A (inside turn) and B (outside turn). Once the individual squares are completed, the covering of the free bars between the squares unites the motifs so that they form one large square. From then on it is smooth sailing; you work rows around the square, making the necessary color changes according to the directions.

━━━━━━

This Greek Key design pillow has a green background with white designs and surrounding frame. (Fig. 7-35.) Pat Rug Yarn: green #569 (36 str.); white #005 (30 str.).

Mark the top of the canvas with a yarn tie. Mark the center crossbar of the canvas with a yarn tie. Fold the canvas in quarters to determine the center. (See Fig. 7-36.) Leave one free row of crossbars of canvas exposed between individual squares. Turn the canvas 90 degrees so that the top becomes the right side. Turn the photograph in the same manner so that numbers 1 and 2 are in the correct readable position. It is very important to start each square in the correct spot.

7-35

Square 1 (Corner A), 1st Row. Use green yarn. Use the center yarn tie marker as your guide to start. Each square is started on the crossbar in its exact center. Not counting the crossbar on which the center yarn tie marker has been placed, count out to the right 7 crossbars and place a finger on that crossbar. Count down 7 crossbars from the center marker and place a finger from the other hand on that spot. Run both fingers in toward the center of the area where the square will be worked and place a yarn tie marker over the crossbar where they meet. This is where the first stitch will be worked. Double-check your count (it will also be 7 diagonal crossbars down to the right from the central marker if correct). Another good check is to place your working sample under the canvas to see if the

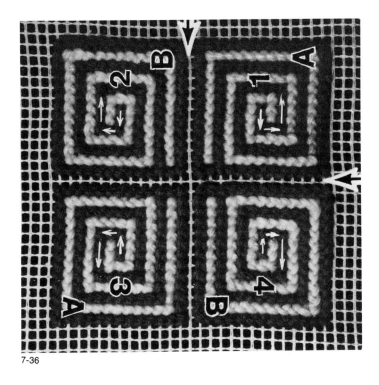

7-36

start matches the one in the sample. Proceed to work the first row following the directions for Pattern 13 and substituting the colors indicated. The arrows in Figure 7-36 will get you started in the correct direction and carry you around the first few turns. Continue until the 13-stitch square motif is completed.

2nd Row. Use white yarn. Fill in the white row between the green stitches. As explained in the pattern directions, the white row is started in the reverse position from the green row.

Square 2 (Corner B). This is the trick which makes it easy to get started in the correct direction. Turn the canvas and the photograph so that they are in the same position as in the start of the first square. Place the working sample next to the photograph in the same position as Square 1. Flop it up and over so the wrong side is up and it becomes a guide for Square 2.

1st Row. Use green yarn. Use the same method to find the exact center as you used for Square 1. Counting out to the right (Square 1 also becomes a guide) and counting up (instead of down), run your fingers toward the middle and place a yarn tie marker over the correct crossbar for the start. Follow the arrows in Figure 7-36 and use your wrong-side-up sample as a guide. Use Corner B (outside corner) to make the turns in the reverse-position squares.

2nd Row. Use white yarn. Fill in the row between the stitches in the green row.

Turn the canvas and the photograph until numbers 3 and 4 are in a readable position (the 2 completed squares will be on the left side).

Square 3 (Corner A). Work Square 3 in the same manner as Square 1.

Square 4 (Corner B). Work Square 4 in the same manner as Square 2.

Filling in Exposed Canvas Between Squares. Use green yarn. Follow the direction of the large arrows. Starting at the right side, work one row of stitches from right to left in a horizontal direction. Turn the canvas 90 degrees so that the top becomes the right side. Fill in the remaining row. Work the stitches in a horizontal direction from right to left, skipping under the center stitch of the first fill-in row. This completes the central square of 4 motifs.

Outside Rows. Start the outside rows at the bottom right and work them from right to left. Use Corner B throughout. The rows are worked one outside the other in the following color pattern: 1st and 2nd Rows, green; 3rd, white; 4th, green; 5th and 6th, white.

7th Row. This is the patterned row of alternate green and white stitches. The design is carefully keyed for a green stitch to fall in each corner. The easiest method is to work the green stitches first.

1. Use green yarn. Start at the lower right. First, work a green stitch on the crossbar directly to the left of the crossbar under the corner white stitch. Work one green stitch. Jump under on the wrong side to start the second stitch, leaving one exposed crossbar between (to be filled in later in white). Continue around the row, skipping one crossbar between green stitches. The green stitches will fall in each corner. If they don't, quickly double-check your placement.

2. Use white yarn. Start at the lower right and work white stitches between the already-worked green stitches.

The 8th and 9th rows are white; the 10th and 11th are green. This completes the pillow design. Each sample has a row of Regular Fill-in Stitches (see Chapter 8) completely around the worked area which were cropped during construction. Use green yarn.

See Chapter 8 for directions for attaching material backing.

The reverse companion pillow has a white background with green designs and surrounding frame. (Fig. 7-37.) The design is worked in the exact same manner as its companion. Since the colors are reversed, you must start each individual square with white and then fill in the exposed row between in green. The two crossed rows between the squares are worked in white. Make a quick list of the outside rows, noting the reversed colors, before you start working those rows. Refer to the list, since it is very easy to forget to reverse colors when you become involved in working the stitches.

Design Note: Reversing colors for companion pieces is an excellent idea because it repeats the pattern but in an

7-37

interesting way. You could add two more companions on the same couch in a bright blue of approximately the same value as the green and have four friends that will live together happily. Another idea is to work the same pattern in four different colors, one for each pillow, using rather deep related colors of similar value, deep enough to produce sharp contrasts when combined with the white. This could produce a stunning effect.

Special Design Note for the Orr Weave Border! If you wish to key a design where a border or frame contains alternate color stitches (as in the green-and-white companion pillows), you must start with a basic center square containing an *odd* number of stitches on each side. The corner stitches will then come out even and all four corners will be uniform, as shown in Figure 7-38. Otherwise, you will end the row around the square containing the alternate colors with 2 stitches of the same color, which would destroy the pattern. You must give advance thought to this factor whenever you work a row of alternate color stitches around a central design area.

7-38

7-39

7-40

Daisies and stripes live happily together on a shocking pink and white patchwork pillow-top. (Fig. 7-39.) Size of sample: 14 in. square. The pillow has a shocking pink velvet backing.
Pat Rug Yarn: white #005 (38 str.); light shocking pink #279 (20 str.); deep shocking pink #239 (24 str.).
    Place a yarn tie marker at the top of the canvas. Follow Figure 7-40 for the order of working the alternate squares. The squares are worked so that one bar of canvas is left

free between all squares. These free bars are filled in after all of the squares are completed by working 4 straight rows of stitches in the directions indicated by the arrows.

Square 1—Daisy Square at Upper Right. Starting along the top of the canvas at a point approximately 5 in. in from the right edge, count *down* 8 horizontal bars from the top and place a finger of the left hand on the eighth bar. Starting approximately 5 in. down from the top, count *in* 8 vertical bars from the right side and place a finger of the right hand on the eighth bar. Run both fingers along the bars toward the upper right corner. The first stitch is worked over the crossbar where they meet. If necessary, tie a yarn marker over the crossbar to indicate the spot until you are ready to start stitching.

Orr Weave Daisy Square. Use white yarn. Working from right to left, work the outside row of a 14-stitch square (14 stitches on each side), turning the canvas when necessary (Corner A). End the yarn. This row forms the outside frame of the daisy square. The 12-stitch daisy square is worked in the center of the white outline. (See Pattern 7, Fig. 7-25.) Use light shocking pink for the background of the square. Use deep shocking pink for the Round Center (worked with a single strand doubled). Use white yarn for the surface daisy petals.

Square 2—Alternate Striped Square. This is also a 14-stitch square but it is worked in straight rows or Orr Weave Stitches. Leave one free vertical bar of canvas on the left side of the daisy square. Start the striped square at the top, directly to the left of the free bar. The stitches are worked from right to left—the rows from top to bottom. Work rows of 14 stitches each in the following color pattern: 1st through 4th Rows, white; 5th, light pink; 6th, white; 7th and 8th, deep pink; 9th, white; 10th, light pink; 11th through 14th, white.

Square 3. Work a daisy square to the left of the striped square, leaving one free vertical bar of canvas along the left side of the striped square.

This completes the top row of squares. The remaining 2 rows are worked in the order indicated in Figure 7-40, alternating the design motifs in each row to produce the pattern. Remember to leave one free bar of canvas between all squares.

Rows Between Squares. Use deep shocking pink yarn. Work rows in the directions indicated by the arrows (2 in one direction and 2 in the other). In the last 2 rows, skip under the stitch in a completed row when you reach a spot where the rows cross. Turn the canvas to the correct position for working the stitches from right to left.

Outside Rows. Use deep shocking pink yarn. Start at the lower right corner. Use outside Corner B. Work one row of stitches completely around the entire area. Do not end the yarn. Work a second row around the first row.

Work one row of deep shocking pink Regular Fill-in Stitches (see Chapter 8) between the outer row of Orr Weave Stitches and the next outer bar of canvas.

See Chapter 8 for directions for attaching material backing. The outer row of Fill-in Stitches is cropped during construction.

8.

Construction and Finishing

After you have worked the Now Needlepoint stitches on the canvas, there are a number of creative decisions for you to make before you can consider the item complete. This chapter contains information to assist you in making choices which will enhance the finished item. The manner in which an article is constructed and such finishing touches as tassels, fringe, and others are extremely important if the end product is to please the eye and have an overall trim, professional effect. Hours of diligent effort on the part of the needleworker can be destroyed by careless construction or incorrect decisions concerning finishing touches. These final decisions you must make as a designer will become easier and easier as your knowledge and creative experience develop.

The following pages include detailed instructions for completely constructing different types of finished items in Now Needlepoint stitches. With the exception of the little sewing required for the lining in the eyeglass case, all of the construction is accomplished through the use of the dutiful Braid Stitch. A typical example of each construction procedure is presented with step-by-step directions for completing the finished sample item. Once you master the technique, you can change the size of the item, the stitch, and the design to suit your desires. For example, the same construction technique with the Braid Stitch is used for pincushions and mini pillows, for average-size pillows and for the extra-large pillows. The backings of the pillows, which are worked on the same piece of canvas as the topside, can be a solid color or very fancy—as you wish. You are assured of exact color harmony since you use the same yarn colors throughout. But first, you must master the Braid Stitch mechanics and learn to work the stitch around corners; after that, you can produce the trim pillows shown in the samples. The Braid Stitch can also be worked around a finished area

and combined with material backing. This assures the exact matching of colors on the top surface of the pillow, since the Braid Stitch eliminates the necessity for material cording. The braid matches the top rather than the backing.

After the basic mechanics for the different versions of the Braid Stitch and the typical sample construction procedures, you will find information which will help you add the magic finishing touches to your Now Needlepoint items.

REGULAR FILL-IN STITCH

The Regular Fill-in Stitch is worked around a completed Now Needlepoint area to prevent the canvas between the worked area and the Regular Braid Stitch from being exposed. It is used on 3 to the inch canvas, but is not necessary on the finer 5 to the inch canvas. It is similar to the stem stitch used for crewel work. You will notice from Figure 8-2, showing the stitch in progress on the green mini pillow with white daisies (see Fig. 5-31) that there is considerable space between the worked area and the next outside bar of canvas on which you will work the Regular Braid Stitch during construction. This can be due to the use of a lighter-weight yarn (Nantucket 6-Ply Cable Yarn was used in the sample) or the very nature of a particular stitch. Use your own judgment to decide whether or not the Regular Fill-in Stitch is necessary. If you work a few Regular Braid Stitches and you see some canvas left exposed, pull out the braid (we all have to "pick out" once in a while), work a row of Regular Fill-in Stitches around and then proceed with the braid. The Regular Fill-in Stitch must be worked around both the top and the back areas before you start the braid construction. Along with properly covering the canvas, it also adds a little decorative touch. If you work the stitches in the color of the background, they seem to disappear. If you work them in the color of the braid, they roll the braid around the edges, making it look wider and heavier.

Regular Fill-in Stitch Mechanics. Follow Figure 8-1. Use 3 to the inch canvas. Work the stitch from left to right completely around the outside edges of the worked area.

   1. Bring the needle up to the surface in 1.

   2. Place the needle down in 2 and up in 3 in one motion.

   3. Place the needle down in 4 and up in 5 in one motion. (Fig. 8-2.)

Continue working the stitch completely around the item, moving one bar of canvas to the right for each stitch.

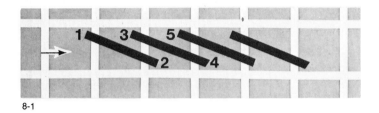

8-1

8-2

THE BRAID STITCH

The Braid Stitch is used for edging and construction and is both decorative and functional.

Personality. Although it is worked with a needle and yarn over a bar (or bars) of canvas, the Braid Stitch simulates the three-strand braid which is so familiar to us all. Worked in the heavy yarn, it gives a very professional look to items because of its firm, trim appearance. It has long been used for edging—mostly in lighter-weight yarn on finer canvas—but it really comes into its own when worked in the heavier yarn for then the pattern and delightful texture of the braid become clearly defined. In addition to pleasing the eye, it literally sews the Now Needlepoint areas together to form pincushions and pillows. After learning the stitch mechanics, you will find out how and when to use the Braid Stitch for edging and construction. Directions for different versions of the Braid Stitch to be used on the two sizes of canvas are included.

Regular Braid Stitch on 3 to the Inch Canvas. (Fig. 8-3.) Because of the deep V formed by the Regular Braid Stitch, there are two starts:

Start A. The stitches are started in such a way that you can weave into them after working around an item with the result that the braid pattern is continuous and the piecing hardly noticeable.

Start B. You will use a straight start on such items as the bellpull or wall hangings, when the stitches are not continuous around on all four sides.

Special Braid (or Cording) Stitch on 5 to the Inch Canvas. (Fig. 8-4.) The Regular Braid Stitch does not work satisfactorily on the finer 5 to the inch canvas, so the Special Braid Stitch was invented. This stitch, which looks somewhat like cording and does not nearly have the definite deep V of the Regular Braid, has a neat appearance and dutifully performs the construction tasks on the 5 to the inch canvas. Only one start is necessary for the Special Braid.

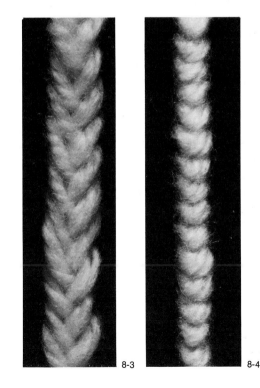

8-3   8-4

Preparing the Canvas. The Regular Braid Stitch is worked over a bar (or bars) of canvas that has been left free along the edge of the completed Now Needlepoint area. There are two different procedures presented for preparing the canvas before working the Braid Stitch that depend on the type of item involved. The following is a quick summary of the procedures.

Bellpulls, wall hangings, edges of rugs. For all items where the Regular Braid Stitch is used for decorative purposes, the canvas must be machine zig zagged and turned under in advance so that all of the stitches near the edges of the Now Needlepoint worked area can be worked through a double layer of canvas. This prevents any loose exposed canvas from peeking through on the right side of the worked area and assures a rather neat appearance on the wrong side. This process must be carried out carefully, to ensure that only the one free bar on which the Regular Braid Stitch will be worked is left exposed. The technique is explained in detail in the directions for the bellpull. (See Fig. 8-30.) Follow the same procedure for other items where a decorative edge is desired.

Pincushions and pillows of all sizes with Now Needlepoint backings. When used for construction as well as decorative purposes, both the top and the back of pillows should be completed before preparing the canvas. This process is explained in careful detail in the directions for the rosebud mini pillow. (See Figs. 8-18, 8-19 and 8-20.) Follow the same procedure for pincushions or pillows of any size or design.

Preparing the canvas for learning purposes. To learn the stitch mechanics, I suggest you use a strip of canvas and machine zig zag it along one bar near the edge. Cut off excess canvas so that the zig-zagged bar becomes the edge. Now, carefully turn back the canvas along the *third bar* from the edge, matching the holes. (See Fig. 8-5.) The two folded-back bars are barely visible in the photograph, but it shows how the third bar forms the edge upon which the Regular Braid Stitch is worked. The canvas is stiff, so it stays folded. For purposes of learning, pretend that you have completed the worked area and that only the one free bar along the edge is now left exposed. (The step photographs were taken without the worked area completed in order to show the steps clearly.) When you work the Regular Braid Stitches on an item where the design area is completed, in many instances the hem will be held in place by the area stitches along the edges which are worked over both layers of canvas.

Note: I always work with the right side of the finished area toward me. I prefer this procedure because I like to have the side which will be visible in the finished item facing me so that I can best achieve an even, trim look.

REGULAR BRAID STITCH MECHANICS (3 TO THE INCH CANVAS)

Let's get down to the nitty-gritty of the mechanics for simulating the braid effect. The photographs—your only guide for this stitch—tell the complete story. The dropped-down letters and numbers identify the sequence you must follow in the working area at the top. You work the stitches in the general direction from left to right, but it is necessary to reverse the direction of certain of the stitch steps as the work progresses in order to define the deep V in the finished braid. It is confusing at first but once you are past the initial starts, you merely take the equivalent of three steps forward (going into the third hole) and two steps backward (going into the second hole). Because of the longer step forward, the row of braid progresses to the right and the deep V pattern forms. After mastering the mechanics, you sail right along. You can complete the correct start and simply follow the two steps outlined in Figures 8-8 and 8-9, repeating them for desired coverage.

Regular Braid Stitch, Start A. This is the usual start to use when you will be working the Regular Braid Stitch completely around on all 4 sides of an article. (The end stitches are worked into the starting stitches after a complete trip around the article.) Since it is a staggered start, the last few stitches can be blended into the first stitches in such a way as to hide the joining.

1. Pull the yarn through to the surface in Hole A. (Fig. 8-5.) (Leave a 6-in. tail for the learning sample. Weave under the worked area for at least 1 in. before you pull the yarn to the surface in a finished article.)

2. Working from left to right, go over the top bar and bring the yarn through from the back to the front in Hole B (directly to the right of Hole A).

3. Go over the top bar, skipping Hole C to the right and bring the yarn through from the back to the front in Hole D. (Fig. 8-6.)

4. Reverse the direction. (Fig. 8-7.) Work from right to left. Go over the top bar and bring the yarn through from back to front in Hole B.

This completes Start A. From now on you repeat the two simple steps which form the Regular Braid Stitch as follows:

1. The yarn is coming through from the back to the front in Hole 1. (Fig. 8-8.) You work the stitch from left to right. Go over the top bar, skipping Holes 2 and 3, and bring the yarn through from back to front in Hole 4.

2. Reverse your direction. (Fig. 8-9.) Work from right to left. Go over the top bar, skipping hole 3, and bring the yarn through from the back to the front in Hole 2.

Repeat these two steps, carefully following the sequence in the photographs for desired coverage.

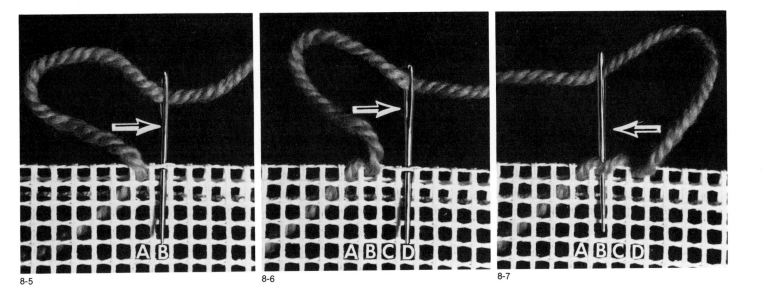

8-5   8-6   8-7

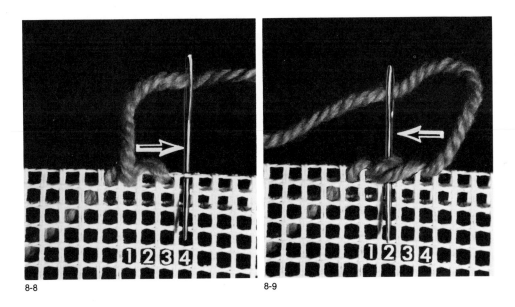

8-8   8-9

Stop! Think of what you are doing and simplify the process in your mind.

1. Forward (left-to-right direction). Skip two holes. Go over the top and bring the yarn through from the back to the front in the third hole to the right (the first free hole).

2. Reverse (right-to-left direction). Skip one hole. Go over the top and bring the yarn through from back to front in the second hole to the left.

Repeat for desired coverage.

Note: The instructions for this stitch are extremely difficult to put into words. Some directions I have read left me swimming with confusion. It is so helpful when a teacher can demonstrate the steps, but since this is not possible, please be a bit patient in the beginning. You will quickly develop an easy rhythm if you concentrate on the two simple steps. Learning this stitch is worth the extra effort, since it makes possible all the marvelous decorative edging—and the construction too—shown in the samples.

Regular Braid Stitch, Start B. This produces the straight-edge start necessary in items such as the bellpull (Fig. 8-30) when the braid does not go completely around all 4 sides of an item.

1. Pull the yarn through to the surface in Hole A. (Fig. 8-10.) (Leave a 6 in. tail for the learning sample. Weave under the worked area for at least 1 in. before pulling the yarn to the surface in a finished article.)

2. Working from left to right, go over the top bar and bring the yarn through from the back to the front in Hole B (directly to the right of Hole A).

3. Reverse the direction. (Fig. 8-11.) Working from right to left, go over the top bar and bring the yarn through from the back to the front in Hole A.

4. Proceed from left to right. (Fig. 8-12.) Go over the top bar, skipping Hole B, and bring the yarn through from the back to the front in Hole C.

5. Reverse your direction. (Fig. 8-13.) Working from right to left, go over the top bar, skipping Hole B, and bring the yarn through from the back to the front in Hole A.

This completes Start B. From now on, you repeat the two simple steps which form the Regular Braid Stitch shown in Figures 8-8 and 8-9.

To End Strands, Regular Braid Stitch. End strands on the reverse motion, as indicated in Figure 8-9. Do not come through to the front. Instead, insert the needle in the same spot, but run the needle under the worked braid on the wrong side in the reverse direction for at least 1 in. The yarn falls in place next to the previous stitch and the pattern is not broken. Snip off the excess tail and tuck it under with the needle.

To Start Strands, Regular Braid Stitch. Run under the worked area on the wrong side for at least 1 in., coming up in the exact spot where the needle entered to end the strand. Bring the needle through from the back to the front in the proper hole so that you are in position to start the next stitch. Snip off the excess tail and tuck it under with the needle.

Note: It is best not to stop and start strands when you are turning a corner. End the strand before you get to a corner if you think you will run out of yarn while turning.

To Weave Into the Staggered Start of the Regular Braid Stitch. Work the Regular Braid Stitch completely around the item right up to the staggered start. Continue working the overlapping stitches until the joining closes. Improvise on the last step or two by holding the yarn in the direction it should follow to conform to the pattern, and inserting the needle at the correct spot. (*Oops!* If your first attempt does not please you, keep loose. Remove the needle and pull out a stitch or two and try again.) On the very last step, hold the yarn across in the correct position

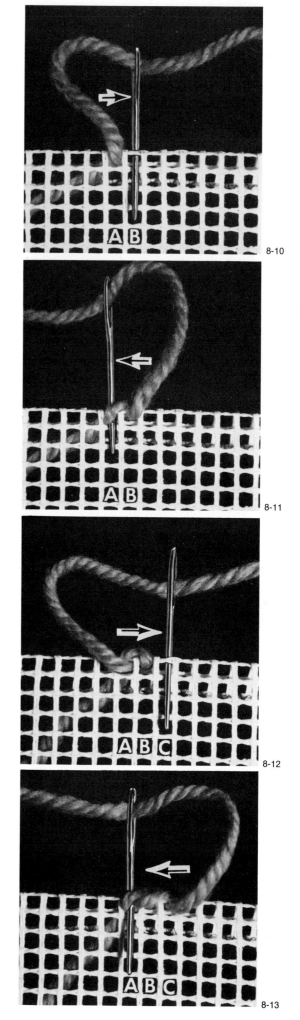

8-10

8-11

8-12

8-13

to preserve the pattern. Insert the needle in the back of the braid and weave under for at least 1 in. Snip off the excess tail and tuck it under with your needle. With a little practice, you can work the joining so that it is unnoticeable.

To End Regular Braid Stitch with a Straight Edge (Used with Start B). When you reach the point where you wish to end the braid with a straight edge, improvise by working several small reverse motion stitches—coming through from the back to the front in the same end hole on the right—until the sides of the V are filled in and a straight line is formed. Follow the pattern of the V. The procedure is similar to the bottom Fill-in Stitches of the Fly Stitch. *Important: Keep the yarn untwisted at all times.* The Regular Braid Stitch can be worked single strand or single strand doubled. It is especially important to keep the yarn untwisted when you use a single strand doubled or the stitches will not lie flat. Use the valuable trick of placing your finger under the spot where the double strand emerges and the stitches will dutifully fall into place side by side. After you have worked a few stitches in this manner, the process becomes automatic.

SPECIAL BRAID STITCH MECHANICS (5 TO THE INCH CANVAS)

There are no unusual starts or stops necessary for this version of the stitch, since the V formed in the Special Braid is very shallow. Happily, you can start off with the basic stitch steps. The stitch is actually a loop of yarn which is worked along the outer double bars of canvas and closes to form the shallow V or corded appearance. You work it in one direction only—from right to left. It is important to make certain the loop is in the exact position shown in Figure 8-15 before you insert the needle. You can easily hold the yarn with the left hand while you close the loop to the size shown. If you do not follow this procedure, you end up with a mess of strange bumps and not the trim edge you wish.

Preparing the Canvas for the Special Braid Stitch. Prepare the 5 to the inch canvas exactly as instructed in the preceding directions for the 3 to the inch canvas, keeping in mind that the double bars are always treated as one. Fold the hem back at the third double bar and work the stitches over this double bar which forms the edge, as shown in Figures 8-14 to 8-16.

Special Braid Stitches are always worked single strand from right to left. The double bar along the edge will be referred to as the top bar in the directions. Always place the needle in the large holes.

1. During the learning process, come up from underneath the hem, insert the needle in a hole directly under

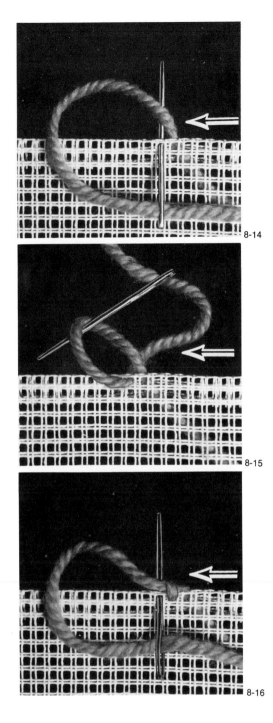

8-14

8-15

8-16

the top bar and pull the yarn through to the back (leave a 6-in. tail to be woven in later). (Fig. 8-14.) For the finished article, weave under the worked area on the wrong side for at least 1 in. and bring the needle through to the back in a hole directly under the top bar.

2. Bring the yarn over the top bar and insert the needle in the large hole directly to the left, going through both thicknesses of canvas from front to back. Hold the yarn with your left hand while you pull the yarn through to the back to form a loop about the size shown in Figure 8-15.

3. Insert the needle through the loop exactly as shown in Figure 8-15. Getting that needle through the loop correctly is the key to the stitch.

4. Slowly pull the yarn through the loop in a left direction to close around the canvas.

Figure 8-16 shows you how to start the next stitch after you have completed the first. It is the same step as shown in Figure 8-14. You use the hole directly to the left to start the next stitch.

Repeat the steps shown in the photographs for desired coverage.

To End Strands, Special Braid Stitch. Complete a stitch. Run the yarn under the worked braid on the wrong side for at least 1 in. Snip off the excess tail and tuck it under with your needle.

To Start Strands, Special Braid Stitch. Run under the worked braid for at least 1 in. on the wrong side (the same section where you ended the strand). Come up in the correct position on the wrong side to start the next stitch (in back of the last stitch worked). The braid becomes a bit heavy at the joining, but you can squeeze it into shape with your fingers. Cut off any excess tail and tuck it under with your needle. After a little practice, you will not be able to detect the joining.

Note: As with the Regular Braid Stitch, it is best not to end and start strands at a corner. End the strand before you get to a corner if you think you will run out of yarn while turning.

NOW NEEDLEPOINT
BACKINGS, PLAIN AND FANCY

Decide whether you want to have a Now Needlepoint backing before you cut your canvas so that you can allow sufficient area for it. You work the backing directly under the frontside, leaving one bar of canvas exposed in between on which you will work the Braid Stitch when you are ready to start the construction. (See Fig. 8-18.) The exact size of the frontside area must be duplicated for the back area. Hole for hole it must be the same. You can key the back easily when you work it directly under the frontside area. The count given is for the number of stitches or rows *down* (depending on how the stitches progress) for each of the samples shown, and the neighboring front keys the distance across. When you do your own designs, you must carefully count down (I double-check after working the first row) to make sure all the holes can be matched with those in the topside area. *Plain backings* are filled in with one solid overall color; you should repeat one of the colors used in the design motif on the frontside in order to integrate the item. *Fancy backings* are worked in different ways, depending on the design and stitch involved. For example, you can work the top and back simultaneously if both involve identical vertical stripes. Detailed instructions for each sample's fancy backing are given in detail in the various chapters. If you design your own backing, you must decide which is the best procedure to follow. Remember that the size of the overall area *must* duplicate the frontside.

Note: When the backing is completed, follow the basic construction directions for the rosebud mini pillow.

CONSTRUCTION DIRECTIONS
FOR THE REGULAR BRAID STITCH
(3 TO THE INCH CANVAS)

The rosebud mini pillow is used as a sample to explain the construction procedure using the Regular Braid Stitch, but you can follow the same steps for any size pincushion or pillow-type of article with a Now Needlepoint backing. The first important step is to learn how to work the Regular Braid Stitch around a corner. If the yarn is extremely heavy, even heavier than the Pat Rug Yarn, you can work the Regular Braid Stitch around the corner with the same two steps used for the straight run. However, I found it was necessary to have a few extra crosses go over the corner area to properly hide the canvas when I used yarn similar in weight to the Pat Rug Yarn, or lighter yarn. Do master the turning before you attempt a corner on a finished item.

The following directions are written with the sincere intention of explaining the steps to you in a clear manner. A drawing showing the yarn runs would look like a nest of baby snakes; therefore, I used words to outline the steps, with the assistance of Figure 8-21. You might find it confusing at first. If you are religious, say a little prayer, or cross your fingers—I use the prayer method myself—and you will be sailing around corners in no time! The first few times you will probably feel much as I did when I learned to "turn heels" while knitting socks. To this day I have not been able to figure out why or how the directions work. I would simply follow the somewhat confusing directions and, all of a sudden, there would be the heel.

With gentle firmness, I emphasize the importance of learning to walk this stitch around corners in a uniform manner, so that you will be able to produce any of the items which involve construction. Diligence and persistence are needed in the beginning, but later comes the joy of designing your own creations with that extra touch of the expert needleworker.

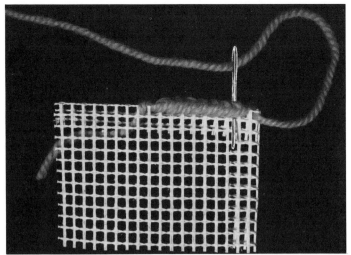

8-17

8-18

8-19

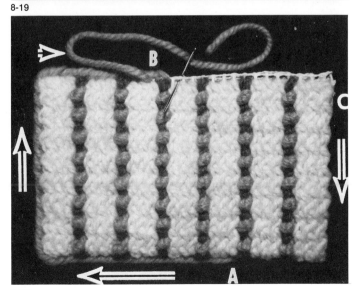

8-20

Learning Corner. I suggest you make up a Learning Corner to help you to master the mechanics before you work on a finished item. Start with a piece of canvas approximately 5 in. × 7 in. Machine zig zag across the top outside and right outside bars. Fold back the canvas along the top and right sides at the third bar from the edge to simulate the sample in Figure 8-17. Line up all thicknesses exactly, especially at the corner where the folds meet and cause a number of layers. Work through all the layers as if they were one. (In a finished item, the Now Needlepoint worked area would be completed before you start the braid construction, but this procedure is for the purpose of learning only.) Work the Regular Braid Stitch until you reach a corner. Then carefully follow Figure 8-21 and the directions for turning a corner. When you have completed the corner, slip the needle off and pull out the corner stitches. Rethread the needle and try it again, and again, until you are ready to work it on a finished item.

Construction Directions for the Rosebud Mini Pillow, Using the Regular Braid Stitch Worked on 3 to the Inch Canvas.

1. Machine zig zag around the canvas on the third bar out from the worked area. Repeat around a second time on the same bar. Cut off the excess canvas outside the machine zig zags. (Fig. 8-18.)

2. Fold in half at the exposed bar between the front and back areas. Fold the canvas back under along the sides; leave one bar of canvas exposed on both front and back areas. (Fig. 8-19.)

Note: Do not be concerned if the edges unfold a bit. You will carefully match the holes as you work each stitch. The raw edges on the long sides will be turned under later.

3. Work the Regular Braid Stitch, using Start A. *Do not start at the corner.* (Fig. 8-20.) The canvas must be turned so that starting spot A is on top before you work the stitches. Unfold the canvas for a minute to weave the yarn under on the wrong side for about 1 in. Bring the needle through to the front at A. Refold the canvas. Follow the direction of the arrow (left to right) and work the Regular Braid Stitch on the exposed bar between the areas up to the corner.

Mechanics for Turning a Corner with the Regular Braid Stitch. Around the corner we go! Follow Figure 8-21. You have worked up to the corner, which means you have gone over the top bar and brought the needle through from back to front in Corner Hole C. Now go over the top in the reverse direction (right to left) and bring the needle through from back to front in Hole A. Now you are ready for the turn.

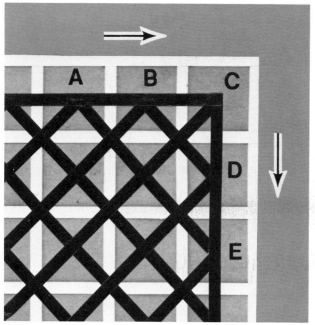

8-21. Black lines indicate worked area.

Forward, Step 1. Go up over the top (left-to-right direction), bringing the needle through from back to front in Corner Hole C.

Reverse, Step 2. Go up over the top (right-to-left direction), bringing the needle through from back to front in Hole B.

Note: Be certain at this point that you have carefully folded inside the excess canvas along the short side edges as in Figure 8-19. Now you must start to fasten the back and front together by matching the holes carefully and working over the 2 exposed bars of canvas as if they were one. Catch the exposed bars of both sides as the needle goes over the top and through from the back to the front. Control the tension so that the pattern of the stitches is uniform with those stitches worked on the single bar.

Forward, Step 3. Go up over the top (left-to-right direction), bringing the needle through from back to front in Hole D. (Remember to catch the bars on both sides under the needle.)

Reverse, Step 4. Go up over the top (right-to-left direction), bringing the needle through from back to front in Hole B (yes, way back in Hole B).

Forward, Step 5. Go up over the top (left-to-right direction), bringing the needle through from back to front in Hole E.

Reverse, Step 6. Go up over the top (right-to-left direction), bringing the needle through from back to front in Corner Hole C.

You are around the corner! Fluff the yarn and correct the tension with your needle if necessary. It is not always possible to actually *see* the canvas holes when you are turning corners, but with a little practice and experience you can determine where the holes are and easily insert the needle in the correct place to assure continuity of the braid pattern. It is what the eye will see that counts. If it looks right, it is right!

Construction Note: I do not find it necessary to baste the exposed canvas bars together with sewing thread before working the Braid Stitches, but I am definitely not a baster by nature. The canvas is stiff enough so that it dutifully stays in place and holds the fold. If you are particular and wish to baste, carefully line up the holes before you sew the sides together. Make certain that you work the overhand sewing thread stitch in a manner that will not interfere with the steps of the Braid Stitch and will not be visible in the completed item. And remember to insert the stuffing before you close up the last side.

Repeat this procedure at each corner. Follow the arrows around the edge in Figure 8-21, turning the work when necessary. Always work from left to right and hold the front side toward you.

Pillow Stuffing. When you use *loose synthetic stuffing,* you must partially stuff when you reach Point B. Push a fair amount of stuffing firmly in the 2 corners already worked. Continue around the next corner to Point C, or a little beyond, and fill in the remaining stuffing before you complete the Braid Stitch around to beginning Point A, where you weave it into the staggered start. To hold its shape, a pincushion or pillow should be firmly packed —but not over-stuffed or it will look tortured.

When you use *already encased pillow forms,* continue the Braid Stitch around the corner just before Point C and insert the form. Continue around the fourth corner to beginning Point A, where you weave into the staggered start. After completing the item, give the pillow several gentle punches and twists with your hands to even up the distribution of the inside stuffing and force it into the corners.

CONSTRUCTION DIRECTIONS FOR THE SPECIAL BRAID STITCH (5 TO THE INCH CANVAS)

Prepare the canvas as outlined under the construction directions for the Regular Braid Stitch. The double bars of the 5 to the inch canvas are considered as one, so you work the machine zig zag on the third pair of double bars outside the worked area. You must leave a pair of double bars exposed between the areas for the Special Braid Stitches.

Start at the same spot A as shown in Figure 8-20, but reverse the working direction, since the Special Braid Stitch is worked from right to left.

Mechanics for Turning Corners with the Special Braid Stitch. Oh happy day! The corners are simple. Walk around with ease following the stitch directions. There are no forward and reverse motions; you only proceed right to left as the stitches progress. You need no special corner since the holes are smaller and the canvas is properly covered by the yarn.

Pillow Stuffing. Partially stuff the pillow at Point B if you use *loose stuffing*. Continue around just past the third corner and insert the remaining stuffing. Continue around the fourth corner to beginning Point A and complete the last stitch next to the first.

When you use an *already encased pillow form*, insert the form just before you reach the third corner. Continue around the fourth corner to beginning Point A and complete the last stitch next to the first.

Separate Now Needlepoint Backing. It is easiest and safest to work a Now Needlepoint backing directly under the frontside so that you can match the exact number of holes, and I would certainly recommend this procedure whenever it is possible. However, should you decide you wish a Now Needlepoint backing *after* completing the front, it is possible to work it on a separate piece of canvas (but carefully match the number of holes in all directions or you will be in trouble) and then attach the two sides with construction Braid Stitches. A single bar of canvas (or a pair of double bars on the 5 to the inch canvas) must be left exposed on all sides when you turn under the excess canvas. You must machine zig zag all 4 edges of each piece twice around on the third bar—or pair of bars—out from the worked area and cut away the canvas outside the zig zags. The difference in this process is that one side will not be attached to the topside, which will make it a bit cumbersome at the start of construction.

Design Note for Now Needlepoint Backings: The rosebud mini pillow construction example which follows is a basic one—much like a basic sewing pattern. The same procedure can be followed with other designs and stitches and the items can vary in size. No sewing is necessary with Now Needlepoint backing and braid construction. All Now Needlepoint from start to finish! You can eliminate those frustrating attempts to match yarns exactly with materials for backings now that you have

discovered this novel formula. Glad you learned to turn that corner? You can now include little fun design touches on the pillow backings for anyone who might look. It is much like the luxury of having a lace binding on the inside of a hem or a kooky inside jacket lining. Although there are a number of fun backings among the finished items in this book, do enjoy the satisfaction of creating some of your own. Avoid designs which "fight" the frontside; keep them fairly simple so that they will complement it.

CONSTRUCTION EXAMPLE 1: A PILLOW OR PINCUSHION WITH NOW NEEDLEPOINT BACKING

This Single Zig Zag Chain pink rosebud mini pillow or maxi pin cushion will delight the young at heart. It is textural, feminine, and pretty too—and has a solid pink Now Needlepoint backing. (Fig. 8-22.) Size of sample: 5½ in. × 9 in.
Pat Rug Yarn: white #005 (14 str.); green #545 (4 str.); pink #279 (35 str.).

The topside is worked first. Work the backing directly underneath, leaving one horizontal bar of canvas exposed on which you will work the Regular Braid Stitch when construction takes place. Work the stitches from top to bottom. The rows are worked from left to right.

8-22

1st Row. Use white yarn. Start at the upper left. Starting with a zig—downward right diagonal—work 17 Single Zig Zag Chain Stitches (ending with a zig).

2nd and 3rd Rows. Repeat the first row 2 more times. Leave one vertical bar of canvas exposed between the third and fourth rows. (The pink rosebuds and green leaves will be filled in later.)

4th, 5th and 6th Rows. Repeat the first row 3 times. Leave one vertical bar of canvas exposed between the sixth and seventh rows.

Repeat the rows across from left to right, working 3 rows of white with one exposed vertical bar of canvas in between until there are 7 groups of 3 rows with 6 exposed bars between the groups.

Rosebud Stripes. Follow Figure 8-23 and detailed directions.

1. Use green yarn (single strand doubled). Work diagonal stitches indicated by the numerals in the diagram from top to bottom on the exposed vertical bars of the canvas.

2. Use pink yarn. Work French Knots indicated by the letters (single strand doubled—around the needle once) from top to bottom between the green diagonal stitches in each row.

Repeat across until all the exposed bars of canvas are covered.

Now Needlepoint Backing. Use pink yarn. Start at the left directly under the completed topside area. Leave one horizontal bar of canvas exposed between the top and back areas. (The Braid Stitch will be worked on the exposed bar later during construction.) Starting with a zig, work 17 Single Zig Zag Stitches down to the bottom of row, ending with a zig. Repeat the rows across from left to right until there are 27 rows which exactly duplicates —hole for hole—the area covered by the top design. (See Fig. 8-18 with construction directions.)

Braid Construction. Carefully follow the directions which outline the steps for construction with the Braid Stitch (See Figs. 8-18 to 8-20.) Use pink yarn (single strand).

Mechanics for French Knot Rosebud Stripes with Suggestion of Green Leaves. Interspersing the straight green diagonal stitches between the pink French Knots immediately suggests leaves and tiny rosebuds resembling the stripes of rosebuds sewn on underwear in the past. Even with the large canvas and heavy rug yarn, you achieve a textural but very dainty effect. This design motif can be worked in rows between numerous stitches as long as it is possible to leave one straight bar of canvas exposed—as for example, with the Fly Stitch and the Orr Weave. You can work stripes horizontally on an item by turning the canvas 90 degrees (the right side becomes the top) while you work the stitches.

Follow Figure 8-23 when working on 3 to the inch canvas. Work the stitch from top to bottom. Keep the yarn untwisted at all times or the stitches and knots will not lie flat and have a uniform look.

Green Diagonal Stitches. 1. Work the diagonal stitches indicated by the striped bars and numbers first. Use green

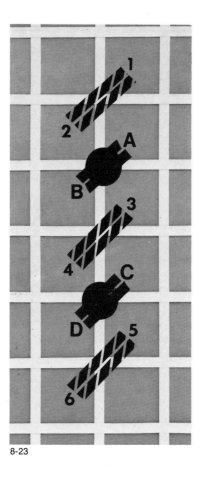

8-23

yarn (single strand doubled). Bring the needle up to the surface in Hole 1. Place the needle down in Hole 2 and up in Hole 3 in one motion, skipping under one crossbar of canvas to leave space for the knot A-B. Use the trick of placing the finger of your left hand under the spot where the doubled yarn comes through to the surface while you pull the yarn to close over the canvas.

2. Place the needle down in Hole 4 and up in Hole 5 in one motion.

Continue down to the bottom of the row, leaving one free crossbar between each green diagonal stitch for the French Knots.

Note: I prefer the down-in-Hole-2 and up-in-Hole-3 in-one-motion procedure. However, you can pull the needle through to the back in Hole 2 and come up in Hole 3 in two motions if you find it easier. The first method is faster, of course.

French Knot Rosebuds. Follow the steps indicated by the letters in Figure 8-23 (the solid bars and circles represent the knots).

1. Use rosebud-color yarn. Bring the needle up to the surface in Hole A. Work one French Knot (single strand doubled—around the needle once), going down in Hole B.

Note: It takes a little practice to make trim-looking French Knots with the single-strand-doubled yarn. Keep that yarn untwisted and learn to use a slow, even pull when you close the knot around the needle. If a little loop appears, give an extra-gentle pull from beneath on the single loose strand and this will usually equalize the tension. And remember, once in a while a knot goes gooney!

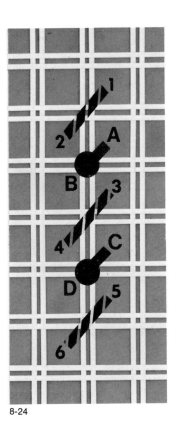

8-24

If it does, pull the needle and yarn back through to the surface, patiently untie the knot and start over again. It happens to the best of us. Do not pull the knots too tight. Let your left hand help by holding the knot in place to prevent it from slipping through to the back. When you complete each knot, ease it in place with your fingers in order to center it as much as possible.

2. Bring the needle up to the surface in Hole C. Work one French Knot as in Step 1, going down in Hole D.

Continue down to the bottom until you have completed the row.

Follow Figure 8-24 to produce the French Knot rosebud stripes on 5 to the inch canvas.

Use single strand yarn throughout. Follow the same procedure you used for the 3 to the inch canvas with one exception when you work the French Knot rosebuds. Bring the needle up to the surface in Hole A. Work one French Knot (single strand—around the needle once), going down in Hole B with the following exception. Hole B as indicated in Figure 8-24 is the small hole formed by the double crossbars of the 5 to the inch canvas. By placing the needle down in this convenient extra little hole, the knot is held secure directly in the center.

Attaching Material Pillow Backing. There are a number of suitable materials. Velvet is a happy companion with the textural look of the Now Needlepoint, but heavy linen or good-quality felt can also be used successfully. If you use other materials, keep in mind the wear and tear which a pillow receives. The material should be durable and heavy enough so that the large canvas will not cause cumbersome bumps along the construction areas. For each of the finished items I have mentioned the type of material used for the backing.

Amount of Material Needed. The very rough drawing in Figure 8-25 is an example of the Think Plan I use to determine the amount of material needed. For a 12 in. square pillow you would cut a piece of material approximately 15 in. × 18 in. You must allow extra material for the insertion of a zipper. Add 1½ in. extra on all 4 sides plus 3 in. extra in one direction for the zipper. You can no doubt do the figuring in your head for the simple square shapes but the Think Plan helps when large or unusual shapes are involved.

Inserting the Zipper. I strongly advise you to use a zipper insert with a material backing. A zipper makes it possible to complete the construction on all four sides before you turn the pillow cover right side out. The heavier canvas can be troublesome if you attempt to turn under the raw edges after you have inserted the stuffing. With a zipper, you can also remove the cover for cleaning when necessary.

Insert the zipper approximately one third of the way up from the bottom of the pillow. Set the zipper in deep enough so that it will not be visible. If you use felt, run

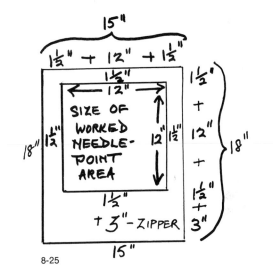

8-25

machine stitching along the edge of the flap to prevent it from stretching.

Zig-Zagging the Now Needlepoint Topside. Remove the masking tape from the canvas. Run zig zag stitches on the machine completely around all 4 sides on the third bar of the canvas outside the worked area. Run a second row of machine zig zags directly over the first. Cut off excess canvas outside the machine zig zagging. No blocking is necessary but at this point it is very important that you carefully pull the worked canvas into proper shape. Make certain it is squared at the corners and that the opposite sides are parallel. You can accomplish this with a few diagonal tugs. Once you have machine-sewed the Now Needlepoint worked area to the backing, it dutifully holds a trim shape. If you use material cording, it must be attached at this point in construction. (See Figs. 8-26, 8-27 and 8-28.)

Attaching the Topside to the Backing. After you have

inserted the zipper, place the backing on a flat surface so that the right side faces upward. Place the canvas with the right side down on top of the backing. If there is a top and bottom to the design motif, the inserted zipper should be one-third up from the bottom. Use the zipper foot on your machine and heavy-duty thread. The zipper remains zipped while you stitch the three sides but it *must be opened before you stitch the fourth side so that the pillow covering can be turned right side out.* I stress this particular step because it is an easy one to forget. And very troublesome when you do! Starting at the lower-right bottom corner, run a line of stitching along the bottom edge so that you catch ⅛ to ¼ in. of worked area, depending on the type of stitch you use. If you have worked a row of Regular Fill-in Stitches completely around the Now Needlepoint area, run machine stitches between the Fill-in Stitches and the next row of stitches in from each edge. The Fill-in Stitches are not visible when the pillow construction is completed, but they hold the backing tightly in place along the construction edge where canvas might peek through. Continue around the three sides. Open the zipper and complete the fourth side. Run a second row of machine stitches directly over the first for increased strength and to correct any irregularities which may have occurred in the first run of stitches. Cut off excess material around the edges to correspond with the width of excess canvas. Carefully turn the pillow cover right side out. Do this slowly since the canvas is heavy. You can ease the edges with your fingers and push the corners into shape by using the blunt end of a pencil. If canvas is exposed at any point along the construction edge, turn it inside out and catch the spot with machine stitches. If necessary, use a needle to fluff and pull wool to the surface in corners so that you completely cover the canvas.

Attaching a Pillow Backing with Matching Material Cording. If you want matching material cording, you must cut bias strips wide enough to allow for at least ½ in. extra material along both edges after folding the strip over a cotton upholstery cording. The cording comes in many weights, so the bias strips must be cut in widths to accommodate the circumference of the cording, plus 1 in. If necessary, piece the strips together before you insert the cording to make one continuous length to go completely around the outside edge of the pillow. A true bias is formed by folding the crosswise thread along the lengthwise thread of the material. Cut along the fold. Mark parallel lines in the width necessary for the strips. Cut out the strips along the lines. Join them together if more than one is needed. (Fig. 8-26.) Place the right sides together and join them by overlapping the diagonal ends so that ¼ in. of each point extends beyond the edges of the seam. Start at the spot where they cross. Stitch a ¼ in. seam across to the opposite crossing. Press the seams

8-26

open. Place your cord in the center. Fold the strip in half over the cord with the wrong sides together (right side outside). Use the zipper foot and run one row of machine stitches close to but not crowding the cording. Attach the bias cording to the right side of your Now Needlepoint worked area. Place the cording side of the strip toward the center. Leave approximately 1 in. free of stitching at the start. Attach the strip, cropping ⅛ to ¼ in. of worked Now Needlepoint along the edges. The amount of cropping depends on the type of stitch involved, or, if there is a row of Regular Fill-in Stitches surrounding the area, run stitches between it and the next row in toward the center. (I very seldom baste but you could do so at this point if it makes you feel more secure.) Work almost up to the corner and then follow Figure 8-27 "around" the corner rather than to a point. Pivot slightly with the needle down, and work several machine stitches. Then slash through both edges almost up to the spot along the stitching where the needle enters the material. Slash again, turn, slash, repeating until you are around the corner. Continue around all 4 sides.

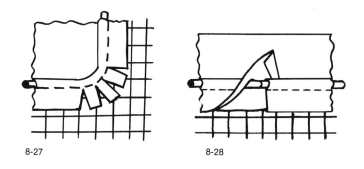

8-27   8-28

To join the beginning and end of the cording, stop stitching about 1 in. before the joining spot. (Fig. 8-28.) Snip open the machine stitches for 1 in. on the starting end. Cut off ¾ in. of cord. Fold under at least ¼ in. of starting edge of bias. Cut the finishing end of bias cord so that it meets with the beginning. Place the folded-back beginning edge over and around the finishing end and complete stitching. Follow the previous directions for attaching the topside to the backing. Run a row of stitching which attaches the topside to the back *close to the cording,* making sure that the previous rows of stitching will not be visible in the finished item. Disregard the instructions for edge cropping of the worked area. Instead, use cording as your guide for placement of the machine stitches. Run a second row of machine stitches over the first.

Stuffing for Pillows and Pincushions. The most luxurious of all stuffing for pillows is down. You can usually purchase a wide variety of standard down-stuffed ready-made forms in department stores and needlework shops which will be rather on the expensive side but delightfully soft and comfortable. However, you are limited to the standard shapes available. On the other hand, many ready-made forms on the market come in a variety of materials which are less expensive and are very satisfactory. I discovered a loose stuffing called Poly-fil which I use for most of my samples and which you can purchase in a large quantity for very little. It has many good features. Not as soft as down, it produces a pillow or pincushion with wonderful resiliency and a trim shape. Because there is no fuzz flying all over, it is extremely easy to work with. With this type of stuffing you can make your own forms in the correct size to use with removable pillow covers and are not limited to the already-made standard shapes available. The poly-fil is also available in pop-in forms in a variety of standard sizes.

Pillows and pincushions with Now Needlepoint backings and braid construction can be stuffed without inner casings or enclosures if you use Poly-fil. I made most of the samples with the needlepoint backings in this manner. The secret is to use the proper amount of loose stuffing and to push it carefully into the corners. The correct amount will produce a trim item which holds its shape beautifully. You have to be careful not to use too much or the item will become tortured looking and, if it is a pillow, it will not be comfortable. Several twists and pulls when the item is completed will distribute the stuffing evenly inside. Poly-fil is excellent for pincushions, too, which should be more on the firm side than pillows, though not so firm that they will refuse to sit flat on a surface. I don't mention rubber foam stuffing for pillows or pincushions since I have never found it to be successful for either item. Too bouncy!

Stuffing for Removable Chair, Bench and Window Seat Pads. For these items I do recommend the rubber foam, which comes by the yard in a variety of thicknesses. Choose the thickness most suitable for each item. Used this way, the foam dutifully behaves, lying flat and trim on a surface.

The following purple-and-white French Stitch pillow design is included in this chapter as an example of how the yarn braid can also be combined with a material backing. This procedure assures the exact matching of the cording surrounding a pillow to a color used in the Now Needlepoint topside rather than having a material cording which matches the backing. It makes a great deal of sense when you think about it. You work the Regular Braid Stitch completely around the outside of the completed design. Then always work a Regular Fill-in Stitch (see Fig. 8-1) around the outside of the braid between the braid and the next bar of canvas. This row of Regular Fill-in Stitches will be cropped during construction so that it is not visible but prevents exposed canvas from peeking through. This also eliminates the necessity of cropping into the Braid Stitches which destroys the formation. Keep in mind that this procedure can be followed for all Now Needlepoint pillow top designs when you wish material backing. When the area stitches require them —an example would be the Fly Stitch—you must even up all outside edges with the Special Fill-in Stitches found in the individual stitch chapters before you work the braid. In some instances when you use a lightweight rug yarn, it might be wise to work a row of Regular Fill-in Stitches around the completed area before the braid is worked as well as after. Work a small portion of the braid to test if it properly covers the canvas. If it doesn't, work that extra row of Regular Fill-in Stitches before you work the braid.

CONSTRUCTION EXAMPLE 2:
A PILLOW WITH YARN CORDING AND MATERIAL BACKING

This pillow has two values of bright purple plus white in easy-to-work French Stitch Zig Zag. (Fig. 8-29.) Size of pattern: 12 in. square. The yarn cording is worked in the Braid Stitch and the pillow has a purple velvet backing. Pat Rug Yarn. *Pillow top*: deep purple #632 (17 str.); light purple #672 (17 str.); white #005 (30 str.). *Braid Stitch and Regular Fill-in Stitches:* white #005 (19 str.).

8-29

See Chapter 4 for the French Stitch. Work stitches from top to bottom. Work rows from left to right. The entire pattern is worked in a Six-Stitch Zig Zag. Follow the general directions for a Four-Stitch Zig Zag (see Pattern 3, Fig. 4-21) but increase the number of stitches in each zig and zag to six and use the following colors.

1st Row. Use deep purple yarn. Start at the upper left. Work one row of Six-Stitch Zig Zags until there are four zig zags from top to bottom, as in Figure 8-29. This first row keys the contour for all rows.

2nd and 3rd Rows. Use white yarn. Work 2 rows.

4th Row. Use light purple yarn. Work one row. Color Pattern. Work one row deep purple, two rows white, one row light purple.

Repeat the color pattern five times across the canvas to the right side. Using the outer points of the side zig zags as guides for the edges, fill in the open side areas, repeating the correct colors to continue the overall pattern. Work Special French Fill-in Stitches around the outer edge in the right colors to preserve the pattern if you will be using Braid Stitch.

Note: French half stitches can be worked at the top and bottom of the rows and to form an even edge. This can be done at the beginning and end of each row while the work is in progress if you are thoroughly familiar with the stitch.

Heavy White Yarn Braid. Use white yarn (single strand doubled). Work the Regular Braid Stitch (Start A) completely around the outside edge of your Now Needlepoint design area. The difference will be that you don't fold the canvas under but work with it flat. You travel around the corners in the same manner as when you use the Braid Stitch for construction. If it helps, temporarily fold the excess canvas back while you work the corner stitches so that it more closely resembles the single bar shown in the directions for turning a corner. Keep the yarn untwisted at all times. Place the finger of your left hand under the spot where the yarn comes to the surface before pulling it to close and the double strands will fall neatly in place next to each other. For the *Outside Fill-in Stitches,* use white yarn. Work the Regular Fill-in Stitch completely around the area between the braid and the next outer bar of canvas. It is a bit of a squeeze. This row of stitches gets cropped when construction takes place but you need it to prevent any canvas from peeking through.

Follow the earlier directions for attaching material backing. Remember that the outer row of Fill-in Stitches must be cropped during construction. Since the white braid is heavy, take a little extra care when you do the machine stitching in order not to catch it in construction. The heavy appearance of the braid adds a trim profes-

sional touch, so it is worth the extra effort to use it.

SIMULTANEOUS CONSTRUCTION

Use a functional new technique for Now Needlepoint wall hangings—large or small—called Simultaneous Construction and completely eliminate the necessity for expensive framing and troublesome mounting. You work a special hem across the top through which you insert an inexpensive dowel or a decorative hanging rod. Either of these holds the top edge securely in a straight line so that the hanging falls evenly. The remaining three edges are folded under before you work the area stitches and the Regular Braid Stitch. A trim, professional item results, with all raw edges of canvas neatly caught under the stitches on the wrong side. You can use simple wooden dowels of various sizes with a decorative knob or ball showing at each end. The white ones shown on the bell-pull (Fig. 8-30) are drawer pulls. You can substitute tassels for the knobs. Marvelous effects can be created with the varieties of metal or wooden drapery rods available in decorator shops or department stores. Choose the type and size of rod you wish to use as soon as you have keyed your basic design. It is important to remember that you must make the necessary top hem allowance for the *size* of the rod you will use. It takes a considerable amount of worked area to run around a rod—much more than you would think—so check your measurements carefully. The best method is to literally hold the canvas around the rod to determine how many rows of Orr Weave Stitches are necessary. Then make an allowance for a very slight shrinkage in size which might take place when the heavy yarn is worked on the canvas. Add at least one extra row of Orr Weave as a safety measure to make certain there will be sufficient room for the pole to slip through. If you wish, you can also repeat the top hem construction on the bottom of a hanging and insert a second pole.

I hope this new construction technique will do much to stimulate your creative awareness, for the possibilities are staggering!

CONSTRUCTION EXAMPLE 3: A BELLPULL WITH SIMULTANEOUS CONSTRUCTION

The French Stitch Special (Pattern 7, Fig. 4-25) has been adapted to a long, skinny bellpull with an oversized macramé tassel. (Fig. 8-30.) Size of sample: 7½ in. × 32½ in. The design is keyed for a ⅜ in. dowel, 7¼ in. long. Pat Rug Yarn: turquoise #728 (39 str.); white #005 (36 str.); yellow #413 (11 str.); shocking pink #279 (12 str.). The tassel yardage is not included above. Approximately 22 extra yards of continuous uncut white yarn #005 would be needed for the tassel.

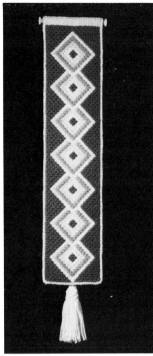

8-30

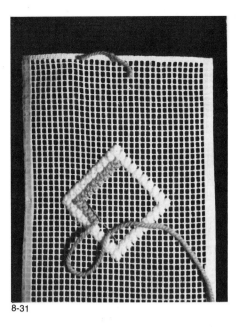

8-31

Starting with the top motif and repeating it down to the bottom, you work each of the overlapping diamonds from the outside white row in toward the center. Find the center hole across the top by folding the canvas in half lengthwise. Place the yarn tie marker at the top over the selvege to indicate the center row of holes. Count down 16 holes from the marker. Work the first white stitch of the top diamond motif around this hole.

Top Multi-striped Diamond. The top diamond has 10 stitches on each side. Start with the outside white row and work in toward the small center turquoise diamond. (Fig. 8-31.)

1st Row.

1. Use white yarn. Work one French Stitch around the center hole. Work 9 additional stitches in a zag direction for making a total of 10 stitches.

2. Work 9 stitches in a zig direction.

3. Work 9 stitches in an upward right diagonal direction.

4. Work 9 stitches in an upward left diagonal direction. This completes the outer white row of the top diamond—10 stitches on each side.

Important Note: Rows can be worked around either in a clockwise or counter-clockwise direction. The counter-clockwise direction is shown and described in the photographs and written directions. Look up the two additional methods for working rows of French Stitches around the diamond in Chapter 4. I suggest you follow the method outlined here until you become familiar with the pattern. Then you can use the method you prefer.

2nd Row. Use pink yarn. Start at the top, inside the white row. Work the first stitch directly under the outside top white stitch of the diamond. Following the same counter-clockwise direction, work a row of pink stitches completely around (8 stitches on each side).

3rd Row. Use yellow yarn. Work a row of yellow stitches completely around (6 stitches on each side).

4th Row. Use white yarn. Work a row of white stitches completely around (4 stitches on each side).

5th Row. This row forms the center diamond which consists of 4 stitches. Use turquoise yarn. Work 4 stitches in a counter-clockwise direction to form the center turquoise diamond.

Second Diamond from the Top. Work this diamond so that it appears to be overlapped by the top diamond.

1st Row.

1. Counting the bottom stitch in the top diamond as one, count up 3 white stitches on the left side. Use white yarn. Work one stitch directly next to this third stitch in a zag direction. (Fig. 8-32.) Work 6 more stitches in the same direction.

2. Work 9 stitches in a *zig* direction.

3. Work 9 stitches in an upward right diagonal direction.

8-32

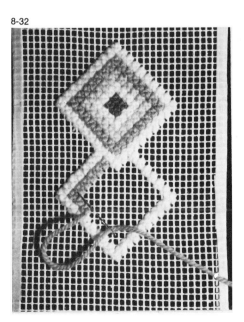

4. Work 6 stitches in an upward left diagonal direction. This completes the outer row of the second diamond. It is the same size as the top diamond except for the overlapping. Start the subsequent rows at the top. Working in a counter-clockwise direction, complete the diamond in the same color pattern of the second through fifth rows of the top diamond.

Repeat the second diamond to the bottom until there are 7 diamonds, including the top one.

Construction. Certain construction processes must be completed before you start the background stitches. See Figure 8-33 which shows the yarn tie markers. It is important that you place the markers *exactly* in the correct spots. Count carefully.

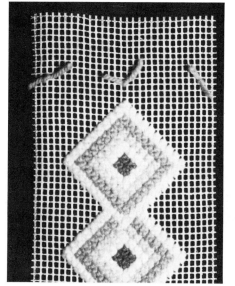

8-33

1. Count up 3 bars of canvas above the center top stitch in the top diamond. Tie a yarn marker over this bar.

2. Count 3 bars of canvas out from the left side point of the top diamond. Place a finger of your left hand on this bar. Place a finger of your right hand on the bar where the center yarn marker is tied. Run your fingers along the bars toward the upper left corner and tie a yarn marker over the crossbar where they meet.

3. Repeat Step 2 on the right side and place a similar marker at the top right.

These markers act as guides for working the background area. The sides will be folded under at the marked bars.

Machine zig zag around the canvas as follows. *Two sides:* Starting at the top, machine zig zag from top to bottom on each side on the second bar of canvas out from the markers or the fifth bar out from the side points of

diamonds. *Top:* Count up 10 bars from the top markers and machine zig zag across on this bar. *Bottom:* Count down 3 bars from the bottom point of the seventh diamond and machine zig zag across on this bar. Machine zig zag completely around a second time directly over the first row of stitches. Cut off the excess canvas on the 4 sides outside of the machine zig zagging. Fold back each side at the bar on which the yarn markers are tied at the top. (Leave this outside bar exposed while you work the background. It will be covered later with the Regular Braid Stitch.) In folding the canvas, the underneath squares must line up exactly with the top squares. Work the background through both layers of canvas, thereby eliminating raw edges. Do not be concerned with the top and bottom edges at this point. The white area across the top which will form the hem for the insertion of the dowel is worked next. Because of the diagonal nature of the French Stitch, the straight white rows across the top are worked in the Orr Weave. Use white yarn. Start at the right. Work one row of Orr Weave stitches from right to left on the bar between the side yarn tie markers (remove the center marker). Work through the double canvas on the sides, leaving free the 2 side bars on which the yarn markers are tied. (Fig. 8-34.) Count up 7 bars and work a similar row across from right to left. (It is easier to work rows from top to bottom in the Orr Weave Stitch. You can work the rows one on top of the other if you wish.) Continue working the rows down until you meet the bottom row and make a solid white area of 8 rows with 3 free bars of canvas on top as shown in the photograph. Fold back the top hem (the white worked area is folded exactly in half), lining up the top excess edge with the holes of canvas directly under the worked white area.

8-34

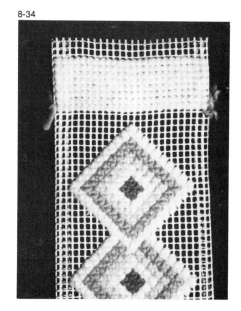

Turquoise Background. Use turquoise yarn. Work one French Stitch directly above the top white stitch in the top diamond, working through both layers of canvas as if they were one. Check in both directions after the first stitch is completed to make certain that the holes of the double layers of canvas are lined up exactly out to both edges. Work through both layers as though they were one when you do stitches in this area. Work the rows of background stitches in downward left and right diagonal directions. (Fig. 8-35.) Remember to leave single bars free along the edges where the Braid Stitch will be worked. Continue working from top to bottom in diagonal rows until you have filled all areas.

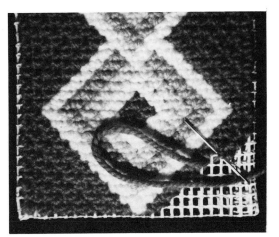

8-36

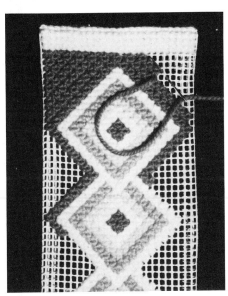

8-35

Fill-in across the top: Work the bottom half of the French Stitch to create an even, straight turquoise area across the top under the white Orr Weave area.

Bottom edge: When you reach the bottom background area, fold up the bottom hem to correspond with the side hems. Fold under the 2 bars of canvas, leaving the third bar exposed for the Braid Stitch. (Fig. 8-36.)

Note: The area stitches in the small sections where many thicknesses of canvas occur—along the sides at the top where the hem construction takes place, and at the two bottom corners—must be worked by pulling the needle and yarn through to the back and then up to surface in *two* motions. Work through all layers as if they were one. These areas are small and so they are worked quickly.

Work French Fill-in Stitches on the 2 sides and across the bottom before you start the Regular Braid Stitch.

Regular Braid Stitch Edging. Use white yarn (single strand). Follow the directions for Regular Braid Stitch, Start B. Start at top of the bellpull, with the wrong side facing you so that the hem for the dowel is on right. First work around the opening for the dowel. Work around, turning the canvas slowly as you progress, until the right side is facing you. The white hem for the dowel will then be on the left side. Work over double bars at the base of the hem. Work down the right side. Turn the corner, working over double bars. Work across the bottom. Turn the corner, working over double bars. Work up the left side, working over double bars at the base of the top hem. Work around the side opening for the dowel, turning slowly as the work progresses until you have worked the Braid Stitch completely around the opening. Except for the tassel, you are finished!

Large White Macramé Tassel. Follow the basic directions for macramé tassels in this chapter. Use white yarn (approximately 22 yards uncut). For the *center inside section* of this tassel, use a 6 in. card. Wind the yarn around 40 times. Cut a 20 in. length of yarn for the top tie. For the *outside macramé casing,* cut a holding cord 30 in. long. Cut 8 lengths of yarn 24 in. each, making 16 lengths of 12 in. when doubled on the holding cord. Work 5 rows of knots around the spool.

Attach the tassel to the bellpull at the center bottom directly under the bottom point of the last diamond. Thread the needle separately with each strand at the top of the tassel, running strands through to the back and catching them securely on the wrong side. Do not let the stitches show on the right side.

OTHER SUGGESTED NOW NEEDLEPOINT CONSTRUCTION ITEMS

Wall Hangings of Any Size or Proportion. As explained before, the pattern for the bellpull is a basic one which can be adapted to any size hanging—small to very large. The size of the dowel or pole you use would depend on the size of the hanging, and proper allowance must be made for the roll around. This is definitely the most potentially exciting area for Now Needlepoint use. Large hangings with a fine art or very decorative approach could be magnificent. Smaller ones using the individual Wiggly Chain Motifs could be made with thin dowels. If you wish, you could eliminate the dowel construction by finishing all four corners according to the directions for the two bottom corners in the bellpull. It would then be necessary to substitute some other device for hanging, such as a brass ring or rings which could be sewed to the top.

Rugs. The corner construction used on the bottom of the bellpull can also be adapted to rugs. Let me remind you that certain stitches are more suitable than others for rug use, and the recommended uses for the various stitches have been pointed out in the individual stitch chapters. Those stitches which produce thick padding on the wrong side are best for rugs, since this will enable the rugs to withstand wear and tear. Stitches with extra-long surface runs are not recommended, because they might catch on a heel. The canvas must be turned under *before* you work the area stitches, as was done along the sides and the bottom of the bellpull. There are two ways to finish rug edges: 1. The Braid Stitch can be worked completely around on all four sides. 2. The Braid Stitch can be worked on the two longest sides, with fringe on the two shorter sides. See directions under the black and white belt (Fig. 8-43) for the method of working fringe over an exposed bar or canvas.

Flat Pads for Chairs and Benches. Most of the stitches are suitable for use on pads for chairs or benches. Moreover, stuffing is not always necessary. The heavy wool acts as a padding by itself, with the result that a flat pad on a hard seat can be very decorative and functional too. Plan the proper size—turn back the edges before you work the area stitches—run a Braid Stitch edging completely around the area and behold, the pad! The Braid Stitch cannot be worked around a curved area as it requires a straight bar of canvas. Therefore, it must be reserved for use on square or rectangular shaped areas. If the area involves a simple curve, see the directions for upholstery which suggest a backing material and perhaps a very thin inner padding. The unstuffed pads might have a tendency to slip if they are not fastened in some mannner. You could make corded twist ties (see the directions for the purple belt, Fig. 8-46) and attach them to each corner. These can be tied to the chair or bench legs and will hold the pad in place.

Double the Impact with Two Now Needlepoint Construction Items. There is something psychologically pleasant about pairs: pairs of people, pairs of leaves, pairs of decorative items. You create a kind of balance immediately when you repeat an item. The repetition of a design can do much to integrate unrelated objects in a room and thereby create a feeling of oneness. The following quickie suggestions for pairs of Now Needlepoint construction items can enhance your décor. Plan one design and color scheme and adapt them to the two items mentioned.

1. A pair of pillows on a couch can be identical for a very symmetrical effect. But, for variety you can use the trick of reversing the colors, as in the green-and-white companion pillows in Figures 7-35 and 7-37. The idea is to repeat something. The color schemes can be different, but then keep the design the same. However, make certain you repeat one dominant color in both items. It is not necessary to limit yourself to a pair of pillows. You can run a row of pillows across a couch, using a different related color for each, with delightful results—but then remember to repeat one color, such as white, in each pillow.

2. A pair of oversized floor pillows make quick extra chairs when company arrives.

3. A pillow and "foot note" rug can make a comfortable lounge chair look so inviting. Design a Now Needlepoint pillow—make it a cozy soft one for comfort—and adapt the same design for a matching small rug which can be placed directly in front of the chair, and which will be wonderful for slippered feet on a cold winter's night. In addition to being decorative, the small rug will save wear and tear on the carpeting in that much-used spot.

4. Give pillows on a couch a matching, long bench top on the opposite side of the coffee table.

5. A pair of square benches could have Now Needlepoint tops.

6. Valance and tiebacks can repeat the motifs used for pillows on a couch or chairs.

7. A bellpull or wall hanging can also repeat the motifs used for pillows on a couch or chairs.

8. A bellpull or wall hanging with a long bench top repeating the motif would be an excellent welcome for an entrance hall.

9. Try a pair of hard chairs with matching seat pads.

10. You can simply repeat and repeat a design on dining room chairs as many times as necessary. An interesting note would be to work pairs of chairs with backgrounds of closely related colors. For example, if you have six dining room chairs, work a pair in yellow, a pair in yellow-orange and a pair in yellow-green backgrounds. Keep the backgrounds close in value and they will appear to match with only a slight variation of color.

Mix them up around the table and the effect will be stunning. A happy addition might be a matching bellpull for the wall or a matching valance and tiebacks. Press your good-taste button, so that you don't get carried away. The right application of these suggestions definitely depends on the design motif and the rest of your décor.

Upholstery. One of the most exciting aspects of the quickly worked Now Needlepoint is that it is so excellent for certain types of upholstery. It is durable (the rug yarn was made to walk on), and, when combined with material, can be adapted to a number of items. There are restrictions, however, so we must understand when and how it can be used successfully. Stick to areas or outlines with straight edges or simple large curves. The Now Needlepoint does not lend itself to upholstery where the basic pattern used by the upholsterer involves intricate small cutouts, such as on French Provincial chairs. The very fine canvas can be tucked under and treated much like heavy material, but this is not true of Now Needlepoint worked on the large canvas in the heavy yarn. Actually this limitation should guide you in using Now Needlepoint. Besides being too bulky for intricate construction, Now Needlepoint would look incongruous used on fancy, dainty pieces of furniture.

With instant designing and fast stitching, you can cover large areas for upholstery that would take months and months to finish in the finer, traditional needlepoint. You can produce glorious eye-catchers. And by combining the Now Needlepoint area with matched upholstery material, you can create fascinating design notes which become dominant focal points in a room.

Although mentioned before, let me emphasize again that unless you are really an expert seamstress who thoroughly understands the intricacies of tailoring and fitting for upholstery, you should let your favorite upholsterer do the constructing and finishing. You know the extent of your own talents, so exercise discretion in this area. Don't spoil professional-looking Now Needlepoint with a botched-up construction job. If there is anything unusual about the piece to be upholstered or if you are planning extensive projects, certainly talk it over with your upholsterer before you start the project. You will probably find him very cooperative, even to the point of providing you with paper patterns as a guide for your Now Needlepoint coverage.

Expert upholsterers are accustomed to the finer, traditional needlepoint, but the large-size canvas and the heavy yarn sometimes startle them in the way that people are surprised by anything new. I have written a note to the upholsterer to introduce the different weight and texture and to outline a few helpful suggestions. Let the person who will work on your project read the note or provide him or her with a xerox copy for reference. This information should answer any questions that might arise. The wonderful woman who does the finishing for my samples assures me there is nothing difficult about working with Now Needlepoint—it's just different.

Note from the Author to the Upholsterer Regarding Construction. Yes, this is needlepoint too! Quite different from the traditional fine needlepoint familiar to us all, it is called Now Needlepoint and is worked on large canvas with heavy rug yarn. Don't let the heavy texture disturb you; it is not difficult to work with if you adhere to the following suggestions.

The first step is an important must and takes place before construction starts. The large canvas unravels easily, so all the edges surrounding the Now Needlepoint area must be machine zig-zagged on the third bar outside the worked area. Repeat the zig zag stitches around a second time directly over the first row. The next step is to cut off the excess canvas outside of the machine zig zags. This leaves enough excess canvas to prevent unraveling but eliminates superfluous amounts which might prove cumbersome.

The instructions to the needleworker state that Now Needlepoint should not be used for upholstered items which require small, intricate cutout patterns. However, straight lines and simple curves can be dealt with easily. I recommend working only the top or front areas in Now Needlepoint. Matching upholstery material should be used for backings and gussets—and cording, if that is desired. Velvet, linen, felt—all in rather heavy weight—are a few suggestions for companion materials. Velvet is the richest looking of all since it is a delightful contrast to the textural Now Needlepoint, but you can substitute many other durable materials with successful results.

If the needleworker requests a paper pattern for the Now Needlepoint area to be covered, I suggest you add ¼ in. along all the outside edges. You can crop this during construction to prevent bare canvas from being exposed along the edges where the Now Needlepoint and the material meet. Providing a paper pattern will be helpful to you in the end. The needleworker will follow it carefully and this will eliminate "size headaches" which might otherwise occur when you start construction. Working with Now Needlepoint will be a different experience for you, but you can make friends with its size in no time.

Suggested Upholstery Projects

Upholstered Bench Top. Now Needlepoint truly shines in this area—made to order for bench tops. The design and color possibilities are endless. The finished item can be traditional or way out, according to your desire. An example of the traditional effect is the purple and blue footstool worked in the French Stitch (Fig. 4-46), while at the other extreme is the hot-colored bench top worked in the Fly Stitch (Fig. 3-38). Only the flat topside of the hot-colored bench top is worked in Now Needlepoint; the sides and cording are made of material. Bench tops of this type are easy to key. Design a rectangular or square shape to size—large or small, whatever the bench demands. Be certain to add ¼ in. extra on all sides for cropping in construction. Tie yarn markers in the corners to indicate the area to be covered. In certain designs it will be necessary to plan the placement so that stripes or motifs will be identical on each side. It depends on the type of design you use. Choose compatible upholstery material for the sides and cording.

Note: The Braid Stitch can be used for the cording as in the purple-and-white French Stitch pillow (Fig. 8-29). If you use the Braid Stitch, you need not add the extra ¼ in. on all sides. Work the Now Needlepoint area to exact measurements. The one row of Regular Fill-in Stitches that you add around on all sides after completing the Braid Stitch will be cropped at the time of construction.

Stuffed, Loose Pads can be designed for bench tops or window seats and can be as thick or as thin as you wish. Rubber foam, which can be purchased by the yard in a variety of thicknesses, is excellent stuffing for this purpose. The flat top can be worked in Now Needlepoint and combined with material for backing and gussets.

Headboards. For example, look at Figure 4-48. The sample happens to be an offbeat, modern design but you can easily produce a headboard for any type of décor if you choose the right stitch design and color combinations. Work the front surface in Now Needlepoint and combine it with material for the sides and backing.

Valances. Figure 4-47 is a companion valance to the headboard. The valance can be custom-made to fit any window or grouping of windows. The headboard-valance combination would of course be for bedroom décor, but the valance can be combined with other items to make a living room sing. Matching tiebacks can easily be produced, using the same technique outlined for the purple and white belt. (See Fig. 8-46.) Tiebacks are simply short little belts with rings sewed on each end. A busy, exciting design for a Now Needlepoint valance and matching tiebacks, used with solid-color material for the draperies, would be a safe and charming combination. But there are other paths of adventure to travel if you are daring. Think of striped drapes, with the valance and tiebacks repeating the stripes but in bold zig zags of Now Needlepoint.

Use the same colors and pattern as in the striped material but zig and zag the stripes merrily across the top—maybe in smaller zigs and zags for the tiebacks. This pattern-on-pattern effect could be stunning. These are only a few of the possibilities. Press your Aware Button and think up some of your own.

Front Side of Loose Chair or Couch Pillows. This would have to be done at a time when you plan to have the couch or chair upholstered. Many types of combinations could be successfully designed, but one of the safest courses would be to choose an overall solid-color material for the item to be upholstered. An exciting Now Needlepoint design could be keyed for the frontside of the loose chair pillow—or pillows, if it is for a couch. The design should definitely repeat the basic material color, so that the pillow front becomes an integral part of the overall effect. The basic color could be combined with harmonious colors which create contrast in the Now Needlepoint area. For such a project, it would be advisable to obtain paper patterns from your upholsterer if possible. Whatever you do, add ¼ in. of extra Now Needlepoint area on all sides for cropping in construction.

CONSTRUCTION EXAMPLE 4: EYEGLASS CASE

This oversized eyeglass case—an eye-catcher in blue, green, turquoise and sparkling white—is an adaptation of the Double Zig Zag Chain Pattern 10 in Figure 5-21. The new construction which includes a lining makes a stiffener unnecessary; Now Needlepoint forms its own protective thickness for glasses. (Fig. 8-37.) Size of sample: 4½ in. × 6½ in.
Nantucket 6-Ply Cable Yarn: blue #61 (10 str.); green #84 (4 str.); turquoise #64 (14 str.); white #1 (6 str.).

8-37

Preparing the Canvas. Cut a piece of 3 to the inch canvas at least 8 in. × 16 in. (cut off the selvedge before measuring). It is always a good idea to allow a bit extra, especially if you are keying your own design; an extra bar or two might be needed for balance. Machine zig-zag on the second bar in from the edge across the top and down the left side only of the cut piece of canvas. Repeat a second row of stitches directly over the first. Cut off the extra bar of canvas outside the zig zag stitches along the 2 edges. Fold the top under at the third bar from the machine zig zag. Fold the left side under at the third bar from the machine zig zag. Match corner holes carefully before you start the first stitch. (Pull the needle through to the back and up to the surface in two motions when you work corner stitches where several thicknesses of canvas occur.)

1st Row. Follow Figure 5-22 for Pattern 10 in Chapter 5. Start at the upper left. (Fig. 8-38.) Use blue yarn. Starting with a zig, work 5 Double Zig Zag Chains (a total of 20 stitches), ending with a zag. Loop over the last chain as at the bottom of a row, but do not end the yarn. Drop under on the back and bring the needle up to the surface in the hole directly under the last stitch, so that one bar of canvas is left exposed. (See the arrow in Fig. 8-39.) Starting with a zig, work 4 Double Zig Zag Chains. Before you work the fifth Double Zig Zag, you must anticipate how many bars of canvas are needed to complete it. Machine zig zag stitches must be run across the bottom and the hem turned under before you work the final stitches in this row. You need a total of 7 bars: 4 bars for the last Double Chain Zig Zag, one bar left exposed for the Braid Stitch and 2 bars extra to be turned under for the hem. Count down and machine zig-zag across the bottom edge of the seventh bar of canvas down from where you worked the last stitch. Repeat a second row of stitches directly over the first. Cut off the excess canvas below the machine stitching. Fold the canvas back at the third bar

from the bottom to correspond with the top. Complete the fifth blue Double Zig Zag Chain down to the corner, carefully matching layers of canvas and leaving one bar exposed along the edge. (Pull the needle through to the back and up to the surface in two motions when you work corner stitches where several thicknesses of canvas occur.)

Note: Cover the raw right edge of canvas with masking tape to prevent the yarn from catching while you work the stitches.

All rows of color pattern which follow are worked leaving the one bar of canvas exposed halfway down as indicated by the arrow in Figure 8-39.

Color Pattern. The first through sixth rows start with a zig. 1st and 2nd Rows, blue; 3rd Row, turquoise; 4th Row, green; 5th Row, white; 6th Row, blue. Reverse rows at this point. The seventh through twelfth rows start with a zag. Follow the right grouping of stitches on Figure 5-22. The sixth row corresponds to Row a. The start of the seventh row corresponds to Row b. The 7th Row is blue (see a following paragraph on Center Motifs); 8th Row, white; 9th Row, green; 10th Row, turquoise; 11th and 12th Rows, blue. (*Note:* The right side of the canvas must be prepared as follows before you work these last 2 blue rows.) Using right points of turquoise zig zags as your guide, machine zig-zag on the fifth bar of canvas to the right of the points (2 bars for blue rows; one bar left exposed for the Braid Stitch and 2 bars extra for the hem). Repeat a second row of stitches directly over the first. Cut off excess canvas to the right of the machine stitching. Fold back the canvas at the third bar from the machine stitching, carefully matching canvas holes. Work the 11th and 12th Rows, catching through the layers of matched canvas, as on the left side. (Fig. 8-40.)

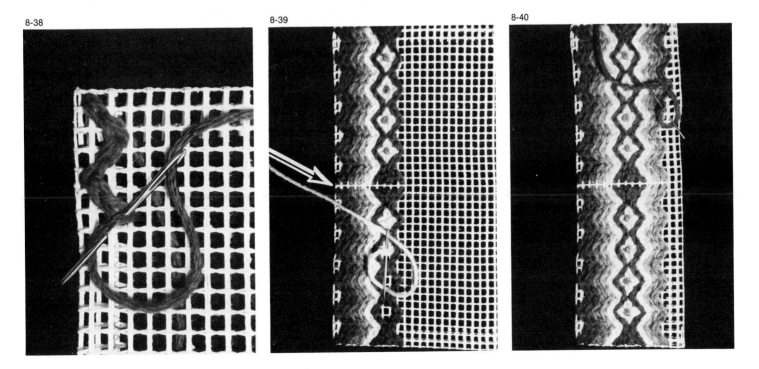

8-38

8-39

8-40

Side Fill-in Stitches to Produce Even Edges. Use turquoise yarn. Work Single Zig Zag Chain Stitches in the open spaces along each side.

Center Motifs. The center motifs can be filled in at the completion of seventh row if you are anxious to see what the design will look like when it is completed, or you can wait until all of the zig zag rows are completed. I find it difficult to wait until the end, as you can tell by the step photographs. Refer to the same grouping of stitches to the right of Figure 5-22. Work the half motif at the top and the half motif at the bottom of each section in blue yarn. The 8 diamond-shaped center motifs are worked in white yarn. Use turquoise yarn to work a French Knot (single strand—around the needle once) in the center of each white motif. The design area is now complete. At this point, the lining is sewed in place.

Lining. A turquoise cotton was used for the eyeglass case-lining but a variety of materials could be used. The material should be durable, since glasses will constantly be stuffed into the case. However, it should not be so heavy as to interfere with construction. Cut 2 pieces of material ¼ in. larger on all sides than the area covered by one side of the case; the two pieces measure 4½ in. × 6½ in. for the sample. (Fig. 8-41.) Attach the lining to the wrong side. Using matching sewing thread, fold the edges of the lining material under and sew by hand with small invisible overhand stitches. Each piece must be attached securely to the edge stitches on the wrong side. Do not let the sewing stitches show on the right side.

Leave ½ in. exposed at the middle section where the case will be folded (indicated by the arrow in Fig. 8-41). The edge bars on all 4 sides must be left free for construction with the Braid Stitch.

Construction Braid. Use turquoise yarn (single strand). Follow the directions for the Regular Braid Stitch, Start B. (Fig. 8-42.) Fold the case in half as shown. Turn the item when necessary so that you can work the stitches from left to right in the direction of the arrows.

Work through both thicknesses of canvas bars on the sides (carefully match them hole for hole). Start at the top right diagonal arrow A. Work down the right side and turn the corner. Work across the bottom exposed bar of canvas and turn the corner. Work up the left side to the top. The 2 sides are now fastened securely together. Use turquoise yarn. Work a row of Regular Fill-in Stitches around the open top before you start the braid to make certain the canvas will be hidden. (If you used a heavier yarn, this will not be necessary.) Work the Regular Braid Stitch, Start A. Use turquoise yarn. Work the Regular Braid Stitch completely around the open top. Weave into Start A in order to hide the joining. Push the yarn down to find the canvas holes if necessary.

Design Note: This basic construction process can be adapted to your own design with the stitch of your choice. You can change the size if you wish. The sample was designed to be large enough for oversized contemporary glasses and sunglasses, but you could easily scale the size down for more conservative-type glasses. You can also go wild with an explosion of color and crazy patterns

8-41

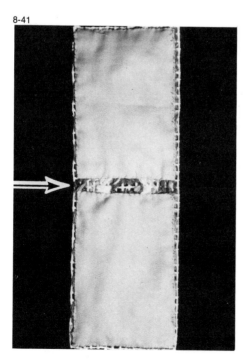

8-42

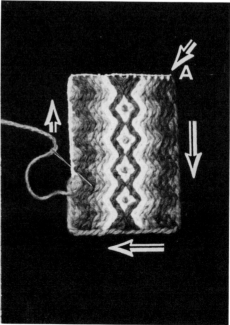

or choose subtle colors and designs for the conservative souls. Here is an opportunity to design distinctive gifts for all kinds of people, yourself included!

CONSTRUCTION EXAMPLE 5: A BELT WITH A BUCKLE AND FRINGE

This Single Zig Zag Chain 2 in.-wide belt with a heavy gold buckle is black and white and wild! (Fig. 8-43.) The worked area shown measures 2 in. × 30 in. with a 3 in. fringe.

8-43

The belt was designed to be worn down on the hips. The fringe can be omitted for a more conservative effect and the length of the belt can be shortened so that it can be worn at the natural waistline. The first step is to purchase a large type of buckle with an attachment bar suitable for construction with the large canvas and heavy yarn. You must purchase this in advance since the size of the buckle determines the width of the belt. If its size varies from that of the sample, you must make the necessary adjustments.

Pat Rug Yarn: black #050 (13 str.); white #005 (10 str.). *Surface Whipping:* white #005 (4 str.). *Topside Braid:* white #005 (5 str.). *Fringe:* white #005 (23 str.).

Preparing the Canvas. The canvas must be prepared to fit the buckle, as shown in Figure 8-44. Make a little Think Plan for the size of the buckle you plan to use if it is different from the sample shown. To duplicate the size in the sample, cut a piece of canvas consisting of 13 bars and running the width of the 40 in.-wide 3 to the inch canvas. Cut off the selvedge at both ends. Run a row of machine zig zag stitches along each of the 2 sides, and across one end, on the second bar in from the edge. Run a second row of stitches directly over the first. Cut off the excess bar of canvas outside the zig zagging on all 3 sides. The strip of canvas will then be 11 bars wide. Fold the canvas back on the 2 sides only on the third bar in from the edge. (Do not fold the end under.) These 2 outside bars will be left free for the Braid Stitch top edging and the bottom fringe.

1st Row. Start at the end with machine zig zagging. Use black yarn. (Fig. 8-44.) Start the first stitch so that at least 5 bars of canvas are left free (approximately 1½ in.) for attaching to the buckle. One bar must be left free along the edge as shown. Work Single Zig Zag Chain Stitches for the length desired. The sample has approximately 30 in. of worked area. Before completing the first row of stitches, carefully measure the length desired (take into consideration the size of the buckle) and mark the distance with a yarn tie marker. Count down 5 bars from the marker and run 2 rows of machine zig zag stitches across the fifth bar. Cut off excess canvas beyond the machine stitches. Work the first row of stitches down to the marker. Remove the marker and work the last stitch. The free canvas beyond the marker will be used to attach the belt to the buckle.

Color Pattern. 1st Row, black; 2nd Row, white; 3rd Row, black; 4th Row, white; 5th Row, black.

Note: If you wish to increase the width, you can add an extra row (or rows) of black after working the third row without disturbing the pattern.

Surface Whipping. Use white yarn. Surface whip down the entire length of each of the two outside black rows to form the pattern. (See Pattern 1A and Fig. 5-8 in Chapter 5.)

Regular Braid Stitch along the Top. Use white yarn (single strand). With the right side toward you, work the Regular Braid Stitch, Start B, the entire length of the worked area along the top.

Note: If you wish Braid Stitch along the bottom instead of fringe, repeat the stitch on the bottom side at this point. Attach the fringe after sewing the belt to the buckle.

8-44

8-45

8-46

Buckle. Figure 8-45 shows how to attach the belt to the buckle. Pull the unworked end of the canvas through the buckle, folding it back so that only the Now Needlepoint worked area shows on the front side. Using white yarn and overhand stitches, sew the buckle securely in place on the wrong side. Cover the raw edges with stitches as much as possible. Try to distribute your stitches in order not to end up with great lumps of yarn. Figure 8-45 shows how it can be done in a fairly neat manner. Repeat this process at the other end.

Note: Because the wrong side of this particular stitch is fairly even and uniform, the sample was not lined. If you are fussy and want a lining, cut a strip of material ¼ in. larger on all sides than the worked area. Turn under the ¼ in. extra and attach the lining to the wrong side of the belt with sewing thread, using invisible overhand stitches. This method is similar to the one used in lining the eyeglass case. You could also use a length of ribbon if you can find one of the correct width.

Bottom Fringe. See the directions for attaching fringe in this chapter.

CONSTRUCTION EXAMPLE 6: A BELT WITH CORDS

Snappy white Fly Stitch chevrons decorate a deep-purple belt. The cords made of yarn make it adjustable; they can be tightened so it can be worn at the waistline or loosened to slide it down on the hips. (Fig. 8-46.) Size of sample: 2¼ in. × 30¼ in.
Pat Rug Yarn: purple #632 (12 str.); white #005 (includes the Special Braid) (16 str.). *Four Cords:* white #005 (8 str.).

Preparing the Canvas. Use 5 to the inch canvas for the Fly Stitch. The length of the belt runs from selvedge to selvedge (the canvas is 40 in. wide). Cut a strip of canvas with at least 16 double bars running from selvedge to selvedge. (Double bars will be referred to as one bar throughout.) Run 2 rows of machine zig zag down the left side on the second bar in from the edge. Cut off the bar outside of the machine zig zagging. Counting the left zig

zagged bar as one, count over to the right and run 2 rows of machine zig zag on the fourteenth bar down the right side. Cut off the canvas to the right of the zig-zagging. Check your bar count. There should be 14 double rows of canvas counting the 2 outside zig zagged rows. Fold the canvas back at the third bar in from the edge along the entire length of each side. Check your count again. With the sides folded back under and counting the 2 edge bars on which the Special Braid Stitch will be worked, there should be 10 rows of double bars.

Working the Stitches. Find the exact center bar of the length of canvas by folding the canvas in half, end to end. Tie a yarn marker over the center bar.

The Fly Stitch is worked in 2 rows, starting at the marked center bar and proceeding out to the ends.

Start in the exact center at the left side. Leave one free bar of canvas exposed along the edge. Work through both layers of folded canvas as if they were one. (See the horizontal arrow to the left of Fig. 8-47 for your start.)

1st Row.

1. Use purple yarn. Work two 4-Bar Fly Stitches with top French Fill-in Stitches. Pull the needle through to the surface on the left, leaving holes free for 2 white stitches.

2. Use white yarn. Work two 4-Bar Fly Stitches.

3. Use purple yarn. Work four 4-Bar Fly Stitches. Repeat Steps 2 and 3 until you complete the eleventh white chevron. The canvas along the end must be folded back before you work the next group of purple stitches and the last twelfth white chevron.

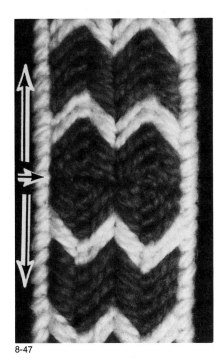

8-47

4. Using the bottom point of the eleventh white chevron (directly under the small tie-down stitch) as your guide, run machine zig zag stitches across on the ninth bar down. Run a second row of stitches directly over the first. Cut off excess canvas below the machine zig zagging. Fold the canvas under on the third bar from the edge, lining up all the layers of canvas.

5. Use purple yarn. Work four 4-Bar Fly Stitches, working through all the layers of canvas as if they were one when necessary.

6. Use white yarn. Work two 4-Bar Fly Stitches. This completes the twelfth white chevron.

7. Use purple yarn. Work the necessary French Fill-in Stitches on each side of the last white chevron to create a straight edge. There should be one free bar along the bottom.

2nd Row. Start at the middle section to the right of the first row. Follow the exact color pattern of the first row. There should be one free bar along the right edge and across the bottom when the row is completed.

3rd and 4th Rows. Turn the canvas upside down and repeat exactly the 2 rows in the opposite direction. Do not leave any canvas exposed at the joining of the rows at the center. Start the rows in the same holes used for the first 2 rows.

Special Braid Stitch. Use white yarn. Work the Special Braid Stitch completely around on all 4 sides. Start anywhere except at the corners.

Cording for Front Ties. Use white yarn. Follow the directions later in this chapter for making and attaching cords.

Design Note: The basic construction method used for this belt can be adapted for use with other stitches and many different types of designs. The length of a belt can easily be keyed to fit any size waistline. The Special Braid Stitch is used for edging on the 5 to the inch canvas which the Fly Stitch requires as shown in the sample. You would substitute the Regular Braid Stitch if the design involved a stitch which must be worked on the 3 to the inch canvas. In this particular design, you start the stitches at the exact center of the belt and work out to the ends so that the white chevrons point toward the two bows in a uniform manner. If the stitch and design can be worked in one continual run (one end to the other), you must machine zig-zag and turn under the canvas along one end before you start the Now Needlepoint stitches. The first row of stitches would then be worked down to within an inch of where the belt will end. Anticipate the exact spot where the stitches will end, count down 3 more bars and machine zig-zag twice across, cutting off excess canvas beyond the machine stitches. Turn the canvas under in the exact manner you did with the first end before you work the final stitches. You can substitute a single tie for the 2 shown in the sample if that type of fastening is better suited to the design you have chosen.

DRAPERY TIEBACKS

How easy! Simply make a short belt! The length will vary depending on how heavy the draperies are. Measure the length needed by holding a strand of yarn around the draperies and make the tiebacks in the size you wish. Sew small brass rings on the ends which can be looped over a hook to hold the tiebacks in place. Single lengths of cording can be attached to each tieback end for use with large decorative tieback fixtures. Tie a bow with the two lengths and slip it over the fixture.

BOUTIQUE FINISHING TOUCHES THAT ENHANCE

As you may have guessed from some of the finished items, I love tassels, especially fat, chunky ones. They seem to dance at the corners of pillows and, as in the case of the bellpull (see Fig. 8-30), they add a special touch of surprise and interest after your eye has traveled the long distance down to the bottom. The oversized ones also produce a custom-made, very expensive effect, and so they should for they do eat up yarn like mad. However, the visual rewards are such that they are well worth the investment of extra time and money.

Tassels can be made in a great variety of sizes. It all depends on the size of the cardboard you use and the number of times you wind the yarn around. The plain tassels can be made in small sizes suitable for pincushions and mini pillows or blown up to extra-large proportions. The tassels with separate outer casings of macramé (decorative knotting) or macrochet (very large crochet) are produced only in the medium to larger sizes.

Plain tassels are pleasing to the eye—that is, until you see how magnificently macramé tassels harmonize with the textural Now Needlepoint. It is a very happy marriage indeed. So if you are wondering what macramé is doing in a Now Needlepoint book, the truth is I simply could not resist including the instructions for macramé tassels. Of necessity, the knot instructions are brief, but there are many books available which outline the procedure in a more detailed manner, such as Virginia Harvey's excellent book, *Macramé: The Art of Creative Knotting.* You might also ask the help of a friend who does macramé. Any experienced knotter can quickly interpret the directions and—who knows—might be happy to know about the tassels too! Do at least give them a try, since they can be used to enhance any pillow or hanging, not only those worked in Now Needlepoint. You work them around an empty spool of thread—a kind of adventure! I also include instructions for macrochet tassels for those who find knotting *too* strange and different. They are easy to make and have a similar look to the macramé tassels (almost as good, but not quite).

Tassels need not only dance at the corners of pillows or hang alone at the bottom of hangings. Bunches or rows of them can be used for texture and interest on large hangings. Press your Aware Button and perhaps you can think of unique design uses for them.

Important Note: Remember to reserve the necessary amount of *uncut yarn,* since all types of tassels are made from one continuous length of yarn.

Plain Tassels. Pat Rug Yarn and Nantucket 6-Ply Cable Yarn were used for the plain tassels shown but other rug yarns of comparable weight could be substituted. Although the basic mechanical steps are given for the small plain tassel, any size tassel can be made by following the same directions. The difference will be in the measurement of the card, the number of times the yarn is wound around the card, and the length of the top tying cord. Special instructions are given for the various sizes plus very approximate estimates of the amounts of yarn used. This makes it possible for you to select quickly the proper size for your item and to know how much extra yarn must be purchased.

Cut Card to Size. Cut out a card made of firm cardboard which will not bend when yarn is wound around it. One measurement of the card should correspond to the size requirements indicated in the directions. The three different card sizes used are 2 in., 4 in. and 6 in.

The basic directions that follow can be used for all sizes of plain tassels.

The *small-size plain tassel* can be used on pincushions and mini pillows. Approximately 4 to 5 yards of yarn are used for each tassel.

1. Cut a cardboard piece with one measurement of 2 in. (or designated size).

8-48

2. Wind the yarn around the card 20 times (or number of times designated) as shown in Fig. 8-48.

3. Cut a 30-in. length of yarn (or length designated). Slip it under the yarn at the top of the cardboard. Tie a secure knot at the top, leaving two equal lengths.

4. Cut through the yarn at the opposite end of the cardboard.

5. Thread your needle with one of the top ends. Run down through the center close to the top knot and bring your needle out a short distance down from the top. Wind the yarn *tightly* around the strands (hold them together with your left hand) 4 times. Weave back and forth several times to catch securely. Run the yarn down through the middle so it becomes one of the strands. (The remaining length of yarn at the top will be used to attach the tassel to the item.)

6. Trim the ends by squeezing the yarn together with your left hand and snipping off the uneven long ends. Give the tassel a good shake and repeat the process. You will usually find a few long ends which were tucked inside during the first trimming.

Attaching a Tassel to Each Corner of the Pillow. Use the remaining length of yarn at the top of the finished tassel, thread a needle and go through to the wrong side at the corner of the pillow. You have to maneuver a bit at this point. I work with the right side of the pillow out and poke the corner through the open zipper when I need to catch on the wrong side. Catch several times on the wrong side by working through Now Needlepoint stitches as close to the corner as possible. To make certain the tassel is secure, I go up through to the right side, catch the yarn through the top of the tassel and then go back through to the wrong side. If the tassel is large, I repeat this process several times until I feel the tassel will stay securely fastened during usage. If these runs of yarn show, a good trick with which to hide them is to bring your needle through to the surface at the spot where the tassel is attached, wind yarn tightly around runs of yarn and go through to the wrong side and catch securely. Snip off the yarn, leaving an end at least 2 in. long. You can always start a new strand of yarn if the top tie is used up before you feel the tassel is secure.

Following are the special requirements for various sizes of plain tassels.

8-50

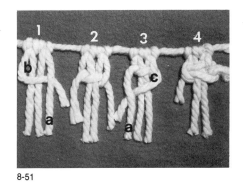

8-51

Note: Yardage requirements for yarn is very approximate, since much depends on how tightly the yarn is wound around the card.

Small-Size Plain Tassel. Cut a 2 in. card and go around the card 20 times. Use a 30 in. length for the top tie. Each tassel requires approximately 4 to 5 yds. of yarn.

Medium-Size Plain Tassel. Cut a 4 in. card and go around the card 20 times. Use a 1 yd.-length for the top tie. Each tassel requires approximately 6 to 7 yds. of yarn.

Medium-Size Extra-Full Plain Tassel (Fat and Chunky). Cut a 4 in. card and go around the card 40 times. Use a 1¼-yd. length for the top tie. Each tassel requires approximately 12 to 13 yds. of yarn.

Large-Size Plain Tassel. Cut a 6 in. card and go around the card 20 times. Use a 1¼-yd. length for the top tie. Each tassel requires approximately 8 to 9 yds. of yarn.

Large-Size Extra-Full Plain Tassel (Fat and Chunky). Cut a 6 in. card and go around the card 40 times. Use a 1½-yd. length for the top tie. Each tassel requires approximately 16 to 17 yds. of yarn.

Plain tassels are worked in one color only. If you try to mix colors by winding 2 or more together on the card, you end up with an unprofessional-looking mix-up, in my opinion. You can successfully achieve a 2-color effect by making 2 tassels of Color A and 2 tassels of Color B. Attach the matching-color tassels to the pillow at opposite diagonal corners. I suggest that you keep the values the same and use closely related colors to ensure balance. Figure 8-49 shows the plain tassel in the small, medium and the medium extra-full sizes. Large and large extra-full tassels are similar to the medium sizes except that the tassel strands are longer.

8-49

Macramé Tassels. The accessories you will need for making macramé tassels are: a firm rubber foam pillow; large size pins such as T-pins or glass-headed pins (used for map making) or hat pins; an empty sewing thread spool of a standard size; and yarn.

The basic mechanics for macramè follow:

Mounting Cords. Each cord is mounted on a holding cord. (Fig. 8-50.) Cut the length of cord specified. Tie a knot at each end and pin it securely to a firm rubber foam pillow. Cut the specified number of lengths of yarn. Start at the left side. Fold the yarn in half. Place the loop *under* the holding cord (Step 1 in Fig. 8-50). Fold the loop over the holding cord and pull the two ends of cord through (Steps 2 and 3). Continue until all the cords are attached as indicated in Step 4 of the photograph.

Note: Each length of yarn is divided in half, so you end up with double the number of lengths cut.

Square Knot. This knot is considered the basis of macramé. Actually it is a Square Knot tied around 2 center cords. You work the cords in multiples of 4. All designs using the Square Knot must contain a number of cords divisible by 4, as in Figure 8-51. Steps 1 and 2 produce a half knot in one direction, Steps 3 and 4 a half knot in the reverse direction. The 2 halves result in the decorative Square Knot. Follow the steps shown in Figure 8-51.

1. Use 4 cords. Place the two outer cords so that the right cord is on top of the left cord. The 2 outer cords form a reverse letter P.

2. The right cord "a" must now go under the 2 center cords and come out through space "b" indicated in Step 1. This completes the first half of the Square Knot as shown in Step 2.

3. For the second half, reverse the procedure. Place the cords as shown in Step 3 so that the cord on the left is on top. This forms a letter P with the long straight side on top.

4. The left cord "a" must now go under the 2 center cords and come out through space "c" indicated in Step 3. This completes the second half and results in a Square Knot when the cords are tightened.

In the following *mechanics for macramé tassel*, Pat Rug Yarn was used for the samples shown here. You will need approximately 12 to 13 yds. of uncut yarn to make each tassel according to the following specifications.

Note: You can substitute comparable or heavier-weight yarn for use with the same specifications. Nantucket 6-Ply Cable Yarn—the lighter-weight yarn—was used for tassels on a number of the pillows in the earlier chapters. The extra turns around the card which are necessary to produce the same bulk and appearance as you obtain with heavier yarn are outlined in the directions.

Tassel Top or Outer Casing. See Figure 8-52.

1. Cut the holding cord 30 in. long. Make 2 knots and pin them on the working pillow as shown at the top left of Figure 8-52. Cut 8 lengths of yarn 24 in. long. Tie them on the holding cord so that there are 16 cords 12 in. long. Work one row of macramé Square Knots. Remove the holding cord from the pillow and untie the end knots.

2. Tie the holding cord around an empty standard-sized spool as shown to the right of Figure 8-52. Tie a fairly loose knot so that it can be opened and tightened later. Using 2 cords from the first knot and 2 cords from the last knot in the first row (they fall side by side on the spool but are the same cords indicated by the bottom stars on either side of grouping 1), work one Square Knot. Continue the second row of knots around the spool, using 2 cords from each pair of adjacent knots of the preceding row to form the pattern. (The 4 X's indicate one grouping to get you started.) Do not drop the knots. Tie them so that they are close up to the preceding row of knots. Third row—repeat the second row, using 2 cords from each pair of adjacent knots of the preceding row. Push the work up the spool when necessary. Fourth and fifth rows—repeat the process 2 more times, always using 2 cords from each pair of adjacent knots in the preceding row. Remove the top casing from the spool.

Note: This all may seem a bit confusing on your first try, but it is not difficult once you have lived through one tassel. The spool is used only as a round firm backing on which to work the seamless top casing. If you are a complete novice at macramé, I suggest you take some scrap yarn and practice the Square Knot on a flat surface as instructed in Step 1. Practice the alternating macramé knots which form the pattern until you are familiar with the mechanics before you attempt to work them on the spool.

Tassel Center. See Figure 8-53.

3. Cut a cardboard 6 in. deep (or the specified measurement). Wind the yarn around the cardboard 16 times (or the specified number of times). Cut a length of yarn 20 in. long. Slip it under the yarn and tie it securely at the top. Cut through the yarn at the bottom.

4. Poke the ends of the top tie on tassel center up through the center of the macramé outer casing, so that the tops are even. Untie and tighten the knot on the

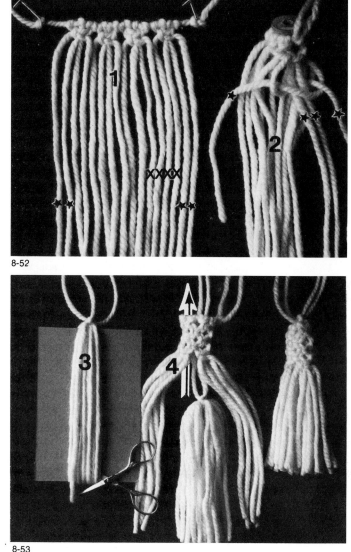

8-52

8-53

macramé casing, so that it closes snugly around the center tassel. Using the 2 cords from the center and the 2 cords from the outer casing, tie a secure knot. Trim the bottom ends of the tassel so that they are even. Use the method of trimming described for plain tassels.

Attaching the Tassel to the Pillow. Thread a large needle with each single strand at the top of the tassel and run them separately through to the wrong side of the pillow at the corner. (Run them through almost in the same spot.) When all of the strands are through to the wrong side, tie them together with several firm knots so that the tassel on the outside is held securely in place. Repeat the procedure at all 4 corners.

Special Requirements for the Extra-Full Macramé Tassel. Cut a 6 in. card and go around the card 40 times. Use a 20 in.-length for the top tie. Each tassel requires approximately 22 to 23 yds. of yarn.

If you want to try your hand at *two-color macramé tassels,* here are some suggestions:

Suggestion 1. Make the outer top casing of Color A and the inner tassel of Color B. An interesting alternative is to make two 2-color tassels as just suggested and two tassels reversing the colors (with the outer top casing of Color B and the inner tassel of Color A). Place the matching tassels at opposite diagonal corners. This scheme would not be advisable if the main design is an extremely busy one, but when used appropriately it can produce a pleasant effect.

Suggestion 2. Make a 2-color outer casing using one of the colors for the inner tassel. An example of this is shown in the turquoise rocket pillow in Figure 3-36. (See also C-31 in the color section.) This type of tassel is very smart looking and creates two entirely different effects, depending on the colors you use. Two closely related colors will blend together beautifully while two sharply contrasted colors produce a startling impact on the eye. You must decide which is best for your pillow or project.

If you wish to produce Suggestion 2, there is a trick you must use to mount the yarn on the holding cord so that the individual knots will be formed by a single color. If you do not follow this procedure, the two colors of yarn will become mixed together in the Square Knots and destroy the macramé pattern. The procedure is simple and you will understand why it is necessary once you start tying the knots with two colors.

Mechanics for Mounting Cords for the Two-Color Outer Macramé Tassel Casing. See Figure 8-54. Follow the preceding directions for producing the macramé tassel top or outer casing. The following instructions refer only to the mounting of the two colors of yarn on the holding cord and the number of cords to cut in each color.

Cutting Cords. Cut ½ number of lengths of yarn as directed in Color A (dark value in Fig. 8-54) and ½ number of lengths of yarn as directed in Color B (light value).

1. Mount one strand of Color A on the holding cord as shown on the right of the photograph. Place a strand of Color B in place under the holding cord so the 2 lengths are on the outside and the loop above as indicated.

2. Pull the loop over the holding cord and place it in a downward position. Pull the individual strands of Color B through on each side.

3. Pull so that you tighten the cords around the holding cord as shown at the left of Figure 8-54. The 2 Color B cords (light value) should fall on either side of the 2 center Color A cords (dark value). Repeat the process for the desired number of cords.

Continue with the regular directions for the macramé outer-tassel casing. When you tie the alternating rows of Square Knots, you will understand why this procedure is necessary to prevent a jumble of knots and colors. The end result is delightful!

Yardage requirements for the 2-color tassels are:

Suggestion 1. The outer top macramé casing requires approximately 6 yds. of uncut yarn in Color A. Deduct that amount from the total yardage requirement for the size macramé tassel you wish to make to determine how many yards of Color B you need.

Suggestion 2. The 2-color macramé outer casing requires approximately 3 yds. of Color A. Deduct that amount from the total yardage requirement for the size macramé tassel you wish to make to determine how many yards of Color B you need.

Macrochet Tassels. Basic crochet mechanics are used for macrochet. Use a crochet hook size Q or #19.

Slip Loop. Hold the large crochet hook in your right hand. With your left hand, loop the yarn over and under the hook so that the short end of yarn is on top, as shown in Figure 8-55 (leave a 12 in. end when working a tassel).

8-54

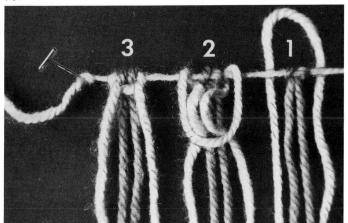

8-55

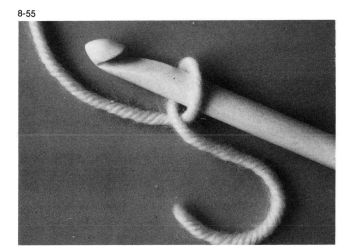

Chain. This is the basis of all crochet stitches. Hold the hook in your right hand and place the yarn over the forefinger of your left hand. Wrap the yarn over the hook, twisting the hook until it catches the yarn, as shown in Figure 8-56. Pull the yarn through the loop. Repeat this process for the desired number of chains.

Note: For practice, make a slip loop and work a length of chain until you can easily produce even stitches. You can use the same pieces of yarn over and over again by pulling out the practice stitches and starting again. When you have mastered the basic chain, the steps involved in the Single Crochet Stitch mechanics are easy to follow.

Single Crochet. 1. (For practice, make a length of chain.) Insert the hook in the correct loop (for practice —the second loop from the last chain). Place the yarn over the hook. (Fig. 8-57.) Pull it through one loop.

2. Place the yarn over the hook. (Fig. 8-58.) Pull it through the remaining 2 loops. Repeat the steps for the desired number of stitches, inserting the hook in the next loop to the left for each new stitch.

Slip Stitch. See Fig. 8-57 (but disregard the black arrow). Place the hook in the correct loop. Place the yarn over the hook. Pull the yarn through all the loops on the hook.

Mechanics for the Macrochet Tassel. Pat Rug Yarn was used for the tassel in Figure 8-59. You need approximately 12 to 13 yards of uncut yarn to make the tassel according to the specifications that follow.

Use a large crochet hook size Q or #19.

Tassel Center. (Fig. 8-59, at the left.) 1. Cut a piece of cardboard 6 in. deep (or the specified size). Wind the yarn around the cardboard 25 times (or the specified number of times). Cut a piece of yarn 18 in. long (or the specified length). Slip it under the strands at the top and tie a secure knot. Cut through the strands at the bottom.

Tassel Top or Outer Macrochet Casing. (Fig. 8-59, center.) 2. Make a slip loop (first loop of the basic chain), leaving an end 12 in. long. Chain 2, 1st Row: Work 6 Single Crochets in the slip loop. Join together by working a Slip Stitch in the top of Chain 2. 2nd Row: Work a Single crochet in each stitch of the preceding row. Join together by working a Slip Stitch in the top of Chain 2. Cut off the yarn, leaving a 12-in. end. Pull the end through the last loop on the hook. Pull so that the last loop tightens around the yarn. Thread a large needle with the bottom 12 in. end. Whip around the bottom through each Single Crochet. Slip the needle off and leave the end loose so that the yarn can be pulled tight later. 3. Poke the top of the tassel center (3) up in the outer Macrochet casing (2) so that the tops are even. Tighten the top slip loop of the outer casing. Tie it securely to the tassel center, using the 2 strands from the top tie. Pull the strand of yarn whipped around the bottom of the outer casing to tighten it around the tassel center. Tie a secure knot, using one of the strands of the tassel center. Hide the knot under the outer

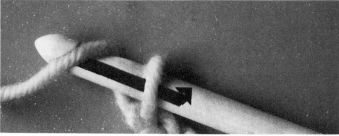

8-56

8-57

8-58

8-59

casing. Trim the bottom ends of the tassel to make them even. Use the method described for the plain tassels.

Attaching the Tassels to the Pillow. Use the same method that was described for attaching the macramé tassel.

Two-Color Macrochet Tassels. Work the tassel center in Color A and the outer macrochet casing in Color B.

Note: After the strand of yarn which has been whipped around the bottom of the outer macrochet casing is tightened and tied to one strand of the tassel center, snip off enough of the loose end of Color B (not so close that the knot will untie) so that the strand will not be visible after you poke the knot under the casing.

Fringe Benefits. Fringe, decorative and fluffy, strikes a happy note when worked on the black-and-white belt shown earlier. (See Fig. 8-43.) It takes on a different personality when you use it along the two short edges of rugs or along the bottom of wall hangings. Although more conservative perhaps in these applications, it is still interesting and pleasing to the eye. Fringe is an excellent finishing touch and easy to produce. You fold the canvas back before you work the area stitches, leaving one free bar along the edge (as for the Braid Stitch) to which the fringe is attached. The fringe will lie flat on a surface or hang down. It simply will not hang up, so do keep this in mind when you create your own designs. Fringe can be successfully combined with the Braid Stitch, as in the black-and-white belt.

Finishing Rugs. Fringe is usually worked on the two short ends of rugs and the Braid Stitch on the two long sides. I say "usually," because you could easily work fringe on all four sides with exciting results. Fringe can also be worked in two or more colors. Be careful that the color changes do not fight the overall Now Needlepoint design but tie in and complement it. A good use of fringe would be a rug with several colors of yarn worked in the

Double Zig Zag Chain Stitch with the zig zag stripes running lengthwise. Fringe matching and continuing the color pattern of the stripes could be attached at the two ends. Work the two long sides in one solid color yarn in the Braid Stitch.

Fringe Mechanics. The following directions are for attaching the fringe on the black-and-white belt. The fringe is worked on the single bar of canvas left free along the bottom. When you want to add fringe, you can follow the same procedure along the edge of any item. Pat Rug Yarn is used in the sample. Cut white yarn in 12-in. lengths. (One length is needed for each vertical bar of exposed canvas along the edge, so you can easily count how many you need.) The sample required 100 lengths for the Now Needlepoint area of the belt plus 4 extra for each side of the buckle, a total of 108 strands. Five 12-in. lengths can be cut from the standard 1¾-yd. strand.

Note: If you wish a different length fringe, reserve uncut yarn in advance, if possible, to eliminate waste.

Fringe is worked as follows after the belt has been attached to the buckle.

1. Thread a large needle with 12-in. length of yarn. Place the belt on a flat surface with the right side up. Start at the left end of the belt directly under the worked area. Place the needle through from *front to back* in the hole to the left of the first vertical bar of canvas just above the exposed bottom horizontal bar. Pull the yarn through to the back, leaving a tail of approximately 4 in.

2. Bring the needle through from *back to front* in the hole directly to the right of the same vertical bar of canvas and above the bottom bar. Pull the yarn through to the front, leaving a large loop as shown in Figure 8-60. Pull the ends even as shown in Figure 8-61.

3. Insert the 2 even ends in the loop, as shown in Figure 8-62. Pull tight until the loop closes around the canvas and yarn.

8-60

8-61

8-62

4. Tie an overhand knot following the directional arrows in the center of Figure 8-63 as follows. Hold the 2 lengths of yarn steady with your left hand. Starting with the directional arrow to the right pointing upward, loop the 2 ends up, over, under and through the loop with your right hand. Tighten the overhand knot so that it falls in place as close to the top of the fringe as possible. You quickly develop a technique for tying these knots which produces a uniform appearance. By attaching the yarn around the vertical bar of canvas, you hold the knots in place, and prevent canvas from peeking through.

Continue from left to right for desired coverage.

Note: The construction of the buckle made it possible to continue the fringe along the bottom for an unusual effect.

8-63

wish. Yarn cording is a delightful, decorative touch around pillows. Along with being decorative, it also can be very functional, when it is used as ties on belts, curtain tiebacks, ties to hold separate seat pads in place on chairs and benches and for hanging purposes at the top of bannerlike wall hangings. The size or thickness of cording depends on the number of strands used together and the weight of the yarn. Figure 8-64 shows 2 weights of

8-64

5. *Haircut Time!* No matter how careful you are, the fringe will need a trimming to even up the ends. Cut a cardboard of the correct depth to use as your guide and you will avoid problems. The fringe in the sample is a bit over 3 in. deep. You travel at your own risk if you rely on your eye as a guide! Shake the fringe and place the belt down on a flat, hard surface. Place the card on top of the fringe while you trim the uneven ends. Shake the fringe a second time and double-check the same section before you proceed to the next. The second shake is the trick. It dislodges and makes evident long, hidden strands of yarn. I sometimes comb the strands with my fingers, replace the card and trim a third time if necessary. The important thing is to get those fringe ends trimmed so that they are even and straight along the bottom. Otherwise, the whole effect will be spoiled.

Tightly Twisted Cording of Yarn. It is trim and even in appearance and you can make it as thick or thin as you

cording with self tassels. Pat Rug Yarn was used for both. The thinner cording was worked using 2 strands as one, the thicker cording using 4 strands as one. Unless you are following specific instructions, I suggest you experiment with short lengths in the particular yarn you plan to use to determine the thickness you desire. Vary the number of strands used together. Measure the amount of yarn involved before you start the cording sample and then make note of the length of cording which is produced. Include the number of strands used together. This will give you the ratio of reduction which can be used to produce any length of cording in the same thickness. Place the different-weight cording samples in separate small plastic bags together with the notes and file them for future reference.

Rough rule of thumb for yarn yardage: It is approximately 3½ times the length of the finished cord desired. This is a very rough estimate. Three times the length will sometimes be sufficient for short lengths, but it is best to allow 3½ times, to be on the safe side. The reduction also varies somewhat with different-weight yarns and much depends on how tightly the cord is twisted. If you make up the suggested samples of cording, you will be able to pinpoint the yardage more accurately. Even then, do not cut it too close or you might unhappily end up with a piece of cording an inch too short to use on your item. Always include an added allowance of yarn, for several extra twists can increase the tension and reduce the length.

Basic Cording Directions. Although the following instructions are specifically for the 4 lengths of cording used on the purple-and-white belt shown earlier (Fig. 8-46), they are basic and can be followed for different lengths and weights of cording. This particular cording is worked with 2 strands of yarn used as one which produces a cord of medium thickness. If a single strand were used, the thickness would be reduced. The cording can be made heavier and heavier by increasing the number of strands used together at the start. By happenstance, the cords for the belt require the same length as the cut strand of 1¾ yds. so that the already-cut standard strands can be used.

Take a deep breath because these instructions are something! You will no doubt wish you had an extra hand while living through them but what fun when that kinking yarn twists back on itself to form the trim, neat, even cording. I have yet to figure out *why* it ends up being so even, but don't question—simply count it as a blessing. All of the directions I have found require 2 people to produce cording. If the cording is extremely long, it is a good idea to have assistance, but being an independent soul and never being able to find another pair of hands at the right moment, I developed this solo style which is not difficult once you have lived through a trial run. Here goes! This is a time when I wish you were here to watch how this is done. Trust me and I'll do the best I can with words and the photograph.

Materials Needed. 1. A small hook attached securely to the wall. (I use a cup hook attached to the side of my fireplace which usually holds a large black antique spoon.) Any small hook which will hold loops of yarn will do. 2. A fairly long pencil. 3. Yarn. You will need eight 1¾-yd. strands of white Pat Rug Yarn to make the 4 lengths of cording for the belt. (This is the standard length of cut yarn strands used throughout the directions.) For other items refer to the previous rough rule of thumb for yarn yardage and reserve sufficient uncut yarn for the desired length.

Cording Mechanics. Make 4 lengths of cording as follows to use as ties for the purple-and-white belt. Use white yarn. Start with two 1¾-yard strands.

1. Tie a secure knot at each end, leaving a loop. (Two strands are treated as one.) Place one loop over the hook on the wall and one around the fairly long pencil.

2. Walk away from the hook on the wall until the yarn

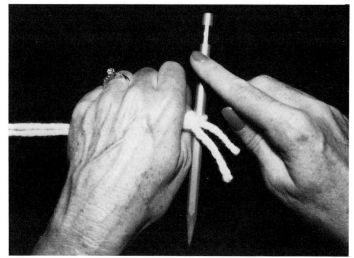

8-65

between the loops is taut. Hold the yarn in your left hand so that the pencil is in the position shown in Figure 8-65. With the index finger of the right hand, start winding, using the pencil as a lever. Keep the yarn taut throughout and wind, and wind and wind (forever, it seems), especially if you are producing a long cord. Test from time to time by releasing the tension very slightly. When it starts to quickly kink, pull it taut again and you are ready for the next step.

3. This is the tricky but fun part. Hold the yarn taut with your right hand (I leave the pencil in place). Find the approximate middle point of the twisted yarn and *grasp it firmly* with the fingers of your left hand (keep it taut between all points or you will have a wiggly mess). Slip the loop around the pencil on top of the loop on the hook. When it is secure, remove the pencil. If you find it easier, you can remove the pencil before placing the loop on the hook, but hang on tight or you will wind, and wind, some more. You have now divided the twisted length in half (still holding it taut with your left hand). Even up the lengths if necessary. Slowly release the tension and watch with amazement as it twists back on itself. Starting at the end away from the hook, ease and help the twisting with both hands, gradually proceeding toward the hook. Like magic the neat cording you see in the belt (Fig. 8-46) is formed.

4. Remove the loops from the hook. Carefully untie the 2 end knots and quickly tie one tight secure overhand knot using all strands as one (see the directions for the overhand knot used for fringe). This must be done quickly or the cord will unravel. Each of the 4 lengths of cording for the belt has a self-tassel at one end. To produce the tassel effect you purposely, but carefully, unravel the cording for approximately 4 in. before tying the overhand knot. This creates long loose ends which simulate a tassel.

Make 3 more cords of similar length. Measure the exact length of the twisted part of the first cord before you tie the overhand knot for the end tassel in order to ensure that all 4 cords will be uniform. The tassel ends can always be trimmed.

Attach cords to each end of the belt at 2 points of the zig zags. (Fig. 8-66.) Sew them on by hand, using heavy-duty sewing thread. Since there will be wear and tear from the tying and untying, sew them on very securely. The stitches should not be visible from the right side.

Cording for Around the Pillows. Measure around the outside of the pillow to determine the length of the cording you will need. Add at least 4 in. extra in addition to the actual measurement. Follow the basic directions for cording using the rough rule of thumb for yarn yardage. Remember to be on the generous side when you cut the yarn. It is far better to have a little excess than to discover the cording is not long enough to go around the pillow. Use matching sewing thread and sew the cording around the outside of the pillow along the construction seam, making your stitches as invisible as possible. Do not start at a corner. Leave a loose end of about 2 in. free when you start the hand sewing. After sewing around the pillow, carefully open a tiny section along the construction edge—just enough to poke the beginning and end of the cording through to the wrong side. Turn the casing inside out and close the opening from the wrong side with sewing thread catching the cording securely in the stitches. Do this so the piecing shows as little as possible on the right side.

Note: You must tie a knot before you cut off excess long ends. A tight overhand knot will usually do the trick, but leave a few inches of tail beyond each knot to prevent it from untying. If the cording is heavy and a knot would cause a cumbersome lump, use sewing thread and tightly wind it around the cording a number of times. Run the needle and thread back and forth through the cording to catch securely. Cut off the excess end, leaving at least 1 in. beyond the sewing thread.

8-66

202

Conclusion

We have reached the end of our visit together. If my hopes are realized, you will increasingly find yourself proceeding with your Now Needlepoint stitches and creative designing on your own and, as time goes by, will refer less and less to the information in this book. But the end is truly the beginning, for the design suggestions you have read about merely skim the surface of the potentials for delightful, creative combinations. There are also many more Now Needlepoint stitches whirling around in my head. If I have inspired you to become more aware of the excitement of design and the magic of color, and have pointed out a way to help you express your individual creative desires, then I am happy! Perhaps you will discover, as I did, that the needle and yarn are forever stuck to your fingers. May the Now Needlepoint stitches help to fill the quiet times in your future with joy and creative fulfillment!

Shopping Sources

Since all of the products I use are distributed nationally, inquire at your local retail needlework shops. The following information is furnished in case you are unable to purchase the material locally. Individuals can obtain the necessary items by mail from the retail firms which are listed as having mail order service, and needlework shop owners and other stores can contact the manufacturer or distributor for wholesale purchase.

While I highly recommend all of the products mentioned in this list, because I have found them excellent for my purposes, my intention is not to exclude other good products that are available. I mention this to be fair to the many companies not mentioned which manufacture high-quality merchandise—canvas and yarns (some with delightful color ranges too)—which could be substituted.

Pat Rug Yarn, 3 to the inch canvas and 5 to the inch canvas

Paternayan Brothers, Inc. (wholesale only)
312 East 95th Street
New York, N.Y. 10028
Note: Upon written request from individuals, Paternayan Brothers, Inc., will provide the name of the nearest store in your area where their products are sold.

Alice Maynard (retail and mail order—write for prices)
724 Fifth Avenue
New York, N.Y. 10019

Jed's Needlecraft (retail and mail order—write for prices)
3959 State Street
Santa Barbara, Calif. 93105

The Naughty Needle (retail)
14 Valhalla Road
Montville, N.J. 07045

Nantucket 6-Ply Cable Yarn, 3 to the inch canvas and 5 to the inch canvas

Nantucket Needleworks (wholesale, retail and mail order—write for prices)
Nantucket Island, Mass. 02554

Poly-fil (loose pillow stuffing and pop-in forms). Available at many fabric stores and variety chains in addition to needlework shops and needlework departments in department stores.

Fairfield Processing Corp. (manufacturer)
Danbury, Conn. 06810
To purchase wholesale, contact the exclusive distributor for needlework shops (a rather large minimum order is required):

Bernard Ulmann Co.
East of Rockies:—
    230 Fifth Avenue
    New York, N.Y. 10001
West of Rockies:—
    3201 Exposition Place
    Los Angeles, Calif. 90018

Belt Buckles

E–Z Buckle, Inc. (wholesale only)
545 No. Arlington Avenue
East Orange, N.J. 07017

IN ENGLAND

Tapestry and rug yarns, canvas, needles
The needlewoman Shop
146 Regent Street
London W1

Yarns
Appleton Bros.
Church Street
Chiswick, London W4

T.M. Hunter
Sutherland Mills
Brora, Scotland

Springbak Handicrafts
8 Springbak Place
Bradford 8   (vegetable-dyed wools)

Wadding and stuffing
MacCulloch & Wallis
25-26 Dering Street
London W1
(also many department stores)

Belt buckles
These are widely available in department stores and shops that sell dressmaking equipment.

IN CANADA

Handcraft House
110 West Esplanade
North Vancouver, B. C.

Georgetown Hobbies & Craft
28 Main N.
Georgetown, Ontario

Craft House
P.O. Box 280
Iroquois, Ontario

Needle and Thread
361 Dundas Street
London, Ontario

The Web
160 Elgin Street
Place Bell Canada
Ottawa, Ontario

Arts and Crafts Centre
4560 Kingston Road
West Hill, Ontario

Condon's Yarns
P.O. Box 129
Charlottetown, P.E.I.

Creative Crafts
4A John Street
Weston, Ontario

Index